Cobbold & Kin

Life Stories from an East Anglian Family

Clive Hodges

THE BOYDELL PRESS

First published 2014
The Boydell Press, Woodbridge

ISBN 978 1 84383 954 5

The Boydell Press is an imprint of Boydell & Brewer Ltd
PO Box 9, Woodbridge, Suffolk IP12 3DF, UK
and of Boydell & Brewer Inc.
668 Mount Hope Ave, Rochester, NY 14620–2731, USA
website: www.boydellandbrewer.com

A catalogue record for this book is available
from the British Library

The publisher has no responsibility for the continued existence or accuracy of URLs for
external or third-party internet websites referred to in this book, and does not guarantee that
any content on such websites is, or will remain, accurate or appropriate.

This publication is printed on acid-free paper

Typeset and project managed by Cambridge Publishing Management Limited

CONTENTS

Foreword by John Blatchly   vii

Family Trees   x

Introduction   xii

1 INDUSTRY AND AGRICULTURE   I

   'Big' John Cobbold   3

   Reverend John Chevallier, MD   9

   John Chevallier Cobbold, MP   I5

   Felix Thornley Cobbold, MP   23

2 FAITH   29

   Reverend William Rust Cobbold   3I

   Reverend Richard Cobbold   36

   Bishop John Coleridge Patteson   43

   Lady Evelyn Cobbold   50

3 THE ARTS   57

   William Cobbold and William Cobbold   59

   Elizabeth Cobbold (née Knipe)   65

   Lillie Langtry   7I

   Dr Martin Edward Fallas Shaw, OBE & Joan Cobbold   77

4 EMPIRE   84

   Horace William Cain   86

   Francis Edward Cobbold   92

   Charles Cobbold Farr   99

   Colonel Ralph Patteson Cobbold, DSO   I06

5 PUBLIC SERVICE   II4

   Sir Thomas Plumer, MP   II6

   Sir Harry Smith Parkes, GCMG KCB   I22

   Field Marshal Herbert Horatio Kitchener, KCMG KG,

      Ist Earl Kitchener   I30

   Cameron Fromanteel Cobbold, KG GCVO, Ist Baron Cobbold   I38

6 SCIENCE and ACADEMIA   144
   Reverend Temple Chevallier, DD   146
   Thomas Spencer Cobbold, MD FRS FLS   153
   Dr Edgar Sterling Cobbold, FGS   160
   Nicholas G. L. Hammond, CBE DSO FBA   167

7 SPORT   174
   William Nevill 'Nuts' Cobbold   176
   Robert Croft Bourne, MP   184
   Gordon Chevallier Cobbold   190
   Colonel John Murray 'Ivan' Cobbold   196

8 MILITARY SERVICE   204
   Field Marshal Herbert Charles Onslow Plumer,
      GCB GCMG GCVO   206
   Bernard Cyril Freyberg, VC GCMG KCB KBE DSO,
      1st Baron Freyberg   213
   Peter Charles Victor Cobbold   221
   Brigadier Simon Fraser, DSO MCTD, 15th Lord Lovat   228

   A Final Word   236
   Sources and Further Reading   237
   Index   247

In selecting images for this book every effort has been made to contact the holders of copyright material; any inadvertent omissions are regretted and will be corrected in future editions if the publisher is notified in writing.

FOREWORD *by John Blatchly*

I am delighted to have been invited to write something to introduce Clive Hodges' *Cobbold & Kin*, having greatly enjoyed previews of several of his lively and compelling biographical essays. Eighteen of his thirty-two subjects have their reward, a tangible taste of immortality, with entries by other authors in the pages of the *Oxford Dictionary of National Biography*, but in that great work there is a formality of treatment by which Clive Hodges was not bound. The jacket text warns us not to expect too many brewers and Ipswich Town directors, and the mixture is far more eclectic. It is fascinating how many great men and women have Cobbold connections, their genes and that surname often discreetly hidden from sight. One is tempted to conclude that if you scratch the surface of a Cobbold life something great and glorious will emerge.

Around Suffolk, and certainly here in Ipswich, there are traces of Cobbolds everywhere. At the civic church of St Mary-le-Tower stands the churchyard cross for the martyred bishop of Melanesia (see page 43), and in the south aisle the large urn memorial in honour of the bountiful and creative Elizabeth (see page 65). At St Clement's church there is a magnificent brass memorial to John Chevallier Cobbold (see page 15) and a headstone, mounted against the west wall of the south aisle, to Thomas Cobbold, the son of the founder, who brought the brewing from Harwich in 1746 and died in 1767. Walking in two very fine parks, Christchurch and Holywells, one cannot but be aware that Cobbolds have made them what they are for us.

I offer two anecdotes. The first headmaster to interview me for a Chemistry post in 1957 was N. G. L. Hammond of Clifton (see page 167). He carried my case to my room, a practice which I have tried to emulate since. Next morning at breakfast his immensely able children needed his help with their prep: Greek irregular verbs. I realised that Hammond had served with Greek guerrillas behind the lines in the Second World War and fell to wondering how regular their verbs had been.

Much later on a north Norfolk holiday, arriving to stay in a barn cottage at the Hall of the Daubeneys, I was greeted by my friend Peter Coke – 'Paul Temple' in the long-running eponymous radio series, but by then an antique dealer of distinction. He said that he was ruined, having paid far too much for two albums containing three hundred scissor-cut Valentines with poems in manuscript written below each. I took them into the cottage and looked for clues. The Ipswich Market Cross was unmistakable and recognising verses in the familiar hand of Elizabeth Cobbold instantly turned his ruin to modest riches, and a framed papercut of the Market Cross was my reward.

> *This antient Mart, fair Lady, shews*
> *That commerce well her wealth bestows,*
> *And give your Valentine to claim*
> *A British Merchant's honor'd name;*
> *Then let the smiles of beauty crown*
> *Integrity and bright renown.*

Abbreviated Family Tree for 'Big' John Cobbold and his First Wife

Subjects in bold type

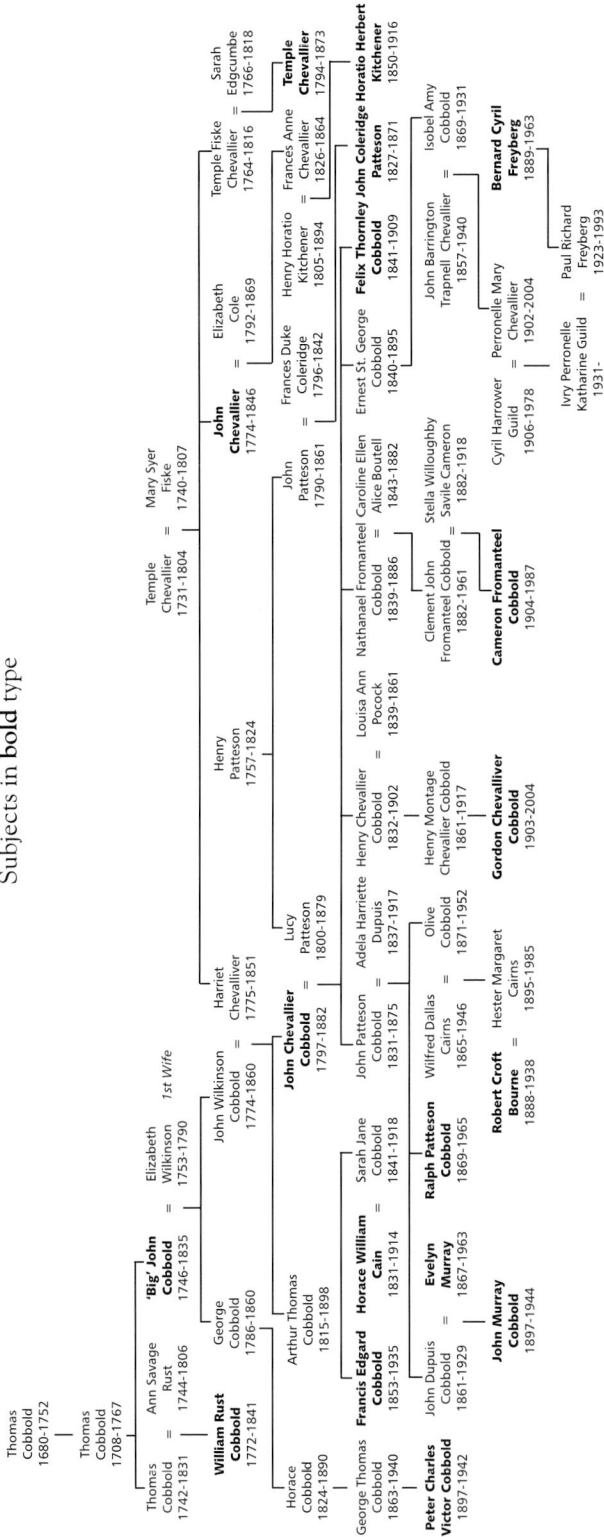

Thomas Cobbold 1680-1752

Thomas Cobbold 1708-1767

Thomas Cobbold 1742-1831

Ann Savage Rust 1744-1806 =

Elizabeth Wilkinson 1753-1790 *1st Wife*

'Big' John Cobbold 1746-1835

William Rust Cobbold 1772-1841

George Cobbold 1786-1860

John Wilkinson Cobbold 1774-1860

Harriet Chevalliver 1775-1851

Temple Chevallier 1731-1804 = Mary Syer Fiske 1740-1807

Temple Fiske Chevallier 1764-1816 = Sarah Edgcumbe 1766-1818

Frances Anne Chevallier 1826-1864 = Temple Chevallier 1794-1873

Henry Patteson 1757-1824

John Chevallier Cobbold 1797-1882

Lucy Patteson 1800-1879 =

John Chevallier 1774-1846 = Elizabeth Cole 1792-1869

Frances Duke Coleridge 1796-1842

Henry Horatio Kitchener 1805-1894

Felix Thornley John Coleridge Cobbold 1841-1909

Horatio Herbert Kitchener 1850-1916

John Coleridge Patteson 1827-1871

Arthur Thomas Cobbold 1815-1898

Horace Cobbold 1824-1890

John Patteson 1790-1861

Ernest St. George Cobbold 1840-1895

John Patteson Cobbold 1831-1875

Adela Harriette Dupuis 1837-1917 =

Henry Chevallier Cobbold 1832-1902

Nathanael Fromanteel Cobbold 1839-1886 =

Caroline Ellen Alice Boutell 1843-1882

Louisa Ann Pocock 1839-1861

Isobel Amy Cobbold 1869-1931

Sarah Jane Cobbold 1841-1918

Horace William Cain 1831-1914 =

John Barrington Trapnell Chevallier 1857-1940

Francis Edgard Cobbold 1853-1935

George Thomas Cobbold 1863-1940

Ralph Patteson Cobbold 1869-1965

Evelyn Murray 1867-1963 =

John Dupuis Cobbold 1861-1929

Wilfred Dallas Cairns 1865-1946 =

Olive Cobbold 1871-1952

Henry Montage Chevalliver Cobbold 1861-1917

Clement John Fromanteel Cobbold 1882-1961 =

Stella Willoughby Savile Cameron 1882-1918

Bernard Cyril Freyberg 1889-1963

Peter Charles Victor Cobbold 1897-1942

John Murray Cobbold 1897-1944

Robert Croft Bourne 1888-1938 =

Hester Margaret Cairns 1895-1985

Gordon Chevalliver Cobbold 1903-2004

Cameron Fromanteel Cobbold 1904-1987

Perronelle Mary Chevallier 1902-2004 =

Cyril Harrower Guild 1906-1978

Paul Richard Freyberg 1923-1993

Ivry Perronelle Katharine Guild 1931- =

Abbreviated Family Tree for 'Big' John Cobbold and his Second Wife

Subjects in bold type

Thomas Cobbold 1680-1752

Thomas Cobbold 1708-1767

'Big' John Cobbold 1746-1835 = **Elizabeth Knipe** *2nd wife* 1765-1824

Thomas Plumer 1753-1824

Robert Knipe Cobbold 1792-1859

Rowland Townshend Cobbold 1821-1895

Thomas Hall Plumer 1795-1852

Richard Cobbold 1797-1877

John Farr 1820-1867 = Emily Caroline Cobbold 1819-1903

Alfred Townshend Cobbold 1852-1934 = Alice Bessie Nunn 1859-1928

Rowland Francis Cobbold 1857-1945

Harry Smith Parkes 1828-1885 = Fanny Hannah Plumer 1832-1879

Margaret Johnstone = Hall Plumer 1827-1888

Edward Augustus Cobbold 1825-1900

Thomas Spencer Cobbold 1828-1886

Charles Cobbold Farr 1851-1914

Edgar Sterling Cobbold 1851-1936

Martin Edward Fallas Shaw 1875-1958 = **Joan Lindley Cobbold** 1890-1974

Lilian Hope Parkes 1872-1946

Marion Plumer Parkes 1860-1949

Thomas Keswick = James Johnstone Keswick 1846-1914

William Keswick 1834-1912

Herbert Charles Onslow Plumer 1857-1932

William Nevil Cobbold 1863-1922

Rowland Hope Cobbold 1905-1986 = Mary Selby Parkin 1908-2000

Anthony Alan Russell Cobbold 1935- (Keeper)

Henry Keswick 1870-1928

William Johnstone Keswick 1903-1990

Simon Christopher Joseph Fraser 1911-1995

Henry Neville Lindley Keswick 1938- = Annebel Teresa Fraser 1942-

Early Norwich Cobbolds

William Cobbold c1530-1586 — Gold & Silversmith

William Cobbold 1560-1639 — Organist & Composer

Hammond and Le Breton

William Le Breton 1773-1853

John Hammond 1801-1880 = Jane Perrose Le Breton 1801-1891

William Corbet Le Breton 1815-1888

Lawrence Nicholas Dijre Hammond 1833-?

Vavasour Fitz Hammond 1842-1897

Emilie Charlotte Le Breton (Lillie Langtry) 1853-1929

Maurice Parkin 1857-1912 = Laura Annie Hammond 1868-1937

James Vavasour Hammond 1871-?

Mary Selby Parkin 1908-2000

Nicholas Geoffrey Lampriere Hammond 1907-2001

INTRODUCTION

In the early spring of 2012, I was mopping up the research for my doctoral thesis, which is concerned with the political aspect of exploration in central Asia during the height of the Great Game, the shadowy cold war played out between Britain and Russia in the region. During the course of my studies I had encountered a Captain Ralph Patteson Cobbold who travelled widely across this dangerous landscape in the closing years of the nineteenth century. Officially he was travelling purely for 'sport and recreation' but he was undoubtedly spying for the Government of India. Having gleaned all I could about Ralph from the India Office Records at the British Library, from the National Archives, the Royal Geographical Society and even from the National Archives of India in New Delhi, there was one last place I felt I ought to look. I sent a hopeful email to the Cobbold Family History Trust and almost immediately received a reply from Anthony Cobbold, its keeper, inviting me to visit him.

I am now embarrassed to confess that, before I first visited the Trust, my ignorance of his family was complete save for that I had learned of Ralph. From the Trust, I learned a little more about his central Asian exploits and much more about other risky missions he undertook later. I immediately realised that here was a man who deserved a biography and, over lunch, I floated my idea. Anthony had other thoughts. He told me that he had approached Boydell & Brewer with a proposal for a biography of another notable Cobbold and that the reply had come that such a book might not have broad enough appeal. Instead, they had remarked that a wider book about the family would be better. Anthony had been beginning to think about who he could ask to write such a book, while I was looking for a project to take up after the conclusion of my studies. The timing of my visit was inspired and we both soon realised that our individual objectives complimented each other perfectly. At this early stage, however, I was unsure whether there would be sufficient family members of interest to warrant writing a book. An hour or two spent browsing the Trust's website when I returned home that evening soon dispelled this concern.

Anthony and I soon decided on eight broad themes or fields of endeavour and then set about populating each chapter with four subjects. This proved quite a challenge, not because of a paucity of good material but because of an abundance of it. After much deliberation we eventually settled on the following thirty-two life stories. The only absolute among our selection criteria was that each subject should be no longer with us. Beyond that, we sought to achieve a balance between Cobbolds and those from other families linked by marriage. That we have been unable to include more stories of the family's women is attributable to the patriarchal nature of past societies. A few of our subjects will be familiar to readers, but most will not. It was this that made the book so enjoyable both to research and to write for, at every turn, I discovered little-known tales of endeavour, tragedy and adventure.

My research was straightforward. In a relatively short period of time, the Trust has accumulated an impressive family archive; this was my starting point for each subject before going on to consult such collections as exist elsewhere: newspaper archives, obituaries and secondary sources. Scholarly secondary works proved extremely useful in helping me boil down to the essentials of each subject's life and I am very grateful to all of the authors and historians whose robust works have helped me in this way. The sources consulted during my research are acknowledged at the end of the book and are recommended as further reading for those who would like to delve into the life of any subject a little deeper than the constraints of this book allow.

There are many people to thank. Writing a family history from outside the family concerned can be daunting and I am grateful to those Cobbolds and their kin who have taken time to review my work and who have made many helpful suggestions. Contributions from the following members of the family have both improved the book and set its author's mind at rest: Nicholas Cobbold, Ivry Freyberg, Angus Sladen, Philip Hope-Cobbold, Barry Chevallier Guild, Henry Lytton-Cobbold, Gillian Oliver, Rowland Cobbold, Isobel Platings, Susan Blount, Christopher Cobbold, Stewart and Ruth Hayward, Richard Cobbold, and Emma and Julian Kitchener-Fellowes. I am also grateful to all those within the family who have provided photographs and who are credited as 'Family member's private collection' – you know who you are. Thanks are also due to the staff at the Suffolk Record Office, Ipswich and to those at other repositories I have visited in the course of my research. Also, I am indebted to the following people who, though not part of the family, have generously given their time, expertise and advice: John Blatchly, Peta and Rob Bruce, Freddie Cohen, Bernie Christian-Bailey, Jeremy Dickson, Lynsey Hughes and Mervyn Russen. Particular thanks are due to Martin Surgey for his technical wizardry with the book's photographs and to the staff at Boydell & Brewer for their kind advice to a novice author.

Cobbold & Kin is as much the Cobbold Family History Trust's book as it is mine. Were it not for the work of the Trust, it would never have been written and many of the life stories told within these pages would remain buried and forgotten. The Trust's archive, which grows daily, has a worth beyond its original intended purpose: much more than a mere accumulation of family records, artefacts, books and memorabilia, it is a collection of real historical value which will, no doubt, be well thumbed by future generations of historians. It has been a privilege to be among the first and I am most grateful to Anthony for guiding me through the Trust's collection and for allowing me to borrow from it: on one occasion he, quite literally, entrusted the family silver with me.

Finally, I am ever grateful to Claire, Caroline and Richard for their unyielding support and patience in all that I do and for allowing me to immerse myself in a family other than my own.

1 INDUSTRY AND AGRICULTURE

The four men considered here, three Cobbolds and one Chevallier, were born into families which were already successful and whose businesses were well established and thriving. Through innovation, entrepreneurship and pure hard work, each built on this success and did very well, making a valuable contribution to the economy of Suffolk in the process. Yet these four were much more than mere businessmen with a narrow focus on profit, intent on securing the futures of their own families. They gave much back to the county of their birth through their engagement with local institutions, participation in civic and national politics and through philanthropy. Each is a giant not just of the family but also of the history of Suffolk.

If the Cobbold family tree is a mighty spreading oak, then 'Big' John Cobbold is its trunk. In his hands, the already successful family brewing business grew steadily and he increased its market share by buying up property from which to sell Cobbold beer. He also oversaw the expansion of the family's interests into coal, corn, shipping and international trade. John had no fewer than twenty-two children and this feat of fatherhood is largely responsible for the remarkable breadth of the family's talents and interests. Over succeeding generations, it also supplied a steady stream of extremely eligible young Cobbold men and women who forged connections through marriage with many other families rich in fascinating stories.

The bond between the Cobbolds and the Chevalliers is among the strongest of these connections, three matches being made within the space of four generations. The Chevalliers have their own extraordinary history and, like the Cobbolds, the family is not short of interesting characters. John Chevallier stands out as a man of many gifts and boundless energy. He was an enlightened physician, specialising in the treatment of the mentally ill, a parish priest and an agriculturalist who discovered a new variety of barley which came to dominate the markets for that cereal all over the world. All the while, he continued to grow the Chevalliers' traditional business, that of cider making, and he made significant improvements to Aspall Hall, which remains the family home to this day.

John Chevallier Cobbold was in his sixties by the time the baton of 'Cobbold & Co.' was passed to him. By this time, JC, as he was known, had already made his mark. A successful solicitor and a driving force behind the family's banking activities, JC is best remembered for his role in infrastructure projects which brought the industrial revolution to Suffolk. Ipswich's wet dock was an impressive feat of civil engineering which gave the town an edge over its local rivals, though it was something of a gamble, its success hinging on the coming of the railway. That the connection was made and that lines soon radiated from Ipswich across the county is JC's greatest legacy. He was also the first Cobbold to enter Parliament, setting a tradition which would be followed by three of his sons.

One of these was Felix Thornley Cobbold. It should come as little surprise to learn that he had a head for business or that, like his father, he should practise law. Yet he was most at home in academia and he might have stayed there had circumstances not required him return to Ipswich to help out in the family business. He did very well, particularly on the banking side of things, and settled at Felixstowe where he became deeply interested in farming. His forefathers (and mothers) had always been energetic supporters of local causes in an age when the poverty gap was more of a chasm. Felix continued this tradition and expanded upon it. He was selflessly public-spirited and the far-sighted gifts he bestowed upon the county of his birth continue to serve the people of Suffolk to this day.

'Big' John Cobbold (1746–1835)
Brewer, Banker & Merchant

Over the last four hundred years or so, more than thirty sons of the Cobbold family have been given the forename John. Many of these did well for themselves and some crop up in the pages of this book. However, there is only one 'Big' John. The 'Big' is a recent addition and serves to distinguish him as a man, big both in stature and in achievement, who is the family's great patriarch. Without him, the story of the Cobbolds would be very different. Under his stewardship, 'Cobbold & Co.' thrived and expanded enormously while, on the home front, he secured the family's future by fathering no fewer than twenty-two children.

In the eighteenth century, a brewer with a head for business was likely to do very well for himself. Drinking water, particularly in towns and cities, was often insanitary and drinking beer was a much healthier option – even children were given 'small

John Cobbold (1746–1835) by Daniel Gardner. (Family member's private collection.)

beer'. As he toured a brewery which was up for sale, Samuel Johnson famously remarked that whoever should buy it would have 'the potentiality of growing rich beyond the dreams of avarice'. Cobbold beer was first brewed by John's grandfather, Thomas (1680–1752), who founded a brewery at King's Quay Street, Harwich in 1723. Thomas was a maltster, and produced his own malt from East Anglian barley for his mash tun. Before long, however, he realised that the quality of his beer was compromised by the brackish water of Harwich. The family owned some land at Holy Wells, Ipswich, and Thomas struck on an idea which was to secure his business for more than 250 years. Holy Wells was, and remains, well known for its natural springs which trickle into a cascade of man-made pools. The waters, pure and crystal clear, were long held to have curative properties and are mentioned in Richard Taylor's *Index Monasticus* (1821) where it is stated that 'in former times pilgrims resorted to them.' The earliest written records of Holy Wells reveal that, from the thirteenth century, it belonged to the manor of Wyks Bishop, held by the bishops of Norwich. It passed into private hands in the sixteenth century and, much later, parcels of it were acquired by the Cobbolds. Thomas decided to replace the unpalatable water of Harwich with the clear spring water of Holy Wells. This improved Cobbold beer immeasurably

though the cost of transporting the spring water from Ipswich to Harwich in large tanks by a small fleet of specially built water schuyts (or shoots) proved expensive. Unable to move the springs to Harwich, Thomas made the excellent business decision to move the brewery to the springs. In 1746, he purchased land at a spot known as the Cliff beside the River Orwell and built a brewery and a new family home, Cliff House, just a stone's throw from Holy Wells (the house is now The Brewery Tap, a thriving waterside pub). The pools at Holy Wells were connected to the brewery by a narrow canal, with a shallow gradient to course the water directly to where it was needed. At about this time, Thomas Gainsborough beautifully depicted the estate and its pools in his only landscape of Ipswich.

Thomas died six years after the move to Ipswich and the brewery passed to his son, also Thomas (1708–67), John's father. John was just seven then and, when not at school at Greenwich, he grew up 'on the premises' where he must have become familiar with many aspects of the brewing industry. This prepared him well to take the helm, aged just twenty-two, when his father died. For the first and the last time in the history of the brewery, responsibility for its running did not pass to the eldest son: Thomas (1742–1831), three or four years John's senior, chose holy orders over Holy Wells, leaving the path open for his younger brother. The decision served both men well: Thomas did very well for himself as a clergyman while John proved to be a master businessman.

John was an imposing man, tall and well built, becoming a little portly in later life. His granddaughter, Emily Caroline (1819–1903) remembered him as having fair hair and blue eyes and it seems he had the physical stature to complement his authority as a businessman. In 1773, he married Elizabeth Wilkinson (1753–90) and the couple set up home in the Manor House on St Margaret's Green, a large house in the heart of Ipswich, which would soon begin to fill up with children. These arrived at quite a rate: John Wilkinson Cobbold was the first in 1774; Frederick, the youngest of fifteen children, was born in 1789. There were seven boys and eight girls and all but two made it to adulthood, a survival rate much higher than the norm for that time: Mary, born in 1781, died in infancy; Henry Gallant died in 1799, aged eleven. Unsurprisingly, this extraordinary feat of motherhood took its toll on Elizabeth who died in 1790, aged thirty-seven, leaving John with fourteen young children to bring up as well as a growing business to run.

In the former of these two tasks he was soon ably assisted by a vivacious new wife, Elizabeth Clarke (née Knipe) whom he married in 1791. Elizabeth (the second) proved to be an excellent stepmother and added to the brood with seven children of her own, though three sadly died in childhood. Elizabeth, as will be shown, was a charming hostess and supporter of the arts. She was the ideal wife for a man of John's growing standing as the couple mixed in Ipswich's politest society. In 1798, the family, still not complete, moved from the Manor House to Cliff House. A year earlier, it had been from the Manor House that Margaret Catchpole, a former servant of the Cobbolds, had stolen John's horse. The ensuing case, Margaret's escape, recapture and eventual transportation, captured the public imagination well beyond the confines of Suffolk. Many years later the story became a literary sensation when it was retold with a generous measure of artistic licence by John's son, Richard Cobbold, who was born in the year the crime was committed (see Chapter 2).

John had clearly been busy at home, and at work he was overseeing an equally impressive expansion as the brewing business continued to thrive. John, like his grandfather and father before him, was a maltster as well as a brewer and he produced his own maltings in Fore Street as well as at the Cliff. He acquired a number of impressive old Tudor properties, which he turned into pubs for selling his beer, and he also branched out successfully into corn and coal. The growth of all these business interests was aided by the rapid enlargement of Ipswich, its population trebling from eleven to thirty thousand during the first half of the nineteenth century. In 1793, after revolutionary France had declared war on Britain, the brewery received a particular boost when the drinking population of Ipswich soared as a garrison arrived to guard the Suffolk coast.

The Brewery Tap and the Tolly Cobbold Brewery, Ipswich 2013. (Clive Hodges.)

By the turn of the eighteenth century, John had already begun planning for his succession. John Wilkinson Cobbold (1774–1860), his eldest, was set to inherit the family businesses and, to prepare him for that responsibility, John sent him off to brew at Eye, where according to his obituary in the *Ipswich Journal*, 'He was also a most useful member of the Corporation of that town.' He remained in Eye until his father's death in 1835, whereupon he returned to Ipswich to assume his position as head of the family's business empire. His position at the Eye brewery was filled by Robert Knipe Cobbold (1792–1859), his eldest half- brother.

John Wilkinson was not the only son to get a leg up in the brewing trade from his father. Recent research by John Blatchly reveals that Big John's efforts to set another son, William (1784–1826), on his way were frustrated by an unscrupulous Manchester brewer named Thomas Caistor. John bought Caistor's brew house and property for £8,760 early in 1805 and set William up in the city. However, Caistor had been less than candid about the state of the business, which was actually heavily in debt. Worse still, echoing the difficulties his great-grandfather had faced in Harwich, William's profits were squeezed by the need to cart good-quality water into the brewery, water from its own well capable of producing only 'ropy' beer. An unscrupulous traveller (sales representative) and disreputable publicans added to William's woes and he wrote to his father on more than one occasion asking for financial help. It is not known how long William persevered in Manchester, but, in 1811, he took over an Epsom brewery and settled in Surrey. In 1817, he moved to Colchester where he ran the North Hill Brewery, which remained the Cobbold Essex branch for more than a century.

In 1814, the family's businesses having gone from strength to strength, John moved the short distance uphill from Cliff House to Holy Wells. The family had continued to buy up land there and, in 1811, John bought Pitt's Farm, the last piece in the jigsaw. The farmhouse formed the basic 'U' shape of the house John built, which back then was far from the imposing residence it would eventually become through the improvements and extensions made by subsequent generations. It was comfortable enough, though, and it commanded a fine view of the estate's rolling landscape and of its gently flowing pools of glistening spring water, the lifeblood of his success. The house at Holy Wells bustled with activity. Elizabeth and John were among Ipswich's most convivial hosts and even when they were not entertaining, their children, young and old, ensured that the house was a lively place. On one occasion, John invited the Bishop of Norwich, Henry Bathurst, to lunch. The bishop, not at all gregarious, hesitated at the offer, no doubt conscious of the Cobbolds' reputation for hosting large gatherings. John reassured him that only his family would be present and the bishop, relieved, accepted the invitation. When he arrived at Holy Wells, he was aghast to find that the house was full and immediately concluded that John had misled him. Of course, John had not. He explained to the unnerved bishop that the sizeable throng *was* just his family.

In 1825, a year of great financial crisis, the Cobbolds went into banking. At that time the banking system lacked robust regulation and the crisis was precipitated in part by private banks over-issuing notes such that they could not be honoured if a number came in for payment together. This problem was compounded by a surge in large speculative investments in Latin America in the early 1820s. Most remarkable among the 'get rich quick' schemes was a fraudulent bond issue for a country named Poyais, somewhere near Honduras. The scam was devised by a colourful Scotsman, Gregor Mcgregor, who had served as a general under Simon Bolívar before returning to England in 1820, claiming to be a senior official of the Republic of Poyais. There never was or ever has been such a country. These dual pressures caused the Stock Exchange to crash and a run on the banks followed, affecting not only the London banks but also the provincial or country banks: six of the former and no fewer than sixty of the latter went out of business.

The shockwaves of the crisis reached Ipswich. The Blue Bank in the town was on the brink of collapse and was only saved by a large injection of cash from the Cobbolds and from William Rodwell, a solicitor in the town. In 1826, a new bank emerged: Bacon, Cobbold, Rodwell, Dunningham and Cobbold. The two Cobbolds were John Wilkinson Cobbold and his eldest son John Chevallier Cobbold; Messrs. Bacon and Dunningham had been bankers in the town for some time. 'Big' John was in his early seventies by this time and though he did not become one of the new bank's partners, he retained absolute authority in the family business. Whichever of the three Johns floated the idea of saving the bank, the final decision to divert funds would have undoubtedly rested with the eldest. The Cobbolds' banking interests continued under various guises into the twentieth century. From 1890, they were run from august new offices in Ipswich's Cornhill, built by Thomas William Cotman. The building was commissioned jointly by two Cobbold banks; Cobbold & Co. took the right-hand side of the development (now Lloyds TSB), while Bacon, Bacon, Cobbold & Co. took the left. The family's banking activities finally drew to a close in 1904 when they were sold to Capital and Counties, which was then itself absorbed by Lloyds in 1918. In 1930 the lower floor of the left-hand side of the building was removed to form Lloyds Avenue, linking Cornhill with Crown Street.

'Big' John was also instrumental in the family's expansion into shipping. The Cobbold fleet grew rapidly in the 1820s, though as Hugh Moffat observes in his *Ships and Shipyards of Ipswich* (2002), records of the day do not make it entirely clear which John (father or son) owned what. Moffat's research suggests that the younger John owned many of the Cobbold ships, which plied the world's trade routes as far as India and China during the 1820s and it was certainly he who oversaw the fleet's further enlargement in the following decade and beyond. As Moffat acknowledges though, 'Big' John certainly had interests in shipping much earlier. By the time he died, the family's fleet was already impressive, comprising schooners, brigantines, brigs and barques. The Cliff was well sited for maritime ventures and, in 1829, 'Big' John extended his riverside landholding when he struck a deal with the town's Corporation for the foreshore down to his brewery and maltings. The timing, according to Moffat, could not have been better as about half the area acquired would soon fall inside Ipswich's new wet dock, making it 'ripe for reclamation and industrial development'. The dock, which opened in 1842, also served the Cobbolds' shipping interests well; at the end nearest to the brewery the family had their own yard where cargo could be landed and repairs carried out.

If his grandfather and father had laid solid foundations for 'Cobbold & Co.', it was unquestionably 'Big' John who turned it into a powerhouse of the East Anglian economy. He grew its core business, brewing, exponentially and by the time he died nearly half of Ipswich's hundred or so licensed premises were Cobbold houses. Not content with a comfortable living from the proceeds of the family's traditional business, this extraordinarily shrewd businessman successfully branched out into coal, corn, shipping, banking and even wine, establishing a merchant's business which survives into the twenty-first century under the name of Barwell Jones Ltd. At the time of writing, Barwell Jones has a Cobbold on its board.

The six Johns and one Patrick who succeeded 'Big' John as heads of the family business certainly had plenty to thank him for. Much more than that, and far beyond the relatively narrow limits of the family's commercial interests, 'Big' John's contribution to the history of the Cobbold family is inestimable. The extraordinary breadth of the family's interests and activities as well as its valued connections to other families stem from his capacity for fatherhood (though perhaps the two Elizabeths deserve a greater share of the credit for this). No fewer than fifteen of the subjects whose life stories are told within these pages were directly descended from him and countless more led lives of note across every imaginable field of human endeavour. Without 'Big' John, the story of the Cobbolds would be very different and not nearly so varied and colourful.

Reverend John Chevallier, MD (1774–1846)
Doctor, Priest and Agriculturist

When John Wilkinson Cobbold married Harriet Temple Chevallier (1775–1851) in 1796, it marked the coming together of two influential Suffolk families. This bond was secured by the couple's fourteen children and tightened in 1854 when their granddaughter, Isobella Frances (Fanny) Cobbold (1834–1917) married Reverend Canon Charles Henry Chevallier (1823–85). A third knot was tied in 1897 by John Barrington (J.B.) Trapnell Chevallier (1857–1940), the son of Fanny and Charles, and Isobel Amy Cobbold (1869–1931), the great granddaughter of John Wilkinson Cobbold. Familial ties apart, the two families had similar commercial interests. The Cobbolds' core business was beer, the Chevalliers' cider. The Cobbolds had maltings, the Chevalliers grew barley. When the two families worked together, as they did in the early days of the East Anglian railways, they were a formidable force.

Revd Dr John (Barley) Chevallier (1774–1846). (Family member's private collection.)

In that particular partnership, the Chevalliers were represented by Harriet's father, Reverend John Chevallier MD, a clever and energetic man of many hats.

The Chevalliers had roots in Jersey, one Jourdam Chevalyir appearing in the parish records of St Mary's, Helir (St Helier) for the year 1274. They were also to be found in Normandy and it was there that Sir Anthony Rudolph Chevallier, tutor to Queen Elizabeth I, was born. They were Huguenots and after Louis XIV's revocation of the Edict of Nantes in 1685, they, like thousands of others, chose East Anglia as a more tolerant place to live. Temple Chevallier, John's great-uncle bought Aspall Hall, near Debenham, from the Brooke family in 1702 and lived there until his death twenty years later. The estate then passed to Clement Benjamin Chevallier (1698–1762), John's grandfather, who moved his family there from Jersey in 1727, bringing with him twelve dozen apple trees and 'the spirit of Cyder-making.' Not long after he arrived in Suffolk, Clement brought in a large circular apple press from Normandy and stones for a great storage trough of similar shape. Orchards were planted, the press was assembled, a mill built and, in 1728, Aspall Cyder began to flow.

Cider is perhaps more commonly associated with the West Country than with East Anglia, but during the eighteenth century it was drunk widely throughout England, accounting for as much as 45 per cent of alcoholic consumption. Clement's business flourished and was in a most healthy condition when he died in 1762, at which point John's father, the Reverend Temple Chevallier (1731–1804), took over. However, within a year, all would change. Britain's involvement in the Seven Years' War had left it broke and the administration of Prime Minister the Earl of Bute, already unpopular, desperately needed to replenish the coffers. The popularity of cider made it an obvious choice for a new tax and a bill to levy four shillings on every hogshead made came before Parliament. This provoked outrage, particularly among small West Country cider makers fearful of the prospect of receiving a knock on the door from the excise men. Riots ensued and the unpopularity of the bill was one of the factors that caused the fall of Bute's government. Nonetheless, the bill was pushed through by Bute's successor, George Grenville. The Cider Act was eventually repealed in 1766, having raised approximately thirty thousand pounds for the Treasury; it had a devastating effect on the industry, putting many out of business, while others uprooted their orchards and decided to grow something else instead.

The tax hit the Chevalliers too, though the estate was not devoted wholly to orchards and the family was sustained by its wider farming interests. Over time, Temple, an industrious man who also tended the spiritual needs of three parishes (Aspall, Cransford and Badingham) in addition to his duties as squire, brought more of the estate under the plough. In his article *The Chevalliers of Aspall Hall*, Walter Tye mentions that Arthur Young, the well-known traveller and agriculturist and a fellow Jerseyman, regularly visited Aspall Hall where he was 'much impressed by his [Temple's] ability and thoroughness in agricultural pursuits, especially in his experiments on the comparative value of turnips and cabbages'. This tradition of agricultural experimentation would be taken up by the next generation of Chevalliers.

John Chevallier was educated at Bury St Edmunds Grammar School and then at Edinburgh University, from where he graduated MD and where he developed a particular interest in mental health. Later, he would employ unusually sympathetic treatments for those afflicted by illnesses of the mind. When his father died in 1804, the running of the Aspall estate fell to John and his brother, Charles, who was two years' his senior. Their two surviving elder brothers, Temple Fiske and Clement had moved away from Aspall Hall, having taken holy orders: the former was the rector at Badingham, the latter vicar of Cransford.

In 1808, John married Caroline Hepburn, the daughter of a Captain with the East India Company. The marriage was short-lived and punctuated by tragedy: three of the couple's six children died in infancy in the space of two years (1812–14) and Caroline herself succumbed to illness in 1815, aged just thirty-nine. A year later, another son, George, died aged three. In October of that same year, 1816, John married again. His new wife was Emily Syer, daughter of Reverend Barrington Blomfield Syer of Kedington in south-west Suffolk. Sadly, she died just three years later having produced two healthy sons, John and Barrington. During this period of his life, it must have seemed to Dr John that every joyful event in his life was followed by one of great sadness. He had better fortune with his third wife, Elizabeth Cole, whom he married in 1821 and who survived him. The family was completed by a further seven healthy children. The second of these was Charles Henry who would later marry Fanny Cobbold; the fourth was Frances (Fanny), the mother of Herbert Horatio Kitchener, the great soldier and statesman.

On 24 November 1816, just two days after John had married Emily Syer, his brother, Temple Fiske died. From 1805, Temple had been the perpetual curate of Aspall as well as rector of Badingham and his death left a vacancy at the former place, which was in John's gift. John decided to fill the position himself. He was ordained deacon in August 1817 and priest three months later. Interestingly, among his fellow ordinees at the latter ceremony was George Elwes Corrie, the noted theologian and academic who became the confidant and best friend of John's nephew, the astronomer and mathematician, Reverend Temple Chevallier (Temple Fiske's son; see Chapter 6). Much later, in 1831, John took on a second parish when he succeeded his second eldest brother, Clement, as vicar of Cransford.

All the while, John and his other brother Charles had been working the land at Aspall, undertaking experiments to improve yields. Experimentation with grains was well established by this time as agriculturists methodically mixed saved seeds to develop new varieties of cereals with names such as Nottinghamshire Long Ear and Old Wiltshire Archer. Chevallier barley, which would come to dominate world barley markets for nearly sixty years, was discovered in an altogether less scientific way. More than one version of the story of its origin exists; the most popular survives from the manuscript, *History of Debenham* (1845), and is worth repeating in full.

> *About the year 1820, John Andrews, a labourer of Mr Edward Dove of Ulverstone Hall, Debenham had been threshing barley, and on his return home at night complained of his feet being uneasy, and on taking off his shoes, he discovered in one of them part of a very fine ear of barley — it struck him as being particularly so — and he was careful to have it preserved. He afterwards*

*planted a few grains from it in his garden, and the following year Dr. And
Mrs John Chevallier, coming to Andrews' dwelling to inspect some repairs, saw
three or four ears of barley growing. He [John] requested it might be left for
him when ripe. The doctor sowed a small ridge with the produce thus obtained,
and from the increase thence arising, he began to dispose of it, and from that
time it has been gradually getting into repute. It is now well-known in most
of the corn markets of the Kingdom, and also on many parts of the Continent,
America etc., and is called the Chevallier barley.*

Another version of the story has Andrews filching a few ears of the barley while
walking home through a field and feeding them to his chickens in his garden
where some sprouted. Chevallier barley was a tall, two-rowed, narrow-eared
variety classified as *Hordeum distichum*, and its proliferation has been charted by
beer historian, Martyn Cornell. By 1833, it was on sale at London's Mark
Lane auction mart fetching thirty-five shillings a quarter, a full three shillings
more than other varieties; within a further year it was being grown all over
England and Scotland, and a Bedfordshire farmer told a House of Commons
select committee that it 'makes the very best malt'. At its peak, perhaps 80 to 90
per cent of British barley was Chevallier and the variety was also grown widely
in Europe, Chile, California, Australia and New Zealand, though it failed under
the tropical sun of South Africa. In 1885, the malting expert, Henry Stopes
wrote of Chevallier barley, 'All the best qualities of every class of barley seem
combined in this one variety, except that it is not awnless.'

Paradoxically, it was the superior quality of Chevallier barley that caused
it to fall out of favour with brewers. In 1880, William Gladstone's government
repealed the tax on malt, levied since 1697, and replaced it with a tax on beer.
As Christine Clark observes in her book, *The British Malting Industry Since 1830*,

WANTED,

FROM 1000 to 1500 bushels of Chevalier
Barley for Malting.
Apply to
DRAKE AND NORTHWO·D,
Wellington Brewery.
Wellington Terrace, January 1, 1847.

Advertisement for Chevallier Barley, 1847. (Courtesy of New Zealand National Library.)

'Previously, with the malt tax levied at a flat rate, brewers had little incentive to use any but the finest malts which yielded the greatest extract.' Gladstone's fiscal tinkering provided a spur for brewers to source cheaper and, consequently, inferior malts. Soon, the demand for premium barley such as the Chevallier variety waned and the market became flooded with cheap imports and malt substitutes such as maize and rice. John, of course, was not around to witness this decline in demand for the crop he had discovered.

John's energies were not confined to agriculture, though it was this that provided the bedrock of the family's prosperity as well as the funds for his substantial redevelopment of Aspall Hall. The additional living space this expansion afforded was put to good use. Despite his avid interest in farming matters and his pastoral responsibilities, John was, first and foremost, a doctor. As master of Aspall Hall, he decided to give much of it over to the treatment of those with mental illnesses. Indeed, over time, much of the first floor of the extended house was given over to the treatment of his patients, the family's children having to settle for quarters on the top floor, which they shared with the family's staff. This sacrifice of the family home was almost unthinkable at the time and perfectly illustrates John's compassion and his enlightened view of mental illness: at that time, 'lunatics' were more commonly kept from view and left to rot in bleak asylums or in the workhouse. John believed that mental illness could and should be treated by kindness, and the patients at Aspall Hall were accommodated very comfortably. Some had a sitting room as well as a bedroom and most were allowed to wander the grounds. Records from the 1840s, not long before John died, reveal that Aspall Hall was licensed to house eleven patients. The private asylum continued to take in patients after John's death when clinical responsibility was assumed by Thomas Radford. John's son, Dr Barrington Chevallier, followed his father into the same branch of medicine and was instrumental in establishing Suffolk's first mental hospital, the Ipswich Borough Asylum (St Clements). He became the hospital's medical superintendent and was known for encouraging his patients to act and sing in organised shows. Between 1873 and 1875, Barrington was Mayor of Ipswich.

If John Chevallier was far ahead of his time in his therapies for the mentally ill, he was also able to foresee that in an age of rapid economic and industrial development the railways were the key to regional prosperity. On 22 February 1825, a public meeting was convened in Ipswich to discuss proposals for a new line linking Ipswich with Diss: John chaired the meeting. This early scheme came to nothing but, a decade later, John teamed up with his brother-in-law, John Wilkinson Cobbold and his nephew, John Chevallier Cobbold to support a scheme which would connect London to Yarmouth via Ipswich and

Norwich – the Eastern Counties Railway. From the start, the plans were beset by difficulties and it was due mainly to the dour persistence of this triumvirate of Johns that any track was laid at all. The younger John (Chevallier Cobbold), in particular, fought stubbornly to keep the scheme alive and see it through to a conclusion.

Squire, doctor, parson, farmer, industrialist – John Chevallier certainly managed to fit plenty into his seventy-two years. His novel attitude towards mental illness, his interest in agronomy and his support for the railways mark him out as an innovator and a man of considerable vision. The family's business interests were safe in his hands and are still going strong in the twenty-first century: Aspall Cyder is still made by Chevalliers on the family estate and, in recent years, the brand has been at the forefront of a cider revival. Aspall continues to innovate: it is the only surviving founder member of the Soil Association (founded 1946) and, in 2014, it was honoured by that association for pioneering organic farming methods. Chevallier barley, which until recently had not been grown for decades, has also had a revival. In 2013, it was resurrected by Dr John Ridout in the laboratories of the John Innes Centre, Norwich. He found the variety to have good disease resistance and the half-acre planted produced malt found to suit beers such as porters and Indian pale ales, which had been popular among Victorian drinkers. Whatever the truth of how it came to be growing in John Andrews' garden nearly two centuries earlier, when John Chevallier first caught sight of it, he instinctively knew he was on to something.

John Chevallier Cobbold, MP (1797–1882)
Brewer, Banker and Railway Pioneer

The blend of Cobbold and Chevallier genes was always likely to produce a man of some substance and John Chevallier Cobbold did not disappoint. During his adulthood, Ipswich developed from something of a provincial backwater to a thriving town of fifty thousand inhabitants, with impressive new docks and a railway connection to London. No individual played a more important part in this development than John Chevallier ('JC') Cobbold; as a solicitor and businessman, as an MP, and in many other civic roles, he was involved in almost every progressive scheme that transformed the town in the thirty years either side of 1850. In October 1882, in its report of his funeral, *The Ipswich Journal* commented, 'The history of the late Mr. J. C. Cobbold's life is the history of the town itself during a period bordering upon a century.'

John Chevallier Cobbold (1797–1882).
(Family member's private collection.)

Little is known of JC's early life, but he certainly enjoyed the benefits and privileges associated with being a son of a successful family engaged in profitable business. He was educated at Bury St Edmunds Grammar School and trained as a solicitor, a profession he followed as a young man. One day he would inherit the rapidly expanding Cobbold business empire, but in a family noted for its longevity this came relatively late in life: he was well into his sixties when his father died in 1860. In the interim, many young men might have been tempted to live an idle life, living off the family fortune until such time as it fell into their hands. JC was quite the opposite. He was a man of enormous energy and ambition, determined to make his own way in the world and to serve not only the interests of his family but also those of the people of Ipswich and Suffolk.

JC was a man of some standing in Ipswich before he had even reached thirty. Already practising law, he entered public service in August 1823 when he was elected a 'Common Councilman' for the Borough of Ipswich. Two years later he was elected one of the town's two bailiffs. In the same year, 1825, he went into banking, joining his father on the board of Bacon, Cobbold, Rodwell, Dunningham and Cobbold at the time of the great banking crisis. He retained banking interests for the remainder of his life and did rather well from them.

In May 1827, JC married Lucy Patteson (1800–79), daughter of the late Reverend Henry Patteson. The ceremony was conducted at Wortham where Patteson had been rector until his death in 1824. The tradition for a large family, set by JC's grandfather and followed by his father, continued as Lucy was delivered of no fewer than thirteen children, three of whom died in early childhood. Among the others were John Patteson Cobbold MP (1831–75), JC's heir, Thomas Clement Cobbold MP (1833–83), first President of Ipswich AFC, and Felix Thornley Cobbold, great benefactor of Ipswich. The union with the Pattesons also brought great colour to the Cobbolds' wider familial connections: Lucy was the aunt of John Coleridge Patteson, first Bishop of Melanesia and, as his name suggests, the Pattesons were connected by marriage to the family of the celebrated poet, Samuel Taylor Coleridge.

JC's banking partner, William Rodwell, was also a solicitor and the pair were in practice together for some time. Together, they advised the Dock Commission, established to oversee the construction of Ipswich's wet dock after an Act of Parliament (1837) gave the scheme the go ahead. Both JC and Rodwell sat on the commission as solicitors and seemed to have been the conduit for negotiations between the town and Parliament, though some of their fellow commissioners grew suspicious that the pair's dealings were not always confided to them fully. Dock Commission meetings were held in public in the Town Hall and received full coverage in *The Ipswich Journal*. Discussions were often lively and sometimes heated, and JC was often at the heart of them, usually giving as good as he got. For example, in late 1837, the banker and dock commissioner, William May, objected to the election of JC and a man named Aldrich as sub-commissioners of pilotage for the new dock. May's preferred candidates, named Finch and Hill, were both experienced Orwell pilots and he sought to overturn JC's selection. He mocked, 'Why, Mr Cobbold could not pilot a vessel in the Orwell so well as either of these two gentlemen [Finch and Hill], and I can say that he should not have the pilotage of one of mine.' JC had earlier asserted that even if he was not a pilot himself, he could spot a good one and concluded, 'I will not give way to any man in that knowledge – to any other Commissioner in the room.' The Dock Commission was comprised of some of Ipswich's most influential men, many of whom (including JC) had specific and vested interests in the scheme. This bred suspicion and gave rise to petty rivalries among the commissioners but, despite these, the dock was built and opened in 1842. JC's father, John Wilkinson Cobbold, was elected to its first committee of management.

At the same time as he was busy with the Dock Commission, JC was deeply involved in an even greater engineering project which he considered essential to the prosperity of not only Ipswich but also of Suffolk and East Anglia as a whole. Without it, many maintained, the wet dock would have become a white elephant. Arguably, it was JC, more than any other, who was responsible for bringing the iron horse to the county. JC, his father and his uncle, Reverend John Chevallier, had supported plans for a railway line from Ipswich to Diss as early as 1825, though these had failed to get off the drawing table. A full decade would elapse before a more ambitious proposal was put forward to connect Ipswich with London and Essex to the south-west and with Norfolk and Yarmouth to the north. The Eastern Counties (Railway) Bill was passed on 4 July 1836. John Wilkinson Cobbold and John Chevallier were on the company's original board of directors, while JC was engaged as a solicitor and provided some of the banking services. However, East Anglians were in a very distinct minority on the board and as investors; most of the proprietors and company directors came from the industrial heartlands of the north-west, where the Liverpool to Manchester line had blazed the trail. Rules requiring a number of directors to retire each year further curbed the influence of East Anglian men and, by 1839, John Cobbold had been retired and John Chevallier had resigned, unable, as a clergyman, to sit on the board of a joint stock company.

Worse still, progress on the line out of London was slow and costs higher than expected and rising all the time, as landowners in East Anglia were hanging out for as much as they could get from the Eastern Counties Railway (ECR). This became a matter of intractable contention between the company's local directors and those from Liverpool, into which JC was to become personally embroiled. Just three weeks after the passing of the Eastern Counties Bill, he bought land at Crane Hall, west of Ipswich. Under the original plans, the new line would run straight through the middle of this land and one of the company's Liverpool directors, Hodgson, accused JC of buying Crane Hall with profit in mind. JC vehemently defended his position, arguing that he had bought the land to secure the route and that he had intended to sell it to the company at cost at the earliest opportunity. Like many others who stood up against JC, Hodgson eventually backed down.

The northern proprietors were, of course, less concerned about the local benefits of a line through East Anglia than they were about seeing a return on their investment. Consequently they concentrated efforts on getting the line between London and Colchester operational and it was becoming increasingly clear to the East Anglian men that the line was unlikely ever to make it to Suffolk, let alone Norfolk. JC took the northern directors on, sponsoring a private amendment bill that aimed to hold the company to its commitments under the original bill. This bold move failed and by July 1840, the ECR had reached only Brentwood. The scheme's supporters in Norfolk decided to take matters into their own hands. In January, 1841, a public meeting of Norfolk residents was convened to discuss the laying of track and a year later a notice was issued to Parliament to construct a line between Norwich and Yarmouth. Soon, JC would lead a similar but much more ambitious initiative across the border in Suffolk.

The Chief Engineer of the ECR, John Braithwaite, estimated that the cost of extending the line from Colchester to Ipswich would be £800,000. Peter Bruff, his junior, thought he could complete the work for a fraction of the cost. However, in 1842, Bruff was dismissed by the ECR for his apparently shoddy work on the Stanway embankment which the company considered was 'of the most discreditable description'. Bruff was undoubtedly a talented engineer but it was held that the embankment was in a poor state because his attention had been diverted by another project. With time on his hands, Bruff independently surveyed a new route to Ipswich which he believed could be delivered for just £270,000, a fraction of the figure arrived at by Braithwaite. Aware of the frustration among the Suffolk supporters of the ECR, he astutely took his plans to John (Wilkinson) Cobbold and JC. The Cobbolds took the scheme up and

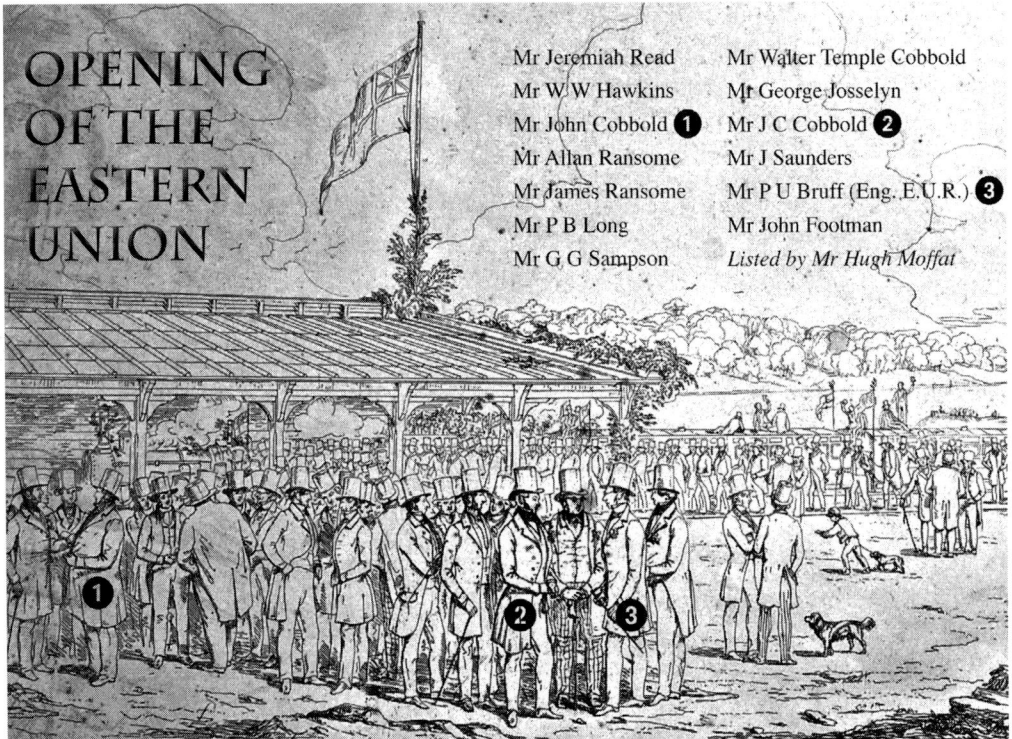

Opening of the Eastern Union Railway at Ipswich Station, 11 June 1846. (Courtesy of Suffolk County Council. Key by Hugh Moffat.)

formed a new company, the Eastern Union Railway (EUR), of which JC became chairman. While Bruff held the position of resident engineer, the project was to be overseen by Joseph Locke, one of the best railway engineers of his day.

Locke engaged Thomas Brassey, the leading railway contractor of the day who had worked under him on a number of other contracts, including the Grand Junction Railway. An act for the line was obtained in July 1844 and, thanks to the formidable combined talents of Locke, Brassey and Bruff, it opened just two years later to great celebrations. JC and his fellow directors were the first to travel on it, from Ipswich to Colchester, where they met up with the top brass of the ECR. The enmity between the rival companies was set aside for the day as they travelled together back to Ipswich. Celebrations continued through lunch and were followed by a river trip to Harwich, speeches, a balloon ascent and fireworks. The ECR directors were still unaware at this point that JC and Bruff had already drawn up plans for extensions centred on Ipswich which would challenge their own ambitions.

Three EUR extensions followed in quick succession; Bentley to Hadleigh, Ipswich to Bury and a branch on that line from Haughley to Norwich via Diss. The Norwich extension enraged the ECR as a rival to its own recently opened route from the Norfolk city to London by way of Brandon and Cambridge. The new route between Norwich and London after the EUR extension was opened in 1849 was 113 miles long, some eleven or twelve miles shorter than the ECR's more circuitous route via Cambridge.

Problematically, the EUR owned only that part of the route as far as Colchester, the final fifty-one miles from there to London being owned by its rival. Out of spite and to maintain passenger numbers on its own line (via Cambridge), the ECR imposed prohibitively high fares for journeys taking the more direct route through Colchester. The two companies failed to reach an agreement on how the proceeds of journeys between London and Norwich by either route might be apportioned between them and a long process of arbitration commenced. Rather than see their profits dwindle while the arbitrators deliberated, JC and Bruff launched a novel new service in 1852. The EUR teamed up with the Ipswich Steam Navigation Company (ISN) to offer its passengers the option of completing their journeys to London by sea from Ipswich. This proved surprisingly popular, despite the fact that it was painfully slow – a journey from Norwich to Ipswich by train and then on to Blackwall in London by ship might take as long as ten hours (though advertising material shamelessly deceived passengers over the duration of the packet service). For those not in a hurry, however, it was cheap and offered a buffet service and toilet facilities, at a time when, as railway historian Hugh Moffat observes, 'such amenities were unknown on the trains'. To augment the ISN service, the EUR purchased its own ships, the *Pearl* and the *Orion* and later took the *Orwell* and the *River Queen* from the ISN when that company went into liquidation in 1853. These purchases were made mostly with Cobbold cash, both ships being re-registered under the ownership of Alfred Cobbold, JC's younger brother who owned other vessels. Shortly afterwards, another steamer, the *Prince Albert* was added to the fleet which sailed under the name of the New Steam Navigation Company.

Though the arbitrators eventually found in the EUR's favour, concluding that it was entitled to have reasonable connections at Colchester, the ECR continued to obstruct. By the end of 1853, the EUR was insolvent and on New Year's Day 1854 it signed over the working of its lines to the ECR in return for one seventh of the profits pooled from all of the lines of the two companies: this despite the fact that the EUR owned a fifth of the route mileage. JC and the other EUR directors continued to feel short-changed by the deal even though their profits increased during the early years of the arrangement, and the two companies continued to squabble until both were subsumed in the Great Eastern Railway in 1862. JC's determination and sheer bloody-mindedness had given East Anglia eighty miles of railway track, sixty-three of which still form part of the East Anglian mainline.

JC's politics were blue and he was returned as Conservative MP for Ipswich in 1847. At that election and the next four (1852, 1857, 1859 and 1865) he accrued more votes than Hugh Adair, his Liberal rival, though both were returned. Adair turned the tables in 1865 and then, in 1868 after twenty-one years, JC lost his seat when Adair and another Liberal, Henry Wyndham West pushed him into third place. JC was a diligent MP, 'though his voice was seldom heard', with a good attendance record in the House where he 'was able to watch over and promote the general welfare of the town he so worthily represented'. As well as championing the town nationally, JC was at the heart of many local institutions, both public and private, to an extent which might reasonably beg the question, 'How did he find the time?' The day after his funeral, *The Ipswich Journal* listed a few:

> *He was a magistrate and Deputy-Lieutenant for the county of Suffolk. He was a trustee of the Ipswich Savings' Bank, a Director of the Waterworks Company, a Vice-President of the Ipswich Mechanics' Institution, a Vice-President of the Ipswich Working Men's College, a patron of the Ipswich School of Art, one of the Ipswich Charity Trustees, a Director of the Suffolk Alliance Company, a Vice-President of the Suffolk Agricultural Society, &c.*

As if Ipswich matters were not enough to fill up his time, he was also responsible for kick-starting the development of Felixstowe where he bought Felixstowe Cottage (later known as The Lodge) overlooking the sea on what became known as Cobbold's Point. The Lodge remained in the family for many years and was developed further in 1885 by the architect, William Thomas Cotman (who also built offices in Cornhill for the Cobbolds' banks) under commission from Felix Thornley Cobbold. The house still commands Felixstowe's seafront from its elevated position and is known today as Cranmer House.

When his father died in 1860, JC took the reins of the family firm, though his eldest son, John Patteson Cobbold, took on much of the day-to-day running of it, leaving JC free to fulfil his political duties and to focus on his banking interests. In 1874, John Patteson avenged JC's earlier electoral defeat when he and fellow Conservative, James Redfoord Bulwer unseated both Adair and West. Among his parliamentary achievements, John Patteson successfully lobbied for a railway line linking Felixstowe with the rest of the Suffolk network. The arrival of the railway in 1877 gave an impetus to Felixstowe's development as a seaside resort, development spearheaded by JC who built the town's first hotel. Sadly, John Patteson died of scarlet fever in December 1876, before the line was opened. At the subsequent by-election, his brother Thomas Clement succeeded him as MP; his son, John Dupuis Cobbold succeeded him as heir to the family's businesses.

In 1879, JC lost his beloved wife, Lucy, after fifty-two years of happy marriage. Two years earlier, on the occasion of the couple's 50th wedding anniversary, JC erected a marquee at Holy Wells and invited Cobbold employees, past and present, and their families to share in the celebrations. Some 350 attended and were entertained generously. *The Ipswich Journal* reported: 'The dinner was evidently much enjoyed, and, after it, there were but very few speeches, and those short, speech-making giving way to various amusements in the open air.' Bells tolled across the town and small cannon were even fired in honour of the couple.

JC died in October 1882, aged eighty-five. For the last seven years of his life he had held the position of high steward of Ipswich, the last honour bestowed upon him by the town. *The Ipswich Journal* broke the news with a short sentence: 'We have lost our leading townsman.' John Chevallier Cobbold, fiercely proud of his home town and county, had been at the forefront of Ipswich's development for sixty years. No man during the same period could claim to have given more to the town, perhaps any town. His influence permeated every sphere of Ipswich life and, though he did very well for himself and his family, so did the ordinary people of Ipswich through his deeds. An example of his generosity came to light at his funeral when a letter was read out. It was written by Richard Makilwaine Phipson, a well-known ecclesiastical architect who completely remodelled the outside of St Mary-le-Tower, the town's civic church, in the 1860s. As part of the renovation, Phipson had hoped to turn the church's ten-bell peal into a twelve-bell peal but had been unable to raise sufficient funds. JC bumped into Phipson in the street one day and, upon learning of the architect's predicament, asked him how much he needed. Phipson replied that the scheme would cost £160. Not long after, Phipson's bank account was credited with that precise sum by a mysterious Mr Johnson. It soon dawned on Phipson that his benefactor was playing with words and that Mr Johnson was, in fact, Mr John-(Cobbold's)-son. Not one individual among the throng that turned out to bid farewell to JC, fittingly at St Mary-le-Tower, had previously known anything of this act of selfless charity. For some time afterwards, each peal of those bells must have conjured fond memories of JC among the townspeople he served so well.

Felix Thornley Cobbold, MP (1841–1909)
Banker, Radical Politician and Philanthropist

So enamoured was John Chevallier Cobbold with his seaside retreat at Felixstowe that he named his youngest son after the town. Felix would also grow up to love the views from The Lodge, though whatever his affection for Felixstowe and its bracing air, it was Ipswich that he always considered home and which would receive the greater share of his benefaction. Today, Ipswich is abundant in public green space, but perhaps its finest public amenity is Christchurch Park with its delightful landscaped gardens and substantial Tudor brick mansion, all in the centre of town. For this invaluable civic asset, the people have Felix to thank. Christchurch, though, was not Felix's only gift to the town or, indeed, to Suffolk. More than a century after his death, his philanthropy continues to benefit the county in many ways.

Felix Thornley Cobbold (1841–1909) by Hon. John Collier, 1897.
(Courtesy of Colchester and Ipswich Museum Service.)

From a very early age, it was clear that Felix was extremely bright and this was borne out by academic performance. He was a King's Scholar at Eton, matriculated at Trinity College, Oxford, and then took a BA (Classics) and MA at King's College, Cambridge. He was called to the bar at Lincoln's Inn in 1868 but practised only briefly as the lure of a return to academia got the better of him. He returned to King's College as bursar in 1871 and became a senior fellow there, a position he would retain for life. Happiest among the hallowed halls of King's, it seems likely he would have remained in Cambridge indefinitely had family tragedy not dictated otherwise. In the New Year of 1876, shortly after the death of his eldest brother, John Patteson Cobbold, his father asked him to return to Ipswich to lend a hand with the running of the family businesses. Felix dutifully answered the call and moved back to his childhood home, Holy Wells.

Felix's talents were employed most notably in the banking side of the family's businesses which, at that time, comprised Bacon, Cobbold & Co., Bacon, Cobbold and Tollemache both in Ipswich, and Cox, Cobbold & Co. based in Harwich. From this point of his life, as Rosalind Thomas, Felix's biographer, notes, 'he seemed destined to spend the rest of his life quietly accumulating wealth and helping the family'. Felix proved himself an able businessman as well as an outstanding scholar and the banks prospered under his guidance. Felix's workload increased markedly after the death of his father in 1882 and of another brother, Thomas Clement, the following year. He shouldered the burden admirably.

Both Thomas Clement and John Patteson had followed their father to Westminster, all three serving as MPs for the Borough of Ipswich. Felix had his own political ambitions and, at some point between 1882 and early 1885, he voiced them. The tradition of politics in the family had always been Conservative and Felix's father and brothers had all represented that party while, at this time, another brother, Nathanael Fromanteel Cobbold and his nephew, John Dupuis Cobbold were both vice presidents of the Ipswich Conservative Association. One can only imagine the gasps from within the family when Felix announced that his politics were of the yellow hue and that he intended to stand for the Liberal Party in the newly created constituency of Stowmarket at the 1885 general election.

A quiet, cultured man, Felix was not obviously made for the cut and thrust of the hustings but he soon learned the trade. Quite apart from his distance from the politics of the rest of his family, he was a radical even among his fellow Liberals and, as a prospective candidate, he campaigned on issues such as corn protection and church reform. On the former subject, he demonstrated his early mastery of the political sound bite during a speech delivered on 6 July in Stowmarket. He said, 'What the Liberals desire to do is to enable the labourers to buy a large loaf at the same price as the Conservatives would make them pay for a small one.' In due course, Felix was selected by his party and then elected with a healthy majority of over a thousand and soon afterwards he took his seat as one of William Gladstone's backbenchers. He did not stay there long as he was among ninety-three rebel Liberals who voted against Gladstone's Government of Ireland Bill (First Home Rule Bill), introduced to the House in April 1886. The rebellion sealed the government's fate: the bill was defeated 311 to 341 and Parliament was dissolved. Felix decided not to defend his seat.

Upon his father's death, Felix inherited The Lodge at Felixstowe. The house had fallen into disrepair and its position atop the cliff at Cobbold's Point was becoming daily more precarious as coastal erosion devoured the land in front of it. Felix engaged the architect, Thomas Cotman, to shore up the site, remodel the house and landscape its grounds. The Lodge became a very comfortable seaside home and in 1885, as he was preparing for his political debut, Felix left Holy Wells to live there permanently. Felix had no children of his own to fill the rooms and corridors of The Lodge and never married, but coming from such a large family he was rarely lonely. He was a gregarious man whose doors were always open to a steady stream of guests. It seems his old friends from King's College, with whom he remained close all his life, were regular house guests at The Lodge.

It was during this period of his life that Felix's interest in agriculture developed. What began as a passing interest soon became a consuming passion. Along with The Lodge, Felix had inherited Villa Farm nearby. He was eager to learn about land management and agricultural techniques from his farm manager. His growing knowledge gave him the confidence to buy other farmland at Hadleigh and Sproughton and he became chairman of the county's Agricultural Association.

Felixstowe, thanks in no small measure to Cobbold investment, was booming at this time. Hotels began to spring up and docks were opened in 1887, two years after Felix moved into The Lodge. Felix took a leading role in the town's civic business as chairman of its district board. In that capacity he oversaw the reinforcement of part of the town's sea defences and laid the foundation stone for a smart new town hall in 1892. The year before, Felixstowe had received a royal seal of approval. In July 1891, Kaiser Wilhelm II of Germany made a state visit to Britain and, while he was engaged in London in

Postcard c.1903. Christchurch Mansion, donated to Ipswich by Felix Thornley Cobbold in 1894. (Cobbold Family History Trust.)

talks with his grandmother, Queen Victoria, his wife, the Empress Augusta, took her children and her entourage for a day at the seaside. The destination chosen was Felixstowe and, almost overnight, it became one of the most fashionable resorts in the country.

After his dramatic flirtation with politics, banking again became the primary focus of Felix's energies, though he also remained active in the brewing business and continued to expand his farming activities. All the while he amassed a large fortune. With no children to indulge, and rich beyond the needs of a very comfortable life, Felix was in a position to bring benefit to those less fortunate than himself. Through history this could be said of countless individuals, many of whom have subsequently gone to their graves, their wallets full. Felix was among the altruistic few who could visualise the good that could come from his fortune. Without doubt already a generous giver to charity, in 1894, Felix provided the land and £1,200 to build public baths on Fore Street. In October of the same year, he bestowed an even greater gift on the people of Ipswich, which has given pleasure to every citizen of the town since.

In 1892, the estate of William Neale Fonnereau, Christchurch, came up for sale. Fonnereau was the grandson of Katherine (Kate) Cobbold (1806–85), daughter of John Wilkinson Cobbold and, therefore, Felix's great-aunt. The estate had been in the Fonnereau family for more than 250 years when it was put up for sale at an asking price of £50,000. The town council proposed buying the park and its mansion but the townspeople of Ipswich opposed the scheme, considering it too expensive. In 1894, a syndicate bought the estate for just £36,000 and soon started to redevelop the land at its fringes, building rows of houses. Realising that the park was rapidly shrinking, the council bought fifty-one acres of it for £16,500, though this excluded the mansion and the grounds to the front and west of it. It transpired that the syndicate had plans to demolish the mansion and to redevelop that part of the estate too. It was at this point that Felix intervened, buying the mansion and the part of the estate adjacent to it. Having struck a deal with the syndicate, Felix wrote to the Mayor, 'I desire to offer the property to the inhabitants of Ipswich as a free gift.' The gift was conditional upon the mansion remaining intact. Later, it was agreed that the house should become a museum, housing archaeological artefacts and paintings.

Two years later, by way of thanks for his acts of generosity, the town council nominated Felix as mayor for the year 1897, the year in which Queen Victoria celebrated her diamond jubilee. The rule that only an alderman of the town could be chosen as mayor was waived in Felix's case. There was no better man to arrange Ipswich's jubilee festivities and he met the challenge with gusto. By tradition, each new mayor was asked to nominate a charity to be supported by the town for his year of office. Felix chose the Ipswich and East Suffolk Hospital in Anglesea Road and a fund was started to pay for its repair and enlargement: he set the ball rolling with a handsome donation of a thousand pounds. The hospital, which already had Cobbold and Patteson wards in honour of Felix's brother, John Patteson Cobbold, would soon have a Felix ward. Regarding the celebrations themselves, the council was strapped for cash and concerned that it would not be able to lay on festivities worthy of such an auspicious occasion. Felix resolved this problem by offering to defray the costs personally.

The jubilee celebrations were a resounding success. The highlights were three non-consecutive days of entertainment laid on by Felix in Christchurch Park. Among the attractions on the first day, 22 June, were a steam circus, races and competitions, a tunnel railway and an evening firework display. The second day was given over to a children's party. More than ten thousand children converged on the park in seemingly endless columns, some carrying banners with slogans such as 'Long Life to Our Mayor'. Not even a violent thunderstorm was able to dampen spirits, though it did disrupt arrangements to feed and water the over-excited young throng. Felix had recruited some of his female relatives to help out with the catering. Three weeks later, a thousand or so from the other extreme of Ipswich's population were handsomely entertained. The qualifying age for an invitation to a patriotic celebratory meal was, strangely, sixty-three. Those unable or too frail to attend each received two shillings with which to treat themselves, a personal gift from the mayor. Felix had done the town proud and the council was warm in its appreciation of both his generosity and his talent as an organiser. A motion was passed thanking him on behalf of the people of Ipswich 'for the eminent services he has rendered to the community during his ever memorable year in office as Mayor of the Borough'. As his year of office drew to a close, a fine portrait of him by John Collier was unveiled at Christchurch Mansion: the portrait, paid for by public subscription, depicts a man of both authority and benevolence and it is still has pride of place there.

In the final decade of his life, Felix re-entered politics. He stood unsuccessfully for the Liberals in the tricky seat of Woodbridge in 1900 but was later returned for his beloved hometown as Henry Campbell-Bannerman led his party to a spectacular landslide in 1906. The Ipswich result, which saw Felix and Daniel Ford Goddard (who polled 6,396 votes to Felix's 6,290) returned, was the first in the entire country to be declared and over the coming days the battle-cry 'Ipswich leads the way!' was to be heard all over England,

Scotland and Wales. The Liberals, successively under Campbell-Bannerman, H. H. Asquith and David Lloyd-George would lead the country for more than a decade. Campbell-Bannerman's administration was truly a government of all the talents, but Felix, sadly, would not survive its full term. He died after a short illness in December 1909. Rather fittingly, the year of his death is perhaps best known as the year of Lloyd-George's radical People's Budget, which (when it eventually passed through the Lords in 1910) taxed the rich to support the poor and which was the forerunner of the modern welfare state. Felix was a strong supporter of the budget, but his own personal schemes for wealth redistribution were not contingent upon legislation.

His will provided for members of his family but it was the people of Ipswich and Suffolk who benefited most. He secured Christchurch Mansion's status as an important repository of art with an endowment of £20,000 Ipswich Corporation Three per Cent stock, which provided year-on-year returns to fund the purchase of artworks. However, in Ipswich, it is not only the generations who have enjoyed and still enjoy Christchurch Mansion and its idyllic surroundings who owe Felix a debt of thanks. Just before he died he had been arranging the transfer of forty-five acres of the Gippeswyk Park estate to the corporation, a transaction that was concluded after his death.

Beyond the confines of Ipswich, he bequeathed his agricultural estates at Sproughton, Hintlesham and Hadleigh, 852 acres in all, to the East Suffolk Council to be administered as private smallholdings and allotments to allow householders to grow their own food. In 1910, the Charity Commission established this bequest as the Felix Thornley Cobbold's Small Holdings and Allotments Trust. Since then, the trust, now shortened to the Felix Cobbold Trust, has evolved to meet changes in agricultural conditions and practices. Today, it states its aims as to 'advance and improve agriculture and, in particular to educate and inform farmers and young persons in agricultural methods, developments and techniques'. At the close of its first century, the trust owned property worth six million pounds, including the site at Otley College where tomorrow's farmers learn their trade. That the trust continues to flourish is a tribute to an extraordinary man.

2 FAITH

It was often the case within noble and well-to-do families that the first-born son would inherit the estate, business interests and any titles, the second would join the military and the third would take the cloth. This convention did not suit Thomas Cobbold (1742–1831), the eldest son (to survive infancy) of second-generation brewer, Thomas (1708–67). The young Thomas passed up the opportunity to take the reins of the family business, preferring to pursue a career in the Anglican Church, despite there being no strong tradition of such ambitions within the family. Thomas has acquired the epithet 'Pious', though scrutiny of his career suggests that he was, perhaps, as much businessman as clergyman. For the last forty years of his life, in an age when the practice of ecclesiastical pluralism was rife, he concurrently held the living of three Suffolk parishes, Wilby, St Mary-le-Tower, Ipswich and Woolpit, delegating many of his duties to curates, one of whom was his son, another his nephew.

Thomas set a trend for religious service which would be followed by generations of Cobbolds. Both he and, interestingly, 'Big' John, through the issue of his second marriage, head branches of the family tree particularly fruitful in producing clergyman. The family's burgeoning clerical contingent was bolstered by unions through marriage with the Chevallier, Patteson, Waller and Dupuis families, all of whom had similarly strong traditions of service to God. Here, three individuals who led remarkable lives as men of the cloth are selected from this rich seam; the fourth subject, a woman, famously defied convention and looked to the crescent rather than to the cross for her faith.

Both William Rust Cobbold and Richard Cobbold took on the responsibility of upholding the spiritual well-being of seemingly idyllic, sleepy country parishes. Both, however, had to contend with a changing rural landscape and discontent among agricultural labourers whose prospects had suffered due to falling grain prices and the introduction of new-fangled machinery. The ways in which each dealt with crises in their parishes largely determined the success, or failure, of their ministries and provide vivid glimpses into the role of the clergy in such matters and in village life in general. William, cantankerous and aloof, lost what little respect his flock held for him over two turbulent days in 1830 and spent the rest of his life taking extraordinary measures for his own protection. Richard's tact and common sense in similar circumstances enhanced his reputation among a village population hitherto suspicious of him. This respect and Richard's affection for his parishioners are conveyed in his studies of village life, which constitute a unique and valuable record of rural Victorian England.

Not all family members who pursued careers in the Church were content with the relative comfort of a rural, or indeed urban, parish. A few were gripped by a sense of mission and travelled to the far corners of the Earth in order to spread God's word. The extraordinary life story of the missionary Bishop John Coleridge Patteson is the stuff of the Victorian adventure novel, replete with accounts of eventful voyages between exotic islands populated by hostile tribes. Patteson's story, however, has no happy ending. The precise circumstances surrounding the brutal murder of the mild-mannered bishop on the South Pacific island of Nukapu in 1871 will probably never be determined, though it is almost certain that some of the more unsavoury commercial activities associated with British imperial expansion played a part.

The combination of a deep spiritualism and a longing for adventure that inspired missionaries such as Patteson was also to be found in the slight yet redoubtable figure of Lady Evelyn Cobbold, one of the most remarkable women of her age. Endowed with all the stubborn adventurous bravado of Freya Stark or Gertrude Bell, Evelyn was the more notable because of her religious convictions; she was an aristocratic English woman who became a Muslim. The story of Evelyn's life is full of the contradictions thrown up by these opposing concepts, yet neither the conventions expected of her class nor of her sex could deter her from following the muezzin's call. Aged sixty-five, she embarked on an historic journey to visit the religion's holiest sites. Evelyn's spiritual adventures demonstrate that determined women of her age could, if they had the means, lead independent and unconventional lives, challenging prevalent paternalistic perceptions of the 'weaker sex'.

Reverend William Rust Cobbold (1772–1841)
Unloved Vicar of Selborne during the Swing Riots of 1830

In the autumn of 1830, a pot of simmering social and economic tensions boiled over spectacularly across swathes of rural southern England. Farm labourers in Kent, impoverished by rising food prices, falling wages, poor harvests and the introduction of labour-saving machinery, were the first to riot in August of that year, but the disturbances quickly spread. In many instances, letters were sent to parsons, magistrates and other village notables demanding pay increases, a reduction in the tithe and the dismantling of threshing machines. Direct action was threatened if these demands were not met. These letters were often signed by a fictitious 'Captain Swing', and the ensuing disturbances became known as the Swing Riots. The southern counties of Kent, Sussex, Berkshire, Hampshire and Wiltshire were most severely affected, accounting for over nine hundred individual incidents, though rioting also occurred in East Anglia and as far north as Nottinghamshire, Lincolnshire and Yorkshire.

East end of St Mary the Virgin, Selborne.
(Courtesy of Robert Updegraff.)

The tithe was commonly held to be a primary cause of poverty among an increasingly destitute labouring class. Levied at a flat rate by the Church, it failed to take into account a farmer's yield causing particular hardships when harvests were poor. During the 1820s it became common practice for farmers to compensate for the burden of the tithe by employing labourers who were in receipt of the Poor Rate, a dole payment given to the unemployed. This enabled the farmers to get labour 'on the cheap' as the Poor Rate subsidised the wages of such men. Of course, as taxes for the Poor Rate were levied on the entire village rate-paying population, this practice was not popular among those who did not farm yet were directly subsidising agricultural labour costs.

The harvests of 1829 and 1830 were particularly poor in southern England and the demands of the tithe on farmers particularly burdensome. Consequently, the pittance farmers were able to pay their workers reduced still further. Poverty-stricken labourers, often with the tacit support of their employers, resorted to direct action against both the new-fangled machinery, which could do the work of many men, and against a Church whose greed denied them a living wage. Historian John Owen Smith's meticulous research reveals that in Selborne, in east Hampshire, the target of this latter frustration was the village vicar, Reverend William Rust Cobbold.

In 1813, William, the third son of 'Pious' Thomas Cobbold and Ann Rust, was given the living at Selborne by Magdalen College, Oxford, where he had studied and in whose gift the parish was. Evidence suggests that, even as a young man, William was not over-blessed with humour or charm. As college schoolmaster at Magdalen he failed to endear himself to his pupils. G. V. Cox, chorister of Magdalen in 1793, remembered him as a humourless pedant who seemed to enjoy dispensing corporal punishment:

> *Having during one or two of his last years been a pupil of Mr Cobbold, I am entitled to speak of the impressions left upon me by his teachings: they are these — that from a bilious constitution, betrayed by his yellow-tinted complexion, he was ill-qualified to bear kindly and patiently with little ignorant boys. 'Alphezibeus, Sir,' he would say; 'don't you know s from z? Listen, Sir, Al-phe-si-be-us;' every syllable, especially the third, being impressed by a sharp cut with a cane, or a sharper twitch of an ear. Indeed, this latter punishment, his favourite one, extended several times to the partial tearing the ear from the head of a dull boy.*

William's irascible character seems not to have been improved by marriage to Maria Mabbott, the year following his arrival at Selborne. From the day he arrived in the village he was almost instantly unpopular and regularly at odds with his vestry. For example, in 1818, he overturned the vestry's appointment of Francis Meggs as churchwarden, arguing that he was unfit for the position on the grounds that he regularly absented himself from church. This typified William's unbending approach to his ministry. He steadfastly refused to compromise his own, often narrow-minded, opinions in order to court the affection of his parishioners. Such adherence to principle might be considered virtuous attributes in a parish vicar; however, William possessed neither the wit nor the tact necessary to gain respect in the village. Relations became so strained between vicar and vestry that the latter took to holding its meetings at the village's only public house, The Compasses, in the knowledge that William, who considered himself Selborne's only 'gentleman', would never cross the threshold of such a den of iniquity.

As the harsh economic realities of the agricultural revolution began to hit Selborne, William's comfortable lifestyle, sustained by the excessive tithe, contrasted ever more sharply with the hand-to-mouth existence of many of his impoverished parishioners. Tensions between the already unpopular vicar and his flock mounted steadily until they erupted dramatically at 11 p.m. on Sunday 12 January 1823. *The London Gazette* reported that upon that evening,

> *Some evildisposed person or persons did wilfully and maliciously discharge a gun or pistol, loaded with shot into the parlour window of the Reverend William Cobbold ... with intent to do him some bodily harm.*

Clearly, William's aloofness and arrogance had antagonised at least one of his flock sufficiently to provoke such a violent attack. Equally telling, perhaps, is that a King's Proclamation offering a reward of fifty guineas for information leading to the apprehension and conviction of the perpetrator was never claimed. Either the identity of the miscreant was a genuine mystery or the village, united against its unpopular vicar, refused to turn him over to the authorities, despite the lure of a handsome reward. Later in the same year, the political reformer William Cobbett spent the night in Selborne during one of his *Rural Rides*. A local man told him that 'he did not believe there was a more unhappy place in England' and that 'there's always quarrels of some sort or other going on ... on matters of rates and tithes mostly'.

It would have been remarkable had the wave of riots of the autumn of 1830 bypassed such a discontented parish. They did not. Many villages escaped the disturbances thanks to the sagacious intervention of their lords of the manor, who were able to avert violent protest by facilitating discussions between opposing sides. Selborne had no such lord, only a sullen pastor who had alienated himself from most of his congregation. On Sunday 21 November rumours of impending disturbances reverberated around Selborne. William was made aware of the gathering storm by Hori Hale, a local farmer, and by Henry Collyer, a churchwarden, who were both seeking his advice in the event of rioting breaking out. The vicar's response was characteristically curt, advising the two men to do as they saw fit, but that he could do nothing. As darkness fell, a watch was kept on the vicarage to make sure that William did not flee.

The following morning, at seven o'clock, William encountered a small delegation of local farm labourers near the vicarage. Prominent among this group were Aaron Harding, a forty-one year old local man with nine children and Robert Holdaway, former landlord of The Compasses, who had been ousted from the public house following a concerted, obsessive campaign by William. Harding said to the vicar, 'We must have a touch of your tithes.' William argued that if his income was reduced he 'could not do the good he was in the habit of doing'. This rather pompous response was dismissed by Harding, who demanded a reduction from six hundred pounds per annum to three hundred, which would allow the farmers to pay improved wages. He asserted, 'The farmers have undertaken to raise our wages, and we have undertaken to reduce the tithes.' William remained unmoved. He later reported that by nine o'clock the vicarage was besieged by 'a mob of three to four hundred' intent upon his submission to Harding's demand.

William was not the only object of the mob's ire. John Harrison, master of Selborne's squalid workhouse, was similarly loathed owing to the appalling treatment dished out to those unfortunate enough to be in his 'care'. Harding informed William that the assembled mob would leave him to consider his proposal while it turned its attention to Harrison. Between fifty and a hundred men remained at the vicarage as the remainder set off to evict the master of the workhouse. Harrison, perhaps having been tipped off by the farmers, was absent from his quarters at the workhouse, though his wife and children were at home and fled hastily as the mob approached. The rioters ransacked the property, stripping the roof within fifteen minutes, destroying furniture and setting fires.

William, hearing the commotion from the workhouse, set off to investigate. He did not get far before being advised by those fleeing the riot to return to the vicarage 'as the mob were coming back and bent on mischief'. William, a corpulent man, lumbered back to the relative safety of his house before, sure enough, the mob, now numbering four hundred, assembled on the adjacent village green. Harding repeated his earlier demands, though in a more threatening manner. If William failed to comply, Harding warned, 'a rush' would be

The mastiff's collar which 'adorned this beast's prodigiously thick neck'. (Courtesy of Robert Updegraff.)

launched against him and his property. William later reported that a number of farmers were present and that they did nothing to restrain the rioters. Indeed, Hori Hale advised the vicar that he should accede to Harding's demands and it seems likely that the farmers supported the mob's actions without wishing to get their own hands dirty; a reduction in the tithe was, after all, very much in their interests. Friendless in the face of an impatient and aggressive mob, William had little option but to submit and he signed an agreement reducing the tithe to three hundred pounds.

Eventually the rioters retired to The Compasses to celebrate with buckets of beer, initially paid for by William, but eventually charged to the Poor Rate. The following day, not content with victory in their own village, Holdaway led many of the rioters out of Selborne towards the neighbouring village of Headley, gathering recruits on the way. There, the Selborne mob, its number swelled to more than a thousand, joined forces with a smaller group from Headley, which had already 'negotiated' a reduction in the tithe from its own rector. The combined Selborne–Headley force then sacked the Headley work-house, draining the wine cellar of its master, James Shoesmith, and causing damage estimated at one thousand pounds.

Retribution was swift. The Selborne and Headley ringleaders were rounded up just two days later and brought to trial within a fortnight, together with more than three hundred other rioters from across Hampshire. Holdaway, Harding and seven others from Selborne and Headley were sentenced to transporta-tion, setting sail for Australia in February 1831. Ultimately the disturbances achieved nothing whatsoever. Tithes returned to their earlier rates and wages for farm labourers remained pitiful.

Selborne quickly returned to normal. Despite his narrow escape, William Cobbold was simply unable to lighten his demeanour or adopt meas-ures to begin mending the rifts between vicar and flock. Rather, he acquired a formidable mastiff to protect himself from his parishioners; the collar which adorned this beast's prodigiously thick neck resides in a glass case in the village church to this day. Selborne continued to be an unhappy corner of rural Hampshire and, unarguably, this mood was in no small measure set by the character of its vicar.

William died aged sixty-eight in November 1841. While visiting London, he was struck by the Oxford Mail cart at the end of Ludgate Hill. His injuries were not immediately considered life-threatening; as *The Gentleman's Magazine* later reported, 'Being a very corpulent man, it was two days before it was discovered that his ribs were broken.' He died six days after the accident – a miserable end to a rather miserable life.

Reverend Richard Cobbold (1797–1877)
Rector of Wortham, Best-selling Novelist and Social Historian

Richard Cobbold as a young man.
(The Cobbold Family History Trust.)

At Wortham, in the far north of Suffolk, a dispute similar to that which beset Selborne was resolved in a far more civilised fashion. This was due in no small part to the tactful intervention of the village's rector, Richard Cobbold, who brokered a deal which secured increased wages for the disaffected farm labourers. Reflecting on the incident many years later, Richard recalled that he cautioned the labourers that if they rebelled he would not support their demands and that subsequently 'never did men behave better'. The incident is significant not only because Richard helped to avert unrest of the sort which blighted Selborne and much of rural England, but also as an indication of a developing mutual respect between rector and villagers.

Richard, the twentieth of 'Big' John Cobbold's twenty-two children and his fifth by his second wife, Elizabeth Knipe, graduated from Gonville and Caius College, Cambridge, in 1820. He was ordained deacon in the same year and priest the year after that, serving as curate to his uncle, 'Pious' Thomas at St Mary-le-Tower in Ipswich. When he married Mary Anne Waller (1801–76) in 1822, his father presented him with the patronage of Wortham as a wedding gift, though Richard was not instituted rector until 1824 after the death of the incumbent, Reverend Henry Patteson. Rather than rush to Wortham to take up his position following Patteson's death, Richard remained in Ipswich for a further four years, having been licensed by the Bishop of Norwich to be non-resident. During this period responsibility for the spiritual care of the parish rested with a curate, James Merest, who had performed the same role for the pluralist Patteson.

Richard and Mary thrived in Ipswich, attending a merry-go-round of functions, dinners and balls 'in the most polite society.' When Merest died in 1827, it was with 'a heavy heart' that Richard prepared to move Mary and their young sons to the rambling village of Wortham, some twenty-four miles from the sophistication of his hometown. To ease the pain of the move for Mary, Richard modernised and built a large extension to Wortham's rectory before taking up residence there in the late summer of 1828, just three months after the birth of his third son, Thomas Spencer Cobbold. Richard was to remain at Wortham for more than fifty years and, from 1842, his duties in Suffolk's north widened when he was appointed rural dean of Hartismere.

Relations between the villagers of Wortham and their new 'town boy' rector were initially strained. Richard was somewhat aloof and demanding of his flock both in terms of their attendance at church and of their behaviour outside of it. He saw himself as the upholder of Wortham's social order as well as its spiritual leader and was openly censorious of those whose conduct fell below his exacting standards. Piety aside, neatness both in personal appearance and in the home, sobriety, moral rectitude and industriousness were the traits he admired most and which he expected in others, whatever their social standing. Once, as a young village girl lay dying having just given birth, Richard frogmarched her seducer to her bedside to impress upon him the consequences of his conduct.

In his liturgical and pastoral duties, Richard was undeniably diligent, only employing curates when his absence at the pulpit was unavoidable. Such commitment was relatively uncommon for the time when many clergymen, such as Richard's uncle, Thomas, were content to enjoy the comforts their living provided while delegating most of their work to subordinates. Despite a tendency to be pompous and prickly, Richard's acceptance at Wortham was won through his commitment to his duties and his genuine interest in the well-being of his parishioners. He was particularly active in promoting education, offering instruction not only at his own Sunday School but also at the union workhouse. At some point between 1842 and 1845, he hired a house on Long Green for ten pounds a year and turned it into the village's first school. Richard, along with the more prosperous of Wortham, met the school's running costs and he eventually bought the property outright in 1862.

However, it was not for such munificence that Richard achieved fame that extended well beyond the borders of Suffolk. He shared his mother's love for the arts and he painted, sketched and wrote prolifically, though with questionable ability. Much of this work, such as the self-illustrated *Valentine Verses* (1827), was produced in order to benefit charitable institutions, again, an instinct inherited from his mother. Despite the noble intentions behind *Valentine Verses*, the work was so fiercely panned by critics that Richard, who was always deeply sensitive to unfavourable reviews of his work, attempted to restrict its circulation by buying back as many copies as he could. He also used his own art to directly support his work. In March 1860, the stage at the Corn Hall, Eye was adorned with no fewer than twenty-four of Richard's paintings and illustrations, used as visual aids for a lecture he was delivering entitled, 'The Horrors of War and the Joys of Peace'.

Richard's greatest artistic legacy, though, was the romantic biographical novel, *The History of Margaret Catchpole, a Suffolk Girl* (1845). Margaret had been in the service of Richard's parents at about the time of his birth. In May 1797, she stole one of John Cobbold's horses and rode it to London, a crime for which she was sentenced to death. She was spared the gallows following pleas for clemency from Richard's mother and her sentence was commuted to seven years' transportation. While awaiting this fate, she made a daring escape from Ipswich Gaol before being recaptured and sentenced to death for a second time. Again, the sentence was commuted to transportation, though this time for life. After the sentence was carried out, Margaret worked as a respected midwife in New South Wales until her death.

Richard's account of Margaret's life became a best-seller, though he imprudently sold the copyright for just a thousand pounds. The book also aroused a fair degree of controversy. In the Author's Preface to the book, Richard wrote,

> *The public may depend upon the truth of the main features of this narrative: indeed most of the facts were matters of public notoriety at the time of their occurrence. The author who here details them is a son of the lady with whom this extraordinary female lived, and from whose hands he received the letters and the facts here given.*

Soon after the novel's publication, the strength of these claims was tested and found to be wanting. Richard's account of Margaret's life, it transpired, was full of embellishment and fabrication. His claims that Margaret could read and write, that she married in 1812 and that she died in 1841 were just some of the 'facts' that were challenged: no evidence exists to suggest that she was educated or that she married, while, indisputably, she died in 1819 from influenza. Interest in the novel and the demarcation within it between fact and fiction continue to excite debate to this day, and the book's enduring popularity can be attributed more to these controversies than to its worth as a great literary work.

Richard became embarrassed by charges that he had been liberal with the truth and his new-found fame did little to enhance his reputation, particularly within his home county. Richard Gowing, in *Public Men of Ipswich and East Suffolk* (1875), wrote, 'I confess I never knew a Suffolk man at home or abroad who would take any pride in being the fellow countryman of this clerical novel-writer.' Even Richard's preaching style came under fire from a steady stream of sermon tasters and journalists who, after the success of *Margaret Catchpole*, began to infiltrate the congregation of Wortham's celebrity rector. In 1858, one commentator reviewed Richard's preaching style as 'more pompous than impressive' and remarked that 'he became verbose and proportionately feeble'.

Though Richard remains best known for *Margaret Catchpole*, his illustrated biographies of the people of Wortham and observations on the workings of village life are infinitely more significant and were genuinely groundbreaking. They provide a vivid insight into the condition of ordinary people, albeit most of them elderly, in rural England during the early Victorian era. Such an undertaking, though unscholarly in nature, was truly pioneering and represents an early example of 'bottom-up' history at a time when only the lives of the great and the good were considered worth recording. This fact was not lost on Richard, who, in the introduction to the biographies which he entitled *Wortham Parochial Associations* (1860), wrote, 'How very few records have we of the poor people among whom we have lived ... not a single monument remains of the poor – their costumes in our day, their habits or their lives.' Almost without exception, Richard's subjects were either elderly or dead when he wrote about them. Given what he had to say about some of them this is perhaps just as well, but it also suggests that he was interested in recording completed lives and, indeed, death. The catalyst for this preoccupation with mortality was the gruesome suicide in a Piccadilly hotel of his younger brother, Edward, in 1860. It was while still consumed with grief at the loss of Edward that Richard determined to begin his 'round of recollection and remembrance' in the parish of Wortham.

A parallel work, *Features of Wortham* (1860), complements Richard's biographies through descriptions and illustrations of the cottages, houses, farms and public buildings of Wortham, providing a setting for the characters introduced in *Parochial Associations*. Most of the buildings Richard painted can be easily identified today as the village has changed relatively little. Richard's rather melancholy introduction to *Features of Wortham* seems to indicate that he had come to consider the village his home, or, perhaps, is a recommendation that one should settle for one's lot.

> *How often do we look for beauties in the features of distant lands, and forget the little nooks and corners of our own happy country. Alas, we often search for happiness and peace where they are never found.*
>
> *Search your own homes and hearts. If not there they are nowhere.*

Both *Parochial Associations* and *Features of Wortham* tell us as much about Richard as they do his rich cast of characters. In the former, he projects his own standards and moral code onto his subjects who are invariably judged by their piety, neatness, sobriety and capacity for hard work. Charlotte Wilby, the wife of Simon, the village's affluent tailor, is portrayed as a miserly, domineering woman without an ounce of charity. One suspects that Richard may have been more generous in his appraisal of her had she once shown her face in his church (she preferred to attend the small chapel on the edge of Long Green). Of the Wilbys, Richard writes,

> *Tailor Wilby I have seen at church, his wife never! There is an austerity of countenance in the latter, which commands even the portly dignity of the former, and deep is the lecture which female conceit can give even to a husband, if he dares go to church.*

Those who failed to live their lives quite as righteously as Richard would have liked were not altogether condemned providing they exhibited redeeming characteristics. John Mattocks, 'a man of colour', village barber and servant to the wealthy Harrison family, received Richard's praise for being 'remarkably clean' and for 'his honesty and many kind acts' despite his weakness for drink 'until even a little became too much for him'. Though acerbic in his criticism of those who could not meet his exacting standards in every part of their lives, he recognised that moral frailty in one aspect could be compensated for by propriety in another. Naturally, he was more inclined to identify good character in those he could count among his congregation but, taken as a whole, Richard's biographies reveal a genuine affection for the good, and not so good, people of Wortham.

The village schoolmaster, George Howlett, is described in affectionate terms as 'a specimen of a gone-by-day, when the fear of God was taught with a competent degree of arithmetic, writing and reading', though he was quite incapable of understanding the 'intricacies of science'. The fact that Howlett tried his best to turn ignorant children into respectable adults was enough for Richard, and his sympathies for the schoolmaster clearly extended beyond the pedagogical challenges of his profession. He observed, 'He [Howlett] must necessarily imbibe the foul atmosphere of a hundred boys and girls assembled in one room, which is not a very enviable situation.' In contrast to his admiration for Howlett, Richard held Rebecca Bobby, who ran the village's preparatory school, in lower esteem. He berates her as 'very ignorant' and her style of teaching as 'imposing rather than enlightening' though, typically, he praises her for her cleanliness and for her insistence on neatness in her pupils.

The tale of the death of one of Wortham's two Waterloo veterans provides a wealth of interesting historical information and conjures a vivid image.

Cobbold relates that Richard 'Soldier' Smith, a war pensioner who had fought in the Peninsular War and at Waterloo, died in 1846 while sitting on Wortham Ling in a wheelbarrow which he had ingeniously converted into a seat. A number of passers-by failed to notice that he was dead, assuming he was taking a rest from his labours on his allotment. Eventually, the dog of a wandering pedlar went up to Smith, sniffed him, barked and, upon getting no response, laid down at his feet. A coroner's inquest later concluded, rather unscientifically, that Smith had 'died by the visitation of God'.

Surprising aspirations for self-improvement are revealed in the tale of Israel Garnham, the donkey-minder, who left Wortham for America to find his fortune only to find that 'sharper fellows than himself do not succeed there better than they do here.' Despite becoming the object of ridicule upon his return, Garnham won Richard's admiration as a man who 'has seen more of the world and gained more experience than I have'. Garnham's voyage

John Mattocks, a Suffolk born black man, painted by Richard Cobbold, 1843.
(Courtesy of Suffolk Record Office, Ipswich branch.)

of discovery and the somewhat comical nature of Smith's demise would have gone unrecorded but for Richard whose descriptions, illustrations and opinions enable hundreds of small details to be assembled to form a colourful tapestry of rural life in the mid-nineteenth century. He tells us, for example, that Poll Parker, who died in 1852, was one of the last women in the parish to use a spinning wheel, while poor Martha Buck was a keen supporter of the 'Clothing Club', a savings scheme for the poor run by the wealthy Harrisons.

The corrupting influences of public houses are considered at length in Richard's writings. There were no fewer than five public houses in Wortham and he conveys the impression that he was locked in mortal battle with them for the soul of the village. In the second volume of *Features of Wortham*, Richard laments, 'There is not a single [public] house in my parish in which my knees have not been bent in prayer.' The Magpie Inn, the Dolphin, the Tumble Down Dick, the Queen's Head and the Cherry Tree, it seemed, were all bent on undermining his good work. Interestingly, Richard remarks that the Cherry Tree had no licence to sell liquor on the premises and operated as a 'beer house', a sort of Victorian off-licence. However, rather than carry beer home as the law intended, the Cherry Tree's clientele preferred to sit at its gate and imbibe by the roadside. The devastating consequences of excessive drinking crop up regularly throughout *Parochial Associations*. He tells us that in 1850 John Flatman was 'accidentally killed by a cart when intoxicated'; that Henry Potter drank himself to death at the age of thirty-one and that many more men lost respect and brought squalor upon their families through 'sotting'.

Despite a tendency to be haughty and judgmental, Richard also had a softer side. He recalled being genuinely touched when a young girl, going away on a short journey, spontaneously gave him a kiss, fearing that she might never see him again. He also possessed an impish sense of humour which he retained well into later life. One day, while out walking, he encountered two chimney sweeps atop a roof. Richard complimented the sweeps on the whiteness of their teeth which were gleaming through their sooty faces. In response, one of the sweeps offered to exchange his own teeth for Richard's for a pound, whereupon the rector began tugging at his own set. To the sweeps' horror, Richard dramatically pulled his teeth clean from his mouth and held them up in the air, proffering them as his side of the bargain. Terrified by such sorcery, the sweeps fled to the Queen's Head where they demanded brandy from the landlady, Mary Allen, claiming they had just seen the Devil. They could not have known that Richard had recently been fitted with a very early set of porcelain dentures.

In the final years of his life, Richard faced increasing ill-health. His sight and hearing began to fail and by the age of seventy-four he was unable to walk, calling himself 'a gouty sufferer who prays for patience'. He died at the age of seventy-nine on 5 January 1877. His beloved wife, Mary Anne had died just eleven days earlier and Richard was so frail that news of her passing was spared him. Both were buried in the churchyard at Wortham. Sadly, in 1862, Richard had felt compelled to sell the living of Wortham to King's College Cambridge for £5,000 in order to raise funds to enable his sons to marry: fifteen years later this step was proved to have been unnecessary as Richard left over twelve thousand pounds at his death.

Bishop John Coleridge Patteson (1827–71)
The Martyr of Melanesia

Just before midday on the morning of 20 September 1871, John Coleridge Patteson, the first Anglican Bishop of Melanesia, stepped out of a canoe onto the white coral beach of the paradise island of Nukapu in the eastern Solomon Islands It was not his first visit to the island and he was accompanied ashore by two chiefs, Moto and Taula, who had been friendly towards him before. The three men crossed the beach together and disappeared from view behind the coconut palms fringing the beach. At half past four that afternoon, a canoe, apparently empty, was set adrift in the lagoon inside the coral reef surrounding the island. Within the boat lay the lifeless body of Patteson wrapped in coconut matting. He had received a crushing blow to the right side of his head which must have killed him instantly. Thereafter, his assailants had inflicted a second wound to his head and one to his chest, while each leg had been pierced by an arrow. Within the matting, a palm, with five

John Patteson, engraved by C. H. Jeens from a sketch by George Richmond RA.
(Courtesy of Macmillan and Co.)

knots in its fronds, had been placed on the bishop's chest. Five wounds, five knots. The islanders of the South Pacific had many reasons to distrust Europeans, yet Bishop Patteson had always travelled among them as a man of peace. It seemed he had simply been in the wrong place at the wrong time.

John Coleridge (Coley) Patteson was born in London on 1 April 1827 to John (later Sir John) and Frances Patteson. His father, the son of Reverend Henry Patteson whom Richard Cobbold had succeeded at Wortham, was a barrister who went on to become a distinguished judge. His mother, John Patteson's second wife, came from the illustrious Coleridge family of Ottery St Mary in Devon and could count the poet Samuel Taylor Coleridge among her uncles. In the year of Coley's birth, his aunt, Lucy Patteson married John Chevallier Cobbold and thus a link was forged between two highly respected and influential East Anglian families.

Coley was schooled first, at the King's New Grammar School, Ottery and then, from age eleven, at Eton, where his uncle, the Reverend Edward Coleridge was his housemaster. He had an easy-going manner and was an able, though not exceptional student, easily distracted by the lure of the river and by cricket, at

which he was unusually gifted. It was while at Eton that he attended a service at Windsor at which the charismatic Bishop of New Zealand, George Augustus Selwyn, friend of his uncle Edward, delivered a sermon. Aged just fourteen, Coley confided to his mother that he had been so moved by the sermon, that his greatest wish was to go out to New Zealand with Selwyn when he was older.

After Eton, John went to Balliol, where his interest in religion deepened. In 1849, he left Oxford with a rather mediocre second-class degree in Classics and spent the next few years travelling through Europe, testing his physical abilities in the Alps and discovering a remarkable gift for languages. While tutoring in Rome, in 1851, he joined a party which was visiting the Vatican and which was presented to Pope Pius IX. When he returned to England in 1852, he obtained a fellowship at Merton which he held for the remainder of his life. His residence at the college, however, was short-lived; a curacy was waiting for him in the village of Alfington, just a few miles from Feniton Court, the home, between Ottery and Honiton, into which his parents had moved in 1841. On 25 September 1853, John was ordained at Exeter Cathedral and preached his first sermon a week later. Though he enjoyed his ministerial duties at Alfington, which had a 'salutary effect' on him, within a year John would be preparing to leave the rural idyll of east Devon for far more exotic climes.

As John was settling into his curacy, Bishop Selwyn was setting off on the long voyage from Auckland to England in search of recruits to take the gospel to Melanesia, a South Pacific archipelago between New Guinea and Fiji, comprising a number of small island groups including the New Hebrides, the Solomons, the Reef Islands and the Santa Cruz Islands. Selwyn corresponded regularly with John's uncle at Eton who, no doubt, would have mentioned John as possible missionary material. The bishop also knew Coley's father as he had been giving him legal advice concerning his proposed New Zealand Church Constitution. Consequently, Selwyn and his wife had scheduled a visit to Feniton, and arrived there in August 1854.

John required little persuading that he should pursue his adolescent ambition. On 28 March the following year, he set sail from Gravesend for New Zealand with the Selwyns. The arduous voyage was a tough initiation for the young clergyman, testing his sea legs for the island-hopping missionary duties which awaited him. Despite suffering from both sea- and homesickness, John arrived at Auckland with his sense of vocation intact. Shortly after the ship docked, he wrote to his sister, Frances (Fanny), 'I do not doubt that I am where I ought to be.'

Selwyn's strategy for the Melanesian Mission was to build a Church from the bottom up. He sought to persuade islanders to entrust the education of their young to the mission at St. John's, six miles from Auckland. There, the children would be taught the gospel and to read and write before being returned to their island communities where, it was hoped, they would gain influence and begin to convert others to Christianity. Selwyn and Patteson agreed that no attempt should be made to impose European values, customs or standards of dress upon the islanders; the aim was to promote the gradual indigenous growth of Christian faith by entwining it with the everyday life of the people. Of course, many recruits who boarded the mission's schooner, the *Southern Cross*, were lured more by the promise of adventure and luxury European goods than by any wish to be educated or converted.

Nonetheless, John was naturally suited to the work. He quickly mastered Maori and a number of Melanesian languages and this, along with his prepossessing manner, endeared him to the islanders and his pupils. For the time, he was unusually free from notions of European racial superiority and this was reflected in his work in the classroom at St. John's, where he recognised the futility of imposing draconian standards of discipline upon his free-spirited charges. Nearly half a century after his death, his successors at the mission considered that, 'His sympathy with the natives and power of acquiring their language were never equalled by any other white man.' Clearly, Selwyn recognised these talents as in 1861 John was consecrated as the first Bishop of Melanesia.

Patteson's diocese comprised no fewer than eighty-one disparate islands, with its centre more than two thousand miles from Auckland. He became the sole director of the mission, which he funded from his income from Merton and from an inheritance from his father who died in the year of his consecration. Every year, he would make a voyage to the islands and would live for a few months on one of the Loyalty, Bank or Solomon Islands. He would barter and trade with the islanders as well as presenting chiefs with gifts in order to gain their confidence. In 1868, he moved the mission's headquarters from Auckland to Norfolk Island, some six hundred miles closer to his diocese. Patteson's energy for his work was boundless and he was not downcast by the mission's limited success, which he considered would be gradual rather than spectacular. In December 1868, an important milestone was reached when he ordained the first native Melanesian deacon, George Sarawia in the small, makeshift chapel on Norfolk Island.

The mission's work was occasionally very dangerous. In 1864, following a visit to the island of Santa Cruz, Patteson and a number of his followers were rowing back to the *Southern Cross* when they came under fire from the beach. The bishop attempted to protect his crew from the hail of bone-tipped arrows by using the boat's rudder as a shield. However, three were struck and Fisher Young and Edwin Nobbs, both originally from the Pitcairn Islands, suffered agonising deaths from tetanus aboard the ship some days later. Though the islanders of Santa Cruz had a reputation for treachery, Patteson had visited the island before and had been warmly welcomed. The incident was an ominous portent of the fate awaiting the bishop on nearby Nukapu.

From the late 1860s, the *Southern Cross* was not the only European vessel cruising the South Pacific islands in the hope of enticing islanders to a new life. The unpleasant business of 'blackbirding', already thriving elsewhere in the South Pacific, reached Melanesia in 1865 with the issuing of the first licence to 'recruit' forty labourers from the New Hebrides to work on the sugar plantations of Fiji. There, and also on the Queensland plantations, the islanders were treated little better than slaves. Typically, they would work for three years in return for just three pounds per year, a few rags to wear, shelter and food. The blackbirders' operations were unregulated and they often employed unscrupulous tactics to entice islanders onto their ships. Gifts would be offered and, once on board, islanders would be locked up and effectively kidnapped. Patteson did not condemn this trade outright, believing that it had the potential to benefit the islanders as well as the traders and plantation owners, but he recognised that it required greater regulation to safeguard islanders from abuses; abuses which devastated families and communities across many islands, including Nukapu.

Patteson had visited Nukapu on at least four occasions prior to 1871, though had failed to gain a single recruit. A mission report, following a visit with Selwyn in 1858, describes the island's people as peaceful and hospitable,

> *We were remarkably struck by the very gentle orderly manners of the people of Nukapu; there was no confusion or noise among the many people who sat or stood around us, but a heartiness of manner and evident desire to do any thing that was in their power to please their strange visitors.*

However, with further visits, this warmth subsided. Nukapu was tiny, capable of supporting no more than about one hundred people and it could ill afford to surrender its young male population to the Melanesian Mission. Having made annual visits for the three (perhaps four) previous years, Patteson reported that the welcome he received in 1859 was noticeably cooler though not particularly unfriendly. It seemed to have dawned on the Nukapuans that trade was not the primary reason for the visits of the *Southern Cross* and that they became frustrated with repeated requests to give up their young men. The mission suspended visits to the island until 1870 (although Patteson might have visited in 1866), when he became irritated at the islanders' continued refusal to volunteer recruits. In a letter to the Bishop of Lichfield, he lamented that he 'could not spend time and property in coming every year and giving presents when they were unwilling to listen'.

It is remarkable, then, that he chose to return the following year. Before approaching the island, he had been made aware that blackbirders had abducted a number of young men from the island and sensed that he and his crew '*may* be exposed to considerable risk'. However, all seemed well as Patteson clambered out of the *Southern Cross*' dinghy and into the canoe carrying the islands chiefs. This transfer was necessary as the barrier reef could not be crossed at low tide, but it also helped to promote the bishop's friendly intentions. Once ashore, as on previous visits, Patteson was led to a hut reserved for visitors, to lie down and rest. Shortly after closing his eyes, he received a violent and fatal blow to the head. The weapon, a club, was normally used for beating mats.

At about the same time, the crew of the *Southern Cross*' dinghy, who were waiting for the tide to rise so that they might head for shore, came under attack. As they loosed their arrows at the Reverend Joseph Atkin and three Melanesian converts, the assailants, in canoes which had earlier escorted the chiefs out to the reef, were heard to cry, 'This is for New Zealand man! This is for Bauro man! This is for Mota man!' Atkin, John Ngongono and Stephen Taroaniara were all hit, but somehow managed to steer the boat back to the safety of the *Southern Cross*. That afternoon, at high tide, Atkin, despite his injuries, led a party across the reef in search of the bishop only to make the grim discovery in the lagoon. John Patteson was buried at sea the following day; within little over a week, Atkin and Taroaniara were also dead, both having succumbed to tetanus.

The precise reason that John Patteson was killed may never be known. Revenge for the abduction of five Nukapuans by blackbirders has long been the most popular theory and seems to be supported by the cries of those who attacked Atkin. Five was the number of missionaries attacked, the number of wounds inflicted on Patteson's body and the number of knots tied on the fronds of the palm placed upon his chest. Eyewitness accounts, taken many years later by the mission, support the view that there was no conspiracy on Nukapu and that the miscreant, whose family had been victims of blackbirding, acted against the wishes of the chiefs. It was said that this man, named Tetule, or Atule, fled to neighbouring Santa Cruz where he was hunted down and shot by that island's people. An alternative theory suggests that the Nukapuans may have simply become fed up with Patteson's attempts to recruit pupils and that his murder may have been a stark message to the mission to leave the island alone.

The Patteson memorial Chapel, St. Barnabas, Norfolk Island, South Pacific.
(Courtesy of St. Barnabas Trustees and Parish Council.)

A short time after the murder, a Royal Navy ship, HMS *Rosario*, which had been cruising in the South Pacific, approached Nukapu with the intention of investigating the circumstances of the bishop's death. The mission had asked the *Rosario*'s commander, Captain Albert H. Markham, not to attempt to punish the islanders. Sadly, the islanders considered the approach of a British warship hostile and fired a volley of arrows at it. The ship returned fire and a number of Nukapuans were killed.

John Patteson's death became a cause célèbre in England. The publicity it received, along with reports of his endeavours, inspired a new generation of Anglican missionaries. His murder also prompted calls to curtail the trade in human misery in the South Pacific, and Patteson's name was mentioned in this regard in the Queen's Speech of 1872. The Pacific Islanders Protection Act followed as an attempt to regulate, rather than eliminate, the human trade between the islands and the plantations, though it proved ineffective as it could only control British subjects and British ships. Blackbirding continued until the inauguration of the Commonwealth of Australia in 1901.

During his time on Norfolk Island, John had cherished the idea that the mission might, one day, be able to build a permanent chapel. In 1880, the mission opened the doors of its impressive stone built chapel, St. Barnabas, paid for from the considerable proceeds of the Patteson Memorial Fund. A brass tablet on the west wall bears a long inscription, written by Coley's cousin, Sir John Duke Coleridge, Lord Chief Justice of England (1880–94). These are perhaps its most poignant lines.

> HE DISPLAYED A CALM RESOLUTION IN THE PRESENCE OF DANGER,
> AN INTUITIVE JUDGMENT IN OVERCOMING DIFFICULTY,
> A TENDER COMPASSION FOR THE SICK AND SUFFERING,
> AND A LIBERAL CATHOLICITY OF SPIRIT AND SYMPATHIES,
> WHICH NOT ONLY WON FOR HIM THE DEEP REVERENCE AND AFFECTION OF
> HIS SPIRITUAL BRETHREN AND CHILDREN,
> BUT MADE HIS NAME BELOVED THROUGH ALL THE ISLES OF THE SOUTH
> PACIFIC,
> UNTIL HE FELL BY THE HAND OF ONE WHO KNEW NOT WHAT HE DID.

Lady Evelyn Cobbold (1867–1963)
First British-born Muslim Woman to make the Hajj

Lady Evelyn Cobbold.
(Family member's private collection.)

Evelyn Cobbold was never able to identify the precise moment she became a Muslim. In the introduction to her book, *Pilgrimage to Mecca*, she muses on the question and concludes that, 'It seems that I have always been a Moslem.' This rather vague declaration reveals that she never made a conscious decision to follow Islam: rather, the religion seeped into her through the experiences of her formative years, long periods of which she spent in North Africa. As a young woman, while visiting Rome, she was asked by the Pope whether she was a Catholic. She replied instinctively, 'I am a Moslem.' She recalled that at this moment 'a match was lit' and she resolved to study Islam thoroughly, reaching the conclusion that it 'was the most practical religion, and the one most calculated to solve the world's many perplexing problems'. Though she never formally converted, in 1933, at the age of sixty-five, she made the Hajj to Makkah (Mecca), a duty incumbent upon every able-bodied Muslim with the means to do so.

Evelyn was born in Edinburgh on 17 July 1867. Her father was Charles Adolphus Murray, 7th Earl of Dunmore (1841–1907), an ebullient minor Scottish peer with a lust for adventure. Dunmore was the epitome of the Victorian amateur explorer, travelling widely throughout Europe, North Africa and North America. His greatest adventure took him to central Asia in 1892 at the height of Anglo-Russian tensions during the Great Game. In common with many British travellers to the region at this time, Dunmore undertook some amateur intelligence work, submitting geographical observations to the Government of India. Unfortunately, he was a less than able surveyor; one critic acerbically suggested that he had seen things 'with the gigantic telescope of exaggeration'.

Evelyn's mother, born Lady Gertrude Coke (1847–1943), was the daughter of the 2nd Earl of Leicester and had been raised at the palatial Holkham Hall on the Norfolk coast before serving as lady-in-waiting to Queen Victoria. Gertrude certainly married beneath her. Shortly after they had married in 1866, Dunmore took her to the Isle of Harris to show off Amhuinnsuidhe Castle, which he had built as a grand sporting lodge. On seeing the imposing house, Gertrude allegedly mocked, 'But it's no bigger than a hen house or a stable at my father's house!' Stung, Dunmore commissioned a further wing to the castle, duly overextending himself and thus losing the castle and estate to his bankers. Thereafter, though not impoverished, Dunmore and Gertrude were required to run their household and their affairs thriftily. The family's comparatively frugal lifestyle was to influence Evelyn's choices in later life.

Gertrude travelled too. After she had married she spent a year in the North African desert with her sister Winifred, Countess of Leitrim, on what seems to have been a spiritual adventure during which she developed leanings towards Islam. Both parents' wanderlust and her mother's spiritualism rubbed off on Evelyn and were reinforced as the family began to winter, for reasons of economy, at a villa near Algiers. Over three winters, the young Evelyn imbibed Moorish culture, learned to speak Arabic and regularly slipped the attentions of her governess to visit mosques with her Algerian friends. She later recollected that, 'unconsciously, I was a little Moslem at heart'. Subsequent winters, spent in Cairo among the British expatriate community, slowed her unconscious drift towards Islam but failed to halt it. The match which had been lit was inextinguishable. Aged twenty-two, she wrote a poem while in Cairo which reveals her deep spiritual connection with the East and foreshadows her eventual personal affirmation as a Muslim woman.

> I stood on the roof in the still of the night,
> And looked my last on my Eastern home,
> The stars above shed their radiant light,
> Those stars would be with me where'er I roam.
> And their weird radiance was as soothing balm.
> That filled my soul with infinite calm.
>
> The city beneath me lay silent in sleep.
> It was the hush that precedes the dawn.
> And my soul yearned to the mighty void,
> To yield its mysteries ere the morn
> Awake, when the toil of the day would begin,
> With its burden of weary sorrow and sin.
>
> And as I gazed into those silent depths,
> The vague longings that filled my soul,
> Took the form of a prayer I upward sped,
> To Him, the One, The essence of all.
> And I felt his presence within and around.
> Divine, soul-enhancing *His Love I Found*.

And even flowed onward the mighty river
To yield its secrets unto the sea.
The mysteries of forgotten nations
The buried past of History.
And the weird cadence of the Mueddin's cry
Bid the faithful prepare for the day that was nigh.

And far in the East where desert and sky
Seemed to meet to welcome the morn.
Came slowly stealing across Abbasiyeh
The radiantly beautiful Dawn
Embracing all things in its tender light.
And I bade farewell to the silent night.

Evelyn's spiritual development, however, was soon to be subordinated to more practical matters. On 23 April 1891, in Cairo, she married the dashing John Dupuis Cobbold, seventh generation brewer; a match which would secure her financial future. The newly-weds arrived at Holy Wells, Cobbold's Ipswich estate, exactly a month later and a great party was laid on to welcome them home. Despite their impressive wealth, Evelyn considered the Cobbolds beneath her and, in echoes of her mother's snobbery, she referred to Holy Wells as her 'little villa'. Nevertheless, she and John appeared well suited, sharing a passion for field sports, enjoying London society and travelling together to Monte Carlo and Cairo. Three children arrived: Winifred (1892), John Murray, known as 'Ivan' (1897) and Pamela (1900). It appeared that Evelyn had it all, but neither motherhood nor the whirl of society life could bring her the spiritual fulfilment she desperately craved.

In 1911, this restlessness got the better of her. While wintering in Cairo, she made a nineteen-day journey into the desert to the Faiyum Oasis in western Egypt with an American friend, Frances Gordon Alexander. The subsequent account of this journey, *Wayfarers in the Libyan Desert*, clearly reveals that her instinctive affinity with Islam had survived the rigid conventions of her life in England. The text of *Wayfarers* is headed with the invocation *bismillāhi r-raḥmān r-rāhīmi* ('In the name of God, Most Gracious, Most Merciful') written in Arabic in her own hand; she refers frequently to herself and Frances as pilgrims, not travellers, and she appears to envy the simple existence of the people she encounters, 'who possess an impregnable faith joined with the power of concentration, who find their happiness in dreamy tranquillity and contemplation'.

Evelyn and Frances certainly did not 'rough it'. Their caravan comprised 'twelve baggage camels, two dromedaries, a sand-cart and pony, and five riding donkeys'. Their Arab retinue numbered twenty-three, not including their dragoman and his son, and they were accompanied by their maids. For the time, such an entourage was unexceptional, though it seems that whatever her spiritual connection with the people of North Africa, Evelyn was not prepared to forego western comforts. Her account is also laced with remarks, again typical for the time, that patronise the Arabs whom she employed and whom she encountered during the journey. If she was a Muslim, Evelyn was a Muslim on her own terms.

Evelyn continued to make regular winter visits to Egypt and while at Petra, immediately after the breakout of the First World War, she bumped into T. E. Lawrence, who had been gathering intelligence in the Sinai Desert. Lawrence borrowed some money from Evelyn so that he could pay off his guides and purchase a train ticket to Damascus. When both had returned to London, Lawrence took Evelyn to dinner by way of thanks and the two met up on at least one further occasion in Cairo the following year.

In 1922, Evelyn and John formally separated. Their children had grown up and it appears both had been unhappy in the marriage for some time. The separation was amicable and Evelyn was granted an extremely generous annual allowance of at least ten thousand pounds per annum. This became difficult for the Cobbolds to maintain, particularly after John's death in 1929. In addition, Evelyn was bought a mews house in Mayfair and the 15,000-acre Glencarron estate in Wester Ross, complete with an eleven-bedroom shooting lodge. It seems the latter purchase was an extravagant way of discouraging her from staying at the Cobbolds' estate near Pitlochry. For the remainder of her life, Evelyn was never more at home than when at Glencarron, indulging her love of field sports. She was a renowned markswoman and the estate became known as a prime spot for deer stalking.

Following John's death, it seems Evelyn felt more at liberty to pursue her faith. In early 1933, she confided to Hafiz Wahba, Sa'udi minister to London and former governor of Makkah, her 'desire to visit the Sacred cities', for which permission was required. This seemingly prudent step belied Evelyn's restlessness and she set sail for the Hejaz before Wahba had had chance to seek the approval of King Ibn Sa'ud, ruler of the recently united Kingdom of Sa'udi Arabia Shrewdly, Evelyn had invited herself to stay with Harry St John Philby at Jidda (Jeddah). Philby, father of the notorious double agent, Kim Philby, had worked for the Foreign Office in the Mandates of Iraq and Palestine before 'going native' in 1924. He was a trusted unofficial advisor to Ibn Sa'ud and

Evelyn clearly thought he might be able to open doors for her. Remarkably, prior to receiving her letter requesting his hospitality, Philby, who formally converted to Islam in 1930, had never heard of Evelyn. This suggests that Evelyn, herself, had not converted publicly; if she had, Philby would surely have been familiar with her name.

Evelyn spent an anxious fortnight with Philby and his wife, Dora, unsure she would be permitted to proceed to Makkah. Her hosts introduced her to Jidda society and she dined at the British Legation with the British minister, Sir Andrew Ryan, who later described her as 'a mighty huntress, and a Moslem ... though a pretty lax one'. Finally, on 12 March, she received word that the king had granted her permission to visit Makkah and Madinah (Medina). Later, Ryan cynically considered that Ibn Sa'ud's kindness to Evelyn was born from the knowledge that her son-in-law, Charles Hambro (Pamela's husband) was deputy governor of the Bank of England. This claim may have some foundation – Ibn Sa'ud's regime was in its infancy and had yet to tap into the nation's oil wealth.

In *Pilgrimage to Mecca*, Evelyn conveys the relief she felt at her good news: 'I had for so long lived in alternate fits of hope and despair, that I can scarcely credit that my great wish is at last to be fulfilled.' The official days of pilgrimage to Makkah did not start until 4 April, so Evelyn prepared to make the 250-mile journey north to Madinah, Islam's second holiest city. The journey required a passport, which bore her Muslim name, 'Sayyid Zainab' – Lady Zainab. Philby decided not to accompany Evelyn to Madinah; she had certainly made the most of his hospitality at Jidda and he feared that he would have to meet all her travelling expenses with little chance of ever being paid back. It appears her parents' requirement to be careful with money had made Evelyn unshakeably parsimonious despite the fortune she continued to receive from the Cobbolds and the fact that she had taken delivery of a brand new Rolls Royce in January.

She reached Madinah on 15 March after a fifteen-hour journey in Dora's car, 'the little Ford which gallantly carried us through those sandy wastes'. Not for Evelyn a suffocating bus journey through the desert or the cramped pilgrim hotels of Madinah: while in the Hejaz she travelled and lived apart from 'ordinary' pilgrims in relative luxury. Ironically she would later write that she 'inwardly prayed that the motor may never replace the camel'. She stayed at Madinah for nine days and became, or so she asserted, the first western woman to visit the Prophet's Tomb under the Green Dome of Al-Masjid an-Nabawi. She took in a number of other holy sites before returning to Jidda to prepare for her spiritual coming of age.

Evelyn arrived at Makkah just before sunset on 26 March. Her quarters in the city, arranged by Philby, were lavish, comprising a suite of rooms which was only let down by a bedstead which 'spoilt the Oriental character' of her bedroom. Philby had his own house in Makkah but seemingly felt that he had earned a further rest from his trying guest, though he escorted her around the city and even managed to persuade her to part with £50 in support of a local hospital. With the temperature rising daily, Evelyn herself was not completely well but was determined to fulfil her long-held religious ambition.

On 4 April, she donned her white pilgrim's *abaya* and made the short car journey to Mina, at the heart of the Hajj's sacred sites on the western outskirts of Makkah. There, she slept on the roof of the house of her hostess, grateful for the cool air of the night. Arriving in the Sacred Territory the following morning, she was struck by the sheer number of pilgrims who had endured great physical and material hardships to get there. Amid this devout throng, Evelyn was entertained in the opulent tent of one of the king's ministers and caught a glimpse of Ibn Sa'ud, of whom she was clearly in awe, as he passed by in his car.

Lady Evelyn in Pilgrim dress. Frontispiece from her book, *Pilgrimage to Mecca*, 1934. (Family member's private collection.)

Later that day, a short drive took Evelyn to the ruined mosque at Muzdalifah where prayers were said and where she and her party slept under the stars before rising at midnight to move on to the 'stoning place' where, in accordance with duty, she hurled seven pebbles at a wall representing the Devil. As the sun rose, she returned to Makkah and the Sacred Mosque, Masjid al-Harām where she performed the Tawaf, circumambulating the Kaaba, Islam's most sacred site, seven times in an anti-clockwise direction. After some sleep, she performed the Tawaf a second time before returning to Mina for the three-day Feast of Sacrifice. However, the heat and her physical and emotional exertions had taken their toll and as she lay down to sleep that night she realised her pilgrimage would have to end prematurely. Though clearly moved by her experiences, she longed 'to see green fields, grey skies, to hear the splash of rain, to escape from the pitiless sun'. On 7 April, Evelyn learned that the king had given her special permission to curtail her pilgrimage. Still, she performed the Tawaf one last time before returning to Jidda and, from there to London.

The closing words of *Pilgrimage to Mecca* are, 'To me an amazing new world has been revealed.' Evelyn had seen tantalising glimpses of this world throughout her life, and her pilgrimage, if not a formal conversion, was a personal affirmation of her faith. It certainly confirmed her as a Muslim in the eye of the western public through the interest of the press and the subsequent publication of *Pilgrimage to Mecca*.

Stubbornly resisting old age, Evelyn continued to travel to North Africa until war intervened and she published a further book, *Kenya: the Land of Illusion*, an entertaining travelogue describing a purely recreational journey she undertook in 1935 with her beloved grandson, Toby Sladen (Winifred's son). After the war, she divided her time between London and Glencarron, moving to the latter after breaking her hip in 1959, before moving into an Inverness nursing home that winter, because Glencarron had no heating. She died on 25 January 1963, aged ninety-five. Forthright to the last, she left detailed, explicit instructions for her funeral, which combined the two defining aspects of her life. She was to be buried on the Glencarron estate 'where the stags will run over my grave', facing Makkah. No Christian minister was allowed to attend and the service was conducted by an Imam. Evelyn's gravestone bears the words,

Allāhu nūr as-samawait wa-'l-ard
('Allah is the Light of the heavens and the earth')

The precise location of Evelyn's final resting place was chosen by Toby Sladen. When Toby died in 1976, he, too, left explicit instructions for his funeral. He was laid to rest alongside his beloved grandmother.

3 THE ARTS

In the words of the great French author Émile Zola: 'The artist is nothing without the gift, but the gift is nothing without work.' The Cobbold family is not particularly renowned for its artists (here considered in the wider sense of the word), though through the generations it has certainly had its 'tryers' – those with perhaps a little of the 'gift' and plenty of the 'work'. For example, the family's best-known book, *The History of Margaret Catchpole, a Suffolk Girl*, by Reverend Richard Cobbold (see Chapter 2), owes its fame more to the controversy surrounding its historical accuracy than to its merit as a work of literature. One of the 'artists' included here might also be considered a 'tryer' with an unexceptional talent who happened to do rather well by exploiting a set of very exceptional circumstances. The others, ironically less well known, represent the cream of the family's artistic crop. They were blessed with genuine flair and their work is still esteemed.

Two Williams, a father and son from Norwich, born during the Tudor age, excelled in very different fields. The elder was Norwich's foremost gold and silversmith whose workshop produced some of the most important provincial pieces of the period, a good number of which survive. His son was an organist and composer, best known for his madrigals and pieces for voices and viols. His compositions continue to stimulate academic interest and one was recorded commercially as recently as 2002. That the work of both father and son is still highly regarded is testament to their abilities.

In the late seventeenth and early eighteenth centuries, Elizabeth Cobbold's artistic talents covered a whole range of disciplines. Her most important artistic legacy, however, comprises hundreds of delicate scissor-cuts, painstakingly crafted to her own imaginative designs. Like filigree on paper, each piece must have required hours of patient concentration and hands as steady as those of the most skilled surgeon. Elizabeth was also an enthusiastic patron of many forms of the arts, providing encouragement and material support to those whose talents required nurturing. Within the family, those descended from this great Cobbold matriarch, including her son, Richard, have tended to have greater artistic leanings than those belonging to other branches of the family tree.

It is generally acknowledged that Lillie Langtry was not one of the most talented actresses of the Victorian and Edwardian era, though she is certainly one of the most famous. Actors are often considered to be emotionally brittle but Lillie could not have been further from this one-dimensional cliché. She was unshakeably determined to succeed and to exploit her talents to the full, though it was her beauty rather than her prowess as an actress that ensured that most of the theatres she played were full. She recognised this, and also that she would not be able to live off her looks forever. In an age when embroilment in scandal would often ruin a woman, her resilience was quite extraordinary. The Cobbold family's slender link to Lillie was not forged until the year of her death when Mary Selby Parkin (1908–2000) the great-granddaughter of her aunt, Jane Penrose Le Breton (1801–91), married Rowland Hope Cobbold (1905–86).

Martin Shaw certainly had the gift. He was a talented composer, one of a confident young group intent on inciting a revolution in English musical tastes in the early twentieth century. Despite the clarity of his vision, Shaw struggled to settle during his early career and, unquestionably, it was Joan Cobbold who provided him with the complementary element of Zola's maxim. The couple met and married in 1916 and, from that point, a life which had been chaotic, became ordered: the 'gift' was given the 'work' and Shaw was able to realise his full potential. Though his name may not be as familiar to audiences as it once was, his work was certainly well regarded in its day and largely remains so.

William Cobbold (*c*.1530–86) and William Cobbold (1560–1639)
Gold and Silversmith; Organist and Composer

These two Williams, father and son from Norwich, pursued very different careers in the arts. The elder, born during the reign of Henry VIII, became one of Norwich's leading gold and silversmiths, the quality of his work rivalling the best of his contemporaries in London. Much of his work was ecclesiastical and a surprising number of plates survive and can still be seen in churches across East Anglia. Secular pieces held – among other places – at Norwich Castle, in the Ashmolean Museum, Oxford, and in Amsterdam's Rijksmuseum are further testament to the extent of his abilities. Some years after his death, his craft was continued not by his heir, William, but by one of his younger sons, Matthew (1564–1604) whose work also seems to have been held in high regard, though as his mark is unknown, no evidence of it survives. William the younger's creative talents lay in a different direction altogether. An exceptionally gifted musician, he played the organ at Norwich Cathedral for many years and composed works of some note including a piece which was included in a remarkable collection of madrigals, a work of great significance in the history of English music.

The smith, William, having completed a seven-year apprenticeship to Thomas Bere, was admitted a freeman of Norwich in 1552. He lived and worked near Swan Lane in Cutlers Row (now London Street) in the shadow of Norwich Castle. He was part of a

The Reade Salt, silver-gilt, Norwich 1568/69. (Courtesy of The Corporation of Norwich.) Inset – the maker's mark of William Cobbold. (Clive Hodges.)

thriving community of goldsmiths in the city at that time, a community loosely bound as the Goldsmith's Company of Norwich. Assaying was not introduced to Norwich until 1565 and the manufactures of goldsmiths were unmarked before this time, rendering any appraisal or even identification of William's earliest work almost impossible but, from his later works and from the prominent role he assumed immediately marks and standards were introduced, it is safe to infer that his young business thrived and that his work was admired by peers and clients alike.

The period in which William sought to establish himself was one of great religious upheaval. The death of Edward VI in 1553 brought Mary to the throne and the restoration of Catholicism. Elizabeth, a Protestant, succeeded in 1558 and in the following year she appointed Matthew Parker, a Norwich man, as Archbishop of Canterbury to secure the Reformation. Among his reforms, Parker gave a great boost to gold and silversmiths throughout the land through an injunction requesting that all 'profane Cups, Bowls or Dishes hitherforeto used at Mass' should be replaced by 'a decent Communion Cup'. This conversion from chalice to communion cup was to keep William's order books full for many years, providing profitable work. One such cup remains the pride of St Andrew's, the parish church of Norwich goldsmiths. Christopher Hartop, expert on silver, observes that, 'Not only are Norwich-made cups often larger than those made in London, in many cases, especially with those from the Cobbold workshop, their quality and decoration are far superior.'

As a result of this boom, and to ensure the integrity of their trade, the Goldsmith's Company of Norwich at last decided that it was time to mark their work, a right which had been granted across the whole country in 1423 but which, up to that point, had not been taken up in Norwich. A petition was presented to the civic authorities in October 1564 and accepted. Of course, the prime reason for assaying wares made of precious metal is to guarantee the quality of materials used. Under the powers granted to the company, its wardens were given rights to seize inferior silver pieces and to enter the premises of any working goldsmith to inspect the quality of their work. These powers were invested in two wardens who were appointed by the company annually: William was nominated and served in the scheme's first year, 1564–65 and again in the following two years, a measure of his standing within the fraternity.

William's own mark was the Orb and Cross set in various shields or on its own. For many years this mark was not recognised as his, but instead, attributed to one of his contemporaries, Peter Peterson. However, a 1567 account was discovered detailing a payment made to William for a communion cup he had made. The cup survives and bears the Orb and Cross mark. William's extant work is far superior to Peterson's or indeed that produced by any goldsmith working in Norwich during the same period. Hartop maintains that William's was the largest workshop in the city and that William and other goldsmiths would have employed immigrant workers from the Netherlands; Norwich was a particularly cosmopolitan place in the late sixteenth century, with a quarter of its population speaking Dutch or French. Certainly some of William's pieces boast features that suggest continental influence.

In addition to ecclesiastical commissions, William was also in great demand for civic and private work. His great surviving masterpiece is the Reade Salt (c.1568), described recently by one expert, Charles Oman, 'as the most important piece of provincial silverware of the period'. The piece's commissioner was Peter Reade, a mercenary, knighted by Holy Roman Emperor Charles V for his part in the defeat of the Ottomans at Tunis in 1535. In later life Reade settled to a more prosaic life as a Norwich mercer. On his death he bequeathed a sum of twenty pounds for 'som piece of plate beying eyther a salte or a boll with a cover', which was to be given to the city of Norwich. To this day, William's exquisite creation, just over fifteen inches high and weighing fifty-nine ounces, remains the treasure of the city's civic regalia. Also in Norwich is perhaps William's next most important work, a silver, parcel-gilt flagon (c.1580), which was given to the city's Castle Museum by the Rothermere family in 1980. This is one of an unmatching pair; the other belongs to All Saints Church in Crostwight, Norfolk. Functional as well as ceremonial items left the Cobbold workshop: wine cups, spoons, jugs and tazzas (shallow dishes mounted on stems), all crafted to William's exacting standards.

It seems William gave up the business before his death as there is no mention of either tools or stock in his will. Matthew was not yet halfway through his apprenticeship to the goldsmith George Fenne at the time of his father's death and was unable, therefore, to take the reins of the Cobbold business. Rather, he set up on his own after he was admitted in 1593. William left a tidy sum but was not phenomenally rich. He was survived by his second wife, Joan Holderness (his first, Emma died in 1568) and by eight of his nine children, four of each sex. The younger William, as heir, was the main beneficiary of his will, receiving 'all my messuages [sic] and tenements in the City of Norwich after my wife's decease', whereupon he was to pay legacies to his younger siblings of between five pounds and twenty pounds.

Of William the composer's early life very little is known save for that which can be inferred from what is known of his father. He was the eldest of his mother's six children. She died when he was just eight and a year later his father remarried and fathered three more girls, William's half sisters. Given his father's standing in the city it is reasonable to assume that William was well educated, though no records of his schooling exist. Indeed, apart from the occasion of his christening, only one historical record of his life prior to 1594 survives. The accounts of Norwich Cathedral, then known as Christ Church, for the year 1581–82, show that the Dean and Chapter paid fees of 6s 8d to William Cobbolde for singing in the choir. Some twelve years later, William would secure more regular work at the cathedral when he was appointed organist. He was already composing his own work by this time, establishing himself as a musician of some note. He wrote a five-part elegy, *For death of her*, for Mary Gascoigne who died in July 1588 and, in 1592, he was one of ten eminent musicians invited by the renowned music publisher, Thomas Este (East) to harmonise the tunes for his *Whole Book of Psalmes, with their wonted Tunes as sung in Churches, composed into four partes.*

Undoubtedly William's most celebrated and enduring work is a five-part madrigal, one of twenty-five composed by no fewer than twenty-three composers, for *The Triumphes of Oriana* (1601). The *Oriana Madrigals*, as they have become known, have long been considered the brainchild of the composer and publisher Thomas Morley (himself, once Norwich Cathedral's organist). They are widely held to have been compiled in honour of Queen Elizabeth I, who was known as Oriana, the intention being to perform them at her court. Elizabeth, however, refused to listen to them and they were not performed in public until 1603, after her death. Recent research challenges the established view that the collection was intended for her. In his introduction to a recent recording of the *Oriana Madrigals*, Dr John Milsom calls to attention the fact that the book was dedicated not to the Queen but to her cousin, Charles Howard, Lord Admiral and Earl of Nottingham and that no mention of Elizabeth is made in Morley's dedicatory preface. Milsom also argues that there was no 'master plan' to bring the work of the composers together and that the madrigals 'were composed individually, and simply began to accumulate'. Doubt over Morley's role as the creative force behind the collection is also advanced by Milsom, though he maintains that it was Morley who put the work to press and who profited most from its success. The collection was instantly popular with singers who were intrigued by the variety of its component pieces which, according to Milsom, is the musical equivalent of a chocolate-box assortment.

William contributed the twelfth composition to the work, *With wreaths of rose and laurel* (SSATB – Two Sopranos, Alto, Tenor, Bass), considered to be one of the collection's superior pieces. The great Georgian musical historian, Dr Charles Burney, certainly thought so: reviewing *The Triumphes of Oriana* in the second volume of his *A General History of Music from the Earliest Ages to the Present Period* (1789), he remarked, 'The most agreeable madrigal in this collection seems to be the twelfth, composed by William Cobbold.' In addition to William, East Anglia was well represented among the work's other contributors: from Norfolk, Richard Carlton, vicar of St Stephen's, Norwich, and John Wilbye, originally from Diss, perhaps the greatest of all English madrigal composers; from Suffolk, George Kirbye from Bury St Edmunds and Michael Cavendish from the village of the same name. John Milton, father of the great poet, also lent his talents to the project.

William's other extant works, music for voices and viols, have recently been the subject of scholarly examination by Dr Ian Payne. *New Fashions* is 'an extended polyphonic composition in four sections' while in *In Bethlehem Town*, William's only surviving anthem, Dr Payne has identified a reworking of his earlier five part consort song, *Amids my bale*. Dr Payne has breathed new life into these compositions, meticulously reconstructing both insofar as the originals exist, and publishing his work in 2002. An early version of *In Bethlehem Town(e)* is preserved in Durham Cathedral's music library.

Norwich Cathedral where William Cobbold was appointed Organist in 1594.
(Courtesy of Hudson media.)

William held the post of organist at Norwich Cathedral until 1608 when he was superseded by William Inglott, son of Edmund, one of the cathedral's longest serving organists. William Inglott had played the organ at Norwich between 1587 and 1591 before taking up a similar position at Hereford. When he headed west, it seems some arrangement was made to enable him to resume his former position whenever he decided to return to Norfolk. William Cobbold resigned to make way, though would still deputise for Inglott and remained part of the cathedral's life as 'a singing man', a position he kept up for the remainder of his life. During the same period he also served as a lay clerk.

William was a man of substance. As organist at the cathedral he would have been reasonably well remunerated and many composers of the age augmented their income through lucrative private commissions for wealthy clients. He had also inherited the bulk of his father's estate and it is known that he had property in Ber Street in Norwich as well as in the parish of his birth, St Andrew's. His will makes interesting reading, providing perhaps the best clues to his character. Among the beneficiaries were the poor of four parishes in Norwich. He also left sums to the cathedral and its choristers and even the 'blowers of the organ' were remembered, each receiving 12d. Norwich Cathedral would have been a fitting final resting place and he had requested that he be buried there alongside his late wife, Alice, who died in 1630. When the end came, however, William was staying with relatives in Beccles and it was there, in the War Memorial Chapel of the parish church, St Michael's, that he was laid to rest. The inscription, now barely legible, concludes with the following rhyme:

> The body rest here
> But the soule above
> Sing heavenly anthems
> Made of peace and love

Elizabeth Cobbold (née Knipe) (1765–1824)
Champion of the Arts and Charity

The notion of the 'accomplished woman' in the higher reaches of society in Georgian England is one that remains familiar today through the works of Jane Austen. In particular, in *Pride and Prejudice*, it is the accomplishments of the Bennett girls that are considered essential to them securing a suitable match. In Chapter 8, Elizabeth Bennett, the Bingleys and Mr Darcy discuss the characteristics that define an accomplished woman, Miss Bingley concluding,

> *No one can be really esteemed accomplished, who does not greatly surpass what is usually met with. A woman must have a thorough knowledge of music, singing, drawing, dancing, and the modern languages to deserve the word; and besides all this, she must possess a certain something to her air and manner of walking, the tone of her voice, her address and expressions, or the word will be but half it deserves.*

Elizabeth Cobbold aged about 30, miniature self-portrait copied by her son Richard.
(Family member's private collection.)

Elizabeth Cobbold was the epitome of this ideal and more. Austen's romantic works conjure images of young ladies honing their accomplishments in order to gain the admiration of gentlemen of standing: for Elizabeth intellectual self-improvement was an end in itself. She was a great patron of the arts and a passionate supporter of those in whom she recognised a talent which required nurturing. Moreover, she was a generous benefactor of good causes and charitable institutions in her adopted county. Though intellectual enlightenment and the support of worthy causes were important to her, Elizabeth herself might have considered these activities subordinate to her most cherished role, that of wife to John Cobbold and mother and stepmother to the family's sizeable brood: in this respect she stands out as one of the Cobbold family's great matriarchs.

Little is known of Elizabeth's formative years. Evidence suggests that she was born in Watling Street, London on 25 February 1765, though some doubt surrounds even this. Her father, Robert Knipe is believed to have been a businessman who hailed from Liverpool and recent research suggests that her mother was Alice Waller whose family had roots in Kendal. It seems Elizabeth was a distant relative of the celebrated portraitist Daniel Gardner, also from Kendal; he was a friend of John Constable with whom Elizabeth later became acquainted.

At some point during Elizabeth's childhood the Knipes moved to Manchester. It was there, aged just seventeen, that, as Eliza Knipe, she published her first work, a collection of poems. She visited London frequently and would often be seen in her favourite bookshop. There, possibly through Gardner, she became acquainted with (Sir) Joshua Reynolds, the great portraitist to whom she dedicated *Six Narrative Poems* (1787). Significant among these, *Atomboka and Omaza* is an emotive condemnation of the slave trade in which the eponymous lovers choose death over a lifetime of bondage. This romantic tragedy reveals the humanity which was at the core of Elizabeth's being and the sympathy she held for life's underdogs.

From Manchester, the Knipes moved to Liverpool where, at St Ann's Church on 16 November 1790, Elizabeth married William Clarke. William, at sixty, was old enough to be her father and was in failing health, yet Elizabeth seemed genuinely in love with him. In a memoir accompanying a collection of Elizabeth's poems, her friend Laetitia Jermyn observed that Elizabeth 'strictly fulfilled all the duties of a wife, with affectionate solicitude and attention'. A Valentine's day verse which Elizabeth composed for her husband provides further evidence of her regard for William and mocks those 'tatlers and tale bearers' who view the disparity in their years with suspicious disapproval. This somewhat unlikely romance, however, was short lived: six months after their marriage William died, leaving Elizabeth a widow at twenty-seven. In the same year, 1791, as Eliza Clarke, she published a two-volume novel, *The Sword, or Father Bertrand's History of his own Times; from the Original Manuscript*.

It seemed unlikely that a young widow 'possessed of such amiable qualities of the heart, and gifted with so many attractions of the mind', as Jermyn put it, would remain on her own for long. John Cobbold, third-generation brewer and *just* twenty years her senior was the lucky man. John's first wife, Elizabeth Wilkinson had died two years earlier: she had borne him no fewer than fifteen children whose ages ranged from one to sixteen at the time of her death. Even with nannies and maids to help, this was a lot for a young woman with no children of her own to take on but such was Elizabeth's energy and kindness of spirit that she rose to the task magnificently. Over the next ten years the family swelled as John and Elizabeth had six boys and a girl, though sadly only four of these seven survived into adulthood.

The Manor House on Ipswich's St Margaret's Green was Elizabeth's home for the first seven years of her marriage to John and it was here that Margaret

Catchpole served the family. Elizabeth and Margaret seem to have been close, a bond strengthened when Margaret saved one of the children from drowning. When, in 1797, Margaret was arrested, tried and convicted for stealing one of John Cobbold's horses, it was Elizabeth's plea for clemency that saved her from the gallows (see Chapter 2, Richard Cobbold). Elizabeth's act of charity towards her former servant illustrates her affinity with those less fortunate than herself. In and around Ipswich, she generously supported existing charities and established new ones, employing her untiring energy and eloquence to great effect in their favour. Her efforts in this regard were wide ranging but she took a particular interest in causes which sought to improve the lot of women and children; the Ipswich Lying-in Charity supported expectant mothers in the town; the Society for clothing for Infant Poor, which she instituted in 1824, was a cause particularly close to her heart and she was the organising force behind Ipswich's 'Annual Charitable bazaar, for the works of Industry and Fancy', first held in April 1820.

This generosity of spirit was not just confined to her work for organised charities. She was a great encourager of nascent artistic talent in the young, regardless of their social standing or educational background. Mary Anne Goward certainly benefitted from her patronage. Elizabeth, recognising the beauty of her voice, took Mary Anne under her wing, cultivated her precocious talent and readied her for a career on the stage. Clearly proud of her young protégée, Elizabeth sent Mary Anne a poem of support when the latter took to the stage of the Ipswich Theatre for the first time. Sadly, Elizabeth did not live to see Mary Anne realise her full potential. She made her London debut in the opera *Rosina* in 1825 and, as Mary Anne Keeley (her married name), she gave up singing and enjoyed great success as an actress.

Another to benefit from Elizabeth's guidance was Ann Candler, a poet known as 'the Suffolk Cottager'. In her sixties by then, she was a woman of humble origin who, earlier in her life, had been forced to put four of her six children into the workhouse. Her poems were brought to the attention of Elizabeth, who was so impressed that she made all the arrangements to have them published. She corrected and arranged Ann's verse, wrote a preface with a short biography of the author and oversaw the volume's publication. *Poetical Attempts by Ann Candler, a Suffolk Cottager; with a short Narrative of her Life* (1803) sold more than five hundred copies; the profits from its success, as Jermyn remarked, 'to a person in the writer's lowly circumstances, afforded a considerable relief'.

Despite the demands of motherhood, Elizabeth continued to write, though inevitably her output was curtailed. She published, under the name of Carolina Petty Pasty, *The Mince Pye, an Heroic Epistle, humbly addressed to the Sovereign Dainty of a British Feast*, a mischievous parody of a pompous poem by Charles

Small Pybus MP, entitled *The Sovereign* which was addressed to the Russian Tsar. She also wrote plays for the children to perform though these remained unpublished until after her death. One such, *The Roman Mutiny* (1810), was a dialogue between two characters named Pompey and Terentius, roles taken by her younger sons, Richard, aged eleven and Edward, ten. In 1805, she persuaded army officers garrisoned in Ipswich to perform *Oronooka*, to which she added her own epilogue, for the benefit of the Lying-in Charity, and she continued to write poetry and to lend her support to theatrical and artistic ventures in and around Suffolk. She dedicated *Ode to the Victory of Waterloo* (1815) to the Prince Regent and donated the profits from its publication to the Waterloo subscription, a fund set up to support the returning wounded and those widowed and orphaned during the Napoleonic Wars. In 1818, she personally presented the Duke of Wellington with a bound copy of the poem. The written word was not her only artistic outlet; she painted and had an excellent ear for music, possessing a particular talent for the lyre. To complete the 'set' of artistic accomplishments she also mastered French, German and Italian.

Cliff House, and later Holy Wells, the family's new home from 1814, were focal points for polite society in Ipswich and Elizabeth was a most vivacious hostess. Foremost among the many parties and other gatherings she arranged was an annual Valentine Ball, held for the first time at Cliff House in 1806 and which became a lavish staple of the Suffolk social calendar. Elizabeth was in her element, playing matchmaker to the unmarried ladies and gentlemen whom she invited to the ball, and she would spend months preparing for it, delicately crafting up to eighty exquisite scissor-cut paper valentines each bearing a short romantic poem of Elizabeth's own composition and mounted on either red or blue paper. These were placed in two baskets, one for ladies, the other for gentlemen, before being drawn in turn by the eligible, once the party was in full swing. Impishly romantic, Elizabeth sought to get pulses racing and to help Cupid on his way. 'The prize', as Jermyn put it, 'was intended to prognosticate to the person, who drew it, marriage or matrimonial engagement in the ensuing year.' The following verse comes from a Lady's Valentine from the party of 1811.

THE ZODIAC
Lady, your horoscope foretells
A Scene where myrth and pleasure dwells;
And ev'ry sign the Zodiac bears
For you a fav'ring aspect wears:
Then chuse, where'er your thoughts incline,
And blessings wait your Valentine.

Every February, these parties became the talk of
Ipswich and provided the town's gossips with much
entertainment. The ball, and its organiser, became
famous well beyond the confines of Ipswich or even
Suffolk. Certainly Charles Dickens was familiar with
Elizabeth's reputation as a poet and hostess and, in
Pickwick Papers, he portrayed her as Mrs Leo Hunter,
the comic character who throws a costume party at
her home at Eatanswill at which she recites her own
memorable poem, *Ode to an Expiring Frog*. Prudently,
Elizabeth produced her valentine cuts by folding
pieces of paper, enabling copies to be made. She
compiled these into four albums, one for each of
her sons. Two of these survive intact, evidence of
her extraordinary dexterity and creative flair. Perhaps
more than her writings, these delightful scissor-cuts,
which provide an enchanting glimpse of polite Georgian society, are her greatest artistic legacy.

Scissor-cut Lady's Valentine by Elizabeth, of Ipswich
market cross, for her 1817 ball.
(The Cobbold Family History Trust.)

    Aside from her artistic accomplishments, Eliz-
abeth took a great interest in the sciences, unusual
for a woman at that time. She was particularly
fascinated by natural history, which Jermyn considered 'her favourite study'.
She was deeply interested in plants native to Suffolk and corresponded with
Sir James Smith, founder and president of the Linnean Society, for whom she
wrote a paper, though as a woman she was not permitted to present it herself.
She was also an enthusiastic gatherer of fossil shells, amassing an impressive
private collection and contributing many specimens to the eminent naturalist
and illustrator James Sowerby. Sowerby honoured Elizabeth's endeavours by
naming a particular variety of shell from the *Nucula* genus, *Nucula Cobboldiae*,
after her: Elizabeth was the first to provide him with a sample of the shell. The
dedication was made in Sowerby's *The Mineral Conchology of Great Britain* (1818).

> *Being desirous of commemorating Mrs Cobbold, whose copious collection*
> *obtained with great industry, in company with several of the junior branches of*
> *her family, whom she delighted to inspire with a love for the works of nature,*
> *from the crag pits of her own estate, evinces a taste and zeal seldom met with;*
> *I have named this rare and withal elegant shell after her.*

Elizabeth seemed to have an intuitive grasp of any subject she chose to turn
her attention to. She was a woman of many 'accomplishments' yet she never

subordinated her family or friends to her own literary, artistic or scientific ambitions, and she tried to instil in her children the same values of good spirit, charity and intellectual enlightenment which defined her life. Jermyn maintains that, despite her love of fun and parties, she was frugal and no slave to fashion: 'Her actions throughout her life shewed that she knew the right use of riches – to encourage merit, relieve the distressed, support the weak and raise the desponding.' Empathy was the defining trait of her character and all those who sought her counsel could count on a sympathetic hearing whatever their predicament, troubles or misdeeds.

Elizabeth died on 17 October 1824 after suffering a relapse from an earlier serious illness from which she had seemingly recovered. She was laid to rest in the family vault at St Clement's, Ipswich. Soon afterwards, a subscription was raised which funded a substantial mural monument at St Mary-le-Tower, Ipswich. It is inscribed with the following introduction: 'As a public testimony of respect for exalted talents and unwearied exertion in the cause of benevolence and charity …'

Lillie Langtry (1853–1929)
Professional Beauty, Actress and Astute Businesswoman

Lillie Langtry remains one of the best-known women of the late Victorian era. Her life has inspired dozens of books, several films and television serials, and few documentaries which assess the British royal family in the second half of the nineteenth century fail to mention her name. Undoubtedly, the continuing public fascination with Lillie is due largely to the very public affair she had with Bertie, the playboy Prince of Wales. Tales of royal indiscretion and scandal seldom go out of fashion, yet Lillie's life would have been scarcely less extraordinary had she never set eyes on the libidinous heir to the throne. She was the great beauty of her age, an extremely popular actress who made the most of her somewhat modest talents and who capitalised on her fame in a very modern way. She had enormous resilience, surviving the scandal of her affair and reinventing herself time and again. The general public loved her for it.

'The Jersey Lily' portrait by Millais, which had to be roped off from the crowds when it was exhibited at the Royal Acadamy.
(Courtesy of Société Jersiaise Photographic Archive.)

Lillie was born Emilie Charlotte Le Breton at St Saviour's rectory, Jersey, the sixth of seven children and only daughter of William Corbet Le Breton (1815–88), Dean of Jersey and his wife Emilie (née Martin). 'Emilie' was always known as 'Lillie' to her family and friends and this is the name, still visible, which she scratched on one of the rectory's windows as a child. With no sisters to play with, the young Lillie grew up a tomboy and, at an early age she learned to sail, swim and ride and seems to have been treated as 'one of the boys' by her exuberant brothers. While they all went off to the local public school, however, Lillie was educated at home, taking to languages particularly well. As the young tomboy grew into womanhood, Lillie's blossoming beauty became renowned across the island and there was no shortage of suitors hanging around the rectory even when she was in her early teens.

Unlike many fathers of the day, the dean seems to have been quite relaxed about the male attention his striking young daughter was receiving, providing the gentlemen in question did not overstep the mark. One overeager suitor was Lieutenant Arthur Longley, the Archbishop of Canterbury's son, who became

William Corbet Le Breton (1815–88), Dean of Jersey,
Lillie's father.
(Courtesy of Société Jersiaise Photographic Archive.)

infatuated with Lillie while garrisoned on the island. When Longley asked the dean for Lillie's hand he refused politely on the grounds of his daughter's minority – she was still just fourteen. Later, Le Breton saw Lillie strolling out with a local lad, a fisherboy. The pair were of a similar age and it seemed that Lillie was quite taken with the boy. The dean, who had seldom raised any objection to Lillie's choice in boyfriends, took her to one side and forbade her from seeing the lad again. For Lillie, her father's insistence was out of character. Whether or not her father confessed his reasons, the rumours that swept over the island could not have escaped her ears: the boy was her own half-brother, the product of one of the dean's many amorous indiscretions across the island. An insatiable philanderer, Le Breton acquired the unholy nickname of 'the Dirty Dean': much later, in 1880 the salacious rumours became too much and caused him to depart the island for good.

An opportunity for leaving Jersey presented itself when, aged sixteen, Lillie went to London with her mother to attend a ball held by Lord Suffield, a member of the royal household who spent summers on Jersey and who had been captivated by Lillie's beauty. Lillie felt distinctly unsophisticated, a country girl among London chic, and she vowed that when she returned to the capital she would take it by storm. Despite the constant stream of admirers, Lillie began to find life on Jersey parochial and tedious. Her glimpse of London life had made her socially ambitious and when a passport to escape the island arrived in the form of the wealthy Irish widower, (Edward) Ned Langtry, she eagerly snatched it.

The couple were married at St Saviour's by Lillie's father in March 1874. Ned was the son of the owner of Belfast's largest shipbuilder and had a luxurious yacht, *Red Gauntlet*, on which his new wife loved to sail. Immediately, they settled at Noirmont Manor on the island but Lillie's long-term ambition was to get to the English mainland and, if at all possible, to London. Ned was set against the idea but Lillie wore him down, first getting him to Southampton, and then in 1877, after a serious bout of typhoid, persuading him to rent rooms in Eaton Place on grounds that London (despite its filthy air) would aide her convalescence.

Cracks had already begun to appear in the couple's marriage. Ned's fortune was being frittered away and, in London, he missed the country life he preferred and quickly grew weary of trotting behind Lillie to museums, art galleries and theatres. Lillie, though, was in her element and her beauty quickly made her a sensation in London society. The breakthrough came at a soirée at the home of Sir John and Lady Sebright in Lowndes Square, to which she and Ned were invited by Lord Ranelagh, who knew her from Jersey. Dressed in a figure-hugging black dress (she was mourning the loss of her brother, Reggie), her hair tied up simply and without any jewellery, Lillie turned the heads of the Sebrights' distinguished guests, who included Henry Irving and James Whistler. She became the talk of the town and Whistler was just one of several well-known artists who queued up to paint her portrait: her favourite, entitled 'The Jersey Lily', was painted by John Everett Millais. Soon her fame spread far beyond the whirl of London society: penny postcards carried her likeness, newspapers reported her every move, the clothes she wore dictated the fashions of the season and the 'Langtry knot' became the hairstyle of choice for thousands of women. She was a celebrity in the very modern sense of the word and was one of the first women to be used to advertise commercial products: she became the face of Pears soap and her endorsement was rewarded to the sum of £132.

Lillie's affair with the Prince of Wales is well documented. A man of many mistresses, Bertie seems to have been particularly fond of Lillie and uncommonly faithful to her (though not to his wife). For other conquests he bought trinkets: for Lillie an imposing residence, The Red House at Bournemouth. He even introduced her to his mother. Yet by 1880 his eyes were beginning to wander again, in particular in the direction of the famed French actress, Sarah Bernhardt, and Lillie was beginning to feel marginalised. Desperate for Bertie's attention, she committed an embarrassing public faux pas in the presence of his wife, Princess Alexandra. This infuriated the prince who ended the affair, leaving Lillie ostracised from his sycophantic circle of friends and from wider society.

Her star falling, Lillie fell into the arms of Bertie's cousin, Prince Louis Battenberg, a German prince and officer in the British Royal Navy. She became pregnant. Battenberg has long been assumed to have been the father, but recent research by Laura Beatty reveals letters between Lillie and another lover, Arthur Jones, which might suggest otherwise. Whatever the case, Bertie stepped in to help contain the scandal, arranging for Lillie to see out her pregnancy in Paris where she was hardly allowed to go out. Louis was sent away to sea and Ned was kept in the dark, Bertie sending him away to America on some concocted princely business. Lillie's daughter, Jeanne, was born in Paris in March 1881: for the first ten years of her life she was told that her mother was her aunt and it was not until she reached adulthood that she learned the identity of the man assumed to be her father, Battenberg.

Lillie returned to London without Jeanne, who was taken to The Red House and placed in the care of Lillie's mother, who had by this time given up on the lecherous dean. Lillie, too, was estranged from her husband and she had realised that she would not be able to live off her looks forever. Encouraged by her friends, Oscar Wilde and the theatre manager Henrietta Labouchère and inspired by her erstwhile rival, Sarah Bernhardt, Lillie decided to pursue a career in the theatre. Her first part was in an amateur production of *A Fair Encounter* at Twickenham Town Hall. Her acting career did not get off to an auspicious start, however. She later recalled, 'When I found myself on the diminutive stage, my mind became a blank. Alas! not a word of the opening soliloquy could I remember.' She overcame her stage fright that day and her career took off when she joined the Bancroft Company. She made her professional debut at the Haymarket on 17 December 1881, taking the part of Kate Hardcastle in Oliver Goldsmith's *She Stoops to Conquer*. In the royal box that night sat the Prince and Princess of Wales. She was a competent actress but it was more her celebrity, or even notoriety, which ensured that the theatres she played were always full. At the Haymarket that day, crowds queued around the block for tickets, bringing sandwiches and camping stools with them. The performance went well, and Lillie later reminisced 'countless bouquets were thrown to me and everything seemed like a dream to me when it was all over'.

Buoyed by her success, Lillie spent three months with the Bancrofts before she was released, and embarked upon an exhausting tour of the provinces. Back in London in September 1882, her performances in *As You Like It* and *An Unequal Match* drew unkind reviews. Clement Scott of *Punch* remarked 'her action is as constrained and mechanical as that of an Eton sixth form boy on speech day'. Laura Beatty, one of Lillie's more recent biographers, maintains that Lillie knew that public curiosity in her would wane and that, sooner or later, she would have 'to fight for bit parts like anyone else'. Rather than slip into obscurity, Lillie decided to form her own company with Henrietta Labouchère and to try her luck in America.

She was a sensation from the moment she stepped ashore in New York, where her arrival had been eagerly anticipated. Traffic came to a standstill and the New York Stock Exchange was closed as thousands craned their necks for a glimpse of Lillie. Oscar Wilde, on a lecture tour of the country, took Lillie under his wing and showed her the sights, including Niagara Falls. On the stage, Lillie played to packed audiences and, though critical reviews were somewhat lukewarm, box office receipts far exceeded expectations. Henrietta, piqued by Lillie's success and by the attention Wilde afforded her left the tour early, though this did nothing to hinder Lillie's rise. She fell in love with a phenomenally wealthy young businessman from Baltimore, Freddie Gebhard, who showered her with expensive gifts and who pestered her relentlessly to divorce Ned so that they might wed. The most lavish of Gebhard's gifts was a sumptuous railway carriage, *The Lalee*, in which Lillie travelled the length and breadth of America and which cost Gebhard a quarter of a million dollars. When Lillie was in America and not touring, she lived in New York with Gebhard.

Among Lillie's biggest fans was Judge Roy Bean, a colourful justice of the peace and saloon owner from Texas. So enthralled was Bean by Lillie when he saw her perform in Chicago that he renamed the land in Texas on which he was squatting, Langtry, and his saloon there, The Jersey Lily. Between 1882 and 1889, Lillie flitted between England and America, doing very well for herself. In 1887, Gebhard persuaded Lillie to become an American citizen so that she could obtain an American divorce from Ned. This Lillie did, but she still refused to marry Gebhard, though she was less reluctant to enter into commercial ventures with him. The following year, with Gebhard, she bought a 6,000-acre ranch in California, Langtry Farms, a string of racehorses on both sides of the Atlantic and even began producing her own wine.

Not long after Lillie had set up home at Langtry Farms, a railway accident in Pennsylvania claimed the lives of seventeen thoroughbreds she had bought and was having transported from the east of the country to her ranch. This loss, compounded by news that her father had died alone and penniless, disheartened her and, not long after, she abandoned California for London, though she continued to own the ranch for some years afterwards. She all but retired from the stage and directed her energies into her new love, the sport of kings. She finished with Gebhard in 1892 and had a brief and tempestuous affair with George Baird, a wealthy racing enthusiast who taught her much about the game. The downside of this relationship was that Baird was a violent misogynist. Once, he put Lillie in hospital having found her in a Paris hotel in the arms of another man. He persuaded her not to press charges by presenting her with a 220-foot racing yacht, *White Ladye*. The affair came to an abrupt end when Baird died suddenly in 1893.

Bertie, the Prince of Wales, was also a racing enthusiast and Lillie would often be seen with him, as a friend, at the Royal Ascot meeting. For a while, Lillie owned stables in Newmarket, though this venture was unsuccessful financially. Still, the horses she owned as 'Mr Langtry' enjoyed some success and none more so than Merman, the promising stayer she bought from Australia. In his first season in England, Merman won the Cesarewitch at Newmarket. Not only did Lillie collect the handsome prize money but she had also backed it to the tune of a thousand pounds at odds of eight to one. That same night, her celebrations were tempered by news that Ned had died in a lunatic asylum having been taken there drunk, destitute and with injuries to his head. Merman went on to further successes at Goodwood and, perhaps most notably, as a 25–1 outsider at Ascot where he won the Gold Cup, the Blue Riband for stayers, in 1900.

On the same day as Merman was galloping to one of his Goodwood wins, Lillie tied the knot again. At St Saviour's, the church most dear to her, on 27 July 1899, she married one of her many suitors, Henry de Bathe, a young aristocrat nineteen years her junior. A return to the theatre beckoned and she opened her own play, *The Degenerates*, at Jersey's new Opera House in July 1900. The following year she turned theatre owner, sinking much of her considerable fortune into London's Imperial, which she bought and refitted. The Imperial, however, was large and difficult to fill and, despite the regular appearances in the royal box of Bertie, from 1901 King Edward VII, the venture lost money and Lillie sold up in 1903. The Imperial was eventually pulled down in 1907. That same year, Lillie achieved perhaps the one thing she had yearned for more than any other, social respectability: she became Lady de Bathe when Hugo inherited his father's baronetcy. In their relationship, however, Lillie was undoubtedly the breadwinner.

Lillie's tenacity and ambition had seen her through some difficult times but even when settled with Hugo and financially secure she did not rest on her laurels. She toured South Africa for six months, performed in Vaudeville in New York, learned to drive and, in 1913, appeared in the silent film, *His Neighbour's Wife*, reprising a role she had played on stage. In between work, she visited Monte Carlo regularly, and in 1907, she became the first woman to break the bank there. During the Great War, she took to the stage in support of the Red Cross and of troops, British and American, raising both moral and money for the cause.

Lillie retired from acting for good after the war and soon after settled in Monaco, where she bought a villa, Le Lys. In 1925, she published *The Days I Knew*, a selective autobiography which circumvented the more stormy periods of her life. The book makes not a single mention of her daughter, Jeanne and their strained relationship. In her final years, she separated from Hugo and lived a rather lonely existence for one so gregarious and longing of attention. She died at home in Monaco in February 1929 and was laid to rest at St Saviour's, the place she always considered home. That she came out of her dramatic and turbulent life on top is testament to her optimism and her refusal to feel sorry for herself when at a low ebb. She looked forward, not back. As she once famously remarked, 'Anyone who limits her vision to memories of yesterday is already dead.'

Dr Martin Edward Fallas Shaw, OBE (1875–1958) and Joan Lindley Cobbold (1890–1974)

Composer and Musical Reformer; Accomplished Musician and Shaw's Guiding Light

Martin Shaw, a contemporary and friend of Gustav Holst and Ralph Vaughan Williams, was a prolific composer who wrote over three hundred pieces. Though his oeuvre is not as well known as those of his illustrious friends, Shaw remains one of the most influential British composers of the last century and was a driving force behind the revival of what he termed 'Englishness' in music. Though he always adhered to this mission, this gifted man's early career meandered somewhat until he met and married Joan Lindley Cobbold in 1916. He considered marrying Joan 'the best thing I ever did in my life'. Joan, herself a talented musician, brought a loving stability to Shaw's life which enabled him to direct all his energies into his music, and it is no coincidence that he was more prolific and creative in the years after their union than he was prior to it. Joan was much more than just a wife and mother; she managed her husband's affairs and collaborated with him in his work. Together they were a formidable team.

Martin Shaw. The frontispiece to his book *Up to Now*, 1929.
(Courtesy of The Martin Shaw Trust.)

Both came from musical families. Martin's father, James Shaw (1842–1907) was a church organist, first in Edinburgh and then in London who, as a very young choirboy in Leeds, had come under the tutelage of Samuel Sebastian Wesley, the renowned organist and composer of church music. His mother, Charlotte James (1850–1912), was a trained pianist. Music was at the heart of Martin's upbringing; in his memoir, *Up to Now* (1929), he mused, 'I cannot remember a time when I couldn't play the piano and the organ.' He and his eight younger siblings were raised in Hampstead, north London, though Martin was born at 3 Camberwell Green within earshot of the bells at Bow and always proudly considered himself a Cockney. He had the sad misfortune to be born with a large birthmark which covered the whole left side of his face, which his friend, Erik Routley, author of *Martin Shaw, a centenary appreciation*, described as 'one of the most alarming facial disfigurements any mortal ever had to bear'.

This did not make him shy, but that he felt inhibited by it is evident in almost every photograph taken of him: he, quite understandably, always offered the right side of his face to the camera.

Joan's grandfather, (Richard) Lindley Nunn (1826–1901), was a well-known Ipswich choirmaster and music teacher; her mother, Alice Bessie Nunn was a virtuoso pianist who had won first prize, a grand piano, in a competition in Paris when she was just sixteen. Alice married Alfred Townshend Cobbold OBE, an Ipswich solicitor, in 1886. Joan was the third of their seven children and grew up in the village of Bramford, a few miles north-west of Ipswich. Joan shared her mother's gift for music and, at nineteen, she took and passed the LRAM (Licentiate of the Royal Academy of Music), which she considered 'the quickest passport to a livelihood'. In the late Edwardian period it was still unusual for a young woman of Joan's class to follow a career but it seems that she did not want to be a burden to her parents. Her father, as was expected of a man of his social standing, maintained a large household, but Joan was aware that this was a considerable financial burden for him. Of the twenty-two mouths he had to feed, she determined that she would be one less. Aged twenty-one she secured a position as lecturer in music at Whitelands College in Chelsea. Whitelands was established in 1841 by the Church of England's National Society as a teacher training college for women; today, it forms part of the University of Roehampton. Joan recorded that her duties at Whitelands included 'directing choral sessions, playing the organ for daily Chapel, organising the Saturday socials' and carrying out the 'demands of the Syllabus for the Board of Education'.

By the time Joan was just starting out on her career, Martin, fifteen years her senior, was well into his. Aged twenty, he had gone to the Royal College of Music where he came under the tutelage of the composer Charles Villiers Stanford, one of its founding professors. It was here that he studied with Holst, Vaughan Williams, Samuel Coleridge-Taylor, John Ireland (best man at his wedding) and others. In *Up to Now*, he remarked, 'I don't suppose there has ever been a time in English music when such a galaxy of young composers studied at the same period under one master.' Martin, however, quickly became disillusioned at the course's lack of 'Englishness' and bemoaned that it was centred on the works of the European masters such as Mozart, Beethoven and Brahms. He later lamented that he had not once heard the words 'folk music' or 'English music' in his whole time at the college. Frustrated, he left the college without taking a degree, 'unhonoured and unsung'.

While studying, Martin also took paid work as organist at Emmanuel Church, Hampstead, where he pulled stops and depressed pedals between 1895 and 1903. If this provided steady work, the opportunity to be more creative came in 1897 when he met and became firm friends with (Edward) Gordon Craig, the theatre reformer. Craig, Martin soon realised, was the perfect theatrical foil to help him advance his own musical agenda, which sought to revive English music from a much earlier age. When Martin founded the Purcell Operatic Society in 1898 he asked Craig to design the *mise-en-scène*, and together they staged a number of groundbreaking productions including *Dido and Aeneas*. Its opening night at the Hampstead Conservatoire was the first public performance of Henry Purcell's music for two hundred years. Indeed, so little was known about Purcell at the time that, following the production's move to the Coronet in Notting Hill, one of the theatrical papers sent three copies of its issue bearing a favourable review to: Gordon Craig, Esq., Martin Shaw, Esq., and Henry Purcell, Esq. Despite receiving critical acclaim, the production was not a financial success, though, as Martin recalled, 'we were not to be deterred by such gross considerations'.

Other productions followed, notably *The Masque of Love* (1901), adapted from Purcell's semi-opera, *Dioclesian* and John Gay's *Acis and Galatea* (1902). In 1903, Martin composed and conducted the music for productions of *The Vikings* and *Much Ado About Nothing*, directed by Craig and staged by the company of his mother, the famous actress Ellen Terry. Hobnobbing with the stars of the day, Martin's face became familiar in bohemian London and he took to wearing a sombrero, sandals and cloak. This offbeat lifestyle was nothing new to him, but in keeping with his upbringing: his father was an eccentric whom he would later describe as 'bohemian to the core'.

In 1904, disillusioned that his gifts were received with indifference by the British public, Craig departed for the continent never to work in England again. In 1906, he invited Martin to join him in Berlin to conduct for the legendary American dancer, Isadora Duncan who was, at the time, Craig's lover. Martin arrived in Berlin three days later. He was initially star-struck in Duncan's presence and captivated by her ability to hold an audience for an entire show on her own. 'Her serenity,' he wrote, 'makes me think of a still, deep lake over which no breeze made the faintest ripple.' He was not quite so enamoured with some of the orchestras he was required to work with during tours which went all over Europe; he caustically described one as 'solid, stolid and squalid'.

After a year or so on the road, Martin's career came full circle in 1908 when Ralph Vaughan Williams suggested that he apply for the post of organist at St Mary's, Primrose Hill. St Mary's vicar, Reverend Percy Dearmer, was a leading Christian Socialist and a kindred spirit who loathed the 'modern' church music of the nineteenth century. Martin and Dearmer had had an earlier association, the former carrying out research into old songs for *English Hymnal* (1906), jointly edited by Dearmer and Vaughan Williams.

At St Mary's, Dearmer introduced Martin to plainsong, or Gregorian chant, which had been banished from the Church of England since the Reformation and which Dearmer was attempting to revive. Along with English folk music, plainsong would become one of the great cornerstones of Martin's future work. Together, he and Dearmer compiled *The English Carol Book* (1913). In his introduction to the book, which he considered a break from the 'banality' of nineteenth century ecclesiastical music, Martin expressed the hope 'that the time is ripe for an attempt to be made to present our national Carols in a manly and fitting way'. In the same year, Martin co-founded the Summer School of Church Music as a vehicle for accelerating the revival of Englishness in music. During this period, he also collaborated with Dearmer's wife, Mabel, on a number of musical plays including *Brer Rabbit and Mr Fox* (1914).

Aged 39 when World War I broke out, problems with his eyesight due to iritis prevented Martin from seeing enemy action. Fiercely patriotic, he diverted his energy into supporting the war effort through his music and by campaigning against the performance of works by German composers. His own wartime tunes were stridently nationalistic and *Six Songs of War* (1914) provided him with his first commercial success, setting his career on an upward trajectory. He followed it up with *Songtime* (1915), which included the first appearance of his setting of 'Royal Oak' to 'All Things Bright and Beautiful'. The influence of Joan, whom he married in 1916, would help ensure that these successes were sustained.

They had met earlier that year through Martin's brother, Geoffrey, also a composer and an inspector of schools for the Board of Education. The principal of Whitelands, Miss C. G. Luard, had arranged dinner with Geoffrey and his brother Martin and she invited Joan to make up the four. Of that first meeting with the man whom she would marry six months later, Joan recorded, 'His physical disfigurement agonized me – his conversation was sheer magic.' She continued, 'Martin was "heady" and all sweetness and calibre.' A short courtship ensued, with music as its backdrop. Their next meeting came when Martin attended the college's May Day celebrations at which Joan performed one of his songs, 'County Guy'. Afterwards, Martin told her it was the first time he had heard it played fast enough. Later, the two met again at a singing rehearsal at St Paul's. Joan recalled, 'A look passed between us, and Life began.' Then, as Martin was working at St Martin-in-the-Fields on the musical arrangement for the S.P.G. (Society for the Propagation of the Gospel) Pageant he was again struck nearly blind by rheumatic iritis: Joan stepped in to help, becoming his eyes. They became engaged in June and were married by Dearmer at St Mary's on 24 July, Martin's bandages coming off just the day before. Two sons, John and Richard (Diccon) and a daughter, Mary Elizabeth later completed the family.

With Joan as his rock, Martin settled down and his career went from strength to strength. He spent the remainder of the war extolling the virtues of English church music at a time when patriotic congregations were particularly receptive to new interpretations of old English songs and when the public at large were ready to reject the German musical hegemony of the nineteenth century. Martin, together with Vaughan Williams, Holst and others, was in the vanguard of this national revolution, which sought to enlighten not only churchgoers but also schoolchildren and theatre audiences. In 1918, Martin co-founded the League of Arts, which organised the armistice celebrations.

Joan Lindley Shaw (née Cobbold) in later life. (Family member's private collection.)

After the war, Martin continued to strive to reintroduce folk songs, traditional carols and Tudor hymns to congregations which had had to settle for what he considered the dreary Victorian compositions of Stainer, Dykes, Barnby and others. Between 1920 and 1924 he directed the music and played the organ at St Martin-in-the-Fields where he ruffled a few feathers with his progressive selections and arrangements. He was also director of music for Maude Royden's Guildhouse Fellowship, a position he held for several years. In 1925, with Dearmer and Vaughan Williams, he edited *Songs of Praise*, a manifestation of everything he held dear in church music, which he promoted with missionary zeal across England as an alternative to the ubiquitous Victorian staple, *Hymns Ancient and Modern*. Three years later the same trio brought out *The Oxford Book of Carols* (1928), a collection of traditional English Christmas songs with a sprinkling of brand new carols, written by English composers. A revised *Songs of Praise* came out in 1931, which was most notable for the inclusion of the traditional Gaelic hymn-tune, 'Bunessan', which was set to a poem by Eleanor Farjeon, specially commissioned by Martin. The hymn became an indispensable constituent of the school assembly for generations of children and a worldwide hit for Cat Stevens. It was 'Morning Has Broken'.

Martin and Joan collaborated to greatest effect on works aimed at children. Together they produced many musical plays and songs to be used in school music lessons. Joan would supply the words; variously this involved selecting poems, writing plays, giving notes on direction and advice for teachers (such as where to buy props) or writing lyrics. Martin took charge of the music, sometimes arranging traditional tunes, sometimes composing new ones. *A Christmas Pageant* (1925) serves as a good example of their work. In its preface, Joan laid out its aims: 'It is planned to meet the needs of those who require something which includes a large number of persons who can give only the minimum of time and talent.' (This, perhaps, encapsulates the desirable characteristics of any piece intended for performance by schoolchildren!) Joan lays out the instructions to those overseeing the production in quite meticulous detail. For example, her first no-nonsense instruction in her 'Notes on Production' was, 'Allow absolutely no talking within so many yards of the stage, and make the boundary quite definite.' Others included the terse 'Keep things moving, but avoid hurry' and 'Take precautions against fire'. Martin's music included arrangements of traditional English carols such as 'The Wassail Song' and 'I Saw Three Ships'. In his crusade to revive English music he saw advantage in catching them young.

The division of responsibility in their collaborative work, in many ways, reflected the nature of the couple's relationship. Joan provided the glue which held things together, her organisational flair and focus on the 'nuts and bolts' giving Martin the artistic freedom he required. Beyond their work together and, in addition to her role as wife and mother, Joan also took charge of the day-to-day running of Martin's career, in effect, acting as his manager. With practical matters taken care of by his wife, Martin's output was prodigious across a broad spectrum of musical styles. He composed hymns and carols, unison songs, popular songs, anthems, cantatas, oratorios, instrumentals and operas, two of which, *Mr Pepys* (1926) and *The Thorn of Avalon* (1931) enjoyed some success. He also collaborated with T. S. Eliot for the pageant play, *The Rock* (1934). As the show was about to open, Eliot wrote to Martin, 'I hope this effort will not be the end either of our acquaintance as human beings, or of our collaboration as workmen.' Eliot also acknowledged the strength of Martin and Joan's relationship, calling Joan 'Mrs Carpenter'.

In 1935, Martin became the director of music for the Diocese of Chelmsford, a position he held until his retirement in 1940. It was recognition that the energetic revolutionary of Church music had become part of its establishment. In 1936, the Archbishop of Canterbury conferred the Lambeth doctorate of music on him, in 1955 he was awarded an OBE and he was elected FRCM in the final year of his life. He continued to work through the Second World War and beyond, composing two of his most acclaimed choral pieces in the autumn of his life. *The Redeemer* (1944) is perhaps his most enduring work and *God's Grandeur* (1948) was commissioned by Benjamin Britten to open the very first

Aldeburgh Festival, staged in June 1948. This was quite an honour and is no mean indication of Martin's stature as a composer.

Martin retired to Southwold, Suffolk, a place dear to him and where he had first met Craig. He saw out the remainder of his years there with his beloved Joan, who survived him by sixteen years and who energetically strived to maintain his position among England's leading composers, endeavours since taken up by subsequent generations of her family. Though not revered in the same way as some of his exalted friends, the breadth and contemporary popularity of Martin Shaw's work provide testament to his rare talent as a composer and an arranger; a talent which reached its peak with the love and support of his remarkable wife.

4 EMPIRE

On the eve of the First World War, the British Empire, 'on which the sun never set', was the largest the world had ever seen. A quarter of the world's land mass was under direct British rule, though Britain's political and commercial influence extended well beyond the territories coloured pink on maps of the day. Any number of Cobbolds or their kin could be considered agents of this vast empire; those who fought for it, traded with it or entered its public service all played a part. Even those who became missionaries were spreading notions of Britishness in far off lands. However, the vanguard of Britain's imperial juggernaut comprised hardy pioneers who embodied the frontier spirit; men for whom a safe, lucrative career and a comfortable life in England were simply not enough.

William Cain, Frank E. Cobbold and Charles Cobbold ('CC') Farr were all such men. Many who left Britain's shores for the colonies and Dominions went in search of their fortune: many returned shortly afterwards with their dreams in tatters. Cain, Cobbold and Farr suffered their fair share of setbacks far from home but simply refused to give in. Frank Cobbold and CC Farr, in particular, overcame great personal adversity during the early years of their adventures: the former at sea, among the wild tribes of the south-west Pacific and in the Australian outback; the latter in the remote reaches of northern Ontario. Indeed, Frank survived more life-threatening episodes during his teenage years than most men of the age could expect to face during an entire lifetime. CC, a risk-taker in more sense than one, sailed for Canada with no firm plans and just a small sum of money in his pocket. Like many, he soon learned the harsh reality of life on the fringes of empire. In order to sustain himself he took on a series of menial, physically demanding and poorly paid jobs which other men from his background might have considered beneath them. The extraordinary tenacity of both men was eventually rewarded with long-overdue strokes of good fortune. Each capitalised fully on his luck and was ultimately rewarded with the sort of success that eluded most emigrants.

William Cain overcame early disappointments following his emigration to Victoria. Fortuitously, at the time of his arrival in Melbourne, the business acumen and flair for construction William had inherited from his father were in demand as the great boom, in the wake of Victoria's gold rush, transformed the city into one of the world's leading commercial and financial centres. His success however, was built as much upon his character as his talents for construction. His integrity and honesty not only ensured his success in business affairs but also made him well suited for public office, and he became one of Melbourne's most respected civic leaders. In later life, he collaborated with Frank, his brother-in-law, on a number of stock-rearing enterprises which reaped handsome rewards for both. Neither forgot their roots: William and Frank were generous in their support of worthy causes, both in the land of their birth as well as in Australia.

William, Frank and CC were all wealth-makers, men with an eye for business who embraced the opportunities provided by Britain's expanding empire. Such men performed an integral role in the Empire's economic development and in the transformation of its obscure outposts into sustainable communities. This chapter's fourth subject, Ralph Patteson Cobbold, served the British Empire in an altogether different way. Ralph was a special agent and spy. He was a maverick, one of a rare breed distinguished by extraordinary bravery and unshakeable nerve. Such men lived life on the edge and were invaluable 'on the edge' of empire, where Britain's interests were vulnerable or ill-defined. Ralph and his kind were employed to penetrate such regions in order to reconnoitre, spy and to both promote and safeguard imperial interests, often alone and usually at great personal risk. They caught the imagination of a public hungry for tales of heroism and adventure. Ralph's remarkable life was as thrilling and incident-packed as any fictional ripping yarn of the day.

Horace William Cain (1831–1914)
Mayor of Melbourne, Builder and Benefactor

William Cain, Mavor of Melbourne 1886-1887
Melbourne Town Hall

30ᴾ   Isle of Man

J. H. NICHOLSON RI   1984   Questa

William Cain, Mayor of Melbourne 1886–87, depicted on an Isle of Man 30p stamp issued in 1984. (Copyright Isle of Man Post Office.)

(Horace) William Cain was destined to become a builder. He was born at Ballasalla, in the parish of Malew, on the Isle of Man, where his father was a successful harbour contractor who constructed a number of quays and piers at ports around the island. Perhaps Robert Cain's most impressive project was the Fort Anne Jetty, a substantial breakwater protecting the inner harbour at Douglas. William was just four years old when it was formally opened in 1835 and he must have been in awe that his father could be responsible for such a formidable structure.

He grew up surrounded by architects' plans and contracts for municipal works, and his father's business acumen and flair for construction soaked into him. However, the buildings and structures which stand as monuments to William Cain's talents are less to be found on a tiny island in the Irish Sea than thousands of miles away in Melbourne, one of Australia's great cities. He was one of a band of pioneers, influential in Melbourne's development from outpost of empire to thriving international city.

William was educated at the Liverpool Mechanics' Institution (Liverpool Institute). Such schools proliferated during the early nineteenth century as centres for the enlightenment of working men, which sought to steer them away from the vices of the public house. The Liverpool Institute, established in 1825, added boys' lower and upper schools in 1840 and William was one of its early pupils. From there, he returned to the Isle of Man where he was engaged for a year with the Admiralty survey of the island before joining the family business. His father, no doubt, hoped he would one day take the reins but William had loftier ambitions. On 6 April 1852, he boarded the *Anna* at Liverpool docks and set off, along with hundreds of other hopefuls, for Australia. Among his fellow travellers was another destined to be one of Melbourne's great builders, David Mitchell.

The *Anna* docked at Adelaide in July and, like many, William joined the rush for Bendigo's Creek (subsequently known simply as Bendigo), ninety-five miles north of Melbourne, where gold had been discovered the previous year. Approximately thirty thousand miners, or 'diggers', descended on Bendigo during this period and not all found their fortune. William enjoyed little success and gave up, turning his attentions towards a much more familiar trade. In 1852, Government Gold Commissioners had been appointed to administer

Victorian colonial law in the ever-growing tented city around the goldfields and William secured the contract to build their offices on Camp Hill (now Rosalind Park), Bendigo's first permanent structure. In addition, he supervised the erection of temporary barracks for the site's new police force.

In 1853, William left Bendigo for Melbourne. The city had been made capital of the new Colony of Victoria, established in 1851, and was expanding rapidly on the back of the gold rush. Opportunities for a talented young building contractor abounded and William fell in with James Lawrence, a respected stonemason who secured a number of prestigious contracts. Lawrence contracted William to work on the construction of Melbourne Hospital's new 'state of the art' west wing, which was opened in 1858. The wing boasted three floors and wards which the Melbourne newspaper, *The Argus* considered 'remarkably spacious and well-ventilated', together with lavatories and bathrooms with hot and cold running water. Later, the pair collaborated on the headquarters of the London Chartered Bank of Australia (1859) and the Bank of Victoria (*c.*1860), cathedrals of capitalism built in the renaissance palazzo style on Collins Street, the city's main commercial artery. Such buildings exuded Melbourne's growing confidence and were fitting for a city of international importance.

With a reputation as solid as the buildings he had worked on, in 1863, William travelled to New Zealand to embark on a project that, no doubt, evoked memories of his childhood and his father's business. He entered into a partnership with James MacKenzie (not the notorious outlaw) to build piers at Bluff Harbour and New River at the southern tip of South Island. The company, MacKenzie and Cain, also constructed railway embankments at Bluff for a branch of the South Main Line to connect the port to Invercargill, some twenty miles north. The South Main Line was eventually opened in February 1867, one of New Zealand's first.

William did not stay to oversee the project's completion; his movements during this period are little recorded, but he certainly visited England in 1865. By 1867 he had returned to Melbourne and had renewed his partnership with Lawrence, securing the contract to build Melbourne's new town hall to the impressive designs of Cornishman, Joseph Reed, perhaps the city's most distinguished architect. Prince Alfred, recently invested as Duke of Edinburgh and second in line to the British throne, the first member of the royal family to visit Australia, laid the foundation stone on 29 November 1867: the building's clock tower was subsequently named after him. A little under three years later, on 9 August 1870, the building, constructed in the Second Empire (or Napoleon III) style, was officially opened by Viscount Canterbury, governor of Victoria.

In 1875, William made an extended visit to England. While there, he took a wife, Sarah Jane, who was also visiting her homeland having settled in Melbourne. Sarah Jane was the daughter of Arthur Cobbold (1815–98) and Sarah Elliston (1813–99) and the elder sister of Francis Edward Cobbold. She had settled in Melbourne with her new husband, William Hill Dickson, partner in his family's import business there, in 1869. Dickson, a Yorkshireman, died during the visit home, aged just fifty, and was laid to rest near his English residence, Marsden Hall, at Great Marsden, Lancashire on 7 March 1876. It is not known whether William Cain was among the mourners but he undoubtedly knew the couple from Melbourne society. Within a year, William and Sarah would set sail for Melbourne together as husband and wife. They arrived, aboard the mail ship RMS *Bangalore* at the end of June 1877, the journey being notable for a smallpox scare when one of the crew fell ill: the sufferer, John Younger, was removed from the ship and was later found only to be afflicted with chicken pox. Once back in Melbourne, William and Sarah set up home at Yarra House, an enormous Italianate house which William built on Anderson Street, Melbourne's 'Millionaires' Row'. They brought their three sons up there, Robert (1879–1935), Willie (1882–1978) and Walter (1884–1950). The couple's first born, Eleanor, died aged just sixteen months in May 1879.

Having played a significant part in Melbourne's development into a city of standing, William entered civic life, serving as a member of the city council from 1880 until 1888 and as mayor in 1886–87. He brought his expertise to his duties and was a particularly strong voice on matters relating to infrastructure and civil engineering. His well-informed and strident views on such subjects regularly brought him into conflict with Melbourne's long-serving town clerk, Edmund Fitzgibbon. On one notable occasion the pair argued over the depth of a storm-water channel which was to be built beneath Elizabeth Street. William insisted the channel should be dug at sufficient depth to cater for the later addition of sewers, arguing that this would prevent the cellars of the whole street from flooding. His views prevailed. In 1891, Fitzgibbon became the first chairman of the Melbourne Metropolitan Board of Works, which oversaw the control of the city's water supply and sewerage system: as a councillor and as mayor, William had been instrumental in preparing the ground for the board's establishment.

William was appointed chairman of the building committee for the 1888 Melbourne Exhibition to celebrate the centenary of Australia's settlement. This involved the erection of temporary annexes to the city's magnificent exhibition building, constructed for a similar event in 1880 by William's fellow emigrant aboard the *Anna*, David Mitchell. The exhibition was a grand affair, attracting more than two million visitors, and its venues reflected the city's growing international status. Earlier, in 1886, William had been invited to serve on the executive council of a commission which organised an event in Adelaide to celebrate the fiftieth anniversary of the foundation of South Australia. William was at the height of his powers and clearly in demand.

Alongside such projects and his civic duties, William's personal business interests continued to flourish. He profited from the land boom of the 1880s which elevated 'Marvellous Melbourne' to the second largest city in the British Empire (after London) and the richest in the world; he invested personally in cattle and sheep stations at Coan Downs in New South Wales and at Inverleigh and Hughenden in Queensland; later, in 1904, he purchased Madowla Park near Echuca in Victoria outright, and the following year he bought Inverleigh in Queensland in partnership with his brother-in-law, F. E. Cobbold; he was a shareholder of Goldsbrough Mort and Co., a leading pastoral house and wool-broker, and of the curiously named Squatting Investment Company which had similar interests; he was on the board of numerous companies, including the Melbourne Tramway Company, the National Trustees, Executors and Agency Company and more than one Newcastle (New South Wales) coal company; he was also a member of the Yarra Dredging Board.

The 1880s saw a rapid expansion in Australia's railway network as lines in South Australia, Victoria and New South Wales were connected up. William, as might be expected, was prominently involved in these projects, constructing part of the Benalla–Wadonga route and securing a number of contracts in New South Wales. Later, in 1895, he was appointed to the board of Victorian Railways, which oversaw the construction, maintenance and management of the colony's network from imposing offices at 67 Spencer Street.

In 1891, Melbourne's boom years came to an abrupt end. A severe depression wreaked havoc with the city's land industries and financial institutions, culminating in the wider Australian Banking Crisis of 1893. In Melbourne alone, sixteen banks went to the wall and 133 limited companies went into liquidation. In 1890, William was elected to the board of Goldsborough Mort and Co., which suffered greatly during the crisis. William incurred heavy losses to the point that rumours abounded, prematurely, of his ruin. The company was ultimately saved by one of its directors, Edward Mitchell, who travelled to England in 1893 to persuade debenture holders not to force the company into liquidation by claiming their money. The company survived and Mitchell became its chairman, though William contributed greatly to its recovery as a director until 1897.

In 1903, public office beckoned again. Supported by the National Reform League, William won a by-election for Melbourne Province's seat on the

Carving on the pulpit of St Paul's Cathedral, Melbourne, commemorating Nellie Cain, who died in infancy.
(The Cobbold Family History Trust.)

Legislative Council, Victoria's upper chamber, following the death of the incumbent, Sir William Sarsgood. He stood for prudence and economy in all public expenditure and was among those the council instinctively looked to in matters relating to construction projects and the railways. He held his seat until May 1910 when he declined to put himself up for re-election.

Ann Hone, author of the article on William for the *Australian Dictionary of Biography*, describes him as exhibiting an 'intense, almost loyalty to any cause or person whose interest he espoused'. Among such causes, he had a deep attachment to Melbourne's cathedral, St Paul's. William's connection with the cathedral, which was consecrated in 1891, was both spiritual and physical, for he had contributed greatly to its construction. At his funeral service, conducted there, Archbishop Henry Lowther Clarke eulogised: 'He gave unstinted time and personal service to its erection. His valuable professional knowledge was given for some years without payment or reward. To no one is the church more indebted to Mr Cain for his long-continued and valuable help.' William bestowed many private gifts upon the cathedral, including an impressive brass lectern and a pulpit on which was carved the face of his daughter, Eleanor (Nellie). He also supported his local church, Christ Church in South Yarra, donating a font in 1886. Two years after his death, a new baptistery there was dedicated to his memory. In later life William became a lay canon and he also served on the council of the diocese and in the synod. William was so highly regarded by the Church in Australia that he was sent as its representative to the Pan-Anglican Conference in London in June 1908, where he was entertained by the Prince of Wales, the Archbishop of Canterbury and the Bishop of London.

William held a great affection for Melbourne Grammar School, serving as a member of the school council from 1894 until his death. Archbishop Clarke remarked that 'His love for the school became an abiding sentiment of his life, and his memory will be cherished for all time as one of its best friends.' William gave four hundred pounds to the school and, five years after his death, his three sons endowed it with one thousand pounds to found the William Cain Scholarship. A house in its middle school, Wadhurst, bears his name.

The Isle of Man also benefited from William's generosity. He returned there regularly throughout his life and 'gave financial assistance to schemes having for their object the betterment of his fellow Manxman'. In particular, he supported religious projects in, or around, Ballasalla, regardless of their denomination. He made significant financial contributions to the building of Abbey Church, a chapel-of-ease for the parish of Malew; he donated a clock to the village's Wesleyan church and contributed one hundred pounds to the Primitive Methodists' building fund. He was also one of the founders of, and the greatest contributor to, the Malew Curates' Endowment Fund. His last gifts comprised 'a striking and useful Church House' together with a gymnasium and a men's club, which he presented to the village in 1909.

William was also free with support and advice for his fellow Manxmen who emigrated to Australia and, in the closing year of his life, he established a Manx Society of Melbourne, his eldest son Robert being its first president. His passing, in October 1914, was mourned both in Melbourne and on the tiny island of his birth: a little over a week after William was laid to rest in Melbourne's Boroondara cemetery, a well-attended memorial service was held at Malew Church. In 1984, the Isle of Man Post Office issued a set of stamps in honour of a local boy who had done well for himself on the other side of the world but who never forgot where he came from; the set was entitled, 'William Cain – Manx Pioneer'.

Francis Edward Cobbold (1853–1935)
Adventurer, Pastoralist and Nostalgic Benefactor

'FE', aged about 40.
(The Cobbold Family History Trust.)

'He is small and thin but you will find him active,' said a reluctant Arthur Thomas Cobbold (1815–98) as he apprenticed his fourteen-year-old son to Captain Birnie of the wool clipper, *Ann Duthie*, in 1867. For young Francis (Frank) Cobbold, the few steps between land and sea marked the beginning of an adventure which would not only see him grow from boy to man but would also determine the course of the rest of his life. Frank had badgered his parents into allowing him to pursue his seafaring ambitions and, as the *Ann Duthie* set sail down the Thames on her maiden voyage bound for Australia, he dreamt that one day he would own his own ship, or even a fleet. However, it would be on dry land, across the mighty expanse of Australia's interior, that Frank Cobbold made his fortune.

Frank's longing for the sea took root with holidays spent on the Suffolk coast, by occasional visits to Ipswich docks where his grandfather (John Wilkinson Cobbold) berthed his merchant ships and through the nautical novels of Frederick Marryat. Aboard the *Ann Duthie* he was quick to learn, willing and cheerful, though he was appalled by the quality of his rations. Mercifully, the weather as far as the Cape of Good Hope was kind, allowing him to find his sea legs and to toughen up for the rigours ahead; for, while crossing the Southern Ocean, the *Ann Duthie* encountered a ferocious hurricane. Standard procedure in such conditions was to stow all canvas and to ride the storm out with bare masts and Frank was sent aloft the fore royal yard to take in its sail. As the ship rolled, he stuck doggedly to this task, his hand bleeding with the effort required to maintain his hold. He survived the terrifying ordeal only to learn that a fellow apprentice and his friend, a boy named Brown, who had been attempting a similar task on the royal yard, had lost his grip and had been hurled into the sea.

The *Ann Duthie* reached Sydney after eighty-four days and remained there for three months before setting sail eastwards for England with a hold full of wool. Storms were encountered around Cape Horn the like of which Birnie had never experienced, breaking two of the ship's masts, which were lost overboard.

This was not an uncommon occurrence for the time and running repairs were made which enabled the ship to continue its passage to England. Back home in Suffolk, Frank reflected on his adventure and concluded that a career at sea merely offered slow progression on wretched pay, quite apart from its physical risks and short life expectancy. Even if he should make captain he would always remain subservient to the ship's owner. From what he had seen at Sydney, there were much better prospects for making a fortune in the colonies on dry land and when he rejoined the *Ann Duthie*, he had already decided that his journey would be one way, though he kept this from his parents.

No sooner had the ship docked at Sydney, in September 1869, than Frank walked off it and boarded another, the SS *Dandenong*, bound for Melbourne. His father had paid sixty pounds for his apprenticeship and so there was no recourse from the captain for this action. Frank was neither hindered nor pursued. When he arrived at Melbourne, he made for the home of his sister, Sarah Jane (1841–1918) who had recently arrived in the city with her new husband, William Dickson (1825–76). Dickson set Frank to clerical work in his import business, Dickson Brothers of Flinders Lane, but the tedium of sedentary employment soon set in and Frank began to consider an altogether more adventurous path. The word around the commercial district of Melbourne was that any ambitious young man not averse to physical hardship should head for Fiji and the South Sea Islands to make his fortune in cotton.

Frank was the seventh son of a seventh son, an indication, so superstition went, that fortune would favour him. However, from the time he left Melbourne in late 1869 to the time he returned in November 1873, just about the only kindness Lady Luck bestowed on him was to spare him his life. He had not turned sixteen when he arrived in the Fijian Islands and, despite his energy and will to succeed, his entrepreneurial efforts repeatedly foundered. His biographer, Arthur Upfield, put this down both to Frank's lack of capital and to his nature, which was 'not sufficiently ruthless and conscienceless to compete with conscienceless and ruthless men'.

At Levuka, at that time Fiji's capital on the small island of Ovalau, he fell in with the Whalley family and visited the land they had recently bought on the larger island of Viti Levu, then being cleared for planting. After a short time working as a bookkeeper at the Albion Hotel where 'the impact of an iron fist against a stubby chin was more often heard than a "beg pardon"', Frank decided it was time to follow Whalley's example. He entered into a partnership with a couple of lads, named Pilbrow and Wetherall, who were a little older than him and just as ambitious. In the early months of 1870, the three embarked on a harebrained scheme that took them to the New Hebridean island of Efate, where they purchased land. They secured the services of a dozen or so natives to clear the land but these were brutally murdered before they had even raised their tools, possibly as a result of tribal feuding. Thereafter the three young entrepreneurs made little progress, suffering repeated bouts of malaria and ague fever before abandoning the island penniless after a year. The ship that 'rescued' Frank was the *Margaret Chessel*, which was engaged in the murky business of 'blackbirding', duplicitously recruiting natives to work in the plantations. The practice was widely held to explain the motive behind the murder, the following year, of John Patteson, Bishop of Melanesia, to whom Frank was related by his eldest uncle, John Chevallier Cobbold (see Chapter 2).

In February 1871, just days after his return to Levuka, Frank survived one of the fiercest hurricanes ever to hit the islands, which levelled all but the town's most sturdy buildings. Later that year, he took work as a second overseer on the Holmehurst plantation on the island of Taveuni, before deciding that he had learned enough of the business to try again on his own. He bought a boat, the *New York*, and sailed for the neighbouring island of Vanua Levu where he purchased 125 acres of land before heading back to Levuka in search of labour. Alas, none was to be found and the money he had saved from his employment steadily dwindled until he was forced to sell the *New York* for a bargain price. Following stints as a clerk to a Levuka solicitor and as a travelling salesman, inopportunely at a time when violence against foreign settlers was at its height, Frank was finally able to sell the land he had bought on Vanua Levu. The proceeds secured his passage back to Melbourne, away from these paradise islands which had brought him so much misfortune.

In Melbourne, Frank secured a clerical position with the Lands Department but took private lessons in surveying in the hope that he might escape the office. His strategy proved successful and he was selected for work in northern Victoria, despite having no experience in the field. The work suited Frank, testing both body and mind, and he might, no doubt, have forged a successful career in surveying had it not been for an encounter with Nicholas Sadleir, manager of Albemarle, one of the largest sheep stations in New South Wales, covering an area of a million and a quarter acres. Sadleir required a surveyor to assess the feasibility of diverting water from the River Darling to irrigate the huge Albemarle run. He was introduced to Frank and was sufficiently impressed by the young man to offer him the work. Frank abandoned his training and set off with Sadleir for Albemarle. Though he quickly established that the watering scheme was impractical, so taken was he by life in the bush that he decided to stay. Sadleir employed Frank as a bookkeeper and storekeeper but found it impossible to confine him to a desk. Frank was eager to learn the rudiments of stock raising, sheep shearing and the financial aspects of pastoralism. Having tried his hand at so much during his young life, he had finally discovered a career which would not only satisfy his wanderlust but which also offered, to those with the necessary drive and business acumen, almost limitless potential. Frank would not be found lacking in either quality.

If he cut his teeth at Albemarle, he won his spurs all over the bush of New South Wales and southern Queensland, establishing a reputation for integrity, durability and common sense. Between 1874 and 1878, working for station owners and managers, he drove herds of cattle over hundreds of miles. The work was tough, and Frank contracted both typhoid and a particularly nasty bout of sandy blight (trachoma), from which he was fortunate to retain his sight. He regularly drove cattle to market at Melbourne and, while there in 1877, he witnessed Chester edge out Savanaka by half a head in the Melbourne Cup. So began a life-long love of the sport of kings.

Having proved himself hard working and reliable, Frank was suddenly in demand. In 1878 he was taken on as manager of the Monkira station in south-west Queensland. He was so highly thought of there that that when the station closed due to a prolonged drought, the owners offered him ten thousand pounds to set up on his own. Instead, Frank decided to take a position with the conglomerate Cobb & Co., managing their pastoral properties south-east of the Gulf of Carpentaria. His annual salary was in the region of two hundred pounds. Cobb & Co. owned two stations in the area, Miranda Downs and The Oaks, which were two hundred miles apart. Frank divided his time between them, alternating every three or four months.

His duties brought him into contact with an Englishman, an Irishman and a Scotsman, Edward Hunt, Patrick O'Brien and William Steele, who owned their own pastoral properties but who had also made a killing through their investment in and subsequent purchase of the Cumberland Goldmine. Recognising Frank as 'a square man', Steele invited him to dinner one evening while the latter was passing close to the mine, which lay midway between Miranda Downs and The Oaks. Steele informed Frank that he and his partners were considering buying the station, Carpentaria Downs, adjacent to The Oaks and asked Frank whether they should buy The Oaks too. Frank thought the scheme a good one. Then, to his astonishment, Steele invited him into the partnership. Steele, O'Brien and Hunt were wealthy men and had just accepted an offer for their mine of £185,000; Frank held savings of just £500. The invitation was an enormous compliment and testament to Frank's reputation. He resigned from Cobb & Co. and took up residence at Carpentaria Downs, quickly implementing a number of changes to increase its profitability. He also managed the Forest Home station, the partners' original holding close to Cumberland. It was 1886 and the combined value of the newly formed O'Brien, Cobbold & Co.'s pastoral holdings was £110, 000; Frank invested just £500 and gave promissory notes for the remainder of his share, £27,000.

Frank, or FE (as he was called by his partners), seemed at last to be set-tled and, in 1890, he married Bessie Fulford (1870–98), the daughter of his closest neighbours at Carpentaria Downs. He added new stations to the com-pany's holding: Authoringa in southern Queensland provided an ideal staging post for herds driven from the north to the markets of Brisbane, Sydney and Melbourne; Waterview, on the north Queensland coast, was added in 1895. However, the growing business suffered a succession of setbacks. The big bank crash of 1893, the arrival of the cattle tick in northern Queensland shortly afterwards, land tenure laws which allotted land to miners so that they could raise their own stock (particularly affecting Forest Home) and seven years of drought between 1895–1902 all took their toll. By 1897, FE, fearing that he would 'lose' the money he still owed the other partners, wanted out. The others, desperate to keep him, proposed a new arrangement and they wiped the slate clean, allowing FE to invest just two thousand pounds while continuing to pay his manager's salary. During this difficult period, FE also suffered a double personal loss. Bessie, who had contracted uterine cancer, died on 10 October 1898; on the other side of the world, Arthur Cobbold, FE's father, passed away on the very same day.

FE sought solace in his work. In 1900 he added two southern Queensland stations to the business, Riversleigh and Lilydale, and shortly afterwards, while at Normanton, he learned that Miranda Downs was about to go under the hammer at Townsville, five hundred miles away. FE was so attached to Miranda Downs that he could not let the opportunity elude him. Travelling day and night, he dashed across northern Queensland in record time to secure the deal. The last station to be added was Magoura on the Gulf of Carpentaria, in 1901.

By 1902, the partnership had run its course. Steele (1899) and Hunt (1902) had died, and O'Brien and FE accepted a lucrative offer from the Queensland Meat Export and Agency Company for their larger holdings, the smaller ones being sold privately. It was the end of a remarkable partnership between four men, which, according to Upfield was 'an association unmarred by jealousy and meanness, suspicion and distrust'. FE had become an extremely wealthy man through it.

In 1904, FE took a holiday, taking a world tour with his second wife, Beatrice, or Bea (1869–1951), whom he had married in 1901. On his return to Australia he directed his efforts into the one station he had purchased outside of his partnership with Hunt, O'Brien and Steele. With William Cain, his sister Sarah's second husband, FE had bought Inverleigh, sixty miles south of the Gulf of Carpentaria at a knock-down price. Between 1905 and 1911, FE transformed Inverleigh from an arid desert to a sought-after, well-watered station, which yielded a handsome profit for each party when it was sold.

At the same time as he was building up Inverleigh, the irrepressible FE was also turning his attention towards sheep farming. In quick succession he purchased three large sheep stations in the heart of Queensland – Langlo Downs, Listowel Downs and Mitchell Downs – securing investment from banks and from his old partner O'Brien. Later, with investment from Beatrice, who sold her shares in the Brisbane Tramway Company, and from Cain's sons (Cain died in 1914), he purchased the huge Hughenden Estate on the Flinders River. All four stations delivered healthy returns for FE and his investors, particularly during the 1920s when the price of wool increased steadily.

By now FE was playing a less active role in the management of his stations, delegating more to managers. Bea, it seems, had tired of the peripatetic lifestyle and, in 1913, FE bought Yarram Park in Western Victoria as a more permanent

FE's favourite and most successful racehorse, Conquistador. (Family member's private collection.)

home though, in truth, this did little to halt the couple's wanderings. Eventually, in 1919, Bea got her way with a townhouse named Tilehurst at 7 Fulham Avenue, South Yarra. Still, FE and Bea would migrate to Hughenden for three or four months during the winter, while taking the longer journey to England and family every four or five years.

In semi-retirement FE found more time to indulge his love of horse racing. Unsurprisingly, he had an eye for a thoroughbred with potential. In 1913, he purchased the colt Conquistador for 190 guineas. A year later, as a three year old, the horse won six of its eight starts in valuable races. Later, Taras won FE £2,500 in prize money, while Danilo and Villius won the Carnival Handicap at Flemington's Melbourne Cup meeting in consecutive years, 1933–34, the latter at odds of twenty-three to one.

FE remained active to the last. In his eighties he would regularly take tours of his stations, though by now resigned to travelling by car rather than on horseback, often travelling two hundred miles in a day. In 1933–34, he acquired two further stations in New South Wales: Table Top and Woorooma West. He died on 31 August 1935, aged eighty-one. He had no children. His Australian and English estates combined were valued at more than half a million pounds, but besides making provision for Bea's future he bequeathed little to his family. He left the remainder of his estate to The Royal United Kingdom Beneficient Association (RUKBA) to provide annuities for the needy of his native Suffolk. Despite his itinerant life, it seems Francis Edward Cobbold never forgot where his roots lay. In 2004, RUKBA valued the F. E. Cobbold Trust Fund at £9.9 million – the largest bequest it had ever received.

Charles Cobbold Farr (1851–1914)
Pioneering Venturer and Founder of Haileybury, Ontario

On 11 May 1871, the mail steamship SS *Nestorian*
set sail from Liverpool bound for Quebec. On board
was a fresh-faced young Englishman, not quite
twenty years old, who was determined to make his
way in the world. As he stood on deck and watched
England's shores dip beneath the horizon, Charles
Cobbold (known as 'CC') Farr had mixed feelings.
Though he knew he would miss his beloved home,
he was full of excitement for the adventures that lay
ahead. More than anything he was already relishing
his new-found independence. He later reflected, 'I
was responsible to no one; free to make friends as
I would and spend my time as I chose.' With just
one hundred pounds in his pocket, given to him
by his family, CC was under no illusion that a fortune would fall into his lap but he could not have

'CC' aged 20 on arrival in Canada from England.
(Family member's private collection.)

imagined how difficult life was about to become. That he ultimately thrived is
testament to his tenacity, optimism and capacity for hard work, characteristics
essential in those wishing to make something of themselves in faraway lands.

To his friends and family, CC's decision to leave England came as little
surprise. He was an adventurous child who could climb almost before he could
walk. As a toddler he would test his physical abilities on chairs, the staircase and
the bannister whenever his father, the Reverend John Farr (1820–67), rector
of Gillingham in Norfolk, was out of the house. His mother, Emily Cobbold
(1819–1903), third child of Robert Knipe Cobbold, 'Big' John's eldest son by
his second marriage, was fortunately calm by nature and 'the various thumps
that occurred did not disturb her in the least'. The more he grew, the wider
extended his playground. After attending Falconberg School at Beccles he went
to Haileybury in Hertfordshire, a school renowned for its encouragement of
athletic pursuits and, prior to 1857, the Indian Civil Service's (ICS) training
college, devoted to producing gentlemen sufficiently robust for the rigours of
imperial service on the subcontinent.

CC was an adventurous boy even by Haileybury's standards, scaling its walls
and scampering across its lofty roofs, though he was otherwise well behaved and
did not break bounds for any reason other than to test his athleticism. On one
occasion, the school's headmaster, the Reverend Arthur Gray Butler, a friend of

the family, stood agog as he caught sight of CC climbing out of his upper-floor dormitory window, edging along a flimsy gutter pipe, opening the window of the adjoining room and hopping through it. There were no restrictions between dormitories and CC could simply have made 'legitimate use of the doors'. Shortly afterwards, Butler summoned CC's father and expressed concern, not for the safety of the boy himself, but that imitators might not be so agile. He concluded 'There was never such a monkey for climbing!'

Clearly, the maturing CC would need a career which would provide an outlet for this exuberance, so the ICS seemed the perfect option. He left Haileybury in 1868 and was placed with a private tutor in order to ready himself for the ICS examination. Competition for India, however, was particularly fierce during this period and CC was unable to secure a position. Not one to sulk at his misfortune and loath to pursue a mundane career behind a desk in England, he decided to head west to test his mettle in the untamed wilds of Canada.

From Quebec, CC made for Toronto, from where, on the advice of an immigration agent, he headed north for the Muskoka district of Ontario, which was being opened for settlement at that time. In June, he arrived at Bracebridge, the district's main developing village, but the ceaseless travelling in searing heat had taken its toll and the novelty of his adventure had begun to wear off. He arrived in the ramshackle village, 'tired and depressed ... unwelcomed and unnoticed by a soul'.

Not inclined to self-pity, CC quickly set about looking for investment opportunities, conscious that delay would see his funds quickly frittered away in hotel bills. He soon learned, however, that money was not easy to make. His first venture involved an arduous hundred-mile round trip to buy fifty sheep and yielded just £5 profit. Next, he bought a blacksmith's business in Bracebridge, which quickly became very busy but which swallowed up all his money because most of his customers 'went on tick' without any prospect of ever settling their bills. Reluctantly, he wrote home asking for a second sum of a hundred pounds to try again. While awaiting a response to this plea, he journeyed into the wilds of Ontario in the company of an old trapper, spending a few weeks canoeing the country's lakes and rivers, trekking through its forests and surviving on its fish and deer. This journey was made as much in the interests of economy as to satisfy CC's adventurous urges.

A draft for a further hundred pounds was waiting for him upon his return. Naively, CC invested these new funds in a hotel venture in Bracebridge without drawing up a legally binding agreement and lost most of his investment to an unscrupulous partner. He purchased a small boat and began fishing on the lakes, but realised that this did not pay. 'For very shame' he was unable to write home for a further bail-out and, in 1872, the realisation dawned upon him that, 'There was nothing for it but to give up all ideas of being a capitalist and employer, and to join the ranks of the employed.' He took work at a lumber shanty for a salary of twenty dollars (four pounds) per month.

A lesser man might have given up and returned to England, but CC could barely contemplate such 'a depth of failure'. Many immigrants were not so resilient. One night CC was walking across the bridge over the Muskoka River when he caught sight of a fellow Englishman, whom he knew, standing outside the bridge's safety railing and clearly intent on jumping into the raging waters below. The man had also been struggling to make his way in Canada and had turned to drink. CC heaved him to safety and restrained him while he shouted for help, no doubt saving his life.

The job at the shanty was short-lived and CC was forced to seek work as a hired hand, which, he lamented, 'threw me into a different class from that to which I had been accustomed'. For eighteen months, 'the roughest time of my life', he took work wherever he could find it, shovelling snow, grooming horses, labouring on farms and working as a common hand at a saw mill. Eventually his luck changed. A friend in Muskoka recommended him to the Government Survey and he was asked to join a party which was about to start for the country north-east of Lake Huron. Though the position he secured was as an unskilled axeman, CC enjoyed the adventurous nature of the work and it was shortly after the survey ended that the 'opportunity of my life' presented itself.

In late 1873, while looking for work at Pembroke, CC was taken on as an axe-man by a surveyor who was heading up the Ottawa River to Lake Temiskaming in order to run a boundary line between the provinces of Ontario and Quebec. The country to be surveyed was vast, the lake itself being sixty-eight miles long. That winter, while walking across the frozen lake towards Fort Temiskaming, an outpost of the Hudson's Bay Company (HBC), CC's gaze was drawn to the gentle gradient of the land at Humphrey's Depot on its sloping western shore. He later recalled, 'I thought, even at that early period, what a magnificent chance lay there for the making of a settlement.'

While with the survey, CC regularly came into contact with representatives of the HBC and wasted few opportunities to badger them to take him on. His efforts paid off: in the late summer of 1874 he was summoned back to Fort Temiskaming to learn fur trading before being sent to one of the company's small outposts, Fort Kipawa in Quebec, as its master, or factor, overseeing the company's trade, mainly in furs, with the indigenous population. The term 'Fort' was applied to all the company's bases but Kipawa was nothing like an army camp, being 'as homely and unmilitary in appearance as any group of dwellings could be'.

At last, CC's future in Canada was secure, though work with the HBC was never likely to make him rich. He spent eight years at Kipawa from where he regularly made visits south along the Ottawa River to Pembroke, navigating rivers with huge bales of furs worth twenty thousand pounds. During one such visit, in 1878, he married Louisa Georgina Probyn, eight years his junior and of Irish descent. Any HBC employee considering marriage required permission from the company; with only a 'half promise' that he could take a wife to Kipawa, CC married Louisa and nonchalantly informed his superiors after the event. Two years later, Louisa gave birth to Emily Ruth Kipawa Farr (1880–1946), CC's only child.

In 1883, CC was relocated by the company to Fort Temiskaming, tantalising close to the land at Humphrey's Depot which he had first noticed ten years earlier. In 1885, the company attempted to purchase a hay crop at the depot but the owner wanted a deal which included his land. This proposition did not

Statue of C. C. Farr erected in Haileybury, Ontario in 2004 to mark the centenary of its foundation. (Family member's private collection.)

suit the HBC but it suited CC perfectly and he purchased the land for himself. In 1887, the provincial government, keen to exploit Temiskaming's agricultural potential, surveyed eight townships in the area and CC's purchase was legalised. He bought a further 1,200 acres at fifty cents per acre and employed a man, Tom Lawlor, to build a house there. Lawlor had already settled on the shore on land adjacent to CC's, which he named, rather unimaginatively, Lawlortown. On 13 May 1889, CC 'abandoned a sure and certain living' and resigned from the HBC. Louisa, Emily and a handful of other settlers travelled up the lake to begin their new lives on the land CC had bought. CC joined them three days later, having handed over his duties at Fort Temiskaming. The town which would bear the name of his *alma mater* was born and, fittingly, it would bear the same motto, *Sursum Corda* – Lift Up Your Hearts.

The venture almost foundered before it had begun. No sooner had the family moved into its new home when a small brush fire threatened to engulf it. Only the united efforts of all those who had landed on Haileybury's shores saved the house from the fire in what was an ominous portent of things to come. A more sustained threat to CC's ambitions came from his erstwhile employers, who opposed all of his plans for development. Few had taken on the HBC in this respect and won, but CC cultivated friendships with government officials and simply refused to yield an inch. His fight with the HBC lasted five years, at the end of which he was left 'master of the field'.

The town's post office opened its doors for the first time in 1890, putting Haileybury on the map, but what were really needed in order to secure its future were people. CC was characteristically energetic in attempting to attract settlers, writing pamphlets extolling the quality of the area's soil, timber and minerals. In 1896, his campaign took him to England where he distributed more pamphlets, gave lectures and 'beat up recruits'. He succeeded in persuading a dozen or so adventurous souls, including his cousin, Paul Cobbold (1862–1922), that their futures lay in Canada. Settlers also trickled in from the Ottawa Valley and from Muskoka, and a group of Swedish emigrants established a farming community on the outskirts of the town. Haileybury's growth, however, was slower than CC had hoped for. He had overestimated the quality of the soil: it was inferior to that further up the lake's shore where a rival settlement, New Liskeard, had been established in 1893 by John Armstrong. Worse, CC had declined Armstrong's offer to buy him out and he became increasingly frustrated at the sight of boats of settlers bypassing Haileybury, heading for New Liskeard just five miles north. CC suffered a further setback when, in 1898, the mill he had established was burned to the ground. The land he had bought seemed particularly vulnerable to brush fires as a rebuilt mill was damaged by another fire in 1902.

Haileybury's future depended on the railway. The town's closest station was sixty-five miles south at Gordon Creek, from where a steamer had to be taken up the lake. Plans to run the line up to Haileybury and New Liskeard were delayed time and again, falling victim to red tape. Eventually, in 1903, the Temiskaming and Northern Ontario Railway was built and it brought with it an unexpected benefit which improved Haileybury's fortunes immeasurably. During the line's construction, large deposits of silver were discovered on the shores of Loog Lake, not far from Haileybury. The discovery sparked a 'silver rush' and prospectors, engineers, investors and miners flocked in. With little accommodation available at Cobalt, the camp established around the site of the discovery, these fortune seekers descended upon Haileybury.

Under Ontario law, the sale of liquor was banned within a five-mile radius of any working mine; fortuitously, Haileybury lay just half a mile beyond the perimeter of this zone of sobriety. Within a year the population had soared to over four hundred and Haileybury was formally incorporated as a town. Mine owners and managers constructed grand mansions along the waterfront, the town's own 'Millionaires' Row' and some of these buildings still stand today. Hotels, churches, schools, sporting clubs, banks, stores and law firms sprang up to meet the needs of Haileybury's burgeoning population; a private telephone service was established in 1905 and electricity was supplied by a steam-driven dynamo at Foster's lumber yard at a price of sixteen cents per kilowatt hour.

Haileybury's first mayor was not Charles Cobbold Farr, but Tom Lawlor, who had settled on the shore prior to CC's arrival. In 1904, Lawlortown was incorporated into Haileybury and Lawlor, nicknamed Protestant Tom because of his determination to keep French-Canadian Catholics from taking up residence in the town, became the new municipality's mayor. He was re-elected in 1905 and served again in 1907, though he died of heart failure in May of that year, aged fifty-one. CC served as mayor just once, in 1906, but during the town's boom years he was certainly the driving force behind its development. He founded its first newspaper, *The Haileyburian and Temiscaming* [sic] *Mining Journal*, which left its readers in little doubt as to which projects in the town he favoured. He could be scathing of schemes he considered unworthy, 'quite often embroiling him in near-fistic encounters'. Away from work, he would often be seen relaxing on the lake aboard his motorboat, *Jinnie M*, accompanied by his faithful four-legged companion, O'Dawg.

Between 1904 and 1907, Haileybury's population increased tenfold from four hundred to four thousand; this despite a serious fire in 1906 which destroyed most of its commercial district. The fire proved a blessing, allowing for a more solid town, comprising three- and four-storey houses built of brick and stone, to rise from its ashes. As mayor, CC urged for and oversaw the introduction of fire protection measures including a modern pump house and waterworks system. The new town exuded confidence and was worthy of the honour bestowed upon it in 1912 when it was made the judicial seat and county town of the newly formed District of Temiskaming.

In 1909, CC built himself a large three-storey brick house at the high point of the west road with sweeping views of the lake and the town. Though Haileybury owed much of its new prosperity to good fortune beyond his own control, CC must have felt an enormous sense of pride every time he looked down upon the thriving town below. Having suffered misfortune after misfortune during his early years in Canada, he had surely been entitled to a large slice of luck. He lived in the house with Louisa until his death on 25 November 1914 following a short illness. He was sixty-three.

The Great War took a great toll on Haileybury's young men. At the same time, the price of silver plummeted, mines closed and the town's fortunes waned. Then, on 4 October 1922, fire returned to the town. During one of Canada's worst natural disasters, brush fires consumed an area of 1,700 square kilometres, ravaged eighteen townships and claimed forty-three lives. Haileybury suffered more than any other town: in under six hours, ninety per cent of its buildings were destroyed and eleven of its citizens perished. Among the dead were Paul Cobbold, who had become divisional court clerk, and his wife, Clara, who was Louisa's sister. The town rose from the ashes again and, today, sustains a population similar in size to that of its commercial heyday. Though CC would now be able to distinguish little of the town he knew, he would no doubt recognise the geography which first drew him to its shores and the majestic views across Lake Temiskaming; views which can be taken in from the road which skirts the lake's shore to the south, Farr Drive.

Colonel Ralph Patteson Cobbold, DSO (1869–1965)
Adventurer and Agent of Empire

R. P. Cobbold suitably attired. The frontispiece of his book *Innermost Asia*.
(Family member's private collection.)

The extraordinary exploits of Ralph Patteson Cobbold epitomise the role played by the 'gentleman officer' in upholding and promoting British imperial interests in far-flung regions of the world. Ralph was a true agent of empire, undertaking risky missions beyond the areas of the globe already coloured pink, often acting alone and with vague orders. He was one of a select band of *Boy's Own* heroes for whom no assignment was too tough, no terrain too harsh, no hardship insurmountable and no adversary too cunning. In an age when imperial interests intertwined with the manly attributes of adventurous travel, Ralph Cobbold and his ilk came to embody the very fibre that held the British Empire together.

Ralph was the fifth of eight children born to John Patteson Cobbold, MP (1831–75) and Adele Dupuis (1837–1917). In 1888, having left Eton, he followed the path prescribed for so many second sons of the great and the good and joined the army. He went to India with the King's Royal Rifles and, in 1891, joined the expedition sent to Wuntho to suppress Burmese rebels. In the same year he also took part in the operations that resulted in the incorporation of Manipur into Britain's Indian possessions. Ralph's military career, however, appeared to have been cut short when *The London Gazette* of 12 March 1895 announced that he had resigned his commission; two years later, the same publication attributed his retirement from the Rifles to ill health.

Ralph's elder brother was John Dupuis Cobbold who, in 1891, had married Lady Evelyn Murray, daughter of the central Asian explorer, the 7th Earl of Dunmore. Though conclusive evidence is lacking, it seems likely that Dunmore's tales of adventure inspired Ralph to consider making his own journey to the 'Roof of the World'. Great Game tensions were at their height during the 1890s as Britain and Russia vied for influence in central Asia. Both

Dunmore and Ralph understood the political implications of their journeys and both understood their duties to queen, country and empire. Though he purported that the sole aim of his journey was to hunt and that he had 'no political programme to fulfil', it is inconceivable that Ralph would not have expected, or have been expected, to gather intelligence relating to Russian movements and to the delicate politics of the region. Very few British travellers to central Asia during this period, whatever their background, passed up the opportunity to report such findings to the Indian authorities. If Ralph travelled to central Asia primarily for adventure, his activities and reports while there squarely put him in the bracket of political explorer and marked him out as a man to be trusted with hazardous, delicate missions.

At this time, travel to central Asia was restricted and those with ambitions to cross the playing fields of Anglo–Russian rivalry required the support of influential figures in government circles able to facilitate the issue of passports and overcome official objections to their plans. In this respect, Dunmore had been able to draw upon the support of no lesser a personage than Tsar Alexander III, with whom he was acquainted; five years later, in 1897, Ralph's rather less illustrious advocate was the son of the 4th Earl of Warwick, Sidney Greville, assistant private secretary to the British prime minister, Lord Salisbury. In India, having obtained all necessary permissions, Ralph was interviewed by the viceroy of India, Lord Curzon before he set off. This strongly suggests that he was charged with explicit objectives which went well beyond the innocent pursuit of the prodigiously horned *oves Poli* (Marco Polo sheep), the largest ovine breed in the world, found only in the rocky mountain habitat of central Asia.

On 13 September 1897, Ralph left Srinagar bound for central Asia via Gilgit. He was accompanied during the early part of his journey by Captain Hugh H. P. Deasy (later founder of the Deasy Motor Company) of the 16th Lancers, another 'private' traveller charged with official objectives. After crossing the Hindu Kush, the two split up. Ralph headed to Kashgar, legendary Silk Road town in Chinese Turkestan (Xinjiang), the westernmost province of China, while Deasy headed for Khotan in the south of the same province. During this period, Chinese Turkestan was at the mercy of Russia, being all but surrounded by Russia's Asian possessions. One strategist described its western towns as 'dissevered, nerveless and forceless limbs', so far removed were they from China proper. At Kashgar it was the indomitable Russian consul, Nikolai Petrovsky who called the shots; the Indian authorities feared that a Russian invasion of Chinese Turkestan would lay the Himalayan watershed open to Cossacks, from where they would be able to peer menacingly down on to the plains of India.

Ralph was alarmed at the extent of Russian influence at Kashgar and lamented the position of Britain's sole representative in the country, the un-accredited George Macartney, who was not even given the dignity of having a uniform. In both his official report to the Government of India and the popular account of his travels *Innermost Asia* (1900), he was scathing of a policy which placed a British representative in such an ignominious position. In an age when travellers tended to sidestep political comment, at least in the public domain, Ralph was notable for his candour. He complained,

> *The position occupied by our own representatives in central Asia is in marked contrast to what it should be, and the weakness of the policy pursued by the Home Government in the furtherance of our interests greatly to be deplored.*

On 5 January 1898, Ralph headed north across the snowy Tien Shan range to Verniy (Almaty) in Russia's Semiretch province, remarkably covering the 464 miles in just twenty days. There he was granted permission to head back to India through Russian Turkestan in order to shoot on the Pamirs, the most contentious area in the entire region. Before heading for the Pamirs, Ralph travelled north-west to the shores of Lake Balkhash. In the jungle near Burkhun he shot his first tiger, saving the life of a fellow hunter, a Russian Cossack, in the process.

While Ralph was enjoying Russian hospitality, Petrovsky had been stirring things up. Shortly after Ralph's departure from Kashgar, the Russian consul informed Macartney that he had received a telegram from St Petersburg relaying the Russian Foreign Ministry's displeasure that the passport which had originally been requested by the London Foreign Office for 'Mr Cobbold' was actually for Captain Cobbold of the 60th Rifles who was likely engaged in espionage. In truth, it was Petrovsky himself who had instigated the complaint. Subsequently, in June, Ralph was arrested by Russian Cossacks at Kala-i-Wamar in the Pamirs despite being in possession of all necessary credentials from the Russian authorities. He concluded that his plans had been undone by Petrovsky, who was fiercely opposed to the ambitions of British travellers and who had, no doubt, been slighted that Ralph had bypassed him in seeking sanction for his onward journey.

Ralph's detention, though inconvenient, was far from an ordeal. He struck up a friendly relationship with his Russian 'captors' and even had his cook prepare them a sumptuous dinner, which included *foie gras*, port wine, mutton chops, chicken, curry and cherry tart with cream. Despite high-level political tensions in central Asia, a mutual respect, even camaraderie, existed between

Russian and British officers whenever they encountered each other in the region, thanks to the unspoken code of gentlemanly conduct of the European officer cadre, which transcended imperial rivalries. Captain Kevekiss, the Russian officer ordered to detain Ralph, invited his 'guest' to accompany him to the garrison town of Fort Charog. There, Ralph was put up in Kevekiss' own rooms and the pair became firm friends, often taking shooting excursions together and sharing opinions on Great Game politics. Ralph later described his detention as something of 'a restful holiday'. After three weeks' honourable confinement, Ralph was escorted back to the Chinese border from where he returned to India. His strategic reports were considered immensely valuable by the Government of India and by the Intelligence Department of the War Office, while *Innermost Asia* became an instant classic of its genre, devoured by a public with an insatiable appetite for tales of derring-do.

Ralph's central Asian adventures acquired for him a reputation for integrity, initiative and resilience. The British military authorities did not have to wait long to re-employ his talents: in January 1900, while attached to the Reserve of Officers, Ralph was selected for 'special service' in the Second Boer War. He set sail for South Africa the following month and served briefly as deputy assistant adjutant general to General John Grenfell Maxwell, military governor of Pretoria, before being invalided back to England in October. He was subsequently mentioned in despatches.

Whatever his injuries, it was not long before Ralph embarked on another extraordinary mission. In February 1901, St John Brodrick, secretary of state for war and the Marquess of Lansdowne, foreign secretary, selected Ralph to assist Major Algernon Hanbury-Tracy on a delicate mission to Abyssinia. The pair had an audience with King Edward VII before they departed and were tasked with conveying gifts and personal greetings from His Majesty to the Emperor of Abyssinia, Menelik II. More importantly, they were to attempt to co-ordinate Abyssinian operations against Mohammed Abdullah Hassan, the 'Mad Mullah', with those of a British-led force under Colonel Eric J. Swayne. In 1898, the Mullah had declared *jihad* against all infidels and, having attracted a fanatical band of followers known as Dervishes, now posed a significant threat to Menelik's Christian regime, to the nominal British protectorate in northern Somalia and to Italian interests in the region. The Abyssinians and the British sought to crush the Mullah's forces in a pincer movement.

Ralph and Hanbury-Tracy arrived at Aden on 17 March 1901. The following morning, while rowing out to the steamer, the *Woodcock*, which would ferry them to Berbera in British Somaliland, they narrowly avoided being run down by a dhow, escaping 'only by the skin of our teeth'. From Berbera, an arduous 260-mile camel trek eastwards took the pair to Harar, Abyssinia's chief trading mart. During this journey, Hanbury-Tracy branched off the road to meet Swayne to obtain details of the colonel's proposed operations against the Mullah. At Harar they awaited the arrival of Ras (a title roughly equivalent to Duke) Makonnen, Menelik's cousin and commander-in-chief, who had been conducting operations against the Mullah's forces in the Ogaden. Ralph and Hanbury-Tracy were able to exchange 'a number of very polite sentences' with the Ras by telephone and Ralph was astonished that the country should possess 'this very modern instrument'. Such communication with Menelik was not possible; Ralph learned that the emperor refused to use the contraption fearing that his enemies might use it to 'suddenly spring a current upon him and so kill him'.

Ras Makonnen arrived at Harar with a large entourage on 20 April. He was immediately suspicious of the two Englishmen and averse to sending his exhausted troops back into the desert in support of a British-led mission. Hanbury-Tracy referred the matter to Colonel John Harrington, british agent to Ethiopia, who persuaded Menelik himself to despatch an order instructing the Ras to allow the two Englishmen to join up with a fresh force being assembled at Jijiga, sixty-five miles west of Harar. The pair accompanied this force between the end of May and September through the Ogaden in pursuit of the Mullah, whom they hoped to drive eastwards towards Swayne's army.

The expedition was poorly supplied and ill-disciplined and Ralph was horrified by atrocities committed by the Abyssinian army, which 'devastated nearly the whole of the country it traversed'. It limped back to Harar, having achieved little beyond 'dissuading' a number of Somali tribes from taking up arms with the Mullah. Though frustrated, Ralph and Hanbury-Tracy were at least able to enjoy some sport during their time with the army, bagging 'twenty-one lions, twelve leopards, twenty or thirty kinds of antelopes and gazelles, and a rhinoceros'. They also captured five lion cubs which were treated as pets. Despite the expedition's failure, Menelik recognised the Englishmen's endeavours and awarded them the Star of Ethiopia (second class). He also had them presented with a zebra, 'a pretty beast in fine condition' as a present for King Edward.

Ralph returned to Abyssinia in January 1903. With the support of Winston Churchill, whom he had happened to meet in the street one day, he presented a plan to the Foreign Office which involved the stationing of an Abyssinian force on the banks of the Shebele River as a blockade to the Mullah's progress south of the Ogaden. Ralph was again received by the king before heading for Berbera to meet up with Colonel A. N. Rochford CB, who would lead the mission. From Jijiga, Ralph and Rochford travelled south and established a

Major R. P. Cobbold, right, and Col. Rochfort leave Berbera, January 1903, to join the Abyssinian column at Harar. (Frank Dadd for *The Graphic*, 21 February 1903.)

zereba, a defensive enclosure formed of concentric circles of felled thorn trees, on the bank of the Shebele. The weeks spent there were largely uneventful save for the occasional skirmish with local tribes. Conditions, though, were uncomfortable; Ralph suffered from the 'damp heat' and was bothered by blackflies and mosquitos 'which seemed of enormous size'.

Not one to be idle, Ralph passed the time angling in the river, landing some good-sized fish which, though similar to carp, were 'not particularly palatable, and wanted a lot of Worcester sauce to get them down'. One day, one of the Mullah's wives, who had fallen out of favour, wandered into the camp. Ralph tried to persuade this young woman, who was 'certainly a good looker', to return to the Mullah's camp and poison him in return for a rich reward. The girl disappeared two nights later and a search initiated by Ralph was unable to find her.

In late June 1903, Ralph left the camp with orders to purchase two or three hundred mules for delivery to Berbera to General William Manning, commander of the Somaliland Field Force, who had recently inflicted a rare defeat on the Mullah's followers. Ralph was unwell and the journey back to Jijiga took six weeks. He continued to Harar and spent a further two months buying up as many mules as he could. Having fulfilled this task, Ralph left East Africa for the last time.

The wily Mullah continued to be a thorn in the side of the British and the Abyssinians and, in 1905, shrewdly struck a deal with the Italian government, which made him the ruler of an Italian protectorate on the Somali coast. He conspired against British interests during World War I before finally succumbing to a post-war British offensive. In late 1920 he escaped from detention only to die of a mystery ailment shortly afterwards.

On 19 January 1904, upon his return to England, Ralph was received by the king at Buckingham Palace. His Majesty remarked that Ralph appeared to have lost a great deal of weight; he weighed just eight stone and was, in fact, extremely ill. Neither a London expert in tropical diseases, nor a Paris 'Nursing Home' could cure him of this mysterious illness. The host of a dinner party Ralph attended, Sir Alfred Beit, a British South African diamond- mining millionaire, was so concerned for Ralph's health that he paid for him to travel first class to Bad Kissingen in Bavaria to be treated at the Sanatorium Dapper, a renowned *Kurhaus* with a distinguished client list. A month later, Ralph emerged two stones heavier and was so impressed by Carl von Dapper's methods that he returned every year, save for the war years.

In 1904, Ralph, now a major, again resigned his commission. In the same year, his eleven-year marriage to Millicent Adela Christy was dissolved, possibly due to his long absences abroad. The following year he married Minnie Diana Pitt (1866–1936), scion of that great political family and widow of Herman Eckstein, eminent diamond magnate and 'first citizen' of Johannesburg, who had died in 1893. Eckstein had been in partnership with Beit and it seems likely that Beit introduced Ralph to Minnie. Shortly afterwards, Minnie bore Ralph's only child, Ralph Hamilton Cobbold (1906–87) who became a fine all-round sportsman and, from 1936, a director of the wine, brandy and liqueur merchants, Justerini & Brooks. A comparative lull in Ralph senior's itinerant life ensued, during which he took a desk job as a stockbroker with Van Cutsem & Co. in London. Interestingly, Ralph was never engaged in the business operations of his own family; it appears he was never at one with the brewing business and that he was considered by other members of the family to be something of a loose cannon. His London job enabled him to spend time with his young family, while away from work he indulged his love of sport: aside from his abilities as a marksman and an angler, he was also a talented rackets player and an owner of racehorses.

In the summer of 1914, Ralph was in Canada, possibly on business. During his stay he journeyed to northern Ontario, almost certainly travelling through Haileybury by train, although it seems unlikely he met up with his distant relative, Charles Cobbold (CC) Farr. In all likelihood he was probably scarcely aware of CC's existence, yet alone his place in Ontario's history. Approximately sixty miles north of Haileybury, near Kirkland Lake, Ralph met a man named Harry Oakes, a gold prospector. At this time, the land surrounding the lake was crowded with prospectors, many of whom had abandoned the silver mines at Cobalt. Oakes confided in Ralph that he believed the richest seam to lie beneath the lake itself, lamenting that he could not afford to drain it. It seems Ralph offered Oakes investment in return for a substantial share of the venture's profits. A deal was struck and Ralph made his way back to civilisation in order to arrange the finance. It was then that he learned that war had been declared in Europe and, ever patriotic, he decided to head back to England rather than invest in Oakes. In so doing, Ralph turned his back on an opportunity which would have made him a very wealthy man. When the lake was eventually drained, Oakes' Lakeshore goldmine became one of the richest in the world, making Oakes himself Canada's wealthiest man. (Having made his millions, Oakes later retired to the Bahamas where, in 1943, he was brutally murdered in mysterious circumstances. The case has inspired a number of books and no fewer than four films.)

For Ralph, king and country came first and he unhesitatingly answered the call, joining up immediately upon his return to England. On 1 July 1916, aged forty-seven, as a captain with the 1st Ox and Bucks Light Infantry, he was on the front line on the first day of the Battle of the Somme when the British Army suffered sixty thousand casualties, the largest number ever sustained on a single day in its history. Ralph's battalion remained on the Somme for the entire course of the battle, enduring heavy losses. He later served at Béthune. Nothing if not durable, he survived the Great War, serving with distinction; he was mentioned in despatches for a second time and won a DSO, before finally hanging up his sword with the rank of colonel.

Ralph's private life was scarcely less colourful than his military career. In 1929, he married for a third time, Rosemary Graves-Sawle (1890–1971) who was more than twenty years his junior. Three years later, the couple took the name, Cobbold-Sawle, when Rosemary succeeded to the family estate, Penrice, at Porthpean, Cornwall, where Ralph lived out his retirement. Late in life, he fell awkwardly in the basement of the sprawling house, sustaining a broken hip. It was some hours before he was discovered and he was later conveyed to a hospital in London. He never fully recovered from the fall. Having diced with death across three continents in the service of empire, Ralph died in 1965, aged ninety-six. At his funeral at Golders Green, the last post was played by a bugler from the (now) Queen's Royal Rifles. His ashes were then conveyed to the family vault at Trimley in Suffolk.

5 PUBLIC SERVICE

The term 'public servant' tends to bring to mind a cadre of no-nonsense individuals working within the machinery of government for the good of the country. The professional lives of the four men considered here certainly correspond to this notion, though their individual careers were very different. What unites them is a resolute sense of public duty which governed all that they did and, even though they all attained high office, the subordination of their own ambitions or popularity to the public good. The achievements or failings of such individuals are judged not just by their contemporaries but also by generation upon generation of historians who rake over their papers and other official records in a process of fluid reappraisal. Few reputations survive this process untarnished, often damned by subsequent events. It is incumbent upon historians not to judge the actions of such men as 'prophets facing backwards' through the convenient prism of hindsight but to examine them in the context of the age in which they lived and of the dilemmas they faced.

For example, the conservatism of the distinguished lawyer of the late-Georgian period, Sir Thomas Plumer, appears positively draconian when comparisons are drawn with today's legal and social structures. Indeed, Plumer was considered something of a stick-in-the-mud by some of his peers, so convinced was he that legal or social reform was both unnecessary and unwise. Structures of government evolve continually and while those who, over centuries, have pressed for or instituted reform are feted as visionaries, those who have resisted it are sometimes unfairly maligned as social Luddites. Though traditional in his opinions, Plumer was certainly a man of principle, and his aversion to reform did little to hinder a career which saw him at the heart of many of the most sensational trials of the age and which led him to the top of his profession.

Sir Harry Parkes' time with the consular and diplomatic services in the Far East coincided with a period of great turmoil in the region as the scramble for China unfolded. Britain's imperial policies there, prosecuted by men like Parkes, now seem unbelievably arrogant and insensitive. However, commercial and political influence in regions where British interference was viewed with immense suspicion could not be attained by being overly sympathetic to the anxieties of one's hosts, and Parkes, like all those who distinguished themselves in such posts, elevated the interests of empire above all other things. That was their job, and Parkes was a master. Parkes married Sir Thomas Plumer's granddaughter, Fanny and the link between both families and the Cobbolds was forged through the marriage of that couple's daughter, Lilian Hope Parkes (1872–1946) to Rowland Francis Cobbold (1857–1945).

Like Parkes, Field Marshal Herbert Kitchener could just have easily been included in Chapter 4, which considers those who served the British Empire; as one of Britain's most celebrated soldiers, he also has undeniable claims to a place in the chapter on military service. He strides the period between 1880 and 1916, the year he died, like a colossus, and few men of that period excite such controversy. Despite many glorious moments on the battlefield, it is as a statesman during the Great War that Kitchener is best remembered.

Cameron Cobbold's twelve-year tenure as Governor of the Bank of England was less controversial and he is widely regarded as one of the more intelligent and able men to have held the position. He steered the bank through the tricky post-war period and guarded its independence closely. After he left the bank he became Lord Chamberlain, a position similarly well suited to a man who, in common with all great public servants, had gravitas, integrity and a flair for leading others.

Sir Thomas Plumer, MP (1753–1824)
Master of the Rolls

Sir Thomas Plumer by Henry Robinson, after Sir Thomas Lawrence, 1847.
(Courtesy of the National Portrait Gallery.)

The judicial system of England and Wales, as we understand it now, bears very little resemblance to the one in which Thomas Plumer operated in the fifty years that straddled the turn of the eighteenth century. For example, in criminal cases in Plumer's time there were no public prosecutions and the office of Director of Public Prosecutions was not created until 1879. Rather, it was the victim of crime who was required to bring his own private prosecution against an accused and who had to foot the bill for the proceedings. It was usual for such cases to be heard before a judge but without barristers, plaintiff and defendant confronting each other across the courtroom. In the 1780s, the decade after Plumer was called to the bar, ninety per cent of Old Bailey trials proceeded without a barrister for either defence or prosecution. In his early career, Plumer established his reputation in other areas of the law; as a commissioner of bankrupts and in the Court of Exchequer, but it was his performances as a defence counsel in a series of high-profile state trials, brought against senior officers of the East India Company, which really brought him to prominence.

Thomas was the son of Thomas Plumer (1711–81), formerly a London wine merchant, of Lilling Hall in the parish of Sheriff Hutton, north of York. His mother, Anne, was the daughter of Henry Thompson of Kirby Hall, Great Ouseburn, also in the North Riding. He was educated at Eton from 1763 until 1771 before going up to University College, Oxford where he was considered one of the college's finest scholars. He graduated BA in 1775, MA three years later and BCL (Bachelor of Civil Law) in 1883. During the course of his studies he was elected Vinerian Scholar, an honour bestowed on the student achieving the highest mark in the examination for the degree of BCL. In 1780 he became a fellow of his college. During his studies, practical experience of the law was gained by assisting the judge, Sir James Eyre, on his circuits. Having first entered Lincoln's Inn in 1769, aged just sixteen, Thomas was admitted to chambers in No. 23 Old Buildings in July 1775 and was called to the bar on 7 February 1778, joining the Oxford and South Wales circuit on which he remained for eight years.

From 1781 until 1793, Plumer was also a commissioner of bankrupts. Attached to the court of chancery, the commissioners were appointed by the Lord Chancellor and were invested with full powers to administer the estate of those declared bankrupt and to dispose of their land and tenements. He also practised in the Court of Exchequer, which dealt with matters of equity, based on the principles of natural law (a set of rules inherent in human nature rather than laws devised by man). He prospered in this work and was in particular demand in cases involving the tithe and in disputes concerning parliamentary elections. In 1785 he was appointed King's Serjeant of the Duchy of Lancaster, a position he held until 1813.

In 1783, Plumer became involved in the first of a string of cases which brought him to the attention of a wider public. Sir Thomas Rumbold, governor of Madras, had returned to England in disgrace in 1781. His suspect dealings with aristocratic Indian landowners (zamindars) and general mismanagement of relations with native leaders had, it was held, precipitated the invasion of the Carnatic by Haider Ali, the ruler of Mysore. A parliamentary committee of secrecy investigated the allegations and recommended a bill 'for inflicting pains and penalties on Rumbold'. He was restrained from leaving Britain and required to pay £100,000 security for himself. When the case was heard before the House of Commons in 1783, Plumer mounted a skilful defence of Rumbold and the bill against the latter was eventually allowed to lapse.

Plumer's performance on behalf of Rumbold secured his engagement as a defence counsel for perhaps the greatest political trial in Britain's history and certainly the longest. A series of unedifying wars in India had led to a loss of confidence in Warren Hastings, governor general, who resigned and returned to London in 1785. The philosopher and MP, Edmund Burke had long been a critic of the rapacious commercial policies of the East India Company in general and of Hastings' conduct in particular. Upon his return from India, Hastings received scant support from William Pitt's government, allowing Burke and his backers to press for impeachment: trial by both houses of Parliament. Proceedings began on 13 February 1788: the verdict was delivered more than seven years later and a third of the Lords who were sitting at the time the trial commenced died before its conclusion. Plumer, along with Edward Law and Robert Dallas, was engaged to defend Hastings. Whether Plumer and Hastings were already acquainted is unclear but it is known that the former was an investor in East India Company stock.

The early sensation surrounding the trial soon subsided as it dragged on and on and as it was overshadowed by events in France in 1789. Gradually, public sympathy began to swing towards Hastings, the target of wave after

Canons, seat of Sir Thomas Plumer, drawn by J. P. Neale. (The Cobbold Family History Trust.)

wave of attack from the over-zealous Burke. Perhaps the decisive evidence came from Hastings' successor in India, Lord Cornwallis, who, when asked if he 'had found any just cause to impeach the character of Mr Hastings', simply responded, 'Never.' Hastings was eventually cleared of all charges and Plumer's reputation was further enhanced.

In August 1794, while still engaged on Hastings' behalf, Plumer married Marianne Turton (1775–1857), daughter of John Turton of Sugnall Hall in Staffordshire. The couple had seven children, five boys and two girls. In 1811, Plumer bought a large estate at Canons, in Stanmore, Middlesex and made substantial improvements to its house and gardens.

More high-profile cases followed in the wake of Hastings' trial. In 1796, Plumer defended John Reeves, whose pamphlet, *Thoughts on the English Government*, was considered an attack on the constitution. Before both Houses, Plumer meticulously dissected the passages of Reeves' treatise that were considered seditious libel and divested them of their revolutionary inferences. Reeves was acquitted. In 1798, Plumer defended two of five Irish revolutionaries who were arrested in Kent and indicted with committing high treason in that they produced 'a certain paper ... containing incitements, encouragements, and persuasions to incite, encourage, persuade and procure the said enemies [France] of our said Lord the King [George III], to make, and cause to be made, such invasion as aforesaid, to prosecute and wage war against our said Lord the King within this kingdom'. Plumer represented the alleged ringleaders, members of the Society of United Irishmen, Father James O'Coigley (or Quigley) and Arthur O'Connor, who were arrested as they were about to sail for France with the petition. Among his adversaries during the trial, which was held at Maidstone, was the great lawyer, William Garrow. Plumer's efforts were not enough to save O'Coigley from the gallows. O'Connor was acquitted but was immediately re-arrested and imprisoned at Fort George on the banks of the Moray Firth. Released in 1802, he eventually made it to France and fought alongside Napoleon Bonaparte in the furtherance of his cause.

Plumer would also appear for the Crown. In 1802, he was one of a distinguished team who secured the conviction of Joseph Wall, colonial governor of the West African island of Gorée. Among the other prosecutors were the Attorney General, Edward Law (later Lord Ellenborough), Spencer Perceval (Solicitor General) and William Fielding, son of the author, Henry. Twenty years earlier, Wall, in a state of drunkenness, had ordered the arrest of Benjamin Armstrong, a sergeant in the African corps. Armstrong's only offence was to lead a delegation asking for a settlement of overdue pay but he was charged with mutiny. Wall saw no reason to convene a court martial and ordered black slaves to flog Armstrong no fewer than eight hundred times with a cat o' nine tails, a punishment which unsurprisingly proved fatal. When Wall returned to England an investigation into the affair was instigated, but stalled when a ship ferrying home witnesses to the crime was lost. Later, as other witnesses arrived back in England, Wall was arrested at his home in Bath but escaped custody at Reading and fled to the continent, taking an assumed name. He thrived in Italy and France until he returned to England in 1797 with the 'distant intention' of giving himself up. Eventually, he surrendered his fate to the courts late in 1801. His trial began at 9 a.m. on 20 January 1802; after just two hours Wall was found guilty of murder and, eight days later, he was hanged at Newgate despite pleas for clemency from the Duke of Norfolk, his wife's relative. The case was a sensation and Wall's execution attracted huge crowds.

A year later, Ellenborough, Perceval and Plumer joined forces again to present the prosecution case at the trial of the Irishman, Edward Marcus Despard, a hero of the American War of Independence whose later shoddy treatment by his own government led him to become involved with the Irish revolutionary movement. In late 1802, Despard was denounced by informers as the leader of a daring plot to seize the Tower of London and the Bank of England and to assassinate George III. He and his five co-conspirators were convicted on flimsy evidence and were subsequently hung, drawn and quartered, the last men in England to be dealt this barbaric sentence. The trial was particularly notable for the appearance of Lord Nelson as a character witness for the defence.

Plumer's association with Perceval continued when, in 1806, he assisted him during the so-called 'delicate investigation' into the romantic conduct of Caroline of Brunswick, Princess of Wales. In the following year he was knighted, appointed Solicitor General by the prime minister, the Duke of Portland, and entered Parliament following a by-election in the borough of Downton. As a politician he was considered a 'languid, confused and inefficient speaker' and he was distinctly conservative, opposing almost any proposal for reform, including the bill to abolish the slave trade, passed in 1807. This conservatism also extended to reform of the law and he opposed measures advocated by the legal reformer, Samuel Romilly, to reduce the number of capital offences, insisting that the security of the state depended upon the severe treatment of those who threatened it. He benefited from his friendship with Perceval, who became prime minister in 1809 and who appointed him Attorney General in late April 1812. Just two weeks later, however, Perceval was assassinated in the lobby of the House of Commons by John Bellingham, a merchant who had been imprisoned in Russia and whose petitions to the government for compensation had been rejected.

Perceval's death put an end to Plumer's political ambitions and he relinquished his seat in 1813 when he was offered the post of Vice Chancellor, a new position created to alleviate the workload of the Lord Chancellor, the Earl of Eldon. Garrow replaced Plumer as Attorney General. The appointment was not universally welcomed. Romilly, in particular, was scathing, arguing that Plumer was unqualified to handle the range of cases which came before the chancery. He wrote; 'A worse appointment than that of Plumer to be Vice Chancellor could hardly have been made. He knows nothing of the law of real property, nothing of the law of bankruptcy, and nothing of the doctrines peculiar to the law of equity.' This was a little harsh. Plumer had certainly served his time as commissioner of bankrupts and in the Court of Exchequer, and Romilly's criticism probably reflects the chasm which existed between the two on matters of legal reform. However, Plumer's appointment did little to expedite the passage of cases through the chancery. He was laboriously slow, perhaps even indolent, though the parliamentary historian, R. G. Thorne maintains that ill-health impeded his capacity for the work. His judgements were notoriously long-winded, giving rise to the rhyme, 'To cause delay in Lincoln's

Inn two diff'rent methods tend; his Lordship's [Eldon's] judgments ne'er begin, his Honour's [Plumer's] never end.'

Nonetheless, Plumer was a safe pair of hands as Vice Chancellor and he was duly promoted to Master of the Rolls on 6 January 1818, succeeding Sir William Grant. Again, the appointment bemused Romilly, who sniped that Plumer had 'great anxiety to do the duties of his office to the satisfaction of every one, but they are duties which he is wholly incapable of discharging'. Plumer was a competent Master of the Rolls, however, perhaps best remembered for his renovation of Rolls House and its chapel in Chancery Lane, work undertaken at his own expense His most enduring judgement, delivered in Dearle vs Hall (1823), set a precedent for determining priority between competing equitable claims to the same asset and was later embodied in statute.

Plumer was a generous giver to charity and a devout Anglican who strictly observed the Sabbath despite having a reputation for being 'savouring of the inns of court'. Like many men of his standing, he took more than a passing interest in science and academic pursuits; he was a trustee of the British Museum and a fellow of both the Royal Society and the Society of Antiquaries. In 1798, as war with France loomed, he had joined the Bloomsbury and Inns of Court Volunteers with the rank of captain. In 1803, when George III learned that a body of men composed entirely of practitioners of the law had been readied to fight Napoleon, he is reputed to have exclaimed, 'All lawyers, all lawyers, call them the *Devil's Own!*' Plumer may never have crossed the Channel to join the fight against Napoleon's armies but he was a formidable adversary for those with whom he crossed swords in the courts of England. He died on 24 March 1824, aged seventy, and was laid to rest in the chapel at Rolls House.

Sir Harry Smith Parkes, GCMG KCB (1828–85)
Diplomatist

Sir Harry, aged about 45.
(The Cobbold Family History Trust.)

During Britain's imperial heyday, the role of 'the man on the spot' was essential. For these adventurous individuals, a narrow path had to be negotiated between asserting the perceived rights of the greatest imperial power the world had ever seen and maintaining cordial relations with their hosts. Nowhere in the mid-nineteenth century did this present a greater challenge than in the Far East and, in particular, China. Although Britain never harboured any ambition to add China (save for Hong Kong) or Japan to its formal empire, the significance of the Far East to informal empire was inestimable (informal empire might be considered as the acquisition of preferential economic rights and political leverage without the need for conquest or annexation). This was usually achieved through strident diplomacy, which let other countries know that it was in their interest to do business with Britain. Many historians hold that such arrangements were preferred by British governments of the day as they were less costly than formal territorial acquisition, which was often a last resort when relations broke down. China was a tricky customer for Britain's informal empire builders. A vast and fading empire, desperate to cling on to its former glories, it had been eclipsed by the technologically advanced European powers which were scrambling to exploit its markets. To the east, Japan was undergoing an altogether different transition: it was both politically unstable and economically ambitious. The challenge to Britain, here, was to cling on to its influence. During crisis upon crisis in Sino-Anglo relations during the mid to late 1800s and through civil war and turmoil in Japan, Sir Harry Parkes was one of the men who faced the unenviable task of both safeguarding and promoting British interests in the region.

Harry's path to the top of the diplomatic service was long and winding. Senior officials of the London Foreign Office during that period tended to come from an extraordinarily narrow elite (usually Eton and Oxbridge) and those from lesser backgrounds who broke into it often had something special to offer. For Harry, the son of a bank clerk turned ironmaster from the parish of Bloxwich in Staffordshire, it was his early mastery of the Chinese language as well as his introduction to men of influence which opened the doors to career advancement.

By the age of five Harry was an orphan. He was then raised in Birmingham by his uncle, John Parkes, a retired naval officer who sent him first to boarding school at Balsall Heath and then, in 1838, to King Edward VI School in the city. That same year, Harry's two older sisters left England for Macau, on the western side of the Pearl River estuary opposite Hong Kong, to join their cousin Mary and her husband, the explorer and missionary, Karl Gützlaff. Harry followed them three years later, aged thirteen, during the latter stages of the First Opium War (1839–42), fought between Britain and China. For the former, the war was more than a dispute over the trade in opium, it was a matter of honour fought for the principles of free trade.

Harry set about learning Chinese immediately he arrived, preparing for a position in the employ of John Robert Morrison, interpreter to Britain's top man in China, Sir Henry Pottinger, plenipotentiary and chief superintendent of trade. Harry joined Morrison in Hong Kong in May 1842 and shortly afterwards sailed up the Yangtze with his master and Pottinger to Nanking. Pottinger immediately took to Harry, taking him everywhere with him, almost as a young mascot, referring to him as 'my boy'. Consequently, Harry witnessed the signing of the Treaty of Nanking (1842), a punitive document which temporarily brought hostilities between Britain and China to a halt. The treaty ceded Hong Kong to Britain, Pottinger becoming its first governor, and provided for the opening of five treaty ports, at Ningpo, Canton, Fuchow, Amoy and Shanghai from where Britons could trade 'with whatever persons they pleased', their business being overseen by British consuls. China was offered nothing in return and Nanking was the first of the many so-called unequal treaties imposed upon it by the Western powers and Russia.

By the time he was eighteen, Harry had worked at all the five treaty ports. In September 1842, Gützlaff was appointed civil magistrate on Chusan, an island occupied by Britain just off the coast of Ningpo, and Harry went with him to serve as his clerk. While there, he studied towards the consular examination in Chinese, passing it in August 1843. Newly qualified, Harry was appointed as interpreter at Fuchow though he was unable to take this position up owing to delays in opening the port. Instead, Pottinger personally arranged for him to spend some months learning consular work, first at Canton and then at the Chinese secretary's office at Hong Kong. Amoy was next, and an appointment as interpreter at the consulate where an enduring professional friendship began with his consul, Rutherford Alcock. At about the same time, Pottinger left Hong Kong and was replaced by John Francis Davis. Harry lamented the departure of the man who had taken such an active interest in his career and, in his journal, he wrote of Davis, 'I am certain that he does not possess many of the frank, generous, kind and endearing qualities of his predecessor.'

Nonetheless, Harry's star, in tandem with Alcock's, continued to rise. The pair were transferred to Fuchow, one of the more volatile treaty ports, in March 1845. In October, Harry was pelted with stones by Manchu soldiers while out walking the walls of the town's Tartar quarter. His six assailants were later apprehended and Alcock meted out harsh punishments; the three youngest were severely flogged with bamboo while their older accomplices suffered the humiliation of having to wear a cangue (wooden collar) around their necks for a month. In August 1846, Harry completed his set of treaty ports when he and Alcock were, again, transferred together to Shanghai, Alcock as consul, Harry his acting interpreter. Alcock was a great influence on Harry, a straight talker who expected China's absolute compliance with its obligations under treaty, no matter how onerous. The careers of each bear many similarities and Harry, no doubt, moulded his own consular and diplomatic career on the example set by his mentor.

Very few made a meteoric rise through the ranks of the consular service and Harry was no exception. Over the next few years he revisited most of the treaty ports as interpreter. This was an important position in any outpost of empire but more so in regions where relations between consulate and host were tense and where even a small error in translation or the wrong emphasis might result in a diplomatic incident. At times, Harry acted as consul to cover absences and took this additional responsibility in his stride. In August 1854, he was appointed consul at Amoy.

The following year, having been part of a delegation which had reached a commercial agreement with Siam, he returned to London bearing the unratified treaty and was received by Queen Victoria. He stayed in England for a year, working out of the Foreign Office. In November 1855 he met Fanny Hannah Plumer (1831–79), granddaughter of Sir Thomas Plumer, who had been Master of the Rolls. The couple were married at Whitchurch, Middlesex on New Year's Day, 1856, and just over a week later sailed for China, stopping at Bangkok on the way to exchange ratified treaties. From there, they went not to Amoy but to Canton, where Parkes was to stand in for Alcock, who was on leave. As his ship docked, he was unaware that he was about to play an important role in events leading up to the Second Opium War (1856–60).

On 8 October 1856, Chinese officials boarded the lorcha, *Arrow*, in Canton and arrested its Chinese crew on suspicion of piracy. The ship had, until a few days earlier, been registered British and still had the right to fly the red ensign.

From the consulate, Parkes remonstrated with the Chinese authorities, claiming the boarding was an insult to the flag and he referred the matter to Sir John Bowring, governor of Hong Kong. The incident provided Bowring with a *casus belli* for asserting Britain's right to enter Canton, a right granted at Nanking yet hitherto denied. A subsequent bombardment by the Royal Navy breached the walls of the city on 29 October, and Parkes and Rear Admiral Sir Michael Seymour proceeded to the *yamen* (office) of Ye, Canton's governor general, with terms. Ye stood his ground and an uneasy stand-off ensued during which Parkes remained at the consulate, practically besieged, drafting dispatches and issuing proclamations to the city's inhabitants. As tensions increased, however, and after the British encampment outside the city was set ablaze, he retreated to Hong Kong. In England, the controversy surrounding the *Arrow* affair led to Prime Minister Lord Palmerston calling a general election: during a debate in the Lords on the situation at Canton, the Earl of Malmesbury severely criticised Parkes, remarking, 'I do not know if I have ever met anything which I should consider more grotesque than the conduct of Consul Parkes throughout these transactions.'

The *Arrow* incident sparked the beginning of the second war. Parkes, attached to Seymour's staff, continued to play a prominent role in measures taken to subdue Canton and led a party of sailors who arrested Ye in January 1858. Parkes joined a commission comprising three Europeans which took over the running of the city and, as the only one fluent in Chinese, he became its effective leader. In June of the same year, the signing of the (unequal) Treaty of Tientsin (1858) failed to bring hostilities to an end. *Inter alia*, the treaty provided for the establishment of British, French, American and Russian legations at Peking, at that time closed to foreign powers. However, in the summer of 1859, when the British and French tried to install their plenipotentiaries in Peking they were repulsed at Taku on the banks of the river Peiho outside Tientsin.

In June 1860, Parkes met Lord Elgin, British ambassador extraordinary in Hong Kong, who had unwisely assumed that the Peking government would comply with the terms of the treaty. Shortly afterwards, Elgin asked Parkes to join him in the Gulf of Pechili, from where the response of Britain and France to the slight at Taku was being coordinated. In July, Parkes, along with Thomas Wade, became Elgin's joint private secretary. The following month, serving under the command of General Sir James Hope Grant, Parkes went ashore at Pehtang beach, south-west of Tientsin and undertook some reconnaissance work which assisted in the taking of the Taku forts. He then headed inland, passing through Tientsin and on to Tungchow, west of Peking, to arrange for land to be allocated for an encampment of British and French troops. There, his work was obstructed by Chinese soldiers, and an engagement ensued during which Parkes and his men were taken prisoner even though they were carrying a flag of truce. Of those captured, Parkes, Henry Brougham Loch, who was Elgin's private secretary, two French soldiers and a Sikh sowar were taken to Peking where they were initially incarcerated in chains. Later, Parkes and Loch were assigned more comfortable quarters where they were urged by their interrogators to intervene in negotiations with British commanders. Elgin later commended Parkes for not compromising the Anglo-French position in order to secure his release, which came anyway on 8 October, six days before the arrival of an order from the emperor demanding his execution. Others, captured with Parkes, were not so fortunate and died in captivity.

At the end of the war, Parkes returned to Canton. In 1861, he sailed up the Yangtze with Grant as part of an expedition to establish treaty ports at three cities along the river, provision for which had been made at Tientsin. Later he became involved in negotiations with the Tai'ping rebels who had been conducting operations in the south of China against the ruling Qing Dynasty since 1850, and then, in early 1862, he made an extended trip to England. His exemplary behaviour during his captivity had made him something of a hero at home and he was made KCB. He was just thirty-four. Having enjoyed holidays in Scotland and Switzerland, Parkes returned to China in 1864 to assume the consulship at Shanghai, a post to which he had been appointed in 1858 but which he had been unable to take up because of the war. He had been there just a year when, while visiting the Yangtze ports, he received a letter from Foreign Secretary Lord John Russell, informing him of his appointment to the court of Japan. The man he was to succeed, and who no doubt recommended him for the post, was Alcock.

The notoriously difficult Japanese language was not a problem for Parkes who had begun learning it in 1847. He held the title of 'Her Majesty's Envoy Extraordinary and Minister Plenipotentiary and Consul General in Japan' for eighteen years. He was a strong supporter of Japanese imperialists and supported, insofar as he was able, the clans which successfully ousted the Tokugawa Shogunate during the civil war of 1868–9. He survived at least three assassination attempts, one of which, in Kyoto (then the capital city), came alarmingly close to succeeding. He described the incident, which occurred in March 1868, in a letter to his wife. 'Yesterday, while proceeding to the Mikado's palace to have my audience, my procession was attacked by several Japanese swordsmen who sprang out as we passed, and commenced their deadly work in a demoniacal way.' One of the assailants ran through the entourage 'cutting frantically at everybody as he ran'. Several men and some horses were wounded: Parkes himself escaped by a whisker – only his belt was cut.

Parkes had 'backed the right horse' in the civil war and he became prominent among Kyoto's foreign statesmen. He attracted British investment for infrastructure projects, including the railways and Japan's first lighthouse and, when a new mint was opened in Osaka in 1870, Lady Parkes (who three years earlier had become the first woman to reach the summit of Mount Fuji) struck the first coin. However, in the latter years of his tenure, as Japan became less reliant on foreign support, Parkes' influence waned and his blunt, sometimes condescending, approach began to irritate his hosts and occasionally caused embarrassment to his subordinates. In that part of the world, however, little was to be gained by having a representative of the British Empire who was meek or a pushover, and those of his countrymen who sought to ply their trade in the region held him in the highest regard.

Three daughters of Sir Harry with their governess Miss Brown, centre, in the clothes in which they climbed Mount Fujiyama in 1880. (The Cobbold Family History Trust.)

In 1869, Prime Minister William Gladstone, tasked the Japanese Embassy with conducting a detailed enquiry into Japanese paper (*washi*), and papermaking. Two years later, more than four hundred samples, collected by Parkes and his staff at Kyoto, Nagasaki, Yokohama and Osaka were despatched to London together with detailed reports on the manufacturing process. This unique collection is of significant historical importance and comprises samples of paper, which now reside at the Victoria & Albert Museum, and products made from paper now held at the Royal Botanic Gardens, Kew. In 1994, the Parkes Collection, as both parts are known, briefly returned to its country of origin for an exhibition staged in Tokyo.

Parkes made another extended visit home in 1879, though in most unhappy circumstances. Having received a telegram informing him that his wife was gravely ill in London, he caught the first ship across the Pacific, dashed across America and then crossed the Atlantic only to arrive four days too late 'to hear her last wishes and injunctions, to smooth her pillow, and to close her eyes'. The loss affected him deeply and he remained in Britain until January 1882; he visited his brother-in-law, Hall Plumer in Torquay, took a yachting tour of Scotland and was in demand at Downing Street for his experience in eastern affairs. On 7 December 1881, at Windsor Castle, he was invested GCMG by the Queen. Before he returned to Kyoto, he made arrangements for his four younger children to stay in England under the care of their aunt, Julia Plumer. He returned with his eldest daughters, Marion, known as Minnie (21) and Mabel (17). Both girls married in 1884: Mabel to a captain in the Royal Navy, Egerton Bagot Byrd Levett-Scrivener; Minnie to James Johnstone Keswick who, like his father, became managing partner (taipan) of the powerful Hong Kong conglomerate, Jardine Matheson. The Keswicks and the Jardines, both Scottish families, were related by marriage. The company, established in Canton in 1832, made its early fortune in opium and its operations were an important factor in the build-up to the First Opium War.

Fittingly, Parkes ended his career where it had begun, in China. Following the recall of Sir Thomas Wade in 1882, Parkes was appointed minister to China on 1 July 1883. Again, he was following in the footsteps of his great mentor, Alcock, who had resigned from the same post in 1871. By this time, 'the man on the spot' had lost much of his decision-making power. When Parkes had embarked upon his career, Britain's representatives in far-flung corners of the world often had to act quickly and decisively without referral to the home government, which might take months. The laying of cables under the sea and the introduction of telegraph communications across even the remotest regions of the world now enabled the Foreign Office to exert much greater control over its overseas agencies and men like Parkes. This irritated Parkes who, no doubt, considered himself a greater authority on Chinese affairs than any supposed expert in Whitehall. Of course, in formulating policy towards China, the Foreign Office also had to take into consideration its relations with other powers in that part of the world, notably Russia, its great imperial rival in the region. The view of the man on the spot tended to be more myopic.

Parkes died in office at the Peking legation on 22 March 1885 from remittent typhoid fever, recovery from which had been hindered by his refusal to slow down in his work. Parkes was a hard taskmaster, irascible and a man whose belligerence and patriotism often manifested itself as an apparent disrespect for his hosts, whether Chinese or Japanese. Some modern historians identify him with all that was worst in Britain's foreign relations at that time – blinkered in his patriotism and operating with scant regard for local sensitivities. There may be some truth in this, but Sir Harry Parkes was a man of his age and, during the height of Britain's world reach, it was men such as him who, for better or worse, sustained its hegemony in world markets and who defended and advanced its geopolitical interests.

Field Marshal Herbert Horatio Kitchener, KCMG KG, 1st Earl Kitchener (1850–1916)

Soldier and Statesman

To those with even a casual inter-est in the history of the British Empire, Herbert Kitchener embodied many of the char-acteristics that enabled a small island to dominate so much of the world. Fearless, determined and uncompromising, Kitchener was born to lead, whether in the army or in public service, and his opinions were difficult to ignore no matter how illustrious the company. His physical appear-ance reinforced his authority: he was unusually tall (6 feet 2 inches) and solidly built, with piercing blue eyes capable of withering any on whom he fixed an icy glare; these and his luxu-riant moustaches dominate the many portraits of him, which depict him as a man not to be trifled with. Of Kitchener's time as secretary of state for war, Winston Churchill, that most persuasive of English states-men, wrote, 'When Kitchener gave a decision it was generally accepted as final. He was never, to my belief, over-ruled by the

'Khartoum' by Spy (Leslie M. Ward) for Vanity Fair, 1899. (The Cobbold Family History Trust.)

War Council or the Cabinet in any military matter, great or small.' Such strength in his own convictions made Kitchener a difficult man to work with but, like all leaders possessed of such confidence, even arrogance, he never sat on the fence or shirked from making tough decisions. All was not blinkered bravado. Kitchener was unquestionably an outstanding military leader and when rank

brought him into the realm of politics he never allowed himself to be cowed by his besuited masters. History has been largely unkind to him. He has often been associated with the worst excesses of imperial expansion and his wartime reputation was quickly tarnished by the memoirs of those who harboured jealousies against him or whom he rubbed up the wrong way. However, in recent years, more balanced studies have emerged and many have reached a more sympathetic conclusion.

Kitchener was born at Gunsborough House, near Listowel, the third child of Lieutenant Colonel Henry Horatio Kitchener (1805–94) and Frances (Fanny) Ann Chevallier (1826–64) of Aspall Hall, Suffolk, whose older brother was married to Isobella Cobbold. The family moved to Switzerland in 1864 for the benefit of his mother's health, though the change of air was unable to save her from tuberculosis. There, the young Herbert boarded at an English-run school where he was generally unhappy. He immersed himself in his studies and became fluent in French and German. In poor health in 1867, he returned to England to stay with a cousin in Cambridge. The following year, having been to a crammer, he passed the examination for the Royal Military Academy, Woolwich, where he was an able if not outstanding cadet. On passing out in December 1870, he immediately headed to France, at that time at war with Prussia, to spend Christmas with his father. Together they discussed the Franco-Prussian War at length. Kitchener was keen to see action and, soon afterwards, he and a friend, Harry Dawson, joined a French medical unit. In January 1871, he witnessed a crushing defeat of French conscripts at Le Mans, a rout which would colour his views on using untrained troops for the remainder of his career. The bloody carnage of that battlefield was enough to dispel any romantic notions of war he may have had and taught him that going into battle ill-prepared was likely to result in defeat. His involvement in the war also brought him his first brush with authority: he was severely reprimanded by Lord Cambridge, commander-in-chief of the army, for violating British neutrality in the conflict.

While in France, Kitchener was commissioned with the Royal Engineers. After he had returned to England he spent three frustrating years clicking his heels, first at Chatham and then at Aldershot, waiting for a call to action. His time, however, was not wasted and he worked hard to perfect his surveying skills, showing a dedication which prepared him well for important assignments overseas. In 1874, he joined the Palestine Exploration Fund as second-in-command on the survey of western Palestine. A year into the work, both he and his commanding officer, Lieutenant Claude Conder, were injured when the fanatical supporters of a rebel sheikh entered their camp. Kitchener was

Kitchener and his surveying staff in Cyprus, 1883. (Courtesy of Rodney Shirley and The Bank of Cyprus Cultural Foundation.)

pelted with stones and badly bruised but fared better than his superior, who was severely clubbed. Kitchener recovered more quickly than Conder and oversaw the completion of the work in 1877, taking much of the credit which Conder thought should have been his. In 1878, on the back of his work in Palestine, he was seconded to the Foreign Office and tasked with compiling detailed maps of Cyprus, which had just been leased to Britain from the Ottoman Empire under the terms of the Congress of Berlin. Philip Warner, one of Kitchener's many biographers, maintains that the appointment was secured thanks to 'a little prodding' by his relative, Thomas Cobbold, MP for Ipswich.

Kitchener's opinion that Cyprus required mapping professionally and in minute detail conflicted with that of the island's first high commissioner, Sir Garnet Wolseley who wanted little more than a rough sketch to help him levy taxes and who considered Kitchener as something of a young upstart. The impasse was broken when both were transferred; Wolseley went to South Africa while, in June 1879, Kitchener was posted as military vice consul to Kastamonu in Anatolia where he witnessed the brutality of Ottoman rule. He remained in Turkey for just eight months before returning to Cyprus to oversee the survey, which was completed in 1882.

Accomplished as he was as a surveyor, Kitchener's real ambitions lay on the battlefield, wherever that might be. In 1882, while looking for trouble, he attached himself unofficially to British forces bombarding Alexandria in an attempt to topple the nationalist regime of Urabi Pasha. Again, he was reprimanded but this failed to hinder him being posted officially to Egypt the following year with a promotion to captain. Egypt was soon subdued, and Kitchener became involved in the reconstruction of the Egyptian Army as well as leading more surveying work. Then, in 1884, he was attached as an intelligence officer to the expedition to relieve General Charles Gordon who was besieged by Mahdist revolutionaries at Khartoum. Though the expedition was famously unsuccessful, Kitchener emerged from it with great credit and was promoted brevet-colonel in 1885. He returned to England a hero and astutely employed his new-found fame to establish a network of connections with politicians and other men of influence whose support might prove useful to his future ambitions.

Senior appointments followed, which required deft political skills in addition to his proven ability as a military commander. He represented Britain on the Zanzibar Boundary Commission and, in 1886, he was appointed governor general of eastern Sudan where he came up against one of the Mahdi's wiliest commanders, Osman Digna (the Mahdi, Muhammed Ahmad, died of natural causes five months after Gordon's demise). During an unsuccessful raid which nearly captured Osman Digna in 1888, Kitchener was shot. He was fortunate to survive: the bullet hit his right ear lobe, splintered his jaw and lodged near his throat. Supposedly, the bullet later moved and might have choked him had he not managed to swallow it.

Kitchener's wound was slow to heal and he returned to London in 1888 on leave. He continued to move in exalted circles and was invited to stay at Hatfield House by Lord Salisbury, the prime minister. He forged a strong friendship with Lady Salisbury, who would remain his champion, showing he understood the importance of petticoat politics more than he is often given credit for. Such associations did his career no harm at all but made him unpopular among his peers, who attributed his swift rise through the ranks to his connections rather than to any particular ability as a commander. He returned to Egypt in 1889 and was made sirdar (commander-in-chief) of the Egyptian Army in 1892; he was just forty-two, young for such a senior command, something which caused additional resentment. He was not the army's choice but was recommended by Evelyn Baring, Britain's consul general in Egypt. The army was furious that its preferred candidate, Colonel Woodhouse, a man of greater experience, had been overlooked.

Kitchener immediately set his sights on one goal – to wrest the Sudan once and for all from the control of the Mahdists. In readiness for this, he retrained the army on a tight budget and recruited a cadre of talented young officers, known as Kitchener's band of boys, who shared his unwavering desire to avenge the death of Gordon. All was not work, however. Contrary to common perceptions of him as a dour, humourless man, Kitchener could be the life and soul of the party. Cairo was a popular winter destination for Europe's aristocracy and Kitchener could be a convivial host who was even known to don fancy dress; he was also a Freemason and he enjoyed the social life provided by the five Cairo lodges he belonged to. Despite a number of flirtations, he never married or had any enduring romantic relationship, leading to unsubstantiated suggestions that he was homosexual.

He equipped the army with new Maxim machine guns and modern artillery and a flotilla was assembled to convey the army up the Nile to take on the Mahdists. The stronghold of Dongola was captured in 1896 and then Omdurman, the Mahdist capital, in 1898. From there, Kitchener was ordered to go to Fashoda where a French officer had claimed much of upper Sudan for his country. Mishandled, the Fashoda Incident may have led to war between Britain and France: Kitchener displayed a surprising light diplomatic touch which went some way to defusing tensions and to persuading the French to abandon their claim.

The Sudan campaign was not universally admired in Britain. Anti-imperialists vilified Kitchener for his crusade against the Mahdists and in particular for ordering the desecration of the Mahdi's tomb and for looting his skull as a trophy. In general, though, he was feted for reasserting British authority in the region, and the British public lionised him, mobbing him wherever he went. The government thanked him with a grant of £30,000 and elevated him to the peerage as Baron Kitchener of Khartoum and Aspall in 1898. He briefly returned to the Sudan as governor general before his services were required at the other end of Africa.

His record during the Second Boer War in South Africa did little to sway the opinions of either his detractors or his admirers. Initially subordinate only to Lord Roberts, his organisational skills soon came to the fore, though his military reputation was dented by a heavy defeat when he led an assault on Boer positions at Paaredeberg. He assumed overall command of British forces in June 1900 and adopted a controversial dual strategy. Firstly, columns were sent into Boer heartlands through tracts of land which had been divided into grids by barbed-wire fences; then, in order to cut off support lines to the Boers, farmhouses were razed to the ground and their occupants, mainly women and children, interned in concentration camps. As many as twenty-six thousand died, prompting the welfare campaigner, Emily Hobhouse, whom Kitchener called 'that bloody woman' to complain bitterly to Henry Campbell-Bannerman's government. A War Office inquiry absolved Kitchener in the matter and his ultimate success in grinding the Boers into submission enhanced his reputation and guaranteed another triumphant reception when he returned home. He was made general and a viscount and was awarded £50,000. He returned with a number of statues, looted from South African cities (though later returned), evidence of a bizarre trait, bordering on kleptomania: he was particularly fond of porcelain.

India was next and the plum job for any officer of the British Empire, commander-in-chief of India. On 28 November 1902, he was greeted at Bombay by the viceroy, Lord Curzon who had welcomed his appointment – the Indian army was in desperate need of reform and Kitchener was clearly the right man to knock it into shape. Before long, however, the relationship between the two men, both obstinate and both with absolute confidence in their own opinions, was to descend into bitter acrimony. On much they agreed: a lengthy reconnaissance of the north-west frontier convinced Kitchener that stronger defences were required if a Russian invasion were to be repelled, and he advocated the construction of railways to speed up the deployment of troops to the region, which broadly concurred with Curzon's thinking.

Instead, the dissension between the two men revolved around the retention of a military member on the Viceroy's Council, who, though junior to the commander-in-chief, had the viceroy's ear. The prospect that his recommendations might be discredited by such a man was intolerable to Kitchener and he demanded that the position of military member be abolished. This would have required constitutional reform and was anathema to Curzon. Neither man was prepared to budge an inch and the dispute escalated, becoming a battle of political will between two great juggernauts of empire. That Kitchener eventually won the day is testament to his mastery of political intriguing, aided by Lady Salisbury and others, working on his behalf at home. Confident in his popularity with the general public, he employed a range of tactics, including political lobbying, briefing the press and a well-timed threat to resign, to foster the notion that, of the two men, he was the least dispensable. Curzon resigned in 1905. Kitchener remained in India until 1909, the year he was promoted field marshal. He bolstered frontier defences and cautioned against the process of detente with Russia, which culminated in the Anglo-Russian Convention of 1907. This set him at odds with the secretary of state for India, John Morley, and impeded his chances of getting the job he coveted most, viceroy of India.

The other position Kitchener had his eye on was that of ambassador at Constantinople, which remained integral to British imperial security despite rapprochement with Russia. This was also denied him as he was not a career diplomat. He did not much fancy Malta, offered to him and reluctantly accepted instead and, after a tour of the Far East, New Zealand, Australia and the United States, he was released from the appointment in April 1910 by King Edward VII with whom he was on friendly terms. In 1911, he bought Broome Park, near Canterbury and extensively renovated its mansion, creating space for the booty he had accumulated and even constructing a long escape tunnel. It was intended for his retirement and to be handed down through future generations of his family. As things turned out, he would never live in it. In the same year, the governorship of Egypt became available and Kitchener was the obvious choice. He remained there for three years and was an effective governor, implementing a number of important reforms. In June 1914, he travelled to England to receive an earldom; he would never return to Egypt.

As Britain declared war, a vacancy existed in H. H. Asquith's government for secretary of state for war. Kitchener filled it on 6 August despite the prime minister's reservations and Kitchener's own distrust of politicians. The appointment was instantly popular with the public and gave a well-needed boost to morale in the country. The transition from soldier to statesman was complete but Kitchener was not used to working in a cabinet and was reluctant to delegate tasks to his staff at the War Office. Neither did his experience of old-fashioned warfare in Africa prepare him for the demands of the new, modern war taking shape on the Continent. Yet he was one of very few who had the prescience to challenge the military and political consensus that the war would 'be over by Christmas' and it was he who persuaded his cabinet colleagues that, consequently, an army on a previously unimagined scale was required. Kitchener set about recruiting a mass volunteer force known as the 'new' or 'Kitchener' armies to swell the ranks of the regulars. David French, author of *British Economic and Strategic Planning, 1910–1915* holds that, 'The raising of the New Armies was one of the most important and far-reaching decisions taken by the British throughout the war. Kitchener's advocacy of raising a continental-scale force must remain his major claim to fame.' Kitchener's steely look and pointing finger on 'that' poster have become almost synonymous with modern perceptions of the war and the senseless loss of a generation of young men: however, without the legions of men who answered Kitchener's call the war would undoubtedly have been lost.

Despite all this, Kitchener's star began to fall in 1915, at least in government circles. He appeared to vacillate over the Dardanelles campaign, and his thinking regarding the deployment of the new armies appeared muddled to his cabinet colleagues, though this was due partly to his failure to explain his rationale adequately, ever reluctant to confide in politicians on military matters. Worse, *The Times* and the *Daily Mail* held him responsible for the shell crisis of 1915. The latter's headline of 12 May read, 'The Shells Scandal: Lord Kitchener's Tragic Blunder'. The scandal, as the historian Keith Neilson points out, was concocted between Sir John French, commander of the British Expeditionary Force, who despised Kitchener, and *The Times*' war correspondent, Charles à Court Repington, a close friend of French, and was deliberately intended to discredit Kitchener. French failed to profit from his scheming and was forced to resign in December 1915. To what extent Kitchener can be blamed for the crisis remains a matter of debate but, in 1916, War Office responsibility for munitions was passed to a new department, headed by David Lloyd-George and, in the wake of the crisis, Kitchener began to become marginalised. At the same time as French was recalled, Kitchener's authority in the War Office was diluted as Major General Sir William Robertson was appointed chief of the imperial general staff and tasked with bringing some order to the department and with advising the cabinet.

Kitchener was not sidelined altogether and, still adored by the public, he continued to be the face of the war effort. In practical terms, he also oversaw the British side of discussions towards the Sykes-Picot Agreement (1916), which would carve up the Middle East into British and French spheres of influence after the war. Then, in the early summer of 1916, he set out from London on a long journey to imperial Russia for discussions relating to the co-ordination of action between the western and eastern fronts. He travelled first to Thurso, at the northern tip of Scotland and then crossed the Pentland Firth. At 4.40 p.m. on 5 June 1916, with Kitchener on board, the HMS *Hampshire* left Scapa Flow for Russia with an escort of two destroyers, *Victory* and *Unity*. Just over three hours later, the Hampshire sank, having struck an enemy mine in rough seas. Kitchener was among the 643 men lost: his body was never found.

The histories of the immediate post-war period judged him badly. His old adversary, Sir John French was particularly swift to 'put the boot in' and, of course, Kitchener had no means of response. More recent works have re-evaluated his career and have afforded him greater credit. George H. Cassar, for instance, in *Kitchener's War: British Strategy from 1914–1916*, concludes that 'his occasional misjudgements pale in comparison to his accomplishments'. He was certainly more at home on the battlefield than in Whitehall, where his reluctance to delegate, his innate secrecy and his shortcomings as an administrator were exposed. Nor was his military career without defeat or controversy. Yet, in the context of the age in which he lived and of the objectives which were assigned to him, it is impossible to dismiss his extraordinary achievements as a surveyor, as a military commander and as a government minister with great foresight. In the latter position, Cassar goes as far as to say, 'One thing is indisputable: without Kitchener, the Entente would have lost the war.'

Cameron Fromanteel Cobbold, KG GCVO,
1st Baron Cobbold (1904–87)
Governor of the Bank of England and Lord Chamberlain

Cameron Cobbold photographed while Governor of the
Bank of England.
(Copyright, Bank of England.)

Cameron 'Kim' (as he was known to friends)
Fromanteel Cobbold was born at 23 Eaton Terrace,
London, the only son of Clement John Fromanteel
Cobbold (1882–1961), a barrister and banker
from Ipswich and Stella Willoughby Savile
Cameron (1882–1918). His unusual middle name,
Fromanteel, was passed down from the Patteson
side of the family and was first given to Cameron's
grandfather, Nathanael Fromanteel Cobbold JP
(1839–66), who, before his untimely death, had
run the family banking business of Bacon, Cobbold
& Co. in Ipswich. Nathanael was the son of John
Chevallier Cobbold and Lucy Patteson and it was
Lucy's grandmother, Martha Fromanteel (1723–
99) who had been the last to bear the distinctive
surname. In order to keep it alive, a tradition was
established to preserve the name through the male
line of John Chevallier Cobbold, a tradition which
survives today.

In the sixteenth century, the Fromanteels had
fled the Spanish invasion of Flanders and settled in East Anglia. Perhaps the
best-known member of the family, Ahasuerus Fromanteel (c.1607–93), was
baptised in Norwich but later settled in London and was the first maker of pen-
dulum clocks in Britain. His son, Abraham, also a clockmaker, was among the
Bank of England's original subscribers when it was granted its Royal Charter
in 1694, stumping up two hundred pounds. This link between the Fromanteels
and the Old Lady of Threadneedle Street would be re-established nearly two
hundred and fifty years later when Cameron Fromanteel Cobbold first joined
the Bank and then, later, became one of its longest-serving governors.

Just ten when war broke out in 1914, Cameron saw his parents do their
bit for their country. His father joined the 6th (cyclist) Battalion of the Suffolk
Regiment and spent the first nine months of the war on the home front patrol-
ling the coastline of his home county. In June 1915, he was attached to the
regiment's 2nd Battalion and went to France with the rank of captain: he ended
the war lieutenant colonel. At Ipswich on 7 August 1914, little over a week after

hostilities had commenced, Cameron's mother established the country's very first medical supplies depot from where hospitals on the front line were restocked. As a correspondent to *The Times* would later observe, 'This example was speedily followed in other places, and many of the largest organisations throughout the country owe their inspiration to meetings addressed by Mrs Cobbold.' In late 1918, Cameron's relief that his father had survived the war was soon displaced by despair when he received the awful news that his mother had died while visiting Boston, Massachusetts, just a month after the guns had fallen silent. She was one of the millions of victims of the global Spanish Flu pandemic, which claimed more lives in a year than had been lost in four years of war on the Continent.

Cameron was already at Eton when his mother died. In 1923, he went up to King's College, Cambridge but academic life proved not to be his bag and he left his studies after only one year to enter the world of accountancy in London, something he took to much more readily. In 1925, during a visit to India, he met (Margaret) Hermione Millicent Bulwer-Lytton (1905–2004) while staying with her father, Victor Alexander George Robert Lytton, 2nd Earl of Lytton, who was governor of Bengal (the 1st Earl had been viceroy of India between 1876 and 1880). A long courtship ensued and the couple were married by the Bishop of London on 3 April 1930 at St Mary's Church, Knebworth, the Lytton family seat. Two girls and then two boys followed, though sadly Jane, the couple's eldest daughter died aged just five. Later, in 1947, following the death of her father, Hermione would inherit Knebworth, her brother (Edward) Antony Lytton, the original heir, having died in 1933; her younger brother, Major (Alexander Edward) John Lytton MBE, was killed in action at El Alamein in 1942.

In the late 1920s, Cobbold made his mark in the City. He was a good linguist and soon found himself working abroad, first in France and then in Italy, where he managed the Milan subsidiary of a British insurance company. This appointment put him in the right place at the right time. In 1929, the Bank of England intervened with financial assistance to support the failing Banco Italo-Britannica, based in Milan, protecting the interests of a number of major British banks which faced exposure during the crisis. As well as much needed cash, the Bank also sent a team of investigators to look into the matter and to seek an individual, preferably English, who could join the board of the Italo-Britannica and untangle its affairs. Cameron Cobbold was their man.

Cobbold helped turn the ailing Italian bank around and this brought him to the attention of the top brass at the Bank of England. It is widely held that the Bank's long-serving governor, Montagu Norman, spotted Cobbold's talents and invited him to join the Bank's staff in 1933; this view is disputed by Forrest

Harts in Herts. Knebworth House and Park. (Photo by Wocko Watkins, courtesy of www.knebworthhouse.com.)

Capie, author of *The Bank of England: 1950s to 1979*, who claims that the deal had been sealed by others before Norman and Cobbold had even met. Capie claims that Cobbold was 'signed up' by three of the Bank's directors: Edward Peacock, Patrick Ashley Cooper and Charles Hambro. This argument is supported by a family connection – Hambro's wife, who had died the year before the appointment was made, was Pamela Cobbold, Cameron's second cousin. Cobbold also later reflected that, at their first meeting, Norman gave the impression that his new recruit had been somewhat foisted on him by others. Common ground between the two was soon found, however, when it transpired that Norman, too, had lasted only a year at Cambridge.

Cobbold, just twenty-nine when he joined the Bank, rose swiftly through the ranks. He became advisor to Norman in 1935 and was appointed one of four executive directors in 1938, new positions created to ease the load of the governor. The 1930s were a time of great economic upheaval; Cobbold joined the Bank not long after Britain had left the Gold Standard and took a leading part in international discussions, particularly with France. These led to the 1936 Tripartite Agreement between Britain, France and the United States, which sought to stabilise the currencies of those three nations both at home and on foreign exchange markets. As Europe lurched from crisis to crisis towards the end of that turbulent decade, Cobbold became increasingly engaged in the Bank's war planning, which commenced in 1937, the point at which the Bank considered war inevitable. From this time, the Bank entered into strategic planning with HM Treasury, made recommendations concerning exchange controls and re-evaluated its financial relations with Britain's presumed backers, most notably the United States.

The Bank played an important role in keeping Britain afloat financially during the war, and Cobbold was prominent in discussions to establish new frameworks as plans for post-war international financial recovery began to take shape. He objected to the American-led recommendations made at Bretton Woods in 1944, wanting instead 'to snap our fingers at the Americans and develop the sterling area'. In this, perhaps, he was misguided and over-estimating of Britain's place in the impending new world order. All the same, Lord Catto succeeded Norman as Governor and, in 1945, Catto appointed Cobbold as his deputy. Cobbold subsequently was closely involved in international discussions leading to the formation of the International Monetary Fund and the World Bank, as well of those concerned with Marshall Aid. At home, he also took a leading role in negotiations with Clement Atlee's government prior to the Bank's nationalisation in 1946.

In 1949, he became governor, though he had not been the preferred choice of Sir Stafford Cripps, Clement Atlee's second chancellor of the exchequer. Cripps first offered the job to Sir John Hanbury-Williams, chairman of Courtauld's and it was only after this offer had been declined that the field was left open for Cobbold. Cripps, it seemed, viewed the now nationalised Bank as an instrument of the government, famously remarking that, 'The Bank is not my advisor, it is my creature.' The notion that politicians might compromise the Bank's integrity appalled Cobbold who, during his twelve-year tenure as governor, fought fiercely against political interference in the Bank's business. Significantly and perhaps more important than the approval of a 'here today, gone tomorrow' chancellor of the exchequer, Cobbold's appointment was welcomed in the City where he was well respected.

It was certainly not the most auspicious time to take the helm of the Bank as Britain faced a long period of post-war austerity. His governorship coincided with the removal of strict economic controls put in place during the war and with the opening of the City's markets, a double-edged sword which left the Bank vulnerable to criticism. Immediately he took up the position, Cobbold had to manage a sterling crisis and a subsequent devaluation of the pound. Later, in 1957, after he had persuaded Harold Macmillan's government that a 2% hike in interest rates was necessary, the Bank came under an unwanted spotlight. A spate of 'inspired selling' in the City, which predated the announcement of the rise, seemed to suggest a leak. The allegations, put forward forcefully by the Labour Party, focused the glare of public attention on the Bank and on its governor, something Cobbold was unused to. According to Capie, 'The affair was enlivened by stories of meetings on the grouse moors, conversations on trains, and gossip at cocktail parties.' Cobbold was called before the Parker Enquiry, set up to investigate the allegations, and he confided to Sir Norman Brook, joint permanent secretary to the Treasury, that he found 'the tone of the proceedings very unpleasant'. In all, no fewer than 132 witnesses were interviewed and 236 written statements received though no evidence of wrongdoing was found. This was much to Cobbold's relief and on receiving the news he wrote to his staff informing them that the Bank had been given 'complete clearance' after what had been 'a very worrying time for all of us'.

The image of the Bank was, nonetheless, tarnished by the affair. In an attempt to restore public confidence, Cobbold used the novel medium of television, becoming the first governor to sit before the cameras. During an interview with Robin Day for ITV's *Tell The People*, he sought to dispel the perception that the Bank operated behind a cloak of secrecy. To this end the programme was filmed not in Cobbold's office at the Bank but in the disarming surroundings of his parlour. During the interview, broadcast on 18 May 1958, Cobbold compared the Bank's relationship with the government to that of a wife to her husband in that 'it offered its advice freely but had been known to nag if the advice was not accepted'. The interview serves as an early example of a venerable institution recognising the utility of fast-developing new media in getting its message across and in moulding its image in the consciousness of the public. The interview could not have been easy for Cobbold who was inherently shy and disliked speaking in public.

Cobbold resigned as governor in 1961, having held the position for twelve years (only Norman had served longer in the post); a year later, he was elevated to the peerage as Baron Cobbold. He was still just fifty-seven and had plenty more to offer public service. Almost immediately, Harold Macmillan selected him to lead a commission of inquiry to determine whether the people of North Borneo (now Sabah) and Sarawak supported joining the proposed post-colonial Federation of Malaysia consisting also of Malaya, Singapore and the Sultanate of Brunei (which pulled out of the agreement). Cobbold's report, filed on 1 August 1962, concluded that the formation of Malaysia should be implemented, though it maintained that a third of the population of North Borneo and Sarawak would object, some because they wanted to remain under

British rule, others because they wanted full independence. The findings of the Cobbold Commission were contentious and remain so to this day: no full referendum was held in Sarawak and North Borneo (as had been in Singapore) and Indonesia and the Philippines both rejected the commission's findings, the former seeing it as part of a British neo-colonialist plot, the latter retaining its own claims to Sabah, claims which, in some quarters, still persist. The United Nations sent in its own commission the following year to evaluate these disputes and reached a similar conclusion to Cobbold's enquiry. Sarawak and Sabah joined the new Federation of Malaysia, which was formed in September 1963, though paramilitary incursions into both territories from Indonesian Borneo sought to destabilise the fledgling state for the three years following the agreement.

From 1963 until 1971, Cobbold served as Lord Chamberlain, a senior position within the royal household reserved for those sworn of the Privy Council (as Cobbold was in 1959). Along with a raft of ceremonial duties, the job came with the responsibility for running all functions of the court. Cobbold, a great administrator, was perfectly suited for this role and turned his organisational flair to arranging state visits, investitures, garden parties and even the care of the queen's swans. One of the more unusual duties given to the Lord Chamberlain was that of statutory authority of censorship, with powers to veto the performance of any play if 'it is fitting for the preservation of good manners, decorum or of the public peace to do so'. This archaic duty had been given to the Lord Chamberlain under the Licensing Act (1737) and later modified under the Theatres Act (1843). Cobbold was instrumental in its abolition in 1968. Famously, the first London performance of the avant-garde musical, *Hair*, was delayed until the new Theatres Act was passed.

Among other public appointments, Cobbold served as one of the lieutenants for the City of London and as a deputy lieutenant for his adopted county of Hertfordshire. In the private sector, he held directorships with a diverse range of companies, including BP and the Hudson Bay Company. He received an Honorary LLD from McGill University, Montreal in 1961 and a DSc (Econ) from London two years later. He was a Fellow of Eton from 1951 until 1967 and was appointed GCVO in 1963 and KG in 1970. He spent a comfortable and well-earned retirement surrounded by his family at Lake House on the Knebworth estate, where he died on 1 November 1987. He is remembered as one of the Bank of England's more able governors, steering it through the difficult post-war period. As a subordinate once said of him, 'He was always the Governor, even when shaving and wearing nothing but his pyjama trousers.'

6 SCIENCE AND ACADEMIA

The Cobbold family and their kin have provided England's elite universities with many talented scholars across a broad range of academic disciplines. Many have attended either Oxford or Cambridge, and strong and continuing associations between the family and particular colleges abound. Nowhere is this connection stronger than at Gonville and Caius College, Cambridge, which has welcomed no fewer than twenty-one (and counting) Cobbolds through its gates over the past couple of centuries. The four men who feature in this chapter were experts in very different fields of study. What binds them together is a desire to push forward the boundaries of knowledge and, perhaps more significantly, a willingness to share their findings and to inform and instruct others for the benefit of academic or scientific progress.

Temple Chevallier, the nephew of the Reverend John Chevallier MD and of Harriet Chevallier who married John Wilkinson Cobbold, was a true academic all-rounder, the archetypal Victorian polymath for whom expertise in just one field of study was not enough. The breadth of Temple's talents was only matched by his industry, for not only did he teach, research and perform administrative duties within Durham University, he was also a devoted churchman in the nearby rural parish of Esh. Remarkably, he was able to pursue two demanding careers concurrently without detriment to either. In the study of mathematics and astronomy he had few equals and had he chosen to devote his entire life to just one subject he might have achieved even greater renown.

The mid-nineteenth century was a time of rapid advancement in many spheres of the sciences. Understanding of the causes of serious diseases and the development of therapies to treat them advanced markedly during this period as medicine emerged from the dark ages. Thomas Spencer Cobbold was among those whose meticulous research and experiments improved the lot of innumerable sufferers. He became Britain's leading authority on internal parasites and worms and published his findings extensively in order to promote advances in treatments and preventative therapies.

Many Victorian gentlemen dabbled in scientific study as a hobby and joined clubs and societies which shared their interests and which acted as fora for exchanging views and maintaining networks. Edgar Sterling Cobbold's passion and talent for geology as an amateur earned him the respect of professionals within the science. His studies, concentrated around the rich geological landscape of south Shropshire, were conducted and recorded diligently and he was rewarded for his endeavours with an honorary doctorate.

Nicholas Hammond was one of Cambridge's brightest classicists. He was also a natural athlete who possessed uncommon reserves of stamina which, in his scholarly career, aided him in his field research in the rugged terrain on the Greek–Albanian border. During the Second World War, the British military authorities would employ Nick's cerebral and physical attributes behind enemy lines in occupied Greece, where he served the Allied cause and the people of Greece with distinction After the war he returned to academia, cementing his position as one of the world's leading authorities in classical history. The Cobbold and Hammond families came together during Nicholas' generation when a son of the former married a daughter of the latter. This marriage also accounts for the Cobbolds' links to Lillie Langtry's family, Nicholas' great-grandmother being Jane Penrose Le Breton, Lillie's aunt.

Reverend Temple Chevallier, DD (1794–1873)
Victorian Polymath

Temple Chevallier, photographed by Heaviside of Queen Street, Durham 1868.
(Family member's private collection.)

When Temple Chevallier was ordained by the Bishop of Ely in 1818, he was following in the footsteps of his father and his grandfather, both clergymen who both bore his unusual and somewhat appropriate forename. It is clear from his correspondence and from the course of his career that Temple saw himself, first and foremost, a man of the Church: he was a hardworking parish priest with traditional views and enjoyed a long association with the magnificent cathedral of the city he adopted as home, Durham. However, it is for his contribution to science and academia that he is best known. His extraordinary intellect and energy did much to establish the reputation of Durham University in its early years and his genius, particularly as a mathematician and astronomer, was lauded well beyond its confines.

Temple received his early education at home at Badingham in Suffolk before going to grammar schools at Bury St Edmunds and Ipswich. In 1814, he went up to Pembroke College, Cambridge with a Bell scholarship. He excelled in mathematics, graduating as second wrangler (the second highest-scoring student in final year examinations) and as second Smith's prizeman. He also began to take a keen interest in astronomy, a science complementary to mathematics. A year after graduating, in 1818, he was elected a Fellow of Pembroke and, a year after that, he became a Fellow of St Catharine's College also. He took his MA in 1821 and BD (Bachelor of Divinity) in 1825 and between these years served three times as an examiner in the mathematics Tripos. At this time, the teaching of mathematics at Cambridge was undergoing fundamental change; in 1820 the university adopted Gottfried Leibniz's conventions for differential calculus, employed for many years on the continent, over Isaac Newton's long-revered methods. Temple embraced these changes.

His star ascendant, he was invited to give the Hulsean lectures at Cambridge for consecutive years, 1826–27. Instituted in 1820 from an endowment given by Reverend John Hulse, the annual lecture was to be delivered by a Cambridge university clergyman, under the age of forty, on a theme encompassing one or more of: 'The evidence of revealed religion; the truth and excellence of Christianity; the prophesies and miracles; direct and collateral arguments; the more difficult texts or obscure parts of Holy Scripture.' Temple's first lecture was entitled, 'On the historical types contained in the Old Testament', while his second, 'On the proofs of divine power and wisdom: derived from the study of astronomy; and the evidence, doctrines, and precepts of defined religion', foreshadowed the entwining paths that his life and career would follow.

On 4 October 1825, Temple married Catherine Wheelwright (1794–1858), the youngest child of Charles Apthorp Wheelwright, a Stoke Newington merchant, who had died bankrupt in 1812. Her mother's side of the family, the Apthorps, had settled in Boston, Massachusetts in the late seventeenth century and had prospered greatly through the slave trade. Three children followed: Catherine (1828–66), Alicia (1831–1910) and Temple (1833–45).

In the autumn of 1834, Temple was offered a professorship in mathematics at the University of Durham which had already engaged him temporarily to assist the acting professor of Divinity, Henry Jenkyns. The university had only been founded two years earlier but Temple considered that it already exhibited 'the germs of a fine establishment' and he was tempted by the opportunity to help mould its reputation. After much deliberation, however, he declined the offer. The reason, as he confided to his best friend from St Catharine's and lifelong correspondent, Reverend George Elwes Corrie, evidenced the primacy of his religious convictions over any academic ambitions. Temple resolved only to accept a permanent position at Durham if he were able to take on pastoral duties as well. He would only make an exception to this rule if he were offered the vacant position of professor of Divinity, which would include a Sunday lecture, equivalent to a sermon. He considered registering his interest for this position with the Bishop of Durham but thought his chances slim because 'as an Oxford man, he [the bishop] is likely to put in a man of his own university'. On 12 February 1835, Temple informed Corrie that he had declined the professorship in mathematics.

The university, however, was determined to get its man. It bolstered its offer with the promise of the perpetual curacy of the parish of St Michael in the small village of Esh, five miles west of the city. Temple accepted the new terms. Shortly after his arrival at Esh, he enthused to Corrie about his prospects, even though 'full half' of the village's population were Roman Catholic. He swiftly established a Sunday school and proved doubters in the village wrong by attracting twenty-four children to it in its very first week. He rented Flass Hall, a large mansion house near the village, from the eccentric and miserly Lady Jane Peat. Temple reported to Corrie that the house was dilapidated and had not been lived in for decades since its previous resident had cut his own throat, having squandered his fortune gambling. 'I hope,' he concluded wryly, 'that 40 years is time enough for his ghost to be thoroughly *laid*.' Temple threw himself into his parochial duties with zeal. Congregations at St Michael's increased and within a year of his arrival he had set up a village school, though shortly afterwards he deemed it necessary to dismiss his schoolmaster when it came to light that the man had, some time in the past, fathered an illegitimate child and now faced 'the prospect of the arrival of another very soon'.

In contrast to the man of science, receptive to new ideas and theories, Temple's religious convictions were entrenched and immovable. He was a traditionalist and uncompromising in his views, abhorring modern trends of the 'current Latitudinarian Age' in which 'half of those who call themselves churchmen seem to have not the slightest notion of what is meant by a church'. He took solace only from the fact that Durham was largely removed from the religious 'newgangledness' which was gaining credence at Oxford and Cambridge.

Temple's unyielding view of Christianity, unsurprisingly, brought him into conflict with the 'Papists' of the parish, 'with their exquisite delusions and unscrupulous ways of winning people over to their creed'. He complained bitterly that some of his young lads were being seduced by Catholics who were distilling whisky illicitly, and was aghast that his Roman Catholic counterpart, Reverend Roger Glassbrook, permitted the playing of cricket on a field adjacent to his chapel immediately after Sunday morning service. One Sunday, as he was making his way to see Glassbrook to protest at such impiety, the wind was taken out of Temple's sails when, as he was passing his own churchyard, he noticed with horror that some of his *own* principal scholars were playing marbles on the Sabbath.

Relations between the two priests were often strained, but Temple's correspondence with Corrie hints that he enjoyed sparring with Glassbrook. In October 1838, Temple tended a young Catholic lad who was dying of consumption and was roundly denounced by his 'Roman Catholic brother … in no unmeasured terms … telling his flock that if they put their souls into my keeping they will all go to (a place unfit to name to ears polite)'. In a dispute with Glassbrook over the Church Rate, Temple wrote sardonically to Corrie, using mixed metaphors, 'I had hoped that I had tamed the Dragon, by facing him boldly, as the American lion tamer does his wild beast.'

Clearly relishing the challenges of his parish, Temple brought the same verve to his academic life. In addition to his pedagogic duties at the university, he served as its registrar from 1835–65, a role pivotal in shaping the fledgling institution and setting its course. He was an energetic promoter of the usefulness of mathematics, using its principles to instruct his students in astronomy.

He insisted his charges study all three books of Newton's *Principia*, though in his early years at Durham, the university lacked the facilities for practical study of the stars.

Incongruous to his main interests, Temple also held a readership in Hebrew at the university from 1835 until 1871. He was a gifted linguist and had, in 1833, published a translation of the *Epistles of Clement of Rome, Polycarp and Ignatius*. After his death the Royal Astronomical Society noted that he shared a talent for the language with one of his distant ancestors, Sir (Anthony) Rudolph Chevallier (1523–72), a renowned Hebraist who, it is believed, also taught French to the young Elizabeth I. The precise nature of the genealogical link between the two men remains unconfirmed.

In 1838, as an extension of the practical uses of mathematics, Temple, together with James F. W. Johnston, reader in Chemistry, founded Britain's first taught course in civil engineering at the university. Temple had argued for the course in the following terms:

> I consider it . . . to be a consideration of no slight moment that the profession of Civil Engineer should take the rank in society which its importance demands, and as a preliminary step, that those who aspire to highest stations should have received the education of Christian Gentlemen.

The burgeoning local mining industry was the primary target for the course, which was initially popular. Its content bore the hallmarks of Temple's influence, with mathematics and both theoretical and practical science at its core, yet the university felt unable to confer degrees on those who completed the course successfully. Instead, they were awarded the 'academical rank of civil engineer', which bore little weight in scholarly circles and even less in industries which continued to prefer practical apprenticeship over theoretical study. The course was also comparatively expensive, costing £80–£100 per year for tuition and accommodation, about double the fees a student of the arts would pay. For these reasons, intake numbers dwindled steadily and the course was discontinued seven years after its inception.

In 1838, Edward Maltby, Bishop of Durham (1836–56) learned that his friend, Reverend Thomas Hussey of Hayes Court, Kent, was giving up practical astronomy due to a 'severe injury'. Hussey was more than just an enthusiastic amateur; he had his own observatory replete with three telescopes, including a Fraunhofer refracting telescope, the best money could buy when it was manufactured in 1825. Hussey was one of the first two British astronomers to observe Halley's Comet and he has frequently been (contentiously) credited as

Temple Chevallier's observatory at Durham University. (The Cobbold Family History Trust.)

the discoverer of Neptune a full twelve years prior to Johann Galle's definitive identification of the planet. Hussey, through Maltby, offered Durham University the chance to buy his equipment. Temple, who had been lobbying for permission to raise funds for an observatory at the museum prior to Hussey's offer, worked feverishly to ensure this fortuitous opportunity was not missed and he was sent by the university to examine Hussey's instruments. In 1839, he started a public subscription to meet the costs of the purchase; he persuaded 143 contributors to support the scheme and within a year nearly £1,200 had been raised. Maltby was the most generous contributor, donating £105, while Temple chipped in with £50 of his own money. The observatory was built at Potters Bank, two miles outside Durham on land made available at low cost by the Dean and Chapter. It opened in 1841 (Hussey's dome was added a year later) and Temple was appointed the university's first professor of Astronomy.

Early observations were primarily concerned with the astronomy of position, pinpointing the latitude of the observatory and checking the accuracy of the equipment against known astronomical objects. Temple then trained his telescope on the limbs (edges of the visible surface) of the Moon and the Sun, Jupiter's moons and, following Galle's discoveries of 1846, Neptune. In the same year, the Duke of Northumberland presented the university with an excellent new 7ft refracting telescope, enhancing the observatory's capabilities.

Encumbered by his other duties, Temple delegated the day-to-day running of the facility to a live-in observer. The post was poorly paid and open only to bachelors and, consequently, few stayed in the position for any long period. The best of these observers during Temple's tenure of the professorship was undoubtedly Richard Carrington, a Londoner who held the position for more than two years between 1849 and 1852. Temple arranged with the Astronomer Royal, George Biddell Airy, for Carrington to be trained at Greenwich and as a consequence the latter felt that the mostly second-hand equipment at Durham was not quite up to the job. Carrington, a man of independent means, offered to install a brand new, first-rate instrument subject to his appointment as director of the observatory, an offer rejected by his employers on Temple's advice. Carrington subsequently resigned. A further opportunity to renew the observatory's instruments would not present itself for the remainder of Temple's tenure. Carrington went on to Redhill in Surrey, where he made many important discoveries relating to solar flares and to sunspots. In this work, he was undoubtedly inspired by Temple who had pioneered the study of sunspots, making important discoveries through his own observations between 1847 and 1849, prior to Carrington's appointment at Durham.

Away from the rigours of academia and church life, Temple was a devoted family man. In 1838, he declined the offer of a parish in Durham, unwilling to forfeit the benefits of country living on his children. When his brother, (Richard) Edgcumbe Chevallier (1794–1853) was retired by the Admiralty due to ill health with a pension of just one hundred and seventy pounds per annum, Temple stepped in, taking financial responsibility for his entire family of nine and making plans for the future careers of his young sons. Temple outlived all of his younger siblings, one of whom, Thomas, died in bizarre circumstances. In the summer of 1835, Thomas had set off for the Continent with friends for a holiday. During the Channel crossing he developed sunstroke and was later admitted to hospital in Rotterdam with 'brain fever'. There, he became deluded that his companions were intent on killing him, slipped the attentions of his carers and was later discovered, drowned, in one of the city's canals.

Neither did Temple's closest family enjoy rude health. Catherine, his wife, was a martyr to numerous ailments and his second daughter, Alicia narrowly survived a serious illness when she was just seven. In early May 1845, he lost his young son who had been unwell for some time. Temple tried to reconcile his son's death with his faith, remarking rather obtusely to Corrie that there was 'something manifestly merciful in death which comes at such an age'. Shortly afterwards he took his wife and daughters on a holiday travelling through Europe, hoping that a change of scenery might ease their sorrow. In 1847, Temple's eldest daughter, Catherine, married Reverend Steuart Pears, whom her father approved of as 'a scholar and a gentleman and a Christian'. Pears became a master at Harrow shortly after the marriage and the couple provided Temple with six grandchildren. Sadly, Catherine also predeceased her father in

1866, aged just thirty-eight. Temple had lost his wife eight years earlier when she succumbed to symptoms which included bronchitis, jaundice and 'bilious derangement'. Poignantly, she died at 5 a.m. on 9 April 1858: exactly thirty years, to the date and time, from the birth of her eldest daughter.

Despite this succession of personal tragedies, Temple's commitment to Church and university remained unchecked. He was made an honorary canon of Durham in 1846, rural dean in 1858 and, in 1865, he was appointed residentiary canon of Durham. The last appointment prompted him to step down as the university's registrar, though he continued to hold his academic posts: he remained reader in Hebrew and professor of Astronomy until 1871 and relinquished his professorship in mathematics the following year, in his seventy-eighth year. He was a prolific writer of learned articles, penning no fewer than thirty concerned with astronomy alone, eighteen of which appeared in the journals of the Royal Astronomical Society. He also published the findings from the Durham observatory, which, from 1843, began to be concerned with meteorological as well as astronomical study.

Mathematician, astronomer, Hebraist, pioneer academic administrator, clergyman: it might be supposed that the extraordinary breadth of Temple's interests and activities precluded him from becoming a true great in any one academic discipline. Certainly, the Royal Astronomical Society rued the fact that he was unable to spend as much time at the telescope as his talent for the science warranted. Following his death at Harrow Weald on 4 November 1873, aged 79, Temple's biographer at the society commented,

> . . . astronomers may perhaps feel disposed to regret that Mr Chevallier's talents were too much occupied by clerical and professional work to admit of the full development of his prowess in the field of original research.

Yet, it is the diversity of his talents and the energy which he employed across so many disciplines which mark Temple Chevallier as an extraordinary Victorian. He excelled in two demanding careers simultaneously and though, academically, he might be considered a 'Jack of all trades' he was also a master of every subject to which he turned his attention. This extraordinary range of talents is still celebrated by Durham University today. The Temple Chevallier lecturers address the subjects most dear to him: theology, mathematics, astronomy and engineering. At Durham Cathedral, a bronze tablet on the rear wall of the Chapel of the Nine Altars memorialises both his contribution to the life of the cathedral and his scholarly achievements. Further afield, a large crater on the Moon bears his name.

Thomas Spencer Cobbold, MD FRS FLS (1828–86)
Eminent Parasitologist and Helminthologist

Of all the advances made in science and medicine during the Victorian age, the meticulous study of parasites and parasitic worms in animals and humans might not be considered among the most glamorous of pursuits. Indeed, the disciplines of parasitology and helminthology (the study of parasitic worms) were almost entirely neglected in Britain until Thomas Spencer Cobbold began his tireless research. Thomas published extensively on the subjects, often on obscure aspects of them, and he became Britain's acknowledged expert on internal parasites, his work acquiring international renown. In 1880, the *Edinburgh Medical Journal* commented that 'of British helminthology it is not too much to say he [Thomas] is the practical founder'.

Thomas was the third son of Reverend Richard Cobbold and Mary Anne Waller and was born shortly before his father took up residence in the village of Wortham. He was schooled at Charterhouse where he decided to pursue medicine and was fortunate, aged sixteen, to be apprenticed to John Green Crosse, surgeon to the Norfolk and Norwich Hospital. Crosse was a Fellow of the Royal Society and held a licence under the Anatomy Act (1832) for the dissection of human bodies. Under Crosse's guidance for three years, Thomas developed a keen interest in comparative anatomy and became a skilled dissector. Interestingly, during the same period, he also became intensely religious. This is, perhaps, not wholly surprising given his father's profession and that his elder brothers, Richard Wilkie (1823–84) and Edward Augustus (1825–1900) also took the cloth. Nonetheless, Thomas' religious conversion seems to have been dramatic; according to an 1884 article in *The Midland Medical Miscellany*, it was 'as pronounced and accentuated as any enthusiast could desire'. Like many scientists of the age, Thomas seems not to have considered his faith at odds with his scientific researches.

In 1847, Crosse recommended Thomas to James Syme, professor of Surgery at Edinburgh University. There, Thomas was deeply influenced not only by Syme, who was at that time Scotland's leading surgeon, but also by Professor

Portrait signed T. Spencer Cobbold.
(The Cobbold Family History Trust.)

Sir John Goodsir, chair of Anatomy at the university. Thomas often assisted Goodsir, preparing dissections for the great man's lectures. Four years later, Thomas graduated, one of five MD gold medallists in his year, but, through his association with Goodsir, he had developed a greater interest in the scientific aspects of medicine than in clinical work. Throughout the remainder of his career, he sat no further medical examinations and he never took up membership of the Royal College of Surgeons.

After a short period of postgraduate study in Paris, Thomas returned to Edinburgh where he was appointed, under Goodsir, curator of the university's Anatomical Museum, a post he held until 1856. It was during this period that Thomas began to take a particular interest in the internal parasites which his animal dissections revealed. His first major discovery came in 1854. While dissecting a giraffe he found a new species of the genus *Fasciola* (a parasitic flatworm) which was much larger than the familiar *Fasciola hepatica*, commonly found in sheep. Thomas named the newly discovered species, *Fasciola gigantica*.

In 1852, Thomas was married by his brother, Richard, to Frances Phillippa (1830–1906), daughter of John and Anne Amys of Palgrave, a Suffolk village just a short distance from Wortham. Sadly, Anne's father died in the year before the wedding; her mother, in the year following it. The marriage produced eight children in equal numbers of boys and girls, though one daughter, Edith Caroline (1860–61), died in infancy. The couple's eldest son, Charles Spencer Waller Cobbold (1852–1932), followed his father into medicine and was elected Fellow of the Royal College of Physicians in 1885. Charles had a special interest in psychology, working for some time at the Earlswood Asylum for Idiots at Redhill, Surrey and he served as honorary secretary for the discipline within the British Medical Association. He later set up practice in Bath.

Back at Edinburgh, Thomas briefly came under the magnetic influence of the dazzling Edward Forbes who was appointed the university's professor of Natural History in 1854, aged just thirty-nine. Like Thomas, Forbes had forsaken a career in surgery for scientific research, acquiring an international reputation in the fields of marine biology, geology and palaeontology. Though he died within six months of assuming his post at Edinburgh, Forbes made a deep impression on Thomas. In particular, Forbes' vivid lectures and regular field trips to the countryside surrounding Edinburgh inspired in Thomas a keen interest in geology.

Edinburgh lost its appeal for Thomas following Forbes' untimely death and, in 1857, he headed for London where he took up the position of lecturer on Botany at St Mary's Hospital, Paddington. In 1861, he took a similar role at the Middlesex Hospital where he also lectured on zoology and comparative anatomy. From the time of his arrival in London, Thomas began to focus more earnestly on parasitology and helminthology, conducting enquiries which elevated him to one of the subject's great experts. Shortly after taking up his position at St Mary's, he obtained permission from London Zoological Gardens to examine the bodies of its dying animals. Between 1857 and 1861, he dissected no fewer than 122 specimens through this arrangement and made some groundbreaking discoveries. For example, while dissecting a Mangabey monkey, he discovered a new species of flatworm, *Bilharzia haemotobia* infesting its urinary tract. It would later transpire that the same parasite could also thrive within the human body, its larvae burrowing through the skin when in contact with contaminated water, causing calcification of the bladder and hydronephrosis, in which the flow of urine from the kidneys is obstructed. Thomas' many findings were published in *The Journals and Transactions of the Linnean Society*, *The Journal of the Zoological Society*, *The British Medical Journal* and the publications of many other learned institutions, cementing his position as Britain's foremost expert on the subject. In 1865, Thomas was elected a Fellow of the Royal Society, following the reading of a paper on Cestode Tuberculosis in calves, which he co-wrote with James Beart Simonds, professor of cattle-pathology at the Royal Veterinary College. A year earlier Thomas had published his first book, *Entozoa: an Introduction to the Study of Helminthology, with Reference more Particularly to the Internal Parasites of Man*.

Significant though they were, Thomas' discoveries did not bring great financial reward and, in 1865, in order to sustain his young family, he entered medical practice, first at 84 Wimpole Street and then in Harley Street. Shrewdly, though, he confined his clinical activities to cases where the presence of internal parasites was suspected, thus enabling him to continue his research while practising. Through the cases he encountered during practice, Thomas succeeded, where others had failed, in developing effective treatment strategies for sufferers. His success in this regard, according to *The Lancet*, was due to the meticulous attention he gave to the method and timing of dosage of worm-killing anthelmintic drugs and to his use of only the best medicines. While practising, Thomas continued to submit papers and to lecture, and in 1866 he published a second book, *Tapeworms and Threadworms*. Two years later, Thomas' reputation as Britain's pre-eminent authority on parasites confirmed, no lesser figure than Charles Darwin offered him specimens of parasitic worms for his research.

Though first and foremost a parasitologist and helminthologist, Thomas also maintained his interest in geology. He supplemented the knowledge he

Fasciola gigantica Cobbold magnified 2½ diameters, drawn by Thomas Spencer Cobbold for the frontispiece of his book *Entozoa*, 1864,
(The Cobbold Family History Trust.)

had soaked up from Forbes with findings from his own enquiries in the field; on Arran, along the Yorkshire and Devon coasts and on the Isle of Wight. He acquired a reputation as a geologist of note, and under the patronage of Sir Roderick Impey Murchison, the father of British geology and president of the Royal Geographical Society, he was appointed Swiney Lecturer in Geology at the British Museum in 1868. He held this post for five years and was a popular lecturer, attracting a cumulative audience in excess of fifteen thousand. He occasionally tackled abstract concepts of the science; among his programme for 1870 was a lecture curiously entitled, 'The Claims of Geology as an Aid to the Acquirement of High Mental Culture'.

Thomas' lectures on geology did not inhibit his activities in his prime area of specialism. While holding the Swiney position, he continued to lecture on botany and he delivered a course of lectures at the Society of Arts entitled 'Parasites of Animals employed as Food'. Nor did he confine his lectures to London. He enlightened audiences across the country, delivering public lectures in large cities and towns such as Birmingham, Manchester, Hull, Norwich, Bath, Nottingham and Stamford. He was an entertaining speaker, able to adapt his manner to audiences whether professional or lay. In 1860, while lecturing on the merits of the study of natural history to a lay audience at the Royal Institution, he enthused, 'Is it not a privilege to commune with those whose minds are imbued with a love of nature, as she attires herself in the ever-varying attitudes of organized existence?' In 1873, his work even received royal attention when he showed specimens from his collection of parasites to a fascinated Edward, Prince of Wales at the opening of the London Medical Society's new headquarters at 11 Chandos Street.

Away from his solitary labours with the microscope, Thomas was a kind, popular man and lively company. He was an entertaining after-dinner speaker and an accomplished musician, possessing a particularly fine high alto voice which, according to *The Lancet's* obituary of him, 'none who ever heard it can forget'. Story has it that on occasions he would attend functions and, quite literally, sing for his supper. He regularly attended the annual dinner at the Edinburgh Club, at which he would often contribute to the musical entertainment.

Throughout his career, Thomas was in great demand with many influential scientific societies. He remained closely attached to Edinburgh, serving as president of the Royal Medical Society and vice president of the Physiological Society; in London he served as president of the Quekett Microscopial Club, and he also served as vice president of the Birmingham Natural History and Microscopial Society. Respected internationally, he was a corresponding member of the Academy of Science at Philadelphia and of the Royal Agricultural Academy in Turin. In 1873, he accepted a professorship in Botany at the Royal Veterinary College, where a chair in helminthology was instituted in his favour shortly afterwards. Here, Thomas added the subject of parasitology to the college's curriculum and took full advantage of fresh opportunities to expand his research and publish its results.

Relentlessly industrious, he updated *Entozoa* (1869) and *Tapeworms* (1875) and published a number new works, including *The Internal Parasites of our Domesticated Animals* (1873) and an anthology of lectures he had delivered while at the Middlesex Hospital. In 1879, rather than revise *Entozoa* again, he produced a brand new volume, *Parasites: a Treatise on the Entozoa of Man and Animals including some account of the Ectozoa*. In the preface to this work, Thomas draws distinction between the noble pursuit of scientific discovery and the ignorance of 'the average mind' which is primarily concerned with commercial and sentimental concerns. He relates a meeting he had with Michael Faraday at which the great scientist mooted that 'there are no people so difficult to instruct as those who are ignorant of their own ignorance'. Thomas asserts that such men, having attained positions of social, political or professional authority, 'contribute to check a nation's trust' and laments that 'There are too few genuine workers at science in this country.' He clearly considered scientific enquiry a noble pursuit which rose above baser human instincts such as the pursuit of wealth or power, and he appears to imply that that those without at least a basic grounding in the natural sciences were unfit to lead or govern. In lighter tone, he concludes the preface with an amusing call to arms, 'I should like to see a small army of helminthologists rise up and lay siege to the fortresses at presently secured by thousands of death-dealing parasites.'

Parasites was perhaps Thomas' most important work; a comprehensive volume which brought together the results of his painstaking and diverse research conducted over the previous thirty years. The first half of the book deals with parasites and worms that inhabit humans; the second half with those found in all types of animal, from fish to birds, from mice to elephants. Thomas did not consider the volume 'professional' in the sense that it did not concern itself with 'therapeutics or the curative treatment of parasitic infections'. Rather it was encyclopaedic, a comprehensive textbook of parasites for the medical profession, intended to inform those who treated sufferers or who were concerned with preventative research. W. D. Foster, author of a 1961 article on Thomas for the journal *Medical History*, concluded that, in some measure, Thomas wrote the book as 'an act of self defence' in order to stem the flow of correspondence from hundreds of enquirers seeking his 'ever forthcoming help in the identification of their "finds"'.

Cruelly, in the same year as *Parasites* was published, tragedy struck Thomas' family for a second time when his second youngest child, Fredrick Forbs died aged just seventeen. Finding solace in his work, Thomas continued to make discoveries which pushed the boundaries of his science still further. In 1882, he completed a new reference manual, *Human Parasites* and also identified and gave his name to a new genus of parasitic fly hosted by elephants; *Cobboldia elephantis* and *Cobboldia loxodontis* lay their eggs in the mouth or at the base of the tusk of Asian and African elephants respectively.

In 1883, a fourth edition of *Tapeworms* appeared, evidence that Thomas was not one to rest on his laurels and that he was constantly seeking to incorporate new findings into his existing works. In the same year, among his public engagements, he delivered a paper entitled, *On the Destruction of Fish and Other Aquatic Animals by Internal Parasites* to the International Fisheries Exhibition held in London. This paper, as with much of his published work, drew widely on the latest findings of other experts working in the field, particularly of those on the Continent, though in the opinion of Francis Day, deputy surgeon-general, Thomas had no equal in Europe on the subject. Commenting after Thomas had delivered his paper, Day concluded jovially that 'It was exceedingly important to know that Dr Cobbold was as good a practitioner in destroying these parasites as he was in finding them.'

Thomas' last work was *Parasites of Meat and Prepared Flesh Food* (1884), derived from two lectures he had delivered on the subject. Gradually, though, overwork was beginning to take its toll on his health. In the summer of 1885, he fainted shortly after speaking at a soirée at the Middlesex Hospital. A subsequent medical examination revealed that he was suffering from aortic disease and cardiac hypertrophy. Through the following winter his health deteriorated rapidly as he began to suffer from angina and extreme breathlessness. He knew his life was coming to an end and, despite his impressive body of work, expressed regret that he had been unable to publish more of his findings. More than anything, he longed to see just one more spring and summer, the seasons most dear to the naturalist. Sadly, this was not be; on 20 March 1886, aged fifty-seven, Thomas died of a heart attack at his London home, 74 Portsdown Road (renamed Randolph Avenue in 1939), Paddington. British medical science had lost a true pioneer, an eminent scientist who made important breakthroughs in the scientific study of parasites and in the treatment of them, which resulted in the relief of unpleasant, often life-threatening symptoms for countless sufferers. *The Lancet* concluded its obituary for Thomas with the Horatian quote – '*Quando ullum inveniemus parem?*' – When shall we look upon his like again?

Dr Edgar Sterling Cobbold, FGS (1851–1936)
Expert Amateur Geologist

Edgar Sterling Cobbold photographed towards the end of his life in his garden at Watling House, All Stretton, Shropshire.
(Transactions of the Caradoc and Severn Valley Field Club 1936.)

The 'enthusiastic amateur' was a common being within the ranks of Britain's scientific community in the late Victorian era and beyond. The nineteenth century saw a remarkable proliferation of clubs, societies and institutions concerned with the natural sciences, and gentlemen of the age joined them in droves, keen to promote their own credentials as men of learning and to sustain and develop influential networks first established through the public schools and universities. Some undertook their own rudimentary research, squeezed in between the demands of career; few, without academic training, acquired reputations which earned the unqualified respect of acknowledged experts in their particular sphere of interest. Edgar Sterling Cobbold's endeavours in the field of geology, particularly in the hills and valleys of south Shropshire, earned him such esteem even though he received no formal education in the subject.

Edgar was born at St Albans on 7 April 1851, the third child of ten and eldest son of Dr Rowland Townshend Cobbold (1821–95), and Sarah Frances Westhorp (1817–91). His father, a surgeon, was eager to introduce his children to the natural world and would regularly lead them on expeditions through the countryside in search of flowers, wildlife and birds. During these instructive rambles, Edgar developed a fascination for rocks and stones, which was further nurtured by frequent visits to his uncle, Reverend Robert Henry Cobbold (1816–93), rector of Broseley in Shropshire. Between 1847 and 1857, Robert had worked as a missionary at Ningpo (now Ningbo), on China's eastern coast, and had come across extensive coal workings during his travels in the region. At the behest of British Foreign Secretary George Villiers, 4th Earl of Clarendon, he compiled a report on his findings for the Geological Society. At Broseley, Robert must have regaled Edgar with tales of his adventures, but it was their common interest in geology that cemented this particularly close bond between uncle and nephew. Shropshire boasts a geology arguably more remarkable than that of any other

English county, and its lure to one with an avid interest in rocks and fossils would, one day, be too great for Edgar to resist.

Edgar was schooled at Brentwood, Uppingham and Tonbridge before, in 1871, gaining the £25 Ashbury Scholarship to Owens College, Manchester to train as an engineer. He emerged from Owens the following year with his Engineering Certificate and was fortunate to secure a position with the firm, Mansergh and Co., owned by the distinguished civil engineer, James Mansergh. Having secured a steady job with prospects, on 21 August 1873, at Dedham on the Essex–Suffolk border, Edgar married his twenty-year-old first cousin Alice Frances Shorting (1853–1925). Alice was the daughter of Edgar's aunt, Elizabeth Harriet Cobbold (1817–1910) and Canon Charles Shorting (1810–64) who had been rural dean and rector of Stonham and an honorary canon of Norwich Cathedral. Edgar and Alice enjoyed a long and happy marriage, though, sadly, their only child died in early infancy.

Mansergh specialised in water and sewage works, designing and building systems for many towns and cities. Among his most famous projects were the Elan Valley dam and aqueduct at Rhayader; the Hury dam and reservoir in County Durham and the Werribee sewage farm for Melbourne, Victoria. Edgar was taken on as a surveyor, supervising the boring of holes and the digging of trenches to assess the suitability of ground for development. During one such excavation at Sandford-on-Thames, just south of Oxford, Edgar noticed a great variation in the strata of the rock that had been dug through. He showed specimens to experts at Oxford University who encouraged him to investigate further. In a subsequent paper, his first on the subject, published by the Geological Society in 1880, Edgar concluded that the variations had been caused by the existence of lagoons in the Jurassic coral reefs in which the sediments had been deposited. Though his findings were initially received with scepticism among professional geologists, they were, much later, borne out by enquiries conducted by Dr William Jocelyn Arkell (1904–58), Britain's leading expert on the Jurassic period.

In 1886, Edgar and Alice moved to south Shropshire. Edgar bought an imposing Georgian residence, Watling House, in the tiny village of All Stretton which nestles in the undulating hills of the Shropshire Marches near England's border with Wales. The location of the couple's new home was chosen carefully, for the hills surrounding the village are formed from some of the oldest rock in the British Isles, while the village's larger neighbour, Church Stretton, sits astride a fault line which bears its name. Church Stretton had been a draw to geologists for almost a century before Edgar and Alice settled there; Edgar could scarcely have chosen a better place from which to indulge his passion.

Edgar threw himself into village life with gusto and became secretary of the Caradoc Field Club, Caer Caradoc being one of the hills that overlook the valley in which Church Stretton lies. Together with the Reverend James Digues La Touche, vicar of nearby Stokesay, he instituted the biannual publication of the club's *Record of Bare Facts*, a list of its members' observations across a range of disciplines including botany, zoology, ornithology, geology and archaeology. La Touche was himself a respected amateur geologist who had been studying the rock formations of south Shropshire since about the time of Edgar's birth; he submitted a number of papers on the subject to the journals of learned institutions and penned a book entitled *A Handbook of the Geology of Shropshire* (1884). In 1883, Edgar and La Touche oversaw the amalgamation of the Caradoc Field Club with the Severn Valley Field Club. The combined Caradoc and Severn Valley Field Club (CSVFC) survives to this day. A little later, in 1891, Edgar edited the first edition of *Church Stretton Illustrated*, which was full of maps, sketches, photographs, many of these his own, and articles of local scientific interest. He oversaw the publication of eight further editions of the town guide, the last being in 1933 when he was eighty-two.

Edgar's early geological investigations in the area were concerned with Caer Caradoc and the Long Mynd (literally, long mountain), a range of hills, seven

CHURCH STRETTON ILLUSTRATED.

Published under the auspices of The Church Stretton Advancement Association.

Edited by
E. S. COBBOLD, F.G.S.

1903.

Printed & Published by
L. WILDING, SHREWSBURY.

Church Stretton Illustrated (1903); the local guidebook was edited by Edgar Sterling Cobbold for over thirty years. (The Cobbold Family History Trust.)

miles long, to the west of the Strettons. He unearthed fossils from which he was able to establish the age of the rocks in each and expounded a theory, later proved, that the valley between the hills in which the Strettons lay was a rift valley floored with Silurian rocks let down by trough faults. He also studied the effects of glacial erosion in the area which, he postulated, explained the formation of Marshbrook Gorge to the south of the Strettons and the curiously severed spurs of the Long Mynd.

Alongside these researches, Edgar also had a keen interest in the archaeology of the area. This, of course, complemented his geological work, requiring the same steadiness of hand, attention to detail and investigative instincts. He was especially concerned with pre-Roman and Saxon antiquities and he became a leading authority on the roads, buildings, camps, tools and relics in the local area from these periods. He shared his archaeological findings in the third edition of *Church Stretton Illustrated*.

In addition to his field trips with the enthusiastic amateurs of the CSVFC, Edgar would often join the parties of notable, professional geologists that frequently descended upon Church Stretton. One such was Charles Lapworth, professor of Geology at Mason Science College, which became Birmingham University in 1900. Through earlier studies in Wales, Lapworth had identified a new geological period, the Ordovician, which lay between the Cambrian and Silurian periods, thus resolving an old academic dispute waged between the revered geologists Sir Roderick Murchison and Adam Sedgwick. Edgar learned a great deal from Lapworth and, according to the obituary of Edgar penned by William Watts, Lapworth's assistant, it was while observing the great man's methods in the field that Edgar resolved 'to devote himself, for the rest of his life if need be and as it turned out, to the elucidation of the Lower and Middle Cambrian of Shropshire'.

In these pursuits Edgar worked tirelessly and with considerable skill, extracting slender bands of rock from around the area in search of fossils which would unlock Shropshire's complex geological history. From 1901, the *Bare Facts* of the CSVFC began to detail his fossil discoveries from the limestone of Comley, a hamlet just north of Church Stretton; his analyses of these formed the nucleus of his work for the first decade of the twentieth century and beyond. He established not only that the Lower and Middle Cambrian rocks contained entirely different suites of fossils (*Olenellus* and *Paradoxides* respectively), but he was also able to divide each into smaller divisions which were used to corroborate findings reached elsewhere, in Europe and in America. Through his Comley enquiries he described no fewer than one hundred new species of fossil.

This work required considerable skill. Comley limestone is difficult to extract and its collection required, as Watts put it, a man, 'with a fair amount of leisure, and with indomitable perseverance and industry, as well as a good eye and skilled hands. Such a man was Cobbold, and it is fortunate for science that the occasion and the man coincided'. Of course, extracting the rock was just half the task; Edgar was equally adept in developing his specimens, delicately chipping away at them with a dental mallet to reveal their characteristics before labelling and cataloguing them and comparing them with other specimens from around the world. In this last respect he developed a close working relationship with the British Museum (now the Natural History Museum) in South Kensington, which he visited regularly. His correspondence with Arthur Smith Woodward, keeper of the museum's Geology Department, reveals that Edgar regularly borrowed specimens from the museum in order to make comparisons with his own finds. On one occasion, having returned specimens loaned, it transpired that two items were missing. A letter from Edgar to Smith Woodward dated 3 December 1910 conveys the former's despair that he might have mislaid these specimens, though Edgar expresses some doubt that they were ever supplied to him. Whatever the case, Edgar searched high and low for the missing items among his own collections and reported that he had even 'instituted a search in my wastepaper accumulations, but to no purpose'. He offered to donate items to the museum from his own collection by way of recompense.

This 'loss' did not sour the friendly relationship between the two men, nor did Edgar's decision to send the greater part of his Comley collection to the Sedgwick Museum at Cambridge rather than to South Kensington. In 1911, when Edgar was looking for an assistant to help him with a heavy workload of sorting and labelling, Smith Woodward offered him the services of one of his own attendants, Thomas Withers. Though grateful for the offer, Edgar declined, concluding, 'I quite see that a man such as Withers would be of great assistance, but I don't think I should be justified in spending as much as £2 a week *and* expenses.' Though some of the work Edgar undertook was sponsored by scientific institutions such as the British Association, much was funded from his own pockets.

Other correspondence with the museum reveals that Smith Woodward assisted Edgar in getting his work published, occasionally putting a good word in for him with academic journals such as the *Geological Magazine*. Over the years, Edgar published numerous articles and these often carried his own photographs and drawings; he was equally adept with camera or pencil, talents which were exceedingly useful in recording his findings. He was also a fair linguist, which proved useful in drawing comparisons between his own work and that of his European peers. Indeed, he and Alice travelled widely on the Continent, despite her being an invalid for many years, visiting Italy, Scandinavia, Bohemia, Poland and France. These journeys were often undertaken in order for Edgar to engage with fellow geologists and thus broaden his knowledge, though undoubtedly he and Alice also enjoyed the recreation of travel; the couple were particularly fond of the Black Forest. When in England, winters were often spent in Bournemouth, where the climate was milder for Alice and from where, no doubt, Edgar would walk the fossil-rich Dorset coastline.

Alice's disability, as Edgar confided to the renowned geologist, Thomas Mellard Reade, in 1895, would sometimes prevent him from undertaking much fieldwork. Far from being frustrated at the constraints his wife's condition put on his activities, Edgar was a patient man and a devoted husband, and Alice's death in 1925 came as a great blow from which he only slowly recovered. Now well into his seventies, he remained remarkably active in the field, which must have afforded him solace, or at least, distraction.

In 1930, in its centenary year, Manchester University, which had evolved from Owens College, recognised Edgar's contribution to geology by conferring upon him an honorary degree of Doctor of Science. The following year, he celebrated his eightieth birthday with the London Geologists' Association and, in 1933, he led a British Association expedition in the county he had adopted as his home. At about this time, he was also engaged by the Geological Survey to collect and identify fossils on the natural exposures of the Wrekin and Charlton Hill, as it sought to update its maps of Shropshire. These enquiries led to the publication of a beautifully illustrated article, co-written by Edgar and R. W. Pocock, entitled 'The Cambrian Area of Rushton (Shropshire)' in the *Philosophical Transactions of the Royal Society*. Edgar was eighty-three when the article appeared, just one of seven articles he put out during 1934.

Throughout Edgar's time at Church Stretton, the doors of Watling House were always open to geologists from all over the world as well as to students from the length and breadth of Britain. Edgar shared his knowledge freely with these guests and would often lead them to his favourite locations and help them interpret their finds. Watts recalls Edgar's 'genius for friendship' and his boundless energy, remarking that even in old age 'his stride was not easy to keep pace with' over the hills surrounding his home. He fondly calls to mind lengthy discussions in Edgar's study 'illustrated where needful with his books or maps or specimens, emphasised from time to time with his pipe-stem or ready pencil'.

Despite weakening eyesight, Edgar continued to gather, examine, develop and catalogue his beloved fossils right to the end, working on his collections to within a week of his death, which came on 20 November 1936 after a short illness. Three days later, St Laurence's in Church Stretton was packed with friends and with representatives from the scientific community, both amateur and professional, from near and far, who came to pay their respects. Edgar's unstinting work, over a period of more than half a century, contributed greatly to the advancement of geological understanding, particularly with respect to the Cambrian period. The description 'amateur' scarcely fits a man whose energy, dedication, methodological precision, knowledge and achievements were, at least, the equal of many a revered professional.

Nicholas G. L. Hammond, CBE DSO FBA (1907–2001)
Classical Scholar and War Hero

When, in 1938, the War Office approached British universities in search of teachers with talents that might prove useful in the event of war, it could hardly have expected to stumble across one man so eminently suited to covert work behind enemy lines. Nicholas (Nick) Geoffrey Lemprière Hammond was thirty and one of the country's leading classical historians when he offered his services. Tall, with an impressive physique, Nick was as agile in body as he was in mind; he spoke modern Greek fluently and could get by in Albanian. Calm and authoritative in temperament, he was made of the right stuff to meld Greek resistance activity with Allied objectives, co-ordinating strikes against the German occupying force. These wartime heroics were in stark contrast to the more sedate life of his distinguished academic career; however, whether in the theatre of war or in the lecture theatre, Nick Hammond's personality, intelligence and physical presence fostered trust in those he was seeking to instruct or advise.

Nicholas Hammond. (Courtesy of Clare College, Cambridge.)

Nick was born at Ayr on 15 November 1907, the second of four children of James Vavasour Hammond (1871–1945), who became rector of the Episcopal Church of All Saints there, and Dorothy May, the daughter of an average adjustor in a shipping firm in Glasgow, where the couple met. The Hammonds hailed from Jersey and were related by marriage to the Le Bretons; James' grandmother, Jane Penrose Le Breton was the eldest sister of the venerable William Corbet Le Breton, the 'Dirty Dean' of Jersey who was Lillie Langtry's father (see Chapter 3). Nick's third given name commemorates a connection to the Lemprières, another Jersey family of note who were linked by marriage to the Le Bretons. The bond between the Hammonds and the Cobbolds was sealed later through the marriage of Rowland Hope Cobbold and Mary Selby Parkin in 1929; Mary's mother was Laura Annie Hammond, James' cousin.

At prep school in Ayr, Nick stood out both for his academic flair and his robust physique, which enabled him to stand his ground in many a schoolyard ruck. In 1921, he won a scholarship to Fettes College, Edinburgh, which honed both sides of his nature; he was a natural sportsman, excelling particularly at rugby, tennis and hockey as well as an exceptional student with a remarkable gift for Classics. In 1926, he went up to Gonville and Caius College, Cambridge, as a Kitchener Scholar, where his seemingly effortless brilliance both on the sports field and in the classroom continued to shine. He became president of the University Hockey Club and treasurer of the Union and achieved first classes in both parts of the Classical Tripos. He gained a distinction in Greek History, and it was this which would determine the precise direction of his academic career.

It is not perhaps surprising that Nick, having graduated, should choose to pursue his research in the field where he could test both his mental faculties and his physical endurance. In 1929, as the first holder of the Sandys studentship of the British School at Athens, he set off on his first expedition to Greece, the first of a number of journeys which not only brought academic celebrity but also gave him a thorough geographical knowledge of terrain which would become of vital strategic importance during the Second World War. He avoided the well-trampled regions frequented by other classical historians, preferring, instead, the north-west region of Epirus, which straddles modern Greece's border with Albania. In classical times, Epirus was on the periphery of the Greek world, rarely peaceful, and far removed from the sophistication of the *poleis* or city-states of southern Greece, its people living in small, scattered villages and speaking a distinct dialect. Its relative obscurity and rugged topography were, no doubt, what attracted Nick to it and he spent many weeks that summer trekking, alone and at breakneck speed, through the region criss-crossing the border between Albania and Greece. Anthony Snodgrass, who wrote Nick's obituary for the British Academy, considers his subject to be one in a long line of topographical historians, mostly British, and that 'like his forerunners, (he) believed that personal autopsy not only was the key to understanding military and other history, but could also result in the discovery of important but hitherto unknown monuments'.

A well-received article was the product of this first visit, to be followed by further expeditions over the next four years. Nick spent a cumulative total of seven months in Greece between the years 1929 and 1933, covering great distances with inexhaustible stamina. He mapped roads, identified ancient sites, copied inscriptions and became friendly with the local people he encountered, employing his mild-mannered charm and linguistic ability. His journeys were not without danger, notably from the savage shepherd dogs which inhabited the slopes of the Pindus range. In his obituary of Nick in the *Annual of the British School of Athens*, his friend and fellow classicist, Frank Walbank, describes how

Nick employed the 'two-stone' method when meeting this threat; he would hurl one stone high into the air and, as the dog watched it, transfixed, he would let off a second at the beast itself in the hope that a direct hit would see the dog retreat, whimpering.

During the second of his expeditions, Nick received a telegram requesting he return to Cambridge. There, he was offered a research fellowship in Classics at Clare College, the university's second oldest, with a hint that a full fellowship would follow. The offer secured his future in academia at the age of just twenty-two. Immediately after the interview, Nick hastened back to Greece but a request that his considerable two-way travelling expenses be reimbursed was tersely dismissed by the university's bursar. Despite his status as a research fellow, Nick was required to take on a heavy teaching schedule for which he exhibited a great flair. In 1936, he became a full, lecturing fellow of the college: this might have been achieved earlier had it not been for objections raised by the same parsimonious bursar: hitherto the college had been getting exceptional value for money from its gifted young researcher. Despite being just half the age of most of the college's younger fellows, Nick was not afraid to speak his mind. Snodgrass recalls an occasion when he attempted to broach the subject of the paltry pay of the college's servants under 'Any Other Business' at a meeting of the governing body. 'That's enough from you, young man!' was the response this elicited from the college's master.

The year 1938 was a watershed in Nick's life for two reasons: not only was it the year in which the War Office came knocking on his door, but it was also when he fell in love with and married, Margaret Townley, a Newnham undergraduate, whom he first met while playing a mixed hockey match. Theirs was a whirlwind romance destined to last. In 1998 the couple celebrated their diamond anniversary and were only separated by Nick's passing three years later. They had five children, two boys and three girls, though sadly one, Caroline Penrose Hammond Bammel, a distinguished Early Christian scholar, predeceased her father in 1996.

Nick was commissioned in 1940, just four weeks before the birth of Caroline, whom he would not lay eyes on until she was four. He was hastily trained in the handling of explosives, though action did not come immediately. In June, the Special Operations Executive (SOE) attempted to deploy him in the regions best known to him so that he could co-ordinate Albanian resistance against that country's Italian occupiers. However, he was refused entry into Greece, which remained neutral until October when the Italian Army marched south across the Albanian border. Instead, he was sent to Palestine where the renowned Classics teacher became a teacher of the art of guerrilla warfare, instructing pro-British Zionists, among them the young Moshe Dayan, in radio operation and in the use of explosives.

He eventually reached Athens in late March 1941, after the Greek Army had repelled the Italians, marking the Allies' first land victory of the war. Within a matter of days, however, he was forced to flee the mainland following the invasion of the German army, which began on 12 April. He remained long enough to destroy stockpiles of cotton, useful to an invading force, at a factory near the town of Aliartus, seventy miles north-west of Athens and, because of this, he made the rendezvous with the caïque which was to evacuate him to Crete with just minutes to spare. The British force, evacuated from mainland Greece, arrived on Crete to find the Germans had already landed there and were about to embark on an air offensive to subdue the island. Nick blew up an SOE arms dump on the island, before sailing for Palestine to resume his training duties. During the crossing, he had a narrow escape when a German fighter fired at the boat, killing two of its passengers before it was knocked off course in an air pocket.

Among his trainees, now, were soldiers of surviving Greek units who had also fled the German invasion of mainland Greece and the islands. These men gave him the nickname *Lochagós Vamvakopyrides* – 'Captain Gun-cotton' due to his expertise with explosives. He also trained units in Syria and on Cyprus as the British began to collaborate with Greek resistance movements to strike back at German targets. The first notable success in this regard was the blowing up of the Gorgopotamos railway viaduct in November 1942. Anxious to maintain the movement's momentum, the British parachuted Nick into Thessaly four months later to co-ordinate the activities of Greek resistance units. He suffered an awkward landing and lost consciousness for a short time but recovered quickly to tackle his dangerous mission head on. In this environment, in contrast to life at Clare, he was, at thirty-five, much older than most of his fellow liaison officers, but was certainly as fit as any of them and possessed a detailed topographical knowledge of the country unmatched by all but a few of the native guerrillas he was sent to aid.

Over the following eighteen months, Nick was at the heart of the Greek resistance movement, operating in Pentalofos and Pindus, his life in danger daily from not only discovery by the enemy but also from squabbling factions within the resistance movement itself. His survival owed much to his talent for disguise: on one occasion, while making a long and dangerous trek to Thessaloniki, so convincing was his imitation of a Greek farmer that he was asked for advice on the art of cheese-making. He grew increasingly frustrated at the bitter in-fighting within the resistance movement: its many factions shared

Nicholas Hammond and his team in the Greek mountains from the cover of his book *Venture into Greece with the Guerrillas 1943–1944*. (Courtesy of HarperCollins.)

little in common politically beyond the immediate aim of expelling the German invaders. Only his engaging geniality, supreme tact and occasional stubborn- ness enabled Nick to preserve some cohesion among these disparate groups and it was as much through these efforts as for action against the enemy that his reputation grew. He developed a particular antipathy towards the largest group, ELAS, which was Communist controlled, but he would not allow these personal views to obstruct his strategic objectives and he was well respected by all sides of the movement. Amusingly he acquired a second nickname among his hosts – 'Eggs', as in 'Hammond-Eggs'.

In January 1944, Nick was awarded the DSO and became the liaison officer for all ELAS units in northern Greece; he was mentioned in despatches twice and in the summer of the same year he was appointed acting commander to the Allied Military Mission supporting the Greek resistance. He left Greece later that summer, suffering from malaria and amoebic dysentery. Nick's exceptionally important and dangerous work with the resistance movement was recognised by the Athens government, reinstalled after the war, when he was awarded the Greek Order of the Phoenix, an honour usually bestowed on Greek nationals for contributions to public service, industry or the arts but occasionally awarded to foreigners who have helped raise Greece's prestige internationally.

His brief, yet dramatic, military career over, Nick returned to Clare as senior tutor. He became the driving force behind reforms that saw the college expand and modernise, raising standards both in teaching and in research. He remained there until 1954 when he, somewhat surprisingly, took the headmastership at Clifton College, a leading public school in Bristol. Again, he raised standards at the school by attracting talented staff and he taught the upper classes himself, so well, that Walbank, when marking 'A' level papers from the school, considered the submissions from Nick's pupils read like Tripos papers. Nick remained at Clifton until 1962, during which time he continued to research energetically and to publish his findings. Notably, he completed *The History of Greece* (1959), a concise companion aimed at 'A' level and undergraduate students.

He remained a regular visitor to Greece's more remote regions during this period and during his next academic post as H. O. Wills, professor of Greek at Bristol University, which he held from 1962 until his retirement in 1973. He then returned to Clare where he was elected to an honorary fellowship. The term 'retirement' is misleading, for in the years after he left Bristol he received and accepted invitations to go as visiting professor to universities all over the world. He spent extended periods at Princeton, the National Humanities Center in North Carolina and at the National Hellenic Research Foundation in Athens, and was also in demand in Australia and New Zealand. Fittingly, and to his great delight, he also went to Ioannina, in Epirus, as visiting Leverhulme professor.

Articles for academic journals continued to flow; he wrote more than 130 during his life. With more free time, he was able to contribute significantly to the canon of literature on Greek history: *Epirus* (1967) was an impressive tome which brought together his extraordinary knowledge of ancient sources with his own discoveries in the field; *The History of Macedonia* (1972–88), in three volumes co-written with his friends Guy Griffith and Frank Walbank, again drew on his extensive topographical knowledge. Among other projects, he edited *The Cambridge Ancient History* (volumes 1–4, 1970–88) and *The Oxford Classical Dictionary* (1970); well into his eighties, he published a biography of Philip II of Macedonia and, in his ninetieth year, another of Alexander the Great.

His contribution to classical study was recognised internationally and rewarded with a string of honorary doctorates and other awards. He was elected a fellow of the British Academy in 1968 and appointed CBE four years later. He served as president of the Hellenic Society (1965–68), chairman of the managing committee of the British School at Athens (1972–75) and, in 1993, he was elected a foreign member of the Academy of Athens. Perhaps the honours that gave him the most pleasure were those conferred upon him by the Greek government and people. He was given the freedom of Thessaloniki, Ioannina and Pentalofos (which he had used as a base for his resistance operations) and, in 1992, he was made a companion of the Society of the Friends of the Greek People.

Nick remained active in mind and body to the last. He sent a manuscript to his publisher for his latest work on Aeschylus just a week before his sudden death from heart failure at Addenbrooke's Hospital, Cambridge on 24 March 2001. Four weeks earlier, he and his beloved Margaret had attended a lunch given in his honour at Clare. Colleagues and former students from his seventy-year association with the college attended to celebrate the life of a unique individual; an internationally renowned expert in the field of classical Greek history, a decorated war hero and, as all who knew him testified, a thoroughly decent and kind man.

7 SPORT

During the Victorian age, sporting activity became recognised as an important constituent in the education of the sons of gentlemen, believed to foster characteristics that would serve them well in adult life when called upon to lead in business, the services or public life. Many Cobbolds and their kin attended schools where this ethos was cultivated and, in turn, passed their own passions for sport on to their sons and grandsons. Consequently, over the years, the family has produced a great number of gifted sportsmen and one or two talented sportswomen, such as that crack shot with a rifle, Lady Evelyn Cobbold (see Chapter 2).

There are gradations of sporting prowess: representing one's first eleven at cricket or fifteen at rugby is, for many, not only a great honour but perhaps the pinnacle of their sporting careers; while a Blue at Oxford or Cambridge certainly sorts out those who excel at a particular sport from those who are simply 'handy' at it. Through the generations, many members of the family have reached the first echelon of sporting success and a considerable number have gone on to play in Varsity matches, those intense contests between Oxford and Cambridge. However, the nature of elite sport dictates that very few get to make it at the highest levels of their sport and that fewer still become genuine legends of them. Three of the four subjects in this chapter satisfy the criteria for the latter; the fourth was the visionary who set the wheels in motion for a legendary journey made by an unfashionable, provincial football club.

William Cobbold, Robert Bourne and Gordon Cobbold were undoubted superstars of their sports. Even though their names may not be familiar to modern sports fans, to those with a deep understanding of the histories of the sports these three men graced, they will forever be considered as pioneers and trailblazers. William Cobbold was, perhaps, the most talented footballer of the game's first half century; Robert Bourne, a four-time winner of the University Boat Race, was one of its toughest and most enduring characters; Gordon Cobbold, a limit-pushing speed merchant, risked life and limb on two wheels around Brooklands' uneven banked track and played a major part in the development of motorcycle racing in Britain. The fourth subject, John Murray 'Ivan' Cobbold, though one of the finest shots of his day, is best known for the part he played in the establishment of the professional football club, Ipswich Town FC and for his example in its leadership which, when followed by his successors, enabled it to punch well above its weight, bringing unimagined glory to Portman Road.

Each of these men made a lasting effect on his sport. Together, they are bound by their competitive spirit, steely determination to make the most of their talents and by the values of gentlemanly sportsmanship, which they scrupulously upheld. Whatever their own personal ambitions or the rewards on offer for success, these four men 'played the game', and though they were all fiercely competitive, they were as gracious in defeat as they were in victory.

William Nevill 'Nuts' Cobbold (1863–1922)
Prince of Dribblers

William Cobbold, from a group photo at West Wratting Park House, 1901, probably in mourning for Queen Victoria.
(Family member's private collection.)

In 2005, the Football Association's historian, David Barber, wrote an article on the history of England's fixtures with (Northern) Ireland. He recounted the story of the second meeting between the two teams at Aigburth Cricket Ground in Liverpool in 1883 which England won emphatically, 7–0. Among the goalscorers that day, bagging a pair on his debut, was William Cobbold, whom Barber referred to as 'the Michael Owen of his day'. Few names from that era of the game remain familiar to the modern fan, but William was one of football's earliest superstars. In their book, *Association Football & the Men Who Made It* (1906), William Pickford and Alfred Gibson, posed the question, 'Who were the greatest three forwards of all time?' They concluded, 'no matter what other two were named, W. N. Cobbold would perhaps come first to the lips'.

William was born at Long Melford, Suffolk, the youngest of six children of Reverend Edward Augustus Cobbold (1825–1900) and Matilda Caroline Smith (1826–1923). His grandfather was the Reverend Richard Cobbold of Wortham (see Chapter 2), bestselling author of *Margaret Catchpole* (1845). Though born in Suffolk, William spent much of his early childhood in Kent as his father took ministries first at Folkestone, then at Dover, Herne Bay and Tonbridge. Having dabbled with the game as a young boy, William went off to Charterhouse School, Godalming when he was fourteen. Charterhouse was an early 'centre of excellence' for association football and played a great part in the game's development. The 'dribbling game', as it was known, became popular there in the 1860s and also at Westminster, Eton and Harrow as a refined alternative to the rugged ball-handling games favoured at schools such as Cheltenham and Rugby. Malcolm Bailey, author of *From Cloisters to Cup Finals: a History of Charterhouse Football*, noted that, by the time the school moved to Godalming in 1872, 'football was flourishing and opponents were delighted to visit the school where the art of dribbling on the fast sandy pitches was perfected'. The school produced no greater exponent of this art than William, a dribbling wizard who could unleash a deadly accurate shot with either foot. It was while at Charterhouse that he acquired the nickname 'Nuts'. Its origins are unclear, though the great double international, Charles Burgess (C. B.) Fry, suggested in his obituary of William that it was awarded 'possibly because he was the very best Kentish cob quality, all kernel and extremely hard to crack'. Fry also quipped that William's 'shooting boots must have been made by Krupp'.

William's favourite position was inside left from where he could terrorise opposition centre halves with his pace and trickery. In the modern game, great dribblers such as Sir Stanley Matthews or George Best are typically slight and wiry in build; William was broad shouldered with a commanding physical presence. One commentator described him as being 'built on ideal football lines, with sturdy legs and hips that could have carried a body far heavier than his'. He swathed his legs in bandages and wore ankle guards to protect himself from the mistimed challenges of bewildered defenders who could only guess which way he would shimmy next. It was remarked that his only 'weakness' was that he never headed the ball, though in those days the lofted pass was still considered something of a crude tactic.

William played for Charterhouse between 1880 and 1882 before going up to Jesus College, Cambridge as Rustat scholar. He was no slouch academically, completing his BA in 1885 and MA in 1889, but it was on the university's football pitch at Parker's Piece that he really dazzled. He won his first Blue in 1883, in the Varsity match played at Kennington Oval, and played in the three following fixtures, captaining his side in both 1885 and 1886. Cambridge won all four of these matches and William netted twice in the 3–2 victory of 1883 and again in 1886 when his team meted out a 5–0 drubbing.

William's sporting talents extended well beyond the football pitch. At Charterhouse, he won trophies in athletics, fives and lawn tennis. He was president of Cambridge's Lawn Tennis Club and played twice against Oxford, partnering Herbert W. W. Wilberforce in doubles and never losing a set; Wilberforce went on to success at Wimbledon, winning the men's doubles in 1887 and 1888. William was also a flashing batsman who played for Cambridgeshire and once for Kent. In 1891, while playing for his local team, West Wratting Cricket Club, he and W. R. Gray put on 440 for the first wicket, the tenth highest opening stand in the history of the game. He was blisteringly quick with or without the ball at his feet and came second in the 100 yards at the Cambridge University Athletics Club sports day, clocking an impressive time of 10.2 seconds.

Football, though, was his first love. During his Cambridge years and until his retirement, he played alongside his old school chums with the amateur side, Old Carthusians. In 1881, Old Carthusians had won England's premier competition, the FA Cup, beating Old Etonians 3–0 in the final, but as the decade wore on, newly founded, well-run professional clubs began to dominate the game. The amateur–professional divide in football was also a south–north divide, and the tide turned decisively in 1883 when underdogs Blackburn Olympic became the first northern side to win the FA Cup, beating Old Etonians 2–1 after extra time at the Oval. Earlier in the competition, at Whalley Grange, Manchester, Olympic had thrashed William's much fancied Old Carthusians 4–0 in the semi-final: arguably this match marked the watershed between the amateur and professional eras of the game.

Always a 'gentleman' rather than a 'player', William became one of the first footballers to sign up for the team that became synonymous with the values of the amateur game, the Corinthian Football Club. The club was founded in 1882 by N. Lane Jackson, assistant secretary of the Football Association, as a means for developing an England squad capable of challenging Scotland, at that time the dominant force among the four home nations. Based in London, the Corinthian FC played friendlies, often for charity, in and around the capital, and drew its talent from the old boys of the leading football-playing public schools. Such were the talents of its players that it would surely have been a match for the professional clubs had it not been for the avowal that the team 'shall not compete for any challenge cup or any prize of any distinction' (these constraints were removed in 1900). It was essentially a gentleman's club, open only to players made of the right stuff who understood the noblest traditions of sport and who eschewed the crude pursuit of 'pot hunting'. The Corinthian player considered himself to have greater individual flair than his professional counterpart, relying on instinct and individual guile rather than on a rigid adherence to team tactics or disciplined, mechanical training. In his book, *On the Corinthian Spirit*, D. J. Taylor asserts that the club's players also felt a moral superiority over professionals, derived 'from an ethic that in the end had very little to do with sport at all'.

In the first thirty or so years of the club's history, approximately one third of those who played for England were Corinthians. From the early twentieth century the team toured abroad and was considered an ambassador for imperial unity, for example in South Africa in 1897 and 1903. It also helped to develop the game in other countries such as Hungary where it did much – according to B. O. Corbett, compiler of the history of the club's first twenty five years – 'to popularise the British idea of true sportsmanship'. William was a model Corinthian: he turned out for the club forty-six times, scoring no fewer than forty goals.

William's England call-up came when he was aged just twenty years and twenty days, and, in scoring against Ireland, he not only notched England's fiftieth goal but he also became the third youngest player to score for the national team: he remains in the top twenty on the all-time list. The first goal, on seventeen minutes, was somewhat scrappy, though William scored neatly through a scrimmage of players; the second, just two minutes later, was reported in the Press as a 'hotshot'.

William was instantly comfortable playing at the very highest level. Vic Wayling, founder-curator of the Football Museum at Hitchin, related a remarkable story of an England trial when William elected to play in goal so that he could assess the form of the players in front of him. After a while, he became so frustrated at the lack of attacking play further up the field that, having made a save, he dropped the ball at his feet and proceeded to dribble past the entire opposition team, including the goalkeeper, to score. Wayling, considered this 'the only time, during an important game, that a "goalkeeper" has scored in such a manner'.

William's debut against Ireland had been a friendly, as was his next appearance, against Scotland (if any game between the two can be considered such). On 10 March 1883 at Bramall Lane, Sheffield (still the home of Sheffield United FC), the Scots edged an end-to-end affair, scoring in the dying seconds to win 3–2. William had scored England's second goal with 'a rapid shot' just before half-time.

In 1884, the annual matches between the home nations, which hitherto had been played on a friendly basis, became full competitive internationals as part of the new British Championship. William, suffering from injury, played no part in the inaugural competition but featured in two of England's three games in both 1885 and 1886, and in all three in 1887. In 1885, he failed to score in either a 4–0 victory over Ireland at Whalley Grange or in a hard-fought 1–1 draw against Scotland at the Oval, though in the latter game he had a number of shots at goal and on one occasion dribbled the entire length of the pitch after intercepting a Scottish corner. England's eleven that day was a blend of amateur and professional players, containing six Corinthian players, four from Blackburn Rovers and one from Notts Forest. This combination of Corinthian flair and professional athleticism was certainly making England more competitive in games against Scotland. In the two years prior to the formation of the Corinthians, the Scots had handed out 6–1 and 5–1 thrashings to the 'auld enemy'. William won four of his nine caps against Scotland but was never on the winning side. Scotland won two of these games by three goals to two, while the others were drawn one apiece. The goal he scored at Bramall Lane in 1883 was the only one of his six international goals to come against Scotland. His other three international goals came in the 1887 season. He scored twice in another 7–0 thrashing of Ireland and once as Wales were beaten 4–0 at the Oval.

After the 1887 British Championship, William gradually began to withdraw from the game and focus on his career. He retired from the Corinthians in 1888 and from Old Carthusians a year later. In about 1886, with his brother Herbert Spencer Cobbold (1856–1904), he had taken over the lease of West Wratting Park, near Cambridge, and turned it into a cram school to prepare students for examinations that would get them into Sandhurst or university. That his work curtailed his footballing is borne out by an article in the *York Herald* of 12 January 1888 which reported that he was unable to play in the forthcoming North versus South match because of 'his duties at West Wratting'.

Following his full retirement from top-level football, he would still occasionally pull on his boots to play in veterans' matches well into his thirties, and though he may have lost a yard or two of pace he could still leave defenders

William Cobbold, second from right of five team members, plays for The Old Carthusians against Preston North End in the FA Cup, 1887.
(S. T. Dadd, *The Illustrated Sporting and Dramatic News*, 1887.)

flailing in his wake. He became an avid spectator of the game, rarely missing a top match, and he remained something of a celebrity long after his playing days were over, receiving invitations to lavish dinners held to honour the sporting greats of the age, such as the cricketers W. G. Grace and K. S. Ranjitsinhji.

William also remained active in other sports, especially cricket, golf and tennis. In 1889, he won the mixed doubles at the South Saxons' Open Tennis Tournament, East Sussex with a Miss Cobbold, presumably his sister Georgiana (1860–1941), who was the only one of his sisters unmarried at this time. For their success, William was presented with a lamp and Miss Cobbold with a toilet set. The ladies' tournament was dominated by the local Arbuthnot girls, two of whom contested the singles final, while three appeared in the final of the doubles. Hester Marion Arbuthnot (1865–1957) did not play, but had clearly caught William's eye: the couple were married the following year at West Hoathly, Sussex. William married well: Hester's father, William Reierson Arbuthnot had served in India as a member of the legislative council, Madras, and as chairman of the Bank of Madras; he was a director of a number of other banks, including the Midland and, in 1874, upon his return from India, he built an impressive country home, Plawhatch Hall, at East Grinstead.

William and Hester had two sons and a daughter, though their middle child, Clive, sadly died in infancy. They raised their young family at West Wratting Park, where the cram school continued to prosper despite the death of Herbert in 1904. With the help of Walter Louis Balzaine Hayter, his Cambridgeshire cricket teammate who became joint principal, the college established a reputation as one of the country's best 'crammers', with students intent on a career in the army benefiting particularly. William and Hayter ensured that a good measure of sport was used to provide relief from the rigours and tedium of the classroom, convinced that the esprit de corps and leadership skills learned on the playing field were at least as important as academic achievement for aspiring army officers. This curricular balance between study and sport produced well-rounded, fit young men – just what the army required for moulding into first-rate officers.

West Wratting Park was more than just a production line for Sandhurst: it was a community, and William formed a close attachment to the students who came under his care. During the Great War he agonised at his role in preparing so many for the squalid misery of trench warfare in France and Flanders, and reports of the deaths of the college's alumni upset him enormously. He was, however, a deeply patriotic man and he bore this burden stoically. William articulated both his despair and his patriotism through poetry, publishing two volumes on themes relating to the war. Underlining his scholarly leanings, he often wrote his poems both in English and in Latin. It seems likely he found the process of writing verse cathartic. The first collection, *De bello et Aliis Rebus: About the War, etc.*, begins with a number of odes to his students who fell in France. Perhaps this is the most poignant:

To my Pupils
Now sadness reigns; in awful war
My bravest boys their life-blood pour;
Thrice fifty now and all the best
Alas! in France are laid to rest;
All heroes these, their souls have sped
To God on high and His abode,
And joined the martyrs who have bled
For His dear sake and Honour's code.
Tho' all looks black and time seems long,
We'll ne'er despair, for list my song;
Our God's above, His arm is strong,
Heaven conquers hell and right the wrong.

The *Aliis Rebus* in this collection dealt with a whole host of themes from political speeches, the weather, sporting events and even the frustrations of looking for his wife's spectacles. The second collection, published in 1919, *Rhymes on the war: March 21st to 11th November, 1918 and after the armistice etc.*, is full of patriotism and triumphalism, yet any jingoism is tempered by his relief that the slaughter has come to end. It also includes a poem lauding the transatlantic achievements of Alcock and Brown. William published two further collections, entitled *Rhymes on Passing Events: September 26th 1919 to June 26th 1920* and *More Rhymes on Passing Events: August 4th 1920 to July 23rd 1921*, which, again, contained a mixture of serious and light-hearted poems. Every collection he published carried odes to those killed in the war and *More Rhymes*, his last volume, bears the following dedication.

> *To my old pupils who fought so gloriously and saved their Country and came through and in memory of those who fought so gloriously and saved their Country and gave their lives.*

Though his poetry may be long forgotten, William's right to a place among football's greats is indisputable. Following his death at Bournemouth on 8 April 1922, after a long period of ill health possibly brought on by overwork, one obituarist wrote, 'We have never seen his equal as a forward of pace and of skill in control of his ball in every imaginable condition of the game.' *The Times* considered him still to be 'probably the most famous Association footballer of all time' and certainly 'the most brilliant individual dribbler' the game had ever seen. Perhaps, though, the tribute paid by C. B. Fry best captured the spirit in which William played the game. Having extolled his talents with ball at feet, Fry concluded, 'Scrupulously fair, with the gentlest of reproofs for halves who tried to trip him, 'Nuts' was the Bayard of the football field, the forward without fear and without blame.'

Robert Croft Bourne, MP (1888–1938)
Illustrious Oarsman and Politician

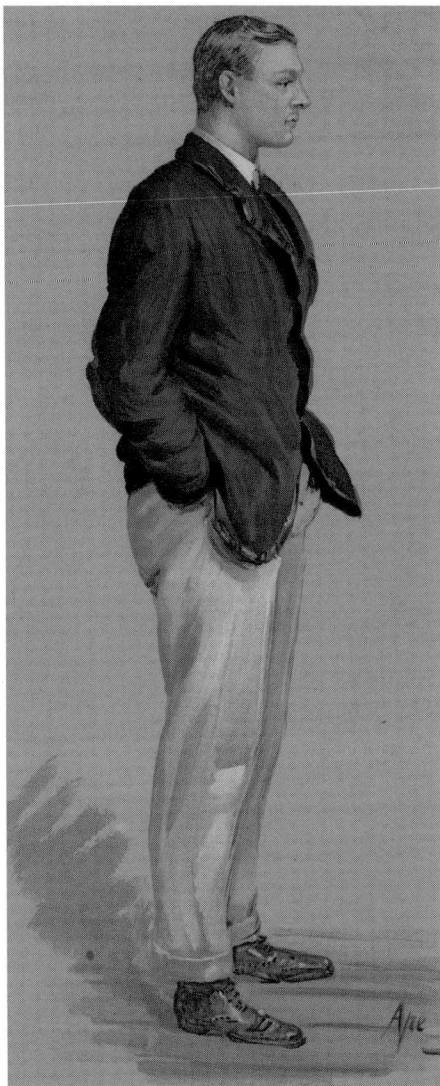

'A good stroke.' R. C. Bourne by Ape Junior for
Vanity Fair Supplement.
(The Cobbold Family History Trust.)

A few of the staples of the British sporting calendar are part of the fabric of national life. Wimbledon, the FA Cup Final, the Derby and the Open Golf Championship are so steeped in history that their very mention conjures up notions of sport's lost heyday when gentlemen played 'not for the sake of a ribboned coat, or the selfish hope of a season's fame'. Little of Henry Newbolt's idyll survives in the modern world in which sport is dominated by money. One event that has managed to cling on to its original Corinthian values better than most is the University Boat Race, contested each spring between crews from Oxford and Cambridge on the River Thames in London. Robert Croft Bourne stroked his Oxford crew to victory in the race no fewer than four times, embodied its spirit completely and remains one of its most enduring characters.

Rowing was in Robert's blood. His father, Gilbert Charles Bourne (1861–1933), had learned to row at Eton before he went up to New College, Oxford. He was bowman in the winning Oxford crews of 1882 (7 lengths) and 1883 (3½ lengths) and later coached the Oxford eight on no fewer than twenty-four occasions between 1885 and 1927, including each of the years of Robert's successes. A favourite son of Oxford rowing, Gilbert is remembered by a memorial stone near the Isis Tavern, Iffley, a place dear to all of the university's oarsmen. Away from the river, Gilbert was a distinguished zoologist and was elected a Fellow of the Royal Society in 1910.

Robert, or Bob as he was widely known, followed his father's route to Putney, the starting point for the Boat Race. The loss of the sight in one eye while playing rounders at school failed to hinder his development as a sportsman at Eton; he won the School Sculling in 1906 and rowed in the eights in that and the following year, before going up to New College to study Modern History. He was an unexceptional student, achieving a second-class degree, but came into his own on the Isis, the stretch of the Thames that runs through Oxford. After eye-catching performances there and at Henley, Bob was first selected to stroke the Oxford crew in the 1909 University Boat Race.

Oxford's prospects seemed inauspicious. Cambridge, and its crack stroke, D. C. R. Stuart, were seeking a fourth successive victory and were hot favourites. Oxford's stroke, the young Bob, was denounced by commentators for having an ungainly style. In his book, *The Boat Race*, Gordon Ross describes why Bob was considered a poor match for Stuart. 'An exaggerated reach forward and an ugly lie back were but two ways in which he failed to conform to the principles of a stylist.' Indeed, many at the time attributed Bob's inclusion in the eight solely to the fact that his father was coach. Such sentiments were dispelled in the 19 minutes and 50 seconds it took Oxford to shock the pundits, crossing the line at Mortlake some three and a half lengths ahead of Stuart's beleaguered crew. The early stages of the race had been close, with little more than a canvass between the boats, when, three hundred yards from Barnes Bridge, Bob upped the stroke rate markedly. This initially took the rest of his crew by surprise and a crab was caught, but once settled into the new rhythm, Oxford stormed to an unlikely victory. Bob had defied his critics and was lauded for his tactics and strength.

The following year's race followed a similar pattern. Cambridge won the toss and took the Middlesex station, forging into a narrow lead after a mile. When the station began to favour Oxford, Bob spurted from thirty-one to thirty-six strokes per minute in the blink of an eye, pushing his boat nearly a length ahead. He spurted again into an unassailable lead, and Oxford won the race by the same margin as the previous year. *The Times* reported that 'Mr Bourne was stroking Oxford with great judgement', biding his time until the bend was in his favour, then striking the killer blow. Bob's sense of timing and tactical aplomb were as impressive as his strength and stamina; on a winding course along which advantages accrue first to one team then the other, strategy is all important. The race was held in Easter week due to the unsuitability of tides at the normal time, and though the Bishop of London gave his consent to the match, the usual lusty post-race antics were significantly curtailed. 'What is a Boat Race without wine, women and song?' wrote Ross much later. No doubt many among the crews of 1910 would have shared this sentiment.

Two victories had silenced the doubters who had slated Bob's technique in 1909. Not that he ever lacked self-belief: on the eve of the 1911 race, one commentator wrote of Bob, who was now president of the Oxford University

Boat Club, 'Ruddy-faced and handsome, with flashing eyes, Mr Bourne looks the confident athlete all over. He is very sure of himself, and has the gift of inspiring confidence in those who row at his bidding.' In fast conditions on a spring tide, he completed a hat-trick of wins in a course record of 18 minutes 29 seconds, this despite the number seven man briefly tangling his scarf in the runners of his slide. The race had a royal audience, with the Prince of Wales (later Edward VIII) and Prince Albert (later George VI) following proceedings closely from the Oxford launch. The race was also noteworthy as being the first to be viewed from the skies as a number of small aeroplanes flitted over the river. A Cockney spectator, when asked about this aerial sideshow, remarked, 'I reckon that skylarking won't ever be so pop'lar as the boat race. It don't seem so English somehow – no, nor so manly neither, guv'nor. Gi' me the good old Oxford and Cambridge.'

Bob's last race, again as president, in 1912 was nothing short of a fiasco, being recorded as the only occasion in the race's history when both boats sank (although strictly speaking, Oxford did not go under). In near-gale conditions Oxford initially fared better, surging ahead of their rivals despite shipping plenty of water. Oxford's cox, Henry Benley Wells, recollected that he had no idea that Cambridge had sunk early in the race, so intent was he on steering a course close to the Surrey shore where the water was slightly calmer. Further on, Wells had to steer back into the middle of the river to pass through the centre arch of Hammersmith Bridge before returning to the Surrey side to hug the shoreline once more. It was clear by this point that the boat had taken on

Oxford beaching their boat to tip out the water in the double-sinking Boat Race of 1912 from *The Boat Race* by Gordon Ross, 1954. (Courtesy of Hodder & Stoughton, London.)

so much water that it would have to be emptied, and Bob instructed Wells to get as close to land as he could. Near Chiswick, the crew gingerly clambered out of the boat and emptied it of water before facing the even more difficult task of taking up their positions again. As this precarious operation got under way, it became apparent that the number two, C. E. Tinne, was nowhere to be seen. Wells later recalled that just as they were beginning to wonder what had happened to him, 'he suddenly appeared from the crowd and apologised for keeping us waiting, explaining that he had spotted a New College friend named Boswell in the crowd, and had gone over to have a chat with him!'

With the crew ready to resume its progress to the finish line at Mortlake, the race umpire, Fred Pitman, who had for some time been overseeing the rescue of the forlorn Cambridge crew, drew up in his launch and yelled through his megaphone, 'No Race!' Wells later remarked, 'I will not repeat what Bob Bourne said to me when he heard this; however he told me to get the crew going again, which I did.' After a few strokes, Pitman drew up close behind and bellowed, 'What are you doing Oxford? Didn't you understand that I have declared "No Race"?' Bob replied, 'We are going to Mortlake,' paused for a few seconds and then added, 'because our clothes are there!' And to Mortlake they went.

The race was declared void and a re-run scheduled for two days later, Monday 1 April. If anything, the weather was even worse but both crews took measures to keep the water out, filling their boats with inflated bladders and fixing outsize washboards: both stayed the course. Oxford won the toss and took the Middlesex station, which offered a distinct advantage in the difficult conditions. They crossed the line six lengths ahead of Cambridge and, in the process, Bob, in his final Boat Race, became the first man to have stroked four crews to victory.

In July of the same year, Bob competed in the eights at the Stockholm Olympics. Of the eleven crews competing, the two favourites for the gold medal were both from Britain and both from Oxford. Bob's New College and Philip Fleming's Leander (composed mostly of students from Magdalen) cruised into the final, the former enjoying a walkover in the semi-final. The course was not entirely straight and one lane required navigation around a protruding boat-house, clearly a disadvantage. Rowing etiquette demanded that whoever won the toss would offer the choice of lane to the stroke of the other team, who would, in turn, politely decline, passing the decision back to the winner of the toss. Bob called correctly and duly offered the choice to Fleming. The Magdalen man flouted the gentlemanly code and snapped up the offer, bagging the more favourable station. The choice proved decisive and Leander triumphed by about a length. As New College trailed in, Bob was heard to utter, 'God damn bloody Magdalen!' The phrase entered Oxford folklore and the foot of the letterhead of New College Boat Club bears the abbreviation 'GDBM' to this day. Fleming's dishonourable behaviour was witnessed by the king of Sweden, Gustav V, who was so dismayed that he offered his favoured colours (though not the colours of the royal house, as often assumed) to New College by way of consolation; the college's crews have worn the same purple and gold ever since.

In 1913, Bob was called to the bar by Lincoln's Inn, though his career in law was interrupted by the Great War. He was commissioned a second lieutenant in the Herefordshire Regiment and saw action in the Dardanelles in August 1915. The landing of British troops at Suvla Bay under the incompetent command of Lieutenant-General Sir Frederick Stopford was a shambles even by the standards of the rest of the ill-conceived Gallipoli campaign. Under heavy enemy fire, Bob lost the use of one hand and sustained a serious injury to a lung. Already an eye short, further active service was impossible and he returned to England to take a desk job with the War Claims Commission. He was promoted captain in 1917.

In the same year, Bob married Lady Hester Cairns (1895–1985), eldest daughter of Wilfred Dallas Cairns, 4th Earl of Cairns (1865–1946) and Olive Cobbold (1871–1952). Olive was the daughter of John Patteson Cobbold, MP and a younger sister of Ralph Patteson Cobbold. Bob and Hester had two boys and a girl. Their eldest, Robert M. A. Bourne (1918–95) went to Eton and on up to New College and rowed at number four in Oxford's winning crew of 1946 and at six the following year when Cambridge ran away with the race, winning by 10 lengths. With Robert's appearance in 1946, the Bourne family became the first in the race's history to have had three consecutive generations in the same boat.

After the war, Bourne increasingly turned his attention to politics. He became a member of Herefordshire County Council and a justice of the peace. In 1923, he was selected to fight the Oxford City seat for the Conservatives at the general election. Bourne lost to Frank Gray, his Liberal opponent, though Gray was later unseated on petition when evidence came to light that he had falsified the account for his election expenses. At the ensuing by-election, held on 5 June 1924, Bourne prevailed with a majority of 1,842, fending off the Liberal Party's new celebrity candidate, the great sportsman, C. B. Fry, world record long jumper and one of a select few to have represented England at both football and cricket.

Bourne entered Parliament, aged thirty-five, and quickly established himself as a rising star of the Conservative party. He was a diligent parliamentarian who set himself the not inconsiderable task of becoming a master of the intricate procedures of the House. This effort was rewarded in 1931 when he was appointed first deputy chairman of Ways and Means in Ramsay MacDonald's National Government, a role in which an expert understanding of parliamentary rules and conventions was essential. In this position, Bourne was required to stand in for the speaker and chair committees of the whole House. He became a privy councillor in 1935 and his name was often touted as a future speaker, not only because of his outstanding knowledge of the procedures of the House but also because he was incorruptibly fair. *The Times*, in its obituary, remarked upon his 'sagacity and confidence', concluding,

> *He had a real facility for 'ruling', was never at a loss and made it his task to expedite business in so far as it was consonant with fairness. He was exceptionally good at keeping debate to the matter in hand and curbing irrelevancies, and could be firm without being arrogant.*

The attributes that made Bourne an outstanding leader of a boat crew served him well in public life. Indeed, it was precisely because of the symbiotic relationship between sport and service to one's country that the leading public schools and universities placed such emphasis on games. Leadership qualities and resilience under pressure, traits honed on the playing field (or on the river), were deemed essential characteristics in the corridors of government, throughout the British Empire, and, for two generations of young men, on the battlefield. Bob Bourne was a prime example of this tradition.

Despite the demands of politics, Bourne remained close to Oxford and to the race he had graced with such distinction as a young man. He coached the Oxford eight in 1927, suffering his only loss in his association with the race as Cambridge won by 3 lengths. In 1935, he became the first Member of Parliament to umpire the race, which Cambridge won. He may have had to mask his disappointment in the interests of impartiality but, for Bob Bourne, sport was all about 'playing the game', and upholding the noblest traditions of gentlemanly competition. He never compromised these values and he usually won. He died suddenly on 7 August 1938 while walking on the moors near Strontian in Argyllshire, aged just fifty.

Gordon Chevallier Cobbold (1903–2004)
Brooklands Motorcycling Ace

Gordon, Sunbeam's star turn, astride his Model 90 in 1926 when he made fastest time of the day. (Courtesy of Mortons Media Group Ltd.)

In 1995, when he was 91, a still spritely Gordon Cobbold promised one of his friends that he would 'crack the ton'. Sure enough, the telegram from the queen arrived on 30 December 2003, just three days before the chequered flag finally came down on the life of this motor racing great. That Gordon should live to be one hundred was particularly fitting because during the heyday of motorcycle racing at the steeply banked Brooklands circuit near Weybridge, an average speed of one hundred miles per hour was the measure that marked out the great from the good. Gordon had cracked that ton as well.

Gordon was educated during the Great War at Westminster School, and was, he later quipped, 'a bit of a dunce', though the death of his father, Monty (1861–1917), when he was just thirteen must have had an adverse effect on his studies. Some aspects of his final school report made painful reading: in Latin he was ranked 18th= (out of 20) 'very poor' and in French 20th, 'very, very weak', though he showed greater flair for Mathematics, 3rd, 'a quick worker'. He was much more at home on the sports field; he played for the school's football and rackets teams and won many races on the athletics track. He was also a good shot, winning the Public Schools' Cadet Trophy in partnership with his fellow pupil D. F. 'Sniper' Knight in 1920. Gordon was popular with both his peers and the school's staff, and the final observation of his headmaster on that report was: 'he leaves a happy memory of himself behind'.

In an interview given to *The Classic Motor Cycle* magazine in 2000, Gordon recalled that his first ride came on a friend's NUT (Newcastle upon Tyne, a British manufacturer) machine during the school holidays. He became immediately hooked and soon acquired various machines of his own, including a Harley Davidson, before eventually buying a brand new Sunbeam Longstroke in 1923. He would often ride his new bike to Richmond Park to meet up with other enthusiasts, one of whom owned a 16H Norton which he was certain was quicker than Gordon's Sunbeam. To settle the matter, the pair joined a club and went to Brooklands; Gordon recalled, 'I won two races at our first attempt – that upset our Norton friend. In those days we just rode to the track and took the mudguards off.'

The Sunbeam Longstroke was fitted with a Wex variable-jet carburettor, which is how Gordon came to meet the company's owner, Harry Weslake. Weslake, just six years Gordon's senior, was a talented engineer who had joined the Royal Flying Corps in 1915. His training required him to attend lectures on the workings of engines. It soon became clear that he knew more than his instructors and he was asked to design two carburettors for testing on aero engines. After the war, Harry returned to his native Devon where he set up Wex Carburettors, later moving the business to Fulham Road, London. Gordon and Harry hit it off immediately and a mutually rewarding partnership ensued: Gordon became Wex's chief tester for motorcycles and cars, while Harry became Gordon's engine tuner as his competitive racing career began to take off.

In 1925, Gordon upgraded from the Longstroke – though quick, it lacked the raw speed to compete at a higher level – to a 500cc Model 90 Sprint, one of the first motorcycles to boast the new overhead valve (ohv) engine. At Sunbeam's Holborn showroom, Gordon handed over the princely sum of 105 guineas for his new bike. During the week, heads would turn as he roared through London's streets, usually with a girl on the back; come the weekend he would strip a few bits off here and there and head to Brooklands for racing.

In 1925, following a few wins on his new bike, the top brass at Sunbeam began to take note and summoned Gordon, together with Harry, to 'Sunbeam-land', the company's headquarters at Wolverhampton. Sunbeam, at that time, was more interested in road racing on the Continent and on the Isle of Man and stopped short of offering Gordon full sponsorship but gave him three bikes, a 350cc and two 500cc, 'to mess about with'. Gordon and Harry began to spend more and more time at Brooklands, testing Harry's carburettors and new parts supplied by Sunbeam, often to destruction. Harry tinkered and Gordon pushed the bikes to their limit and beyond, striving to eke out a few extra miles per hour or miles per gallon. Gordon reckoned they must have cost Sunbeam at least half a dozen good engines. Not all was hard work, though: in winter, when snow lay on the track, the pair would toboggan down its steep banking and on one occasion they took a joyride with the famous transatlantic aviators, Alcock and Brown, whose Vickers aircraft was built at Brooklands. The social life around the track was lively. There were tea dances and parties and then, as now, motorsport attracted a fair amount of glamour, including the girls from London's Windmill Club.

The obsessive quest for maximum performance reaped rewards. Gordon won a number of races in 1926 and finished third in his class in Brooklands' prestigious end of season Grand Prix. He also set an MCC (Motorcycle Club) One Hour record. By now, he was a works rider for Sunbeam and had also secured sponsorship deals with oil, plug, chain and tyre manufacturers and with John Bull knee-grips, essential wear for Brooklands' bumpy banking which, Gordon later reminisced, 'wasn't exactly like a billiard table'. He had also become a member of the BMCRC (British Motorcycle Racing Club, later Bemsee) which had its headquarters in Brooklands' elegant Edwardian club-house. In those days, not just anybody could join the club, and prospective members were required to have at least two registered sponsors before their applications would even be considered.

More success followed in 1927, the year that marked the peak of Gordon's career. He chalked up a number of wins at Brooklands and joined an elite band of riders who had earned the BMCRC Gold Star for lapping the two and a half mile outer circuit at an average speed in excess of 100 mph. Gordon achieved an average of 102 mph on his own Sprint Sunbeam, becoming only the third rider to achieve the feat on a 500cc machine. Such speeds were not for the faint-hearted on Brooklands' uneven surface and with 'safety' wear comprising no more than a World War I leather flying helmet, great coat, army surplus boots and those knee-grips.

In the same year, Gordon began to have a crack at setting world records at Brooklands, breaking no fewer than seven. Arranging record attempts was no straightforward business. Gordon recalled, 'You had to get hold of the clerk of the course, Percy Bradley first, book the course and get hold of 'Ebby' or George Reynolds, the Brooklands timekeepers. Their fee was twenty guineas for sitting there for twelve hours.' After a number of attempts which faltered due to mechanical failure, Gordon, co-riding with Ron Gibson, broke three records in one day on 23 August 1927. At average speeds touching 75 mph (including fuel stops and changeovers), the pair set new bests for distance covered, first in seven and then in eight hours; continuing, they completed 1,000km in a new record time of 8 hours 16 minutes. The following month, Gordon, this time in partnership with Percy Brewster, beat the seven-hour record again and added the eleven- and twelve-hour records to his haul. In those twelve hours Gordon and Brewster covered a staggering 879 miles, some of them in the dark when headlamps from parked cars were used to illuminate parts of the track.

Though best known for his Brooklands performances, Gordon also enjoyed success away from the track. He entered, and won, many speed tri-als and hill climbs across the south of England at venues such as Brighton, Eastbourne and Essendon Park, pocketing decent prize money. One record set on a hill climb near Brands Hatch in Kent will never be broken: the track was closed shortly after Gordon tore up it because it was considered too dangerous. He also travelled to the Continent, appearing in the Belgian Grand Prix in 1926 and the French the following year. He was going well in the former, at Spa, until his fuel tank sprang a leak. Both he and the machine became soaked in petrol and both caught alight. A reporter for *The Motor Cycle* magazine reported how Gordon dealt with the situation: '[Cobbold] somehow disengaged himself from his machine, rolled down a steep bank, put out the flames and returned to his burning Sunbeam, which he extinguished by beating it with his body belt.' He fared better in France in 1927, finishing fourth.

Another close shave came at Brooklands in 1928. While lapping his Sunbeam at close to 100 mph, Gordon's racing line took him close to the lap-scoring box, positioned on the outside of the track at the end of the Vickers sheds. As he approached the box he saw a flash in front of him, something shooting out of the door of the box right under his wheel. At the time he had no idea what it was and carried on with the task in hand. Only later was he told that a young lady, visiting the track for the first time, had seen enough of the race from that particular vantage point and had decided to cross the track to the other side. She, and Gordon, escaped disaster by the narrowest of margins. The next edition of *The Motor Cycle* carried a cartoon of the incident with the caption, 'Cobbold: "I don't mind breaking my neck, but I do hate to be ignored!"'

Sunbeam's interest in racing was on the wane and it pulled out altogether in 1929. Gordon, though still often competitive, suffered more disappointments than he had been used to, often due to mechanical failure, riding machines which were less reliable than his trusty 'Beams. He simply did not get on so well with other marques and later remarked that he found one 500cc Raleigh so stable compared to his quirky Sunbeams that he found it difficult to ride. He had a final spree of record-breaking in July 1929 astride a Rocket J.A.P. with a tiny 75cc engine. In all, ten time and distance records fell at more sedate speeds than he was accustomed to, peaking at about 35 mph!

In 1930, Gordon entered the world of professional dirt track racing (now known as speedway), signing for Crystal Palace. He earned good money, £5 per night, racing up to six nights a week at London tracks such as Haringey, West Ham, Stamford Bridge and White City. Handsome prize money was on offer and, still in his twenties and a single man, Gordon was as fast and free with his earnings as he was on the track. He recalled, 'I once won £90 at Crystal Palace and blew the lot that night, throwing a party at the Castle Hotel in Richmond.'

In late 1930, a fellow rider, Arthur 'Westy' Westwood who rode for West Ham, invited Gordon to join him in a venture to launch dirt track racing in Paris. Given Gordon's last school report, it seems unlikely that Westwood wanted him on board for his language skills. The pair based themselves in the French capital, flying out old dirt track bikes to Orly and hiring them out. Once their customers had caught the bug, they would sell them new machines. As interest in the sport began to grow in France, Gordon and Westy took a leap of faith and organised a so-called 'world championship' at Paris' new Buffalo Stadium, inviting riders from as far afield as Australia and New Zealand. The scheme was extremely risky. Without decent gate receipts, Gordon and Westy would have no means of paying the wages of the competitors, and on the night of the event they even parked an escape van just outside the stadium in case things went wrong. Fortunately, the gamble paid off and the stadium was full. Gordon and Westy paid the riders and were left with a suitcase full of francs. Rather than reinvest this handsome profit, they headed south to Monte Carlo and 'blew the lot' within a couple of weeks before returning to London. Gordon wryly recollected that he had left England in 1930 with £20 in his pocket and returned in 1932, after a roller coaster ride of fun and trouble, with £15 in his pocket, though he 'wouldn't have changed a bloody thing'. He clearly enjoyed living life on the edge, off the track as well as on it, and he certainly liked the odd flutter. On one occasion he won £100 on a car race at Brooklands and, while rushing to claim his winnings before the bookie disappeared, he tore his trousers on a car door. He recounted, 'This gorgeous girl in a Hispano Suiza

Gordon Cobbold's 100th birthday with his family and a royal greeting. (Family member's private collection.)

said I better go round to borrow a pair of her husband's trousers – I won't go any further with that story!'

Such impetuosity came to an end upon his return from his French adventure. Gordon hung up his racing goggles for good and settled down to a more prosaic life, buying a petrol filling station, the Ideal Garage, in Fulham. At about the same time, an old school friend who had raced cars at Brooklands, introduced him to a Scottish girl, Rita Smith (1903–96) and the couple were married in September 1933 in Bognor Regis. A daughter, Gillian, completed the happy family in 1936. When war broke out, Gordon's garage was requisitioned and he went to work for General Aircraft at Feltham, Middlesex, which was owned by ex-Brooklands car racing driver, Gordon England. The factory made spitfires and gliders, and Gordon worked as a night superintendent, though he longed to join the RAF and became frustrated at the company's refusal to release him. After the war, he returned to the motor trade, eventually running Parade Motors, a successful MG and Austin dealership in Mitcham, until his retirement in 1969.

Gordon always remained close to the sport he had lit up in his youth. He took a leading role in the post-war revival of the BMCRC and served on its board for many years. In 1993 he was elected president of Bemsee and became president for life in 1999. He never lost his love of speed, memorably flying to New York with his daughter aboard Concorde when he was in his nineties and insisting they take a helicopter ride over the Statue of Liberty. He continued to drive a car until he was ninety-eight and attended Bemsee race meetings almost to the very last. He was held in the highest regard by followers of the sport and by riders, young and old, who were captivated by his tales of Brooklands' vibrant heyday. When he died, peacefully with his family around him, having completed his second 'ton', the remarks made by his old headmaster some eight-five years earlier were as apt as they had ever been: 'he leaves a happy memory of himself behind'.

Colonel John Murray 'Ivan' Cobbold (1897–1944)
Soldier, Brewer, Sportsman and Founder of Ipswich Town FC

Photograph of Captain Cobbold with his elder son and daughter.
(F. H. Meads for the front of *Country Life*, 14 September 1935.)

Despite the extraordinary breadth of the family's interests through the generations, the name 'Cobbold' is still most likely to conjure associations with one of two occupations – brewing or football. No single member of the family could be considered synonymous with both of these interests simultaneously more than John Murray Cobbold, eighth generation brewer and the man responsible for bringing professional football to the town of his birth. The family's connection with Ipswich football dates back almost to the beginning of the sport itself, but it was 'Captain Ivan', as he was affectionately known, who moulded the club familiar to fans of the modern game. John Murray Cobbold, though, was far more than just 'Mr Ipswich Town': in his hands the family's brewing business continued to thrive; he was an outstanding field sportsman, particularly with shotgun in hand, and he served his country admirably in both world wars, making the ultimate sacrifice.

The nickname 'Ivan' was given to John as an infant, supposedly because of his 'terrible' behaviour, and it stuck for the remainder of his life. He had a colourful childhood with colourful parents, being the only son of the dashing John Dupuis Cobbold and his restless wife, Lady Evelyn Cobbold, the first western woman to complete the Hajj to Makkah (Mecca). Ivan was the couple's second child and first son. He was born in the year of Queen Victoria's Golden Jubilee and, to commemorate both events, his father bought ten acres of land near Ipswich Racecourse on Nacton Heath and presented it to the town for use as a public recreation ground. Ivan, in the tradition of his branch of the family, went to Eton, where, like his father, he excelled at rackets. He was also a fine cricketer, playing for the first eleven in his final year, 1915. From Eton, he might have expected to follow his father to Trinity College, Cambridge but the Great War blocked this path. Instead, he was commissioned into the Scots Guards and went off to France, aged just eighteen. He returned, two years later, with a minor injury and the rank of captain.

Upon his recovery, Ivan joined the family brewing business and settled into a comfortable life in which his love of sport played a large part. In 1914, his father had paid £140,000 for estates around Rannoch in the central Scottish Highlands which comprised over forty thousand acres and boasted some of the best fishing, stalking and grouse shooting to be had anywhere in the Britain Isles. Ivan was a frequent visitor to Rannoch and soon established a reputation as one of the country's leading shots, largely due, it was considered, 'to his exceptionally quick footwork'. On one occasion, in 1919, he killed two woodcock with one shot, an extremely rare feat. In addition to spending time on the family's estates, Ivan would also test his aim at Millden, Lord Dalhousie's estate in Angus. There, the Knocks beat was, according to *Country Life*, 'productive of the most difficult grouse to be met on any single day's driving'. Ivan took the estate for nearly twenty consecutive summers and invited friends up to shoot with him.

For generations, Cobbolds had married well, but few married as well as Ivan. On 30 April 1919, he wed Lady Blanche Cavendish (1898–1987), daughter of Victor Cavendish, 9th Duke of Devonshire, one of the wealthiest men in Britain from one of its best-known families. Though Ivan was a commoner, the duke approved of the union, having heard good things about his prospective son-in-law. Unusually, the two did not meet until some time *after* the wedding: since 1916 the duke had been governor-general of Canada and his duties, particularly onerous in the aftermath of the war, precluded him from travelling home for the ceremony, which was conducted at the Guards' Chapel, Wellington Barracks in London. It was one of the society weddings of the year. Among the gifts the couple received were a diamond and pink enamel brooch from the king and queen and a coffee set from their daughter, Princess Mary.

The post-war housing shortage affected rich and poor alike and for the first four years of their marriage Ivan and Blanche lived in 'furnished houses'. Two daughters, Pamela (1920–94) and Jean (1921–2001), arrived during this period before Ivan put an end to the family's itinerant lifestyle with the purchase of Glemham Hall from the 8th Earl of Guilford. This grand new home, set in three hundred acres of parkland near Woodbridge, Suffolk, was perfectly situated for Ivan's work at the Cliff Brewery, Ipswich and plenty big enough for a growing family: the couple's two sons, John (1927–83) and Patrick (1934–94) were born there. In June 1929, Ivan took over the reins of the brewing business after his father died suddenly, shortly after returning from a trip to India.

The Cobbolds had had a close connection to Ipswich Town from its very foundation as an amateur side in 1878, when Thomas Clement Cobbold, MP for Ipswich, was elected the club's first president. His brother, Nathanael Fromanteel Cobbold, became vice president in 1885 but served only a year before his untimely death; he was replaced by John Dupuis

Cobbold, Ivan's father. In 1905, the club's ground, Portman Road, came under the control of a new company, The Ipswich Cricket, Football and Athletic Ground Co. Ltd. John Dupuis' youngest brother, Philip Wyndham Cobbold (1875–1945) was appointed vice chairman of this company. Remarkably, the top man at Ipswich Town was either a Cobbold or someone married to a Cobbold from the day it was founded right up until 1991.

Ivan became president of 'Town' in 1935 following the death of Herbert Jervis-White-Jervis, the son of Lucy Cobbold (1828–1916), the eldest sister of Thomas Clement and Nathanael Fromanteel. By this time, professional football was thriving in England yet Ipswich Town remained an amateur club. All that was about to change. Ivan counted Sir Samuel Hill-Wood, chairman of Arsenal, among his shooting friends and, one day, the pair went to Highbury together. So impressed was Ivan with the quality of the football on show and the fervour of the support that he resolved to turn his own club professional.

Among Ipswich's supporters, calls for a professional club reached a crescendo in 1936, a year after Ivan became president. During that year many letters were sent to the local press demanding the move to professionalism, calls that had hitherto been rejected by the committee of the amateur club. One particular correspondent, Leonard P. Thompson, harnessed the public mood and, in March 1936, a new professional club, Ipswich United FC, was formed. Shortly afterwards, 1,500 people packed a public hall to hear Thompson's father, a prominent local businessman, appeal to the amateur club, Town, to join the new venture. A week later, after much deliberation, the committee of Town declined the offer to amalgamate with United. Ivan, Town's president, was absent from all these discussions. He had been in Canada and, in all likelihood had not the faintest inkling of these developments. On 24 April, shortly after his return, he made clear his feelings on the subject in a letter to the local press:

> *On my return from Canada today I am delighted to hear that the question of professional football has at last come to a head.*
>
> *For many years I have been convinced that a town the size and importance of Ipswich must have professional football and it is distressing for supporters to have to go to London or Norwich to see a match.*
>
> *Being interested in the game in general and particularly in this endeavour to introduce better football at Ipswich, I shall certainly be pleased to give the scheme my utmost support.*
>
> *Yours faithfully,*
> *J. M. Cobbold, Glemham Hall*

This letter proved decisive. The two sides reconvened on Friday 1 May and issued a statement later that day confirming the coming together of Town and United to form a new professional club, Ipswich Town FC Ltd., which would compete in the Southern League. Ivan became the new club's president and was joined on the board by Robert Nevill Cobbold (1904–44), son of Philip Wyndham Cobbold. The club's home would continue to be Portman Road, but a new manager was appointed: Nick O'Brien, a former Northern Ireland international. On the morning of Saturday 29 August 1936, all those connected with the new venture assembled at the Great White Horse Hotel in the town where Stanley Rous, secretary of the Football Association, proposed a toast to 'Football' to which Ivan responded. That afternoon, John Luckie, captain, led Ipswich's first professional eleven out onto the pitch in front of 14,211 spectators. The home team, in its new strip of blue shirts, white sleeves and shorts, strolled to a 4–1 victory against Tunbridge Wells Rangers. John Eastwood and Tony Moyse, authors of the official history of the club, maintain that having resisted professionalism for so long, 'a reservoir of energy' was released when the dam of amateurism eventually cracked. The club's debut season as a professional side certainly supports this view: Town cruised to the Southern League title, beating their closest rivals, Norwich City Reserves, by five clear points.

The next step was to get the club playing in the Football League. In those days, promotion was not automatic and those clubs wishing to move up from either the Southern or Northern Leagues had to receive the support of those already in the Football League. Two places were up for grabs in the Third Division South, to be contested between Town and the two teams who finished bottom of that division (who were required to seek re-election). Exeter City received forty votes, Aldershot thirty-four and Town just twenty-four. Promotion would have to wait.

O'Brien left after that first season for personal rather than professional reasons: he had sadly lost his wife during the season. The appointment of a replacement demonstrated to English football just how serious Ivan was about making Town a force to be reckoned with: the new manager, A. Scott Duncan had been lured to Portman Road from no lesser a club than Manchester United. Having arrived in Suffolk with Duncan, Ivan reportedly phoned Old Trafford and informed United, 'We have your manager and we're going to keep him – but there will be two cases of vintage port arriving in due course.' Duncan remained in charge of the team for seventeen seasons. At the end of his first, Ivan led a delegation to London, which persuaded the Football League that Ipswich Town was worthy of its place in the Third Division South. In its first season in that division (1938–39), the last to be played before the game was interrupted by war, Town finished a respectable seventh.

The close season for football corresponded with the open season for grouse. Come the Glorious Twelfth, Ivan would invariably head for Scotland where he would entertain guests at Millden. As a shot he had few equals and he was considered to be among the best half dozen in the country. He was in great demand for shooting parties and regularly joined those of King George VI at Sandringham. Neville Chamberlain was also a regular shooting companion. In early September 1938, as the crisis surrounding the German occupation of the Sudetenland deepened, Chamberlain, was staying with the king at Balmoral. The situation was considered so serious that the king made arrangements for Chamberlain to be flown back to London at a moment's notice in an aircraft of the royal flight should this be deemed necessary. Chamberlain declined the offer on the grounds that he had never before flown and had no wish to start now. Resisting all calls for him to expedite his return to London, Chamberlain lingered in Scotland. From Balmoral he went, not directly to Westminster, but the short distance to Millden where he shot with Ivan. The *London Evening Standard* reported this and remarked of Ivan that he 'enjoys sufficient leisure from city activities to enable him to fire as many as 40,000 cartridges in a season, at grouse in Scotland, and at partridges and pheasants at his estate in East Anglia'.

Arguably, Britain and Europe might have been better served had Chamberlain stayed at Millden a little longer, rather than returning to London and boarding the plane for Munich, his first flight, where he appeased Hitler's policy of *Lebensraum*. 'Peace in our time' proved illusory and exactly a year after Chamberlain and Ivan had taken aim at grouse at Millden, Britain and Germany were at war. Ivan, aged forty-two, immediately rejoined the Scots Guards with the rank of lieutenant-colonel. He saw no fighting but was employed in a number of key positions in London. He was appointed aide-de-camp to Lieutenant General Sir Bertram Sergison-Brook, general officer commanding (GOC), London District, a post he held until 1942. Thereafter he briefly joined the staff of the APM (assistant provost marshal) before becoming a liaison officer with the United States forces.

With football suspended and with no gate receipts, Ipswich Town, like many clubs, soon ran up a sizeable debt. Ivan presided over a board meeting in 1943 at which the liquidation of the club was considered. Desperate to avoid this, he persuaded other directors to chip in to meet the club's debt which stood at £14,195. Most chipped in with £250 or £500: Ivan's contribution was £11,195, nearly eighty per cent of the total owed. Closing the meeting, Ivan remarked that there was now nothing to prevent the club from resuming play as soon as the war was over and assured the board 'that if I am spared I shall endeavour to get the club started again and producing reasonably good football as soon as possible'.

These proved to be poignant words. On Sunday 18 June 1944, Ivan was attending a church service at the Guards' Chapel in Birdcage Walk where, twenty-five years earlier, he had married Blanche. The chapel was packed and shortly after 11 a.m. some in the congregation heard a faint buzzing in the distance. The buzz became louder and louder until it reached a roar overhead, drowning out the hymn singing. Then, the engine of the VI rocket cut out and it fell directly onto the roof of the chapel, detonating on impact. The entire roof fell onto the worshippers below. Ivan was one of 121 military personnel and civilians who lost their lives; a further 141 were injured, many seriously. The only person to escape unscathed was the Bishop of Maidstone who was conducting the service: a portico over the altar protected him from the falling debris.

This tragedy for both the family and the football club came within a month of the death of the other Cobbold on the Ipswich Town board. On 26 May, Major Robert Nevill Cobbold was killed in action at Monte Piccolo in Italy while serving with the Welsh Guards. At Portman Road, Philip Wyndham Cobbold stepped into the breach despite being in poor health, overseeing the club's affairs until the end of the war. Play resumed in 1945 and, after Philip Wyndham's death, that Christmas, his son, Alistair Philip Cobbold (1907–71), Major Robert's brother, stepped in to help out. The following year Cobbold & Co. Ltd stepped in to settle further debts of £6,000, which had accumulated since Ivan had bailed the club out in 1943. In November 1948, Ivan's son, John, joined the board, becoming, at just twenty-one, the youngest football club director in the country. Alistair became chairman of the club a year later and remained on the board until his death in 1971, though he gave way to John, who became chairman at the end of the 1956/57 season. Around the club, Ivan had always been known as 'Captain Ivan' even after he had attained a higher rank; his son would always be known as 'Mr John'.

John was one of the most colourful chairmen the game has ever known. His charismatic style of leadership is perhaps best illustrated by the oft quoted, 'There is no crisis at Ipswich until the white wine runs out in the boardroom'. In 1964, John and Alistair were joined on the board of the club by Patrick, John's younger brother. ('Mr') Patrick would become chairman in 1976 as John stepped down to battle cancer. He held the position until 1991. At about the same time as Patrick joined the board, his mother, Ivan's widow, Lady Blanche, became honorary president.

Reduced to rubble. The Guards Chapel where Col. Cobbold died during morning service on Sunday 18 June 1944.
(Courtesy of The Reverend Kevin Bell, Chaplain to the Household Division.)

Ivan had recognised the importance of attracting the best managers to the club and the Cobbolds who followed him also chose their managers well: Sir Alf Ramsey and Sir Bobby Robson, the England national side's most successful managers, both made their names at the club. Ramsey (1955–62) led Town to its only First Division title in 1962 in its very first season in the top flight. Robson (1969–82) blended home-grown talent and European flair to produce a team with an attractive passing game and which won the FA Cup in 1978 and the UEFA Cup three years later. Flair on the pitch matched the spirit in which the club was run. When 'Mr John' eventually succumbed to illness in 1983, Robson paid the following tribute:

> *When we won John Cobbold had a bottle of champagne and when we lost he had two bottles of champagne. That was his civilised way of looking at defeat. He was a remarkable guy, an outstanding fellow.*

Few families can boast an association with a football club as strong as that of the Cobbolds to Ipswich Town. The family's recent history is entwined with the history of 'Town', the successes of which are, in no small measure, attributable to the vision, determination and faith of those who have guided it since its formation as an amateur club in 1878. Today, two of Portman Road's stands are named after the club's great managers, Ramsey and Robson; a third is named the Cobbold Stand. Though his sons oversaw the remarkable achievements of a small provincial club fighting above its weight, it was undoubtedly Ivan who set the ball rolling for these successes and who instilled the gentlemanly principles by which the professional club was run by those who succeeded him.

8 MILITARY SERVICE

On a cold Sunday morning in November 2007, nine members of the Cobbold family spanning three generations mustered outside the old War Office building in London's Whitehall. From there, having observed two minutes' silence with the thousands of others gathered to remember, they marched to the Cenotaph with a wreath of poppies. At the centre of the wreath was a card bearing the family crest, *Rebus Angustis Fortis*, 'Strength in Adversity'. Attached to the wreath was a remembrance card which simply said '48 Cobbolds'; tucked behind this card was a list of the names of the family members killed in the world wars. The list makes poignant reading. That forty-eight members of the same family lost their lives during the two world wars is extraordinary enough, but for the Cobbold family this is only part of the story. The list of forty-eight records only those with the surname, Cobbold: scores of the family's kinsmen also lost their lives for their country.

No fewer than thirty-five of the '48' were killed during the First World War, many of them young and of low rank: the youngest, Private Reginald Louis Cobbold of the Suffolk Regiment, was just seventeen when he was cut down. Two of the subjects considered here served as officers during the 1914–18 war. General Herbert Plumer had few superiors in the British Army and was among a minority of such elevated rank who emerged from the Great War with their reputations untarnished. In particular, he seems to have had a genuine regard for the thousands of men under his command. Bernard Freyberg, whose son would marry the granddaughter of a Cobbold, was a dashing young officer who, for a while, was subordinate to Plumer. Freyberg was one of that war's great heroes, highly decorated for acts of outstanding bravery and wounded so many times that his mere survival gave him an air of immortality. In the Second World War, he led his New Zealand troops from the front throughout North Africa and the Mediterranean and, improbably, survived again before going on to a distinguished career in public service both in New Zealand and in Britain. Few men could claim to have been present at so many momentous battles.

If Plumer and Freyberg were conventional soldiers, assiduously working their way through the ranks, Lord Simon Lovat was precisely the opposite, though certainly no less brave. This maverick from the Scottish Highlands, distantly related to the Cobbolds through the Keswick family into which Sir Harry Parkes' daughter married, saw just a few days of action in the Second World War, yet his seemingly cavalier attitude, extraordinary disregard for his own safety and inspirational leadership has assured his standing as one of the British Army's most irrepressible and charismatic characters. Among all the graphic stories surrounding the D-Day landings, Lovat's is one of the most colourful.

Four of the '48' were civilians who were simply in the wrong place at the wrong time. One was a thirty-nine year old woman, Barbara Elizabeth Cobbold, victim of a German air raid on London in December 1940. Another was Peter Cobbold, a veteran of the First World War who had gone on to do reasonably well for himself working for a British company in Sarawak on the tropical island of Borneo. The colonial idyll of his life was shattered when the Japanese invaded the island in December 1941. The harrowing story of Peter and those who fled the Japanese invasion with him is one of ordinary people in a most desperate situation. Defenceless and posing no threat, they were hunted down and massacred without pity, victims of one of the war's most barbaric atrocities.

Field Marshal Herbert Charles Onslow Plumer, GCB GCMG GCVO (1857–1932)
'The Soldier's General'

Field Marshal the Viscount Plumer, from the painting by René de l'Hôpital in the possession of the Viscountess Plumer, from *Plumer of Messines* by General Sir Charles Harington GCB GBE 1935.
(Family member's private collection.)

The generals who commanded British troops in the First World War have not been sympathetically treated by history, often with good reason. The image often conjured is of buffoons, sipping claret at a safe distance from enemy lines while dispassionately ordering legions of innocent young men 'over the top' to be cut down by enemy fire. This cliché is certainly not without foundation: more than one million men of the British Empire were killed during the Great War, many during poorly planned offensives ordered by tactically incompetent commanders. Herbert Plumer bore the appearance of the archetypal bumbling general so maligned by subsequent generations: by the end of the war he was the wrong side of sixty; he was plump with a shock of white hair and sported a bristly walrus moustache of the same colour. He bore a striking resemblance to Colonel Blimp, the pompous, irascible cartoon character created by David Low for the *London Evening Standard* in the 1930s and he may well have provided the inspiration for this caricature. However, despite his appearance and his association with a command structure long identified with ineptitude, Herbert Plumer was one general who emerged from the horrors of the Great War with his reputation largely intact and one who still enjoyed the respect of those who had served under him: the most recent biography of him, written by Geoffrey Powell in 1990, bears the subtitle 'The Soldier's General'.

Herbert Plumer was raised at Malpas Lodge, Torquay, the second of four children of Hall Plumer (1827–88) and Louisa Turnley (1830–1903). The family's connection with the Cobbolds was secured in the year of his mother's death when Herbert's cousin, Lillian Hope Parkes (1872–1946) married the Reverend Rowland Francis Cobbold (1857–1945). In September 1876, shortly after leaving Eton, Herbert was commissioned sub lieutenant in the 65th Foot, which, in 1881, amalgamated with the 84th Foot to become the 1st and 2nd Battalions, the York and Lancaster Regiment. He arrived in India with his regiment six months later and was stationed first at Lucknow, then at Dinapore and finally at Morar near Gwalior. He saw no action in India, but became popular with his men who came mostly from Yorkshire. This respect endured and was reciprocated. Herbert was a skilled horseman and India afforded him the opportunity to display his ability: he earned a reputation as a fearless 'race-rider' and he also played polo for his regiment.

In 1882, just after he had been promoted captain, Herbert's battalion was posted to Aden, remaining there until 1884. Remarkably, during this two-year tour, not one incident of crime was recorded among the battalion's number of five hundred or so men, an achievement which Geoffrey Powell considers as 'possibly a unique feat in that or any other era'. As Herbert and his men were about to set sail for England aboard HMS *Seraphis*, the colony's governor praised the battalion's conduct and this, no doubt, reflected well on its young adjutant. Herbert took two periods of furlough while in Aden, returning home on both occasions. On the second of these he became engaged to his second cousin, Annie Constance Goss (1858–1941), with whom he had been corresponding ever since he left for India. The couple were married in London on 22 July 1884, though Herbert's journey home was dramatically interrupted.

Two days into the voyage from Aden, the *Seraphis* received a signal from a warship in the Red Sea instructing it to make for the Sudanese port of Trinikat. Herbert and his men were about to see action for the first time. At this time, large tracts of Sudan had been wrested from Egyptian control by the fanatical Muslim leader, the Mahdi, Muhammed Ahmad. The British, with a garrison in Egypt, leant support to the Khedive's operations against the Mahdi. Early in 1884, an Egyptian force under the command of General Valentine Baker was annihilated at El Teb by Mahdist troops, though Baker himself escaped. Having reached Sudan, Herbert and his men joined a force led by General Sir Gerald Graham that would exact retribution. At El Teb on 29 February and at Tamai a fortnight later, Graham routed the Mahdists. Herbert saw action at both battles, was mentioned in despatches and was awarded the Mejidiye, fourth class (an honour bestowed by the Ottoman sultan for bravery) as well as the Khedive's star.

Back in England, Herbert settled comfortably into life as a married man. He and Annie had a daughter, Eleanor, in 1885 and shortly afterwards Herbert learned that he had passed the entrance examination for the Staff College at Camberley, where future commanders were groomed. There, Herbert enjoyed the camaraderie and the games, particularly cricket and drag hunting. He enjoyed the latter perhaps a little too much: he drag hunted for four successive days immediately prior to his first-year examinations and only just scraped through them. He eventually passed out, after two years, a rather undistinguished nineteenth of twenty-six officers in his year. A second daughter, Sybil, had arrived in the meantime and within three further years two more children came along, Marjorie and Thomas.

Regimental duty followed until, in May 1890, he was appointed assistant adjutant-general to the lieutenant governor of Jersey, a position he held for three years. Life at St Helier was comfortable and towards the end of his stay he was offered the non-military position of government secretary, a tempting and lucrative offer. After careful consideration, Herbert declined the offer, reluctant to abandon his chosen profession and fully expecting a further staff appointment. Despite being strongly recommended for such a post, these hopes were dashed and it was with a heavy heart that, in November 1893, having recently been promoted major, he went off to join the 2nd battalion of his regiment (not his beloved 65th Foot) in Natal. Not long after his arrival, he and his battalion were transferred to Wynberg in Cape Colony where Herbert rented a pleasant house from Cecil Rhodes' secretary. Annie joined him there in August 1894, though the couple's children remained in England.

In January 1896, following an extended period a leave when he again failed to secure a coveted staff position, Herbert's big chance came when General W. H. Goodenough, for whom he was acting military secretary, sent him on a mission to limit the damage from the calamitous Jameson Raid, an unedifying scheme to incite an uprising against Paul Kruger's Transvaal government. The raid – conceived by Leander Starr Jameson of the British South Africa Company with the backing of its chairman, Rhodes – failed utterly, and Herbert's task was to head for Bulawayo, capital of Matabeleland (now part of Zimbabwe), to disarm the company's officers lest they were considering further action. Herbert carried out his orders successfully, but no sooner had he returned to Cape Town than he was ordered to return to Bulawayo to quell an uprising of the Ndebele (Matabele), which had erupted almost immediately after he had left. Jameson's withdrawal of some three hundred white policemen from Matabeleland prompted the revolt, incited by the Ndebele's spiritual leader who blamed white settlers for the drought and pestilence which blighted the country.

En route to Bulawayo, Herbert raised a force of 750 mounted riflemen and two hundred Zulu and Xhosa infantry. The force arrived at Bulawayo on 24 March 1896 and a fierce and brutal war ensued. Both sides employed guerrilla tactics until, in August, the Ndebele were eventually worn down. The terms of their surrender were notoriously onerous and led to the formation of Rhodesia. In modern Zimbabwe, the Second Matabele War has since become known as the First War of Independence. From British perspectives, the war is perhaps best remembered for the early activities of Robert Baden-Powell. While scouting the Mtobo Hills under Herbert's command, Baden-Powell was taught woodcraft by the American, Frederick Russell Burnham, the British Army's chief of scouts. It was these adventures which inspired Baden-Powell to form the scouting movement.

At the end of 1896, his reputation enhanced, Herbert returned to England with the rank of brevet lieutenant colonel and was appointed a deputy assistant adjutant general at Aldershot by Sir Redvers Buller. There he remained until the summer of 1899 when, with war in South Africa again imminent, he was sent back to Bulawayo in order to raise a force of irregular troops. Now *under* the command of Baden-Powell, who had become a brevet colonel, Herbert was to repel any attempt by the enemy to cross the Limpopo into Rhodesian territory and to mount diversionary raids into Transvaal. When Baden-Powell became cut off at Mafeking, Herbert and his men became involved in operations to break the siege, and Herbert sustained an injury during a skirmish at Vryburg, being shot in the wrist. Geoffrey Powell relates that he then 'put someone else up on his horse and made his way on foot in the blinding heat with the men who had had their horses shot under them'. Such bravery no doubt inspired those under his command. Later Herbert's battalion joined up with the main column, which eventually brought about Mafeking's relief. Thereafter, Herbert commanded Australian and New Zealand units around Pretoria. In early 1901, he doggedly pursued the talented Boer commander, Christian de Wet, all over Orange Free State, and he succeeded in capturing thirty of de Wet's men and forty wagons of his supplies, though the wily Boer evaded him. Herbert returned home from South Africa with a reputation as a brave, reliable, though perhaps not brilliant, commander.

After Britain's Pyrrhic victory, Herbert's star continued to rise and then suddenly fell. He was promoted major general and in 1904 landed the plum job of quartermaster general on the new army council. However, he fell out of favour when the Liberals came to power the following year and was dismissed by R. B. Haldane, the new secretary of state for war. This impressed upon him the political nature of senior military command and he spent the next years diligently rebuilding his career. By the time the First World War broke out, he was leading northern command at York with the rank of lieutenant general.

In the early weeks of the war, Field Marshal Sir John French, commanding the British Expeditionary Force (BEF), wanted Herbert to succeed Sir James Grierson, who had recently died of a heart attack, as commander of his II Corps (Sir Douglas Haig commanded I Corps). French was overruled by Secretary of State for War, Lord Kitchener, and General Sir Horace Smith-Dorrien who had served under Kitchener at Omdurman in 1898 was appointed instead. When Herbert finally reached the western front at Ypres early in 1915, he came under Smith-Dorrien's command, leading V Corps, a newly established division of the 2nd Army, comprising the 27th and 28th Divisions composed of regular army battalions from all four corners of the empire, including Herbert's own 1st York and Lancasters. Conditions on the Ypres Salient, an eastward bulge in the front line, were unspeakable: Herbert's men moved into trenches dug by the French which were poorly constructed, lacked drainage and provided inadequate cover. The stench of death hung over the place, which was littered with bodies from earlier battles. Herbert's concern for the welfare of his men was conveyed in letters to his wife in which he expressed his wish to do everything in his power to improve their lot: among the measures introduced to this end were the installation of baths behind the lines, facilities to wash and press clothes (thereby killing the lice infesting them) and the introduction of a rum ration.

In April 1915, the Germans launched an assault on the northern curve of the Ypres Salient, held by French troops. The ensuing battle is now known as the Second Battle of Ypres. For the first time, chlorine gas wafted across no man's land and its effects punched a four-mile hole in Allied defences. The Germans, not expecting gas to be quite so effective, failed to capitalise and the hole was plugged by Canadian troops under Herbert's command, who protected themselves from the gas by covering their mouths and noses with urine-soaked cloth. In response to the German assault, a series of ill-judged counter-offensives, ordered by Field Marshal French, weakened the Allies' hold on the Salient and cost countless lives. French laid the blame for the fiasco squarely on the shoulders of Smith-Dorrien who had begun to advocate a tactical retreat. On 27 April, French instructed Smith-Dorrien to cede command to Herbert. Herbert then initiated a rearguard action along the lines proposed by his erstwhile superior, conceding ground at the tip of the Salient and consolidating the defensive line further west. The new line held and a stalemate ensued.

The 2nd Army enjoyed relative peace for the next two years, occasionally engaging in diversionary operations and training. ANZAC soldiers, who had fought under Herbert at Ypres before witnessing the horrors of the Somme in 1916, were known to sing a ditty 'Take me back to Daddy Plumer's Army' within earshot of their senior officers. This was probably prompted by the relative ease of the 2nd Army's duties rather than by any sentimental attachment to its commander, though Herbert was undoubtedly popular among the men under his command, who gave him the nickname 'Old Plum and Apple' on account of the jam he included in their rations. Herbert himself was considered as a replacement for French in late 1915 following the latter's resignation, but lost out to Haig. Relations between Herbert and Haig were cordial though a little strained, due (according to Powell) to the fact that, early in Haig's career, Herbert had given him a low mark in a Staff College examination.

From June 1916, Herbert was ably assisted by the brilliant Major General Charles Harington, who became his chief of staff. The two worked well together and some historians consider Harington the brains of the formidable partnership. In assessing their professional relationship, Brigadier General John Charteris, Haig's senior intelligence officer, concluded: 'nobody knows where Plumer ends and Harington begins'. In June 1917, the pair masterminded a devastating attack at Messines, on the Ypres front. Tunnellers, who had worked on the London Underground, and miners had long been employed to dig under enemy positions, and Herbert employed them to devastating effect. Chambers under enemy positions at Messines were packed with 450 tons of explosives and detonated on 7 June. At the time, the explosion was the loudest manmade noise ever made and its shockwaves were felt as far away as London. In its wake, the Allies drove through the German line, advancing nearly two miles. This was the prelude to Third Ypres, or Passchendaele; after a slow start to the battle proper, Haig put Herbert in charge of the offensive at the end of July. In September and October, further significant breaches of German defences were made. However, poor weather inhibited a decisive breakthrough, which

Field Marshal Plumer delivers his speech, without a single note, to dedicate the Menin Gate, Ypres on Sunday 24 July 1927, containing the legendary words 'He is not missing. He is here!' (Courtesy of CWGC, Maidenhead.)

might have caused the enemy to capitulate altogether. Third Ypres ended on 10 November; casualties on each side numbered hundreds of thousands.

Three days before the guns fell temporarily silent at Ypres, Herbert and Harington had left to command British troops engaged on the Italian front. They returned to Ypres in March 1918 and Herbert confirmed his reputation as an able defensive tactician during the German 'Georgette' offensive in April, when Haig issued his oft quoted 'backs to the wall' order. All the gains made at Ypres the previous year were lost. Thereafter, the 2nd Army played only a peripheral role in the Allies' final decisive offensive.

After the war, Parliament awarded Herbert a grant of £30,000 as thanks for his contribution to victory. Immediately, he was put in charge in the British occupation at Cologne, where he stayed until April 1919. He then went to Malta as governor. He returned to England in 1924, staying a year, before he accepted the challenging role of high commissioner for Palestine. He was, by now, in his late sixties and in increasingly fragile health. He eventually retired to his Kensington home in 1928 and indulged his love of cricket, becoming president of the MCC. He was created Viscount Plumer of Messines in June 1929 for 'his long and distinguished public services'. When he died at home on 16 July 1932, tributes were led by King George V, who remarked that,

> *My people throughout the Empire, will, with me, mourn the loss of one whom history will ever gratefully remember not only as a distinguished commander in war, but as a great administrator.*

Herbert Plumer was given a state funeral and laid to rest in Westminster Abbey. He destroyed his papers before he died and this has impeded an objective analysis of his career. A sycophantic biography by Harington portrays Herbert as a brilliant commander and loyal friend. However, his abilities as a general are not indisputable and some historians have suggested that his successes owed much to his knack of surrounding himself with able deputies, such as Harington. This seems a little harsh, for is not one of the marks of a talented commander his ability to make the best use of such men? What seems irrefutable is the esteem in which he was held by those who served under him. He certainly cared about his men, from the small battalions he led during his early career to the fifty thousand or so he commanded in the mud of Flanders. This alone sets him apart from many of his contemporaries.

Bernard Cyril (Tiny) Freyberg, VC GCMG KCB KBE DSO, 1st Baron Freyberg (1889–1963)

Decorated Soldier and Governor General of New Zealand

The military career of Bernard Freyberg spanned both world wars and he was at the heart of some of the most fiercely fought battles in each: in the First he was at Gallipoli, on the Somme and at Passchendaele; in the Second, in Greece, on Crete, in North Africa and at Monte Cassino. Few men could have seen as much action as he; certainly, very few ended their careers more highly decorated. As a commander, he stood shoulder to shoulder with his men on the front line and was wounded on so many occasions that barely any part of his body was unscarred. He fought for both Britain and for New Zealand, the latter being the country he called home and where, in later life, he held the highest office.

Bernard's nickname, 'Tiny', was given to him because he was the youngest of five boys. It stuck, even though he grew up to be six foot one and a half. He was born in Surrey but his family moved to New Zealand when he was just two. The Freybergs settled on the slopes of Mount Victoria overlooking Wellington Harbour, a perfect spot to raise boys for an outdoor life. Bernard developed a particular

Bernard Freyberg. An end-of-war photograph taken in April 1945 by George Kaye on the eve of the final offensive in Italy.
(Family member's private collection; courtesy of Hodder & Stoughton.)

talent for swimming and would often swim in the harbour and across it to Eastbourne, more than six miles away. At Wellington College he did not excel academically but beat all-comers in the water, a contemporary describing him as 'seal-like'. In 1906, he became swimming champion of New Zealand and came third in the 250-yard race in the Australasian championships in Sydney.

On leaving school in 1904, Bernard apprenticed as a dentist, though he was never fully enthusiastic about the career. During the same period he joined the field artillery volunteers in Wellington and, in 1911, he was commissioned second lieutenant in the territorial 6th Hauraki regiment. Yearnings for adventure beyond the dental surgery were given a boost by the heroic and ultimately tragic efforts of Robert Falcon Scott and his team to reach the South Pole. Scott used New Zealand as a base and Bernard took an avid interest in every facet of the expedition, dearly wishing he could have been part of it.

In 1913, the opportunity for adventure came. Practising dentistry in Levin, up the coast from Wellington, Bernard was called to act as a special constable during a bitter strike by the town's dockworkers. He subsequently answered the government's call for volunteers to work the boats to Sydney in place of the strikers, soon joining the crew of the *Maunganui* as a stoker. It seems Bernard had few qualms about crossing the picket line: when one of the ship's stewards called him a 'bloody scab', Bernard punched him, sending him reeling 'from one end of the saloon to another'. The journey fuelled his ambition to see more of the world and, in March 1914, with the encouragement of an old swimming friend who had settled in America, Bernard resigned from the Levin surgery and boarded the RMS *Tahiti* for San Francisco.

Little is recorded of Bernard's time in America, but it seems that he was hired as an armed guard to the New Zealand National Film Unit, which was reporting on the Mexican Civil War. Remarkably, it appears that he then offered his services as a mercenary to the revolutionary General Francisco 'Pancho' Villa and that he saw action, albeit briefly. For as soon as he heard of the outbreak of war in Europe, he deserted, with a price on his head, and hitchhiked three hundred miles back to San Francisco, from where he sailed to Britain.

In London by late August 1914, Bernard made straight for the War Office where he met Major G. S. Richardson, New Zealand's liaison officer. He also met Winston Churchill, first lord of the admiralty, who had been instrumental in the recent establishment of the Royal Naval Division (RND), and this meeting may have helped Bernard secure a commission as a second lieutenant in the Royal Naval Volunteer Reserve. He was posted to the Hood Battalion of the 2nd Royal Navy Brigade, where he was almost immediately put in command of 'A' Company, which comprised two hundred men. Among his junior officers were Arthur 'Oc' Asquith, the prime minister's son, the composer Patrick Shaw-Stewart, the scholars Rupert Brooke and Denis Browne, and Johnny Dodge, Churchill's cousin and the great escaper of World War II who became the inspiration for Steve McQueen's character in the epic film. The group became known as the 'Argonauts', often being described as representing the cream of British manhood.

Within six weeks Bernard had been landed at Dunkirk, his brigade having been sent to assist Belgian troops lift the German siege of Antwerp. Nothing could be done to save the city and the decision was made to withdraw. While reconnoitring an escape route, Bernard accidentally put his hand on a defensive electrified fence. It was some time before the current could be switched off and Bernard's hand was severely burned, leaving scars which would stay with him for the rest of his life. During the withdrawal, part of the brigade was cut off in the

Netherlands and, of the fifteen hundred Royal Naval Division men who landed at Dunkirk, more than nine hundred were taken prisoner. Despite being in great pain, Bernard, led 'A' Company away from the enemy to Ostend and evacuation.

In February 1915, the RND sailed for Gallipoli. On the way, Brooke died from sepsis, and Bernard played a prominent part in arrangements for his funeral on the Greek island of Skyros. The Gallipoli campaign itself was an unmitigated disaster, though for Bernard one formidable heroic act earned him a reputation as an outstanding soldier. The RND was tasked with deceiving the enemy into thinking that a landing was imminent at Bulair in the Gulf of Saros. The scheme hinged on the lighting of flares on the beach as guides to landing craft which, of course, would never follow. The Turks, it was hoped, would divert troops to Bulair away from the actual landing beaches. Rather than sending the flares ashore by boat, which he considered risky, Bernard argued that swimmers should be used. Both he and Asquith volunteered, but his commanding officer, Colonel Quilter, baulked at sending the prime minister's son on such a dangerous mission; Bernard, however, an unknown New Zealander, was altogether more expendable.

Just after midnight on 26 April, smothered in thick grease, Bernard slipped into the icy sea from a dinghy two miles from shore. He was towing a heavy waterproof bag containing three oil flares, five calcium lights, a signalling light, a knife and a revolver. An hour and a quarter later he waded ashore and lit his first flare. He then took to the water again and swam eastwards for a further three hundred yards to light a second flare further along the coast. He saw no sign of the enemy and discovered that what had looked like trenches from the sea were, in fact, just mounds of earth or dummy trenches. Having lit his last flare, he swam back out to sea, suffering with severe cramp, where he was picked up in the nick of time by his own cutter just after 3 a.m. The feint worked: Turkish troops *were* diverted to Bulair, though this failed to prevent heavy Allied losses at the main landing sites at Cape Helles and Ari Burnu (ANZAC Cove). For his remarkable feat of endurance, Bernard received a DSO.

In early May, Bernard joined the failed assault on Achi Baba. At Krithia, an intermediate objective vulnerable to an enemy holding higher ground. The RND sustained heavy losses. Bernard himself was shot in the abdomen and was evacuated to Egypt. He returned in mid-June just as the earlier slaughter at Krithia was being reprised: among the thousands killed was Bernard's eldest brother, Oscar, who had recently joined the RND's Collingwood Battalion. In July, Bernard was wounded in the stomach again, but returned to his battalion just twenty-five days later having been 'brilliantly operated on'. As both sides dug in, the Gallipoli campaign became simply a matter of survival in conditions which were every bit as bad as those on the western front. Bernard, and what remained of the RND, were eventually evacuated in January 1916.

In May, Bernard, now a temporary lieutenant commander, led Hood Battalion on the western front. In November, at the Battle of Ancre, the last major engagement on the Somme, Bernard displayed extraordinary bravery and inspirational leadership. As he led an assault on the village of Beaucourt, he received two minor wounds and then a much more serious wound to the neck. Though in great pain and in need of urgent medical attention, he led his men on and refused to relinquish command until he was certain that the attack had succeeded and that the village had been secured. He was awarded the Victoria Cross, 'For most conspicuous bravery and brilliant leading as a Battalion Commander'. General Sir Henry de Beauvoir de Lisle considered Bernard's conduct that day as 'Probably ... the most distinguished personal act in the war.'

Bernard returned to the Hood Battalion in February 1917. Two months later he was given command of 88th Infantry Brigade, becoming, at twenty-eight, the youngest brigadier general in the British Army. In September, he was wounded yet again during the Battle of Menin Road, Ypres. Shrapnel punctured his body in five places after a 5.9-inch shell exploded at his feet, yet he continued to direct his troops by telephone from brigade battle headquarters. After another period of recuperation he fought again on the Somme and then at Bailleul, south of Ypres, under General Herbert Plumer, as the Germans made their last big push of the war in the spring of 1918. The line at Ypres held, and Bernard was awarded a bar to his DSO for his part in its defence. Later, on 3 June, he sustained 'serious' shrapnel wounds to his leg and head which were treated at a field hospital. Bouncing back again, he fought bravely right up to the end, receiving a second bar to his DSO for capturing a bridge at Lessines moments before the armistice.

After the war, Bernard reverted to the substantive rank of captain and went to the Staff College at Camberley. He continued to swim and between 1925 and 1926 he made several unsuccessful attempts to swim the English Channel: in August 1926 he was thwarted by a turn in the tide just five hundred yards from Dover. He dabbled in politics, coming second for the Liberals in Cardiff South at the 1922 general election. In the same year, he married Barbara McLaren, née Jekyll (1888–1973), widow of Francis McLaren MP, who had been killed while serving with the Royal Flying Corps in 1917. Barbara was a great support to Bernard in all his subsequent endeavours and, in 1943, she was awarded an OBE for welfare work in Cairo. The couple had one son, Paul, who wrote an authoritative biography of his father, *Bernard Freyberg VC: Soldier of Two Nations* (1991). In 1960, Paul married Ivry Guild, granddaughter of Isobel Amy Cobbold.

During the interbellum, Freyberg took on a number of staff appointments and was made major general in 1934. The chances for further advancement, however, seemed to have been dashed when, the following year, the offer of a senior position in India was withdrawn after a medical examination revealed an irregular heartbeat. This came as a great blow to Freyberg, who was subsequently placed on retired pay in 1937. When war broke out in September 1939, he was declared fit only for service at home and was appointed general officer commanding (GOC) on Salisbury Plain. Bernard Freyberg, however, would not settle for being deskbound while others took the fight to the enemy. To the astonishment of the War Office, on 11 October, he contrived to get himself declared fit for action, albeit only in temperate climates, by a Salisbury medical board. Within a month, having impressed New Zealand's acting prime minister, Peter Fraser, who was in London, and with the support of Churchill, Freyberg was put in charge of the Second New Zealand Expeditionary Force (2NZEF). Uniquely, he was an officer of the British Army on loan to the New Zealand government.

After a spell in Egypt, 2NZEF was ordered to Greece as part of Anthony Eden's over-optimistic plan to create a Balkan front. When Greece fell, Freyberg was commended for leading a brave rearguard action and for his role in the evacuation to Crete. There, he was appointed commander of British and Commonwealth forces (CREFORCE), with orders to hold the island at all costs. That he failed to do so is perhaps the one blemish on an otherwise exemplary service record, though to what extent he can blamed for the fall of Crete remains open to debate. The controversy centres around his possible misinterpretation of ULTRA intelligence received from Bletchley Park and his (not unreasonable) assumption that the main thrust of a German invasion would be seaborne. Decisively, a formidable strike by German paratroopers of the 11th Air Corps captured the airbase at Maleme on the second day of the battle, 21 May 1941, which all but ensured victory. Whether or not Freyberg misjudged the situation, CREFORCE, under-equipped and with inadequate communications, stood little chance of repelling an enemy that commanded both the sea and the skies in the region. The attack on Maleme was the first large-scale airborne attack in the history of warfare and it was executed devastatingly.

If Freyberg's reputation had been dented by Crete, it was fully restored during the desert campaign in North Africa between 1941 and 1943, and subsequently in Italy. Always ready to put himself in the firing line, Freyberg became an inspiration to his New Zealanders and won the admiration of his peers and superiors. Promoted lieutenant commander in 1942, he cheated death again when he was struck by a shell fragment near El Alamein. From his hospital bed in Helwan, he described the nature of his wound: 'A piece of shell the size of an egg entered below my left ear and passed through my neck. I had a hole that they passed a piece of gauze through the size of a handkerchief.' Freyberg seemed indestructible and the alacrity with which he recovered from his wounds and returned to action prompted Churchill to describe him as 'the salamander of the British Empire'.

For his part in victory at El Alamein, Freyberg was made KCB. Next, he led his forces through Italy. In 1944, at Monte Cassino, he was instrumental in the decision to bomb the monastery, having set a limit on the number of New Zealand casualties he was prepared to accept on the exposed slopes beneath German positions. The welfare of his men was always to the fore in his thinking and when, early in June 1944, the New Zealand Division entered Rome with the Fifth US Army, it was Freyberg who commandeered the city's best hotel, the Quirinal, for use as a club by his troops. Though intimidating in stature, he was something of a gentle giant, approachable and extremely popular with troops proud to call themselves 'Freyberg's men'. From Rome, he led them north to Florence and then to Venice which was liberated at the end of April 1945. Again, he ensured his men had every possible comfort, billeting them in the city's Danieli Hotel. During the closing days of the war he earned a third bar to his DSO in a tense stand-off with Tito's partisans at Trieste. Earlier, on 24 August 1944, during its progress, the New Zealand Division was paid a visit by Churchill. Of the division's record, the prime minister remarked: 'Its career and record is one that will live not only in the history of New Zealand but in the history of the British Empire as an example of duty, valour and honour.' Just over a week later, Freyberg survived a crash-landing at Eighth Army headquarters on the Adriatic coast. One of the plane's wings broke through the fuselage, piercing his abdomen deeply, though missing his vital organs; within three weeks he was swimming again.

In September 1945, Freyberg became governor general of New Zealand, the first person with an upbringing in that country to hold the position. He relinquished command of his beloved 2NZEF in November, was made GCMG in early 1946, and then sailed in May with his family for Wellington, where he was sworn in on 17 June. He considered his six years as governor general as the happiest of his life. He and Barbara embraced their constitutional duties enthusiastically, visiting all parts of New Zealand and its Pacific dependencies and warmly welcoming foreign dignitaries. Astutely, he remained aloof from party politics and kept his own counsel on political matters relating to the services. He took a strong interest in the production of the official history of New Zealand's contribution to the war and it became clear to historians working on the project that he remained preoccupied with the fall of Crete. Immensely

As governor general of New Zealand, Freyberg visits Niue in the Cook Islands, July 1948.
(Family member's private collection; courtesy of Hodder & Stoughton.)

popular as both a war hero and as governor general, huge crowds turned out to wave Freyberg off when he left Wellington for the final time in August 1952. He had been raised to the peerage the previous year as Baron Freyberg of Wellington, New Zealand and of Munstead in the county of Surrey.

Back in England, he was appointed lieutenant governor and constable of Windsor Castle, where he took up residence in the Norman Tower. This was a prestigious position, which entailed many ceremonial and constitutional duties: for example, it was he who conferred the Order of the Garter upon Winston Churchill. As a member of the royal household, he played a part in the coronation of Queen Elizabeth II and attended the state banquet afterwards. He was also active in the House of Lords and represented New Zealand at reunions and at the dedication of memorials at Athens, Malta and El Alamein. In 1956, he proudly commanded a parade in Hyde Park of the surviving 297 holders of the Victoria Cross. He saw his life out at Windsor where he died on 4 July 1963 following the rupture of one of his old Gallipoli wounds.

That Bernard Freyberg lived well into his seventies is in itself remarkable. In the 1920s, Churchill was staying with him at a country house and asked Freyberg to show him his wounds: Freyberg stripped and Churchill counted no fewer than twenty-seven scars and gashes, a number which would be added to significantly in the Second World War. Despite debates surrounding the effectiveness of his command on Crete, his reputation as a fearless soldier and as an inspirational commander in both world wars is secure and unquestionable. German records reveal that, in North Africa, Rommel respected the New Zealand Division of Montgomery's Eighth Army more than any other, while Montgomery himself described Freyberg in the following terms: 'His example and infectious optimism were an example to the whole army. Such outstanding leadership can rarely have been seen in the history of the British army.'

Peter Charles Victor Cobbold (1897–1942)
Victim of the Long Nawang Massacre on Borneo

When Japan entered the Second World War with its spectacular assault on Pearl Harbor on 7 December 1941, the imperial interests of Britain and its allies in South East Asia became sitting ducks. Within a week, the Japanese Imperial Army had landed at Miri on the coast of Sarawak, which for nearly a century had been under the British rule of the Brooke family, the so-called 'White Rajahs'. Neither the meagre British force in Sarawak nor Dutch troops in the south of Borneo, which was part of the Dutch East Indies, could hope to repel the invaders. Sarawak's western population, predominantly British, faced a stark choice: to surrender or to flee. Down the coast at Sibu, yet to fall to the Japanese, Peter Cobbold was among twenty-six westerners who decided to take the latter course.

Peter left England for Borneo aboard the MV *Glenapp* in 1919 when he was just twenty-two. His great uncle on his mother's side, John Charles Templer, had been one of the founders of the Borneo Company Ltd., and this probably explains why Peter went to work in one of the most remote corners of Britain's informal empire. Templer had been a friend of James Brooke, the first 'White Rajah' of Sarawak. In 1842, the Sultan of Brunei,

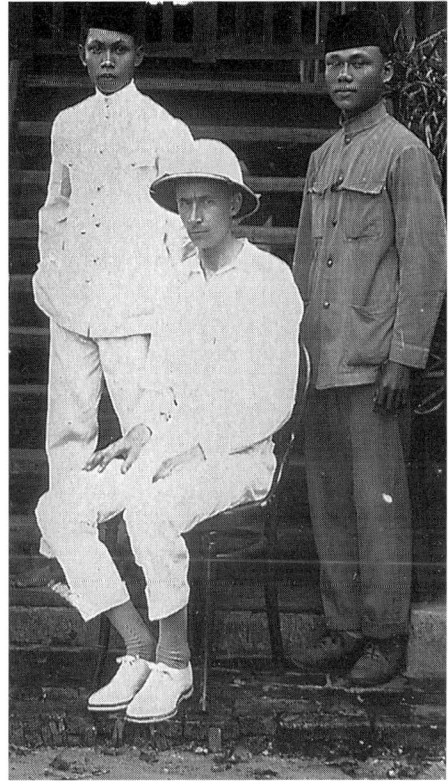

Peter Cobbold and some of his staff at Kuching.
(Family member's private collection.)

Omar Ali Saifuddin II, ceded Sarawak, a vassal of Brunei, to Brooke by way of thanks for the Englishman's help in suppressing the piracy that had blighted the seas in the region for many years. Thereafter, the territory was ruled by three generations of Brookes and had a relationship with Britain similar to that of India's princely states. The last 'White Rajah', Charles Vyner Brooke, ceded Sarawak to the British Colonial Office in 1946.

Little is known of Peter's life before he arrived at Kuching in Sarawak on 2 June 1919. He was born in Dedham, Essex in 1897, the youngest of three sons of George Thomas Cobbold and Mabel Frances Down. His mother died when he was just six. He served with the RAF in the Great War with the rank of aircraftman first class, the equivalent of private in the army. His service record shows that he joined up in December 1916 and his trade is listed as 'Labourer'.

Details of his career with the Borneo Company are similarly sketchy. The company's main interests were in mining 'seams of all descriptions of minerals', the rights to which it had been granted in 1852 in return for royalties paid to the Sarawak Treasury. Its headquarters were in Kuching in the south of Sarawak and this is where Peter began his career with the company. Most likely he would have been groomed for senior management, learning the business from the bottom up. Mentions of Peter in the *Sarawak Gazette*, a monthly newspaper edited by the Rajah's civil service, provide the only glimpses into his life as part of a European elite in Sarawak. For example, in February 1922, the *Gazette* reported that he departed for Singapore on a fifteen-month secondment to his employer's branch there. He also made visits made to the company's operations elsewhere in Sarawak; to Sadong and Sibu and to its Brooketon mine in Brunei. He also occasionally returned to England on leave, for example in 1924 and again in 1937, when he is known to have visited his brother, Horace John Templer Cobbold (known as Jack), in Essex. Peter's other brother, Robert (Robin) George, emigrated to Vancouver as a young man and fought with Canadian forces during the First World War.

Peter never married and had no children. It would have been perfectly normal for him, as a bachelor in Sarawak, to have a local girlfriend or mistress who might have lived with him, though no evidence exists to support this.

Peter Cobbold's bungalow home, Kuching, in the 1930s. (Family member's private collection.)

The hub of Kuching society was the Sarawak Club, which provided entertainment, fine dining and sporting activities for its select membership. The *Gazette's* reports of club business reveal that Peter was an enthusiastic, if not particularly talented, bowls player and that he also played tennis. On one occasion he played in a doubles match against His Highness the Tuan Muda, literally translated as 'the Little Lord' and none other than Charles Vyner Brooke's younger brother, Bertram.

Peter's progress up the career ladder was steady rather than spectacular. At some point in the 1930s he was appointed manager of the company's Sibu branch, an important position with considerable responsibility and prestige. The position afforded a very comfortable lifestyle and came with a large house built on piles over water, replete with a native staff. For Peter and for many westerners life in Sarawak was good. Hard work reaped handsome rewards and the whirl of civilised colonial society offered refinement, camaraderie and enormous fun. This enviable way of life came to an abrupt end in December 1941.

When news reached Sibu of the Japanese landings at Miri, Peter and the other westerners there had to decide whether to remain in post or try to escape. Stories of Japanese atrocities in China and elsewhere convinced the majority that fleeing into the jungle was the best of their unenviable options. The closest safe haven was Java, not yet under Japanese control, but the long sea voyage there from Sarawak would be fraught with dangers as the Japanese commanded both the seas and the skies. Instead, the group decided to travel into Borneo's mountainous interior in the hope that they might find a way to Banjarmasin on the immense island's southern coast from where the voyage to Java or even northern Australia was much shorter. An account of the trials of those attempting to flee the Japanese from Sibu was written by W. McKerracher, one of very few of Peter's companions to escape to safety.

The top man in Sibu was the Rajah's resident, Andrew MacPherson, and it was under his authority that escape plans were made. On Christmas Day, the Japanese Air Force began its bombardment of Sibu, a sure indication that ground troops were on the way. More of the same followed on Boxing Day and when news was received that the enemy were coming up the river from the south it was considered unsafe to remain in Sibu any longer. Motorboats had been readied and MacPherson led Peter and the other westerners, mostly government staff, up the Rejang River to the relative safety of Kapit, some fifty miles inland from Sibu. There, on 27 December, other evacuees joined the party and preparations were made to head on for the Dutch Borneo border. The boats were loaded with drums of benzine and sacks of rice, while personal effects deemed inessential were discarded and destroyed. The group numbered between twenty-four and twenty-six and included three women, among them MacPherson's wife who was six months pregnant. Another, a Mrs Bomfrey of the Island Trading Company, took her two sons, one aged five and the other just nine months old.

Early on 28 December, the party set off upstream in a northerly direction. The aim was to get as far as possible in the motorboats and then to proceed by lighter paddling boats and on foot. At about midday the ferocious Pelagus Rapids were reached and Peter and the others disembarked to walk around them while their guides steered the boats, laden with stores, through the raging waters. One boat capsized, its motor having stalled from taking in water. Twenty drums of benzine, four bags of rice and the clothes and possessions of Peter and three of his companions were lost. It was a sorry blow on the first day of an arduous journey, though thankfully the boat's crew were all able to swim ashore.

After three days the party reached Belaga, the highest up and last settlement on the Rejang, where they stayed in the comparative comfort of the Rejang Timber Concession's (RTC) forest station; two of the party, Messrs Miles and McKerracher worked for the RTC, which was a subsidiary of the Borneo Company Ltd. Thanks to local goodwill towards the RTC, the next seven nights were spent in longhouses, the traditional homes of the native Kenyah population. Beyond these small settlements lay uninhabited country where the river became shallower and too narrow to be navigable by the motorboats; these were duly sent back to Kapit. Miles and A. F. R. Griffin, district officer, Kapit, had earlier secured the use of eleven paddling boats together with paddlers, ten to each boat, to convey the party as far up the shallower reaches of the Rejang as possible. The paddlers, native Kayans, would then act as bearers and guides to the party through the jungle up to the border. Two of the government servants, Philip Jacks, a fair linguist able to speak the local languages and J. A. Schotling, a Dutchman, went ahead to alert the Dutch authorities of the party's approach. They were successful in their mission and the Dutch officials, under instruction from Java, sent forty Kayans into Sarawak to clear a path through the jungle for the now beleaguered party. The going had become extremely tough, through thick jungle where even their guides lost their way, and across fast-flowing rivers, one of which was crossed no fewer than thirty-six times, 'a raging mountain torrent sometimes knee deep, sometimes armpit deep, and particularly powerful'.

Eventually, twenty-eight days after leaving Sibu, Peter and his companions reached Long Nawang, a Dutch military post just over the border from Sarawak. They were in a sorry state and reached the base in the nick of time: food was running low, medical supplies had been exhausted and their guides were becoming increasingly disgruntled. Three of the party, including MacPherson, had contracted malaria, while Peter was suffering with dreadful sunburn, which had turned septic. Long Nawang boasted a four-bed hospital with a native dresser, a good supply of drugs and enough food to last the party a year. The Dutch had evacuated the post and headed to the coast on military duties and the party moved into the officers' vacant bungalows and the barracks, welcome comfort after a month in the wilderness. Unfortunately, the day before the party arrived, two-way radio communications to Long Nawang had been cut. The refugees were safe for the time being but had no way of calling for help.

From Long Nawang the most viable route of escape from the island was a daunting trek across the mountains and through almost impenetrable jungle to the east coast port of Samarinda. This journey would take at least a fortnight, following a route never before taken by a westerner and was considered 'very difficult' even by the group's native guides. An advance party of some of the fittest men was selected to try the route out. This group comprised Jacks, McKerracher, Schotling, A. W. Anderson and T. E. Walter. On 28 January, two days before these five were due to set out, news came over the radio that Samarinda had fallen to the Japanese. The same day, a native arrived at the camp bearing an SOS from a Dutch flying crew who had spent thirty-six days in the jungle having had to make forced landings after raiding Japanese positions at Miri and Brunei. The crew had two 'Britishers' with them and reached Long Nawang on 3 February.

The advance party's route proved every bit as difficult as the locals had foretold. Eventually, they reached Long Eran (Longiram) on the Mahakam River, seventy or so miles from Long Nawang and halfway to Samarinda. The plan, now, was to avoid the major ports and hope to make the crossing to Java undetected on a small vessel. This might entail a further two months' exhausting trek and the group was already suffering badly with jungle sores, mainly caused by leech bites which had turned septic. Fortuitously, while at Long Eran, they learned that they were close to a Dutch aerodrome, which remained operational, despite having been bombed by the Japanese. Eighteen days after leaving Long Nawang, the five men reached the aerodrome by fast launch and were flown across the Java Sea to Bandung and from there to Batavia (Jakarta). There, they tried to persuade the Dutch to fly a relay of rescue missions to save Peter and the others, arguing that seaplanes could land on a river at a place close to Long Nawang and rescue the party two or three at a time, women and children first. The Battle of Java, and its subsequent fall to the Japanese in March, precluded the sending of any such missions.

The escape of McKerracher, Jacks and the others did, at least, allow for news of the refugees' condition to be sent to their families. Peter's brother, Jack, received a letter from the Borneo Company Ltd., dated 19 February 1942, informing him that Peter was 'fit and well' in Dutch Borneo where he was awaiting evacuation. Not long after arriving at Batavia, Jacks and McKerracher sailed (separately) to Australia; Schotling was conscripted by the Dutch forces, Anderson joined the Royal Navy at Batavia while Walter was confined to hospital. Walter and Schotling were both subsequently taken prisoner by the Japanese.

Of course, those who remained at Long Nawang had no idea of the fortunes of the advance party, though they must have harboured hopes that plans to rescue them were in hand. It had become clear that Japanese forces would soon hold the entire island and some, including Peter, made plans to return to Sibu to surrender. Possibly because he was not well enough to undertake the journey, Peter decided not to leave the camp with Griffin and R. N. Baron, who both returned to Sibu where they were interned. Miles had also been imprisoned by the Japanese, having decided to return to Kapit long before the party reached Long Nawang.

Peter's decision to remain at Long Nawang is understandable. The hill station was three hundred miles from the nearest Japanese, was well stocked with rice, fruit and tobacco, and living conditions were comfortable. At an altitude of 2,500 feet, it was also pleasantly cool. In April, forty or so Dutch soldiers from the Royal Netherlands East Indies Army (KNIL) under the command of Lieutenant D. J. Westerhuis arrived at the camp, swelling its population to about seventy; this number included Mrs MacPherson's baby who was born there. Later, three American missionaries, Reverend Jackson and Reverend and Mrs Sandy and their child reached the camp. Though no account of the time the party spent at the base survives, (after McKerracher's departure) it can be imagined that routines were established, food was rationed and those who were ill were able to recuperate. Each member of the party must have lived, day in day out, with emotions alternating between hope for their rescue and fear of discovery by the Japanese. Sadly, it was foe rather than friend that reached their refuge first and what followed was brutal almost beyond imagination.

The party's hiding place was betrayed by a local tribesman. On 25 July, a detachment of seventy-two marines led by Captain Mora Shima set off from Samarinda for Long Nawang. As the refugees had failed to surrender when the Japanese originally invaded Borneo, Mora's orders were to treat them as enemy fugitives and this, perhaps, explains why they were not simply captured and marched back to Samarinda or Kuching as prisoners of war. The details of what happened when the Japanese reached Long Nawang were related by two witnesses, native policemen there, to Lieutenant F. R. Oldham of the Services Reconnaissance Department who was sent to investigate the massacre after the war.

The Japanese stormed the camp at 8:30 a.m. on 20 August, the day after the American missionaries had arrived. It seems likely that the troops of the KNIL tried to defend the party's position and, during the assault both MacPherson and Westerhuis were killed. Mrs MacPherson sustained bullet wounds to both thighs. Once the Japanese had established control, the men were imprisoned in the camp's fort while the women and children were removed across the river to Kampong Kenyah some distance away. At 5:00 p.m. on 26 August, the men were led to a hill behind the barracks where mass graves had been prepared. There, they were shot, bayoneted and thrown into the graves. Peter was among the victims. Captain Mora left the camp the following day with forty-five marines, leaving a Lieutenant Okino to guard the six women and four children who, for the time being, had been spared, but whose ultimate fate was even more horrific. For nearly a whole month after the execution of the men, the women were repeatedly molested by Okino's men. Then, on 23 September, they were horribly mutilated and murdered, probably by bayonet. The children suffered unimaginably cruel deaths. They were forced to climb, or placed on, the trunks of areca nut trees until, exhausted and unable to cling on any longer, they slipped down onto the upraised bayonets of the Japanese marines. Not a single refugee who was there when the Japanese marines marched into the camp survived.

Oldham compiled his report in 1945, citing Mora, Okino and a Private Higasi Kumobun among the perpetrators. However, despite the assertion that 'no effort should be spared' to trace them, none of the three or indeed any of the Japanese marines responsible for the atrocity ever faced trial. After the war, plans to move the bodies of the victims to Kuching were rejected on the grounds that identification of individuals would be difficult. Instead, crosses were set above the mass graves at Long Nawang and a priest sent to consecrate the ground.

Brigadier Simon Fraser, DSO MCTD, 15th Lord Lovat (1911–95)

Chief of the Clan Fraser and Hero of the D-Day Landings

Brigadier the Lord Lovat during the winter of 1939, from his memoir, *March Past*, 1978.
(Family member's private collection.)

When he died in March 1995, the *Independent* published an obituary of Lord Lovat written by Sir Max Harper Gow, who had been his staff captain during the Normandy landings. The piece provides a fascinating insight into the character of Lovat, who was about as unconventional a soldier as one could imagine. Gow describes him as 'Gay, debonair, inspirational, and yes, lovable – arrogant, ruthless, at times terrifying, his personality is too complex to explain. Perhaps we should try not to, and simply remember that he was a Lovat.' Larger than life, Lovat was also fearless. He emerged from the war a great hero – this despite the extraordinary fact that during its full six-year duration he saw less than two weeks' action.

Lovat, known to his friends as 'Shimi' an anglicised form of his Scottish Gaelic forename, was born in Beaufort Castle, Inverness-shire. His father, Simon Joseph Fraser (1871–1933), 14th Lord Lovat (though commonly known as the 16th Lord) was, himself, something of a maverick in military circles. In 1899, two years after he had resigned his commission with the Queen's Own Cameron Highlanders, he persuaded the War Office to allow him to muster what was essentially a private army to fight in South Africa against the Boers. Highland countrymen, versed in spying, stalking and shooting were, the 14th Lord maintained, precisely what the British Army needed to defeat the Boers in the similarly wild terrain of their homeland. He presented his unorthodox proposals to the War Office in December 1899 and, to some surprise, received the go-ahead to raise two companies, one of mounted infantry and one of foot. These were to be employed 'primarily for scouting purposes' and would be attached to the Black Watch. Volunteers for the Lovat Scouts came from all over Scotland and almost all of the large clans were represented. Originally, the two companies comprised 236 men, eighty of whom were chosen with stalking ability as their primary qualification. The Scouts were the first British unit to wear Ghillie suits, heavily camouflaged uniforms designed to resemble dense foliage, and they soon earned their spurs in playing the Boers at their own game. They contributed greatly to improvements in intelligence gathering, using spyglasses to observe, and semaphore and heliograph to communicate. Later, during World War I, the Scouts saw service at Gallipoli and in Egypt and Macedonia, and a crack sniper unit was formed from their ranks for service on the western front.

Shimi Fraser was commissioned second lieutenant in the Lovat Scouts in 1930, aged nineteen, while still at Magdalen College, Oxford where he failed to distinguish himself, emerging with a lowly fourth-class degree in Modern History. The adventurous side of his nature had already gained the upper hand over the scholarly; between school and university Shimi had travelled to South America to work on a coffee and cattle ranch. In 1931, he transferred to the Scots Guards and was promoted lieutenant in 1934. A year earlier, Shimi's father had died after collapsing at a point-to-point meeting near Oxford, having just watched his son win a race. At just twenty-two, Shimi became the 25th chief of the Clan Fraser, and 15th Lord Lovat, inheriting Beaufort and its two hundred thousand acres, though his mother ran the estate on his behalf until he resigned his commission in 1937. In June of the same year, Beaufort was nearly destroyed by fire: its library and picture gallery were completely gutted and many valuable paintings were lost.

In October 1938, Lovat married Rosamond Delves Broughton (1917–2012) at Brompton Oratory in London. It was the first big society wedding after the Munich crisis and a large crowd of sightseers turned up to see the handsome couple. The *Angus Evening Telegraph* reported that a stampede ensued and that 'The bride and her five-yard-long train only just managed to precede the crowd of women who surged in her wake.' Rosamond was the daughter of Sir Henry John (Jock) Delves Broughton, 11th Baronet. He and Rosamond's stepmother, Lady Diana (née Caldwell) would later be the central characters in one of the scandals of the age. In 1940, the couple moved to Kenya, taking a house in Happy Valley, an enclave north of Nairobi populated by licentious, aristocratic British and Irish expatriates. Diana, almost immediately, embarked upon a very public affair with Josslyn Hay, 22nd Earl of Erroll, the languid unofficial leader of what was known as the 'Happy Valley set'. On 24 January 1924, having spent the evening with Diana, Erroll was found dead at a Nairobi crossroads, having been shot in the head. The cuckold, Broughton, was arrested and charged. The resulting trial made the headlines not just in Kenya and Britain but all over the world as the salacious details of the case came to light. Ultimately, ballistics evidence proved inconclusive and Broughton was acquitted, though many doubted his innocence in the matter. He left Kenya shortly afterwards, his wife having taken another lover, and days after his arrival in England in December 1942, he was found dead from a morphine overdose in his room at the Britannia Adelphi Hotel in Liverpool.

Shimi and Rosamond, it seems, had a less tempestuous marriage. Immediately upon moving into Beaufort Castle, Rosamond directed her energies into overseeing the restoration of its damaged rooms. Three children followed between 1939 and 1942 and another three after the war. Sadly, two of the couple's three sons predeceased their father. Their youngest, Andrew was fatally gored by a charging buffalo in Tanzania while on safari with his family in 1994; a few weeks later, Simon Augustine Fraser, Master of Lovat and heir to the title, died of a heart attack while hunting in the grounds of Beaufort. Only the couple's three daughters have survived both parents.

After resigning his commission in 1937, Lovat transferred to the Supplementary Reserve of Officers. He resigned this commission in June 1939, just three months before the outbreak of war. In August, as war seemed unavoidable, he was mobilised as a captain with the Lovat Scouts, though he soon fell out with his commander and did not stay with them long. In early 1940, while the Scouts were preparing to leave for the Faroe Islands, which they were tasked with defending, Lovat joined the commandos, taking some of his best men with him. He was initially posted to Achnacarry, near Fort William, where he led commando training for exiles from France, Poland, the Netherlands, Belgium, Norway and Czechoslovakia as well as for his own countrymen. It was here that he first met Bill Millin, the piper with whom he will forever be associated. As an instructor, according to Max Harper Gow, Lovat was intolerant of any inefficiency in his men. Dashingly handsome and with a deep, booming voice which he never had to raise, Gow maintained, 'there was a debonair, almost romantic air about him, which intrigued and brought the best out of one'.

It was not until March 1941 that Lovat first saw action. He took part in Operation Claymore, a daring assault on the Norwegian Lofoten Islands where factories processed fish oil and glycerine for use in the German weapons industry. The raid was an unqualified success: eight hundred thousand gallons of oil and glycerine were destroyed, eighteen factories put out of operation and eleven merchant ships sunk. More significant still, the commandos recovered an Enigma machine, together with ciphers from the armed trawler, *Krebs*, before she went down. This enabled the code breakers at Bletchley Park to decipher German naval codes for some time, supplying intelligence which would enable the transatlantic convoys to steer clear of U-boat concentrations.

In April 1942, Lovat was in action with the commandos again. This time, he was in overall command of a reconnaissance raid on the French coast at

Hardelot, south of Boulogne. As a temporary Major, he led a hundred men of No. 4 Commando as well as a detachment of fifty Canadians across the Channel. Under darkness on 22 April 1942, No. 4 Commando landed to the north of Hardelot, though due to a navigational error the Canadians were unable to get ashore further south. Lovat and his men were caught in searchlights and came under moderate fire, though this was returned with interest from the landing craft support (LCS) vessels, which were providing cover fire. A successful reconnaissance of German defences was made before Lovat and his men slipped back into their LCSs. For his action at Hardelot, Lovat was awarded the Military Cross. The mission, Operation Abercrombie, was an important component in plans for a much larger raid on the French coast – Operation Jubilee, the raid on Dieppe.

The Dieppe Raid, launched in the early hours of 19 August and planned by Vice Admiral Lord Louis Mountbatten, failed in almost all its objectives. The plan was to hold Dieppe for at least two tides and to destroy its military installations. A 'hit and run' raid, it was supposed to boost morale and to test the water for further large-scale assaults on the French coast. Of the six thousand troops – mostly Canadian – who landed at Dieppe, more than sixty per cent were killed, wounded or captured. Lovat, now acting lieutenant colonel, led No. 4 Commando and fifty US Rangers to the raid's only notable success, destroying a battery of six 150mm guns at Varengeville, six miles west of Dieppe. Lovat received a DSO for his efforts, while one of his men, Captain Patrick Porteous received the Victoria Cross: Porteous refused to take a backward step despite having been shot and wounded twice 'under withering fire'. The Dieppe Raid was one of the most costly Allied debacles of the Second World War. Arguably, Mountbatten's reputation only survived due to the timely release, just after Dieppe, of Noël Coward's film, *In Which We Serve*, which dealt sympathetically with Mountbatten's naval career. Coward himself played Mountbatten in the film. Mountbatten would later rather lamely claim that, through lessons learned, for every life lost on the beaches of Dieppe, ten were saved on D-Day.

Nearly two years would elapse before the Allies would risk another assault on the French coast, though when it came it was on an almost unimaginably larger scale. The daring Lovat was, unsurprisingly, at the forefront of operations on D-Day – 6 June 1944 – and was not found wanting, displaying his own unique blend of courage and swagger. He had, by now, been promoted brigadier and was the commander of the newly formed No. 1 Special Service Brigade, comprising Nos 3, 4 and 6 Commando and No. 45 Royal Marine Commando. On the morning of 6 June 1944, Lovat (wearing a white jumper with his name embroidered into the collar under his battledress) and his crack brigade waded

Commandos of 1st Special Service Brigade led by Brigadier Lord Lovat (in the water to the right of his men) land on Queen Red beach, Sword area, c.0840 hours 6 June 1944. Bill Millin is in the foreground about to disembark.
(Photograph by Capt. J. L. Evans.)

ashore at Ouistreham in Queen Red sector on Sword Beach, the most easterly point of all the D-Day landings. About half of Lovat's band became casualties before they had even emerged from the water. Once on the beach, Lovat turned to his piper, Bill Millin, and asked, 'Would you mind giving us a tune?' Millin, aged twenty-two, was unarmed save for a knife and was wearing the kilt his father had worn in Flanders in World War I; he was the only man who landed on the beaches that day thus attired. He initially baulked at his commander's request, citing army regulations which forbade such frivolity. Lovat reasoned,

'Ah but that's the English War Office. You and I are both Scottish, and that doesn't apply.' Stunned, Millin then asked Lovat, 'Would you want me to walk up and down, sir?' Lovat replied, 'Yes that would be nice. Yes, walk up and down.' While men were being cut down all around him, Millin played *Hielan' Laddie* and *The Road to the Isles* and, miraculously, escaped the beach without so much as a scratch. In later life, he met up with some of the German snipers who were picking off his comrades that day. They told him he had been spared because they thought he was crazy.

Lovat mustered those who managed to clear the beachhead and then led them through the Atlantic Wall, crossing a clearly marked minefield. The commandos then bravely fought their way six miles inland along the Canal de Caen to the village of Bénouville. The canal ran parallel to the River Orne with a 400-metre strip of land running between the two. At Bénouville a bascule bridge crossed the canal while further east another bridge, at Ranville, crossed the Orne. The capture of both bridges was essential to cut off any German counter-attack and was one of the key strategic objectives of that day. Just after midnight on D-Day, the 6th Airborne Division, led by Major John Howard, landed six Horsa gliders in the area, each bearing about thirty men whose task it was to hold the bridges until support arrived. Some lost their lives while landing but, with the element of surprise weighing in their favour, both bridges were soon seized and the 6th Airborne dug in, their numbers soon being swelled by the arrival of men from the 7th Parachute Battalion.

Lovat was due to reach the Caen canal bridge at noon on D-Day, but arrived just over an hour late, having been delayed by enemy mortar fire and marshy terrain. What followed must have seemed incredulous to both friend and foe. Lovat's men marched boldly across the Caen bridge to the strains of *Blue Bonnets Over the Border*, played by Millin. This was either a show of great bravado or utter madness, but was done with a flourish typical of Lovat. Alerted by Millin's rendition, the Germans levelled their sights on the commandos and twelve were killed, shot through their berets. Lovat's recollection of the scene, recorded, in his memoir, *March Past* (1979), captures its incongruity; 'Several other ranks became casualties, but the good music drowned the shooting and we managed to strive over in step – almost with pomp and circumstance!' Later, Lovat and the remainder of his brigade fought fiercely and established defensive positions around Ranville, which they held until they were relieved by elements of the British 3rd Infantry. The battle for the bridges became one of the most celebrated episodes of D-Day. The Bénouville bridge was subsequently renamed Pegasus, the emblem worn by British airborne forces: the bridge at Ranville became known as Horsa. Today, the former is a major tourist attraction.

On 12 June, Lovat was leading 6 Commando during an attack on the village of Bréville, a few miles east of Ranville. The village came under heavy fire from German artillery and, during the melee, as Lovat later wrote, 'It was my turn to bite the dust.' He was seriously wounded in the back and side. As he lay receiving a blood transfusion, he gave instructions to his second-in-command, Lieutenant Colonel David Mills-Roberts; 'Take over the brigade,' he said, 'and whatever happens – not a foot back.' The order was followed but, for Lovat, the war was over.

He made a full recovery but never saw action again. Churchill made good use of his urbane charm, sending him as his special emissary to Moscow where Lovat, still only thirty-three, had talks with Stalin. The prime minister sent an advance letter of introduction to the Soviet leader in which he described Lovat as 'the mildest-mannered man that ever scuttled a ship or cut a throat', a quotation from Byron's *Don Juan*. After the war, Lovat remained with the army, transferring to the reserve in 1949 until his formal retirement in 1962, though he retained the honorary rank of brigadier for the remainder of his life. He was active in politics, serving briefly as parliamentary under-secretary of state for foreign affairs in Churchill's caretaker government before the Labour Party came to power in July 1945. Thereafter, he remained active in the House of Lords, speaking on highland affairs and was a member of Inverness County Council, a position he held from 1932 until 1974. At Beaufort, he reared shorthorn cattle and he became chairman of the Anglo-Scottish Cattle Company. He travelled widely in this role and as chief of his clan to countries including Argentina, Australia, Canada, and South Africa. He was also in great demand as a show judge. Returning to Normandy in 1962, he was an advisor on the film, *The Longest Day*, in which he was portrayed by Peter Lawford. Interestingly, Richard Todd, who played Major John Howard, commander of 6th Airborne, had actually fought with the 7th Parachute Battalion alongside Lovat at Ranville and Bénouville.

In 1970, Lovat handed Beaufort Castle, to his eldest son, Simon. Over the next twenty-five years, the estate accumulated debts of £7,400,000 as a series of business initiatives, including the construction of a bottling plant for Lovat spring water, failed. In 1995, shortly after Lovat's death, Beaufort Castle and its land were sold to meet these debts and inheritance taxes. It went in thirty-nine lots, the house itself fetching £1,500,000. It had been in the family's hands for over six hundred years.

Though perhaps sometimes cavalier, Lord Lovat was undoubtedly a brave soldier and an inspirational leader of his men, who were among the Allies' finest. Max Harper Gow recalled that, 'Under fire, he seemed to be completely at ease; almost contemptuous of the enemy's worst efforts.' Such confidence, bordering on arrogance, coupled with his physical demeanour created an aura of invincibility about him, which secured the unconditional loyalty of those around him in the most extreme circumstances. Beneath all the show, however, he was an exceedingly intelligent man and astute tactician who never took the dangers of battle lightly, despite appearances to the contrary. At once flamboyant and considered, he was an outstanding officer. His appearances in battle may only have been fleeting but they were immeasurably telling. He was a true hero of the Second World War.

A FINAL WORD

The Cobbolds are, of course, best known for brewing and for their long association with Ipswich Town FC. I hope that the life stories presented here illustrate that ale and the family's long presence in the Portman Road boardroom form but a small part of the story of a family with enormously diverse interests and activities.

The football club's two most successful managers, Sir Alf Ramsey and Sir Bobby Robson, both went on to manage the England team. One of the most difficult tasks facing the manager of a national side is the selection of a squad to take to one of the big tournaments. From a wide pool of talent, the manager has to select those he thinks will cohere as a squad and, inevitably, many do not 'make the plane'. Similarly here, the selection of our 'squad' was among the most difficult tasks Anthony Cobbold and I faced and there are many life stories which we excluded reluctantly and with heavy hearts. In the same way that Sir Alf and Sir Bobby were unable to satisfy everyone, some readers may disagree with our squad selection, or feel aggrieved that their favourite 'player' has been overlooked. Our aim, for better or worse, has always been to shine a light on the immense patchwork of the family's talents and interests and to relate stories of remarkable lives. In this we hope to have achieved some success.

Though no longer brewing, the family is still flourishing and the lives of today's generation of Cobbolds and their kinsfolk continue to shape the story of the family. None of the subjects of this book is still with us, but the work of the Cobbold Family History Trust is just as concerned with the living as the dead and with life stories that are still unfolding. The family tree, like the archive, continues to grow and is enriched by each new addition.

The Cobbold Family History Trust was settled in 2004 and became a charity in 2011. Its purpose is to encourage the study and understanding of family and local history using the Cobbold and related families as an example. Contact details as at 2014:

Cobbold Family History Trust
Charity No. 1144757
14 Moorfields, Moorhaven
Ivybridge
Devon, PL21 0XQ, UK.
+44(0)1752 894498
anthonycobbold@tiscali.co.uk
www.cobboldfht.com

SOURCES AND FURTHER READING

Industry and Agriculture

John Cobbold

Arnott, C., *Britain's Lost Breweries and Beers: Thirty Famous Homes of Beers that have Brewed their Last Pint* (London, Aurum Press, 2012)

Bishop, P., *The History of Ipswich: 1500 Years of Triumph and Disaster* (London, Unicorn, 1995)

Blatchly, J. M., 'The Cobbolds meet their match', *East Anglian Daily Times*, 29 January 2011

Maltster, R., *250 Years of Brewing in Ipswich* (Holbrook, Malthouse Press in association with Tollemache and Cobbold Brewery Ltd, 1996)

Moffat, H., *Ships and Shipyards of Ipswich, 1700–1970* (Holbrook, Malthouse Press, 2002)

Walton, F., *Souvenir of the Bi-centenary of the Cliff Brewery Ipswich, Cobbold & Co., 1723–1923* (Ipswich, 1923)

Reverend John Chevallier, MD

Clarke, C., *The British Malting Industry Since 1830* (London, Hambleden, 1998)

Cornell, M., 'Zythophile. Beer now and then' (available at: http://zythophile. wordpress.com/2013/04/15/revival-of-ancient-barley-variety-thrills-fans-of-old-beer-styles, accessed 6 February 2014)

Davidson, A., 'The MT Interview: Henry Chevallier Guild', *Management Today*, 1 November 2012

Evans, G. E., *The Horse in the Furrow* (London, Faber & Faber, 1960)

Oliver, G. (ed.), *The Oxford Companion to Beer* (Oxford, Oxford University Press, 2012)

Sandon, E., *Suffolk Houses: A Study of Domestic Architecture* (Woodbridge, Antique Collectors Club, 1977)

Stone, M. (ed.), *The Diary of John Longe, Vicar of Coddenham, 1765–1834* (Woodbridge, The Boydell Press, 2008)

Tye, W., 'The Chevalliers of Aspall Hall, their Cider Press and Barley Corn', *Société Jersiaise Annual Bulletin* (1968), pp. 307–14

John Chevallier Cobbold, MP

Lindsay, M., 'The Eastern Union', *The East Anglian Magazine* (November 1960), pp. 2–9

Moffat, H., *East Anglia's First Railways* (Lavenham, Terence Dalton, 1987)

Moffat, H., *Ships and Shipyards of Ipswich, 1700–1970* (Holbrook, Malthouse Press, 2002)

Obituary, *Ipswich Journal*, 10 October 1882

Felix Thornley Cobbold, MP

Thomas, R., *A Farming Legacy 1910–2010: Celebrating the centenary of the Felix Thornley Cobbold Agricultural Trust* (Ipswich, Old Pond, 2012)

Thomas, R., *To Suffolk With Love: The Life of Felix Thornley Cobbold* (Stowmarket, Cobbold Family History Trust, 2009)

Obituary, *East Anglian Daily Times*, 6 December 1909

Faith
Reverend William Rust Cobbold

Hobsbawm. E., and G. Rudé, *Captain Swing* (London, Lawrence & Wishart, 1969)

Smith, J. O., *One Monday in November... and Beyond: The Selborne and Headley Workhouse Riots of 1830* (Headley Down, John Owen Smith, 2002)

Reverend Richard Cobbold

Blatchly, J. M., 'Cobbold, Richard (1797–1877)', *Oxford Dictionary of National Biography* (Oxford University Press, 2004; online edn May 2005)

Cobbold, R., 'Wortham Parochial Associations', Suffolk Record Office, Ipswich, HD368/1

Cobbold, R., 'Features of Wortham', Suffolk Record Office, Ipswich, HA42/1–2

Cobbold, R., *The History of Margaret Catchpole, a Suffolk Girl* (London, Oxford University Press, 1929)

Dymond, D. (ed.), *Parson and People in a Suffolk Village: Richard Cobbold's Wortham* (Wortham, Wortham Research Group and Suffolk Family History Society, 2007)

Fletcher, R. (ed.), *The Biography of a Victorian Village: Richard Cobbold's Account of Wortham, Suffolk 1860* (London, Batsford, 1977)

Bishop John Coleridge Patteson

Fremantle, W. H., 'Patteson, John Coleridge (1827–1871)', Revd David Hilliard, *Oxford Dictionary of National Biography* (Oxford University Press, 2004; online edn, October 2006)

Gutch, Sir J., *Martyr of the Islands: The Life and Death of John Coleridge Patteson* (London, Hodder and Stoughton, 1971)

Kolshus, T., and E. Hovdhaugen, 'Reassessing the Death of Bishop John Patteson', *The Journal of Pacific History*, vol. 45, no. 3 (December 2010), pp. 331–55

Page, J., *Bishop Patteson, the Martyr of Melanesia* (New York, F. H. Revell, 1890)

Yonge, C. M., *Life of John Coleridge Patteson, Missionary Bishop of the Melanesian Islands*, 2 vols (London, Macmillan, 1874)

Lady Evelyn Cobbold

Cobbold, Lady E., *Pilgrimage to Mecca* (London, Arabian Publishing, 2009)

Cobbold, Lady E., *Wayfarers in the Libyan Desert* (London, Humphreys, 1912)

Gilham, J., 'Cobbold, Lady Evelyn (1867–1963)', *Oxford Dictionary of National Biography* (Oxford University Press, October 2007)

Porter, V. (ed.), *Hajj, Journey to the Heart of Islam* (London, British Museum Press, 2012)

Shepherd Moorhead, E., 'The Muslim Aristocrats: British Converts to Islam at the Turn of the Century' (unpublished BA Thesis, Harvard University, 2011)

The Arts

William Cobbold (Goldsmith)

Barrett, G. N., *Norwich Silver and its Marks 1565–1702: The Goldsmiths of Norwich 1141–1750* (Norwich, The Wensum Press, 1981)

Hartop, C. (ed.), *East Anglian Silver 1550–1750* (Cambridge, John Adamson, 2004)

William Cobbold (Composer)

Burney, C., *A General History of Music from the Earliest Ages to the Present Period* (New York, Harcourt, Brace & Co., 1935)

Hipperson, L., 'William Cobbold, Madrigalist', *East Anglian Magazine*, no. 11, vol. 33 (September 1974), pp. 594–5

Josephs, N., 'William Cobbold' in S. Sadie (ed.), *The New Grove Dictionary*, Vol. IV (London, Macmillan, 1980), pp. 507–8

Milsom, J., *The Triumphs of Oriana* (Colchester, Chandos Records, 2002)

Payne, I., 'Recomposition and Rearrangement in William Cobbold: In Bethlehem Town', *The Musical Times*, vol. 143, no. 1881 (Winter 2002), pp. 42–55

Payne, I., *William Cobbold: The Music for Five Voices and Viols* (London, Fretwork Editions, 2002)

Elizabeth Cobbold, née Knipe

Records pertaining to Mrs Elizabeth Cobbold, Suffolk Record Office, Ipswich, HA231/3

Blatchly, J.M., 'Cobbold , Elizabeth (1764–1824)', *Oxford Dictionary of National Biography* (Oxford University Press, 2004)

Cobbold, E. (introduction by Jermyn, L.), *Poems by Mrs Cobbold* (Ipswich, J. Raw, 1825)

Lillie Langtry

Aronson, T., 'Langtry, Lillie (1853–1929)', *Oxford Dictionary of National Biography* (Oxford University Press, 2004; online edn, May 2008)

Beatty, L., *Lillie Langtry: Manners, Masks and Morals* (London, Chatto & Windus, 1999)

Birkett, J. and J. Richardson, *Lillie Langtry. Her Life in words and pictures* (St Clements Bay, Rupert Shuff, 1979)

Brough, J., *The Prince and the Lily: the story of Edward VII and Lillie Langtry* (London, The Leisure Circle, 1975)

Coleman, T., *Lillie the Legend: the Life of Lillie Langtry* (Jersey, Société Jersiaise, 1999)

Langtry, E., *The Days I Knew* (St John, Redberry Press, 1989)

Dr Martin Edward Fallas Shaw, OBE and Joan Cobbold

Craig, E., *Gordon Craig, the Story of his Life* (London, Victor Gollancz, 1969)

Martin Browne, E., *The Making of T. S. Eliot's Plays* (Cambridge, Cambridge University Press, 1969)

Nunn, L., Music *Recollections of More than Half a Century* (Ipswich, W. E. Harrison, 1899)

Routley, E., *Martin Shaw: A centenary appreciation* (London, Martin Shaw Centenary, 1975)

Shaw, M., *Up to Now* (London, Oxford University Press, 1929)

Tomes, J., 'Shaw, Martin Edward Fallas (1875–1958)', *Oxford Dictionary of National Biography* (Oxford University Press, 2004; online edn, May 2011)

Martin Shaw: Music & Song, www.martinshawmusic.com

Empire
Horace William Cain

Hone, J. A., 'Cain William (1831–1914)' *Australian Dictionary of Biography*

Obituary, *The Argus* (Melbourne), 30 October 1914, p. 6

Memorial Notices, *The Manx Quarterly*, vol. 2, no. 15 (1915), p. 303

Francis Edward Cobbold

Upfield, A. W. (ed. S. Berry), *The Gifts of Frank Cobbold* (New Malden, Number 11 Publishing, 2008)

Obituary, *The Argus* (Melbourne), 2 September 1935

Charles Cobbold Farr

Angus, C. and B. Griffin, *We Lived a Life and Then Some: The Life, Death and Life of a Mining Town* (Toronto, Between the Lines, 1996)

Farr, C. C., *The Lake Temiscamingue District, province of Ontario* (Toronto, Warwick Bros. & Rutter, 1893)

The Life of Charles Cobbold Farr (published privately by his granddaughters, 1967)

Mason, S. J., *Haileybury* (Cobalt, Highway Book Shop, 1974)

Colonel Ralph Patteson Cobbold, DSO

Ralph P. Cobbold Papers, MS 1663, Yale University Library (copy held by The Cobbold Family History Trust)

Report by Mr Cobbold on his Journey in the Pamirs and Chinese Turkestan, *Political and Secret Memoranda*, The British Library (BL), India Office Records (IOR), L/PS/18/A135

Kashgar Diaries, *Political and Secret Home Correspondence*, BL, IOR, L/PS/7/114–5

Cobbold, R. P., 'My Travels in central Asia', *The Wide World Magazine* (1899).

Cobbold, R. P., 'A Sample of Chinese Administration', *The Nineteenth Century*, vol. XLV, no. 266 (Apr., 1899), pp. 590–7

Cobbold, R. P., *Innermost Asia: Travel and Sport in the Pamirs* (London, Heinemann, 1900)

Deasy, H. H. P., *In Tibet and Chinese Turkestan. Being the record of three years' exploration* (London, T. Fisher Unwin, 1901)

Hodges, C., 'The Politics of Exploration, with Specific Reference to Eastern or Chinese Turkestan, 1865–1908.' (PhD Thesis, University of the West of England, 2013)

Hopkirk, P. *The Great Game: On Secret Service in High Asia* (Oxford, Oxford University Press, 1990)

Skrine, C. P., and P. Nightingale, *Macartney at Kashgar: New Light on British, Chinese and Russian Activities in Sinkiang, 1890–1918* (Oxford, Oxford University Press, 1987)

Public Service
Sir Thomas Plumer, MP

Dean, D., 'Joseph Wall of Goree Island', *African Affairs*, vol. 57, no. 229 (October 1958), pp. 295–301

Howell, T. B., *Cobbetts complete collection of state trials and proceedings for high treason and other crimes and misdemeanours from the earliest period to the present time* (London, Bagshaw, 1813)

Marshall, P. J., 'Hastings, Warren (1732–1818)', *Oxford Dictionary of National Biography* (Oxford University Press, 2004; online edn, October 2008)

Polden, P., 'Plumer, Sir Thomas (1753–1824)', *Oxford Dictionary of National Biography* (Oxford University Press, 2004; online edn, Jan 2008)

Romilly, S., *Memoirs of Sir Samuel Romilly*, 3 vols. (London, John Murray, 1940)

Sir Harry Smith Parkes, GCMG KCB

Papers of Sir Harry Parkes, Cambridge University Library, GBR/0012/MS Parkes

Dickins, F. V., and S. Lane-Poole, *The Life of Sir Harry Parkes*, 2 vols (London, Macmillian, 1894)

Lane-Poole, S., *Sir Harry Parkes in China* (London, Methuen, 1901)

Leiper, S., *Precious Cargo: Scots and the China Trade* (Edinburgh, National Museums of Scotland, 1997)

Loch, H. B., *A Narrative of Events in China* (London, John Murray, 1900)

Wells, J., 'Parkes, Sir Harry Smith (1828–1885)', *Oxford Dictionary of National Biography* (Oxford University Press, 2004; online edn, May 2011)

Field Marshal Herbert Horatio Kitchener, KCMG KG, 1st Earl Kitchener

Cassar, G. H., *Kitchener's War: British Strategy from 1914–1916* (Washington DC, Brassey's, 2004)

Cohen, S. P., 'Issue, Role and Personality: The Kitchener–Curzon Dispute', *Comparative Studies in History and Society*, vol. 10, no. 3 (April 1968), pp. 337–55

Esher, R., *The Tragedy of Lord Kitchener* (London, John Murray, 1921)

French, D., *British Economic and Strategic Planning, 1910–1915* (London, Allen & Unwin, 1982)

Neilson, N., 'Kitchener, Horatio Herbert, Earl Kitchener of Khartoum (1850–1916)', *Oxford Dictionary of National Biography* (Oxford University Press, 2004; online edn, January 2011)

Pollock, J., *Kitchener, Saviour of the Realm* (London, Constable, 2001)

Warner, P., *Kitchener, the Man Behind the Legend* (New York, Atheneum, 1986)

Cameron Fromanteel Cobbold, KG GCVO, 1st Baron Cobbold

Capie, F, *The Bank of England: 1950s to1979* (Cambridge, Cambridge University Press, 2010)

Fforde, J., *The Bank of England and Public Policy, 1941–1958* (Cambridge, Cambridge University Press, 1992)

Hennessy, E., *A Domestic History of the Bank of England, 1930-1960* (Cambridge, Cambridge University Press, 1992)

Taylor, P., 'Cobbold, Cameron Fromanteel, first Baron Cobbold (1904–1987)', *Oxford Dictionary of National Biography* (Oxford University Press, 2004; online edn, May 2005)

Report of the Commission of Enquiry, North Borneo and Sarawak, 1962 (London, HMSO, 1962)

Sarawak, Report for the Year 1962 (London, HMSO, 1963)

Science and Academia
Reverend Temple Chevallier, DD

Chevallier/Corrie Correspondence, Durham University Library, GB 033 ADD–837

Knight, D., 'Chevallier, Temple (1794–1873)', *Oxford Dictionary of National Biography* (Oxford University Press, 2004; online edn, October 2007)

Rochester, G. D., 'The History of Astronomy at the University of Durham from 1835 to 1939', *Quarterly Journal of the Royal Astronomical Society*, vol. 21 (1980), pp. 369–78

Thomas Spencer Cobbold, MD FRS FLS

Bettany, G. T., 'Cobbold, Thomas Spencer (1828–1886)', Rev. Peter Osborne, *Oxford Dictionary of National Biography* (Oxford University Press, 2004; online edn, May 2006)

Cobbold, T. S., *Entozoa: an Introduction to the Study of Helminthology, with Reference more Particularly to the Internal Parasites of Man* (London, Groombridge, 1864)

Cobbold, T. S., *Tapeworms and Threadworms* (London, Longman's Green & Co., 1866)

'T. S. Cobbold, MD, FRS', *Midland Medical Miscellany and Provincial Medical Journal*, vol. 3 (March 1884), pp. 65–8

Dr Edgar Sterling Cobbold, FGS

E. S. Cobbold correspondence with the Natural History Museum, NHM Archive, DF100

Cobbold, E. S. and R. Woodhouse, 'The Cambrian Area of Ruston (Shropshire)', *Philosophical Transactions of the Royal Society of London*, vol. 223 (1934), pp. 306–404

Watts, W. W., 'Edgar Sterling Cobbold', *A Paper read before the Caradoc and S. V. Field Club*, 4 December 1936

Nicholas G. L. Hammond, CBE DSO

Hammond, N. G. L., *The History of Greece to 322 B. C.* (Oxford, Oxford University Press, 1959)

Hammond, N. G. L., *Venture into Greece: with the guerrillas, 1943–1944* (London, Macmillan, 1983)

Hammond, N. G. L., 'Travels in Epirus and south Albania before World War II', *The Ancient World*, 8 (1983), pp. 13–45

Walbank, F., 'Nicholas Hammond', *The Annual of the British School at Athens*, vol. 96 (2001), pp. 445–9

Obituary, the *Independent*, 28 March 2001

Obituary, the *Guardian*, 5 April 2001

Sport

William Nevill 'Nuts' Cobbold

Bailey, M., *From Cloisters to Cup Finals: A History of Charterhouse Football* (Hindrigham, JJG Publishing, 2009)

Johnston, F. (ed.), *The Football Encyclopedia* (London, Associated Sporting Press, 1934)

Taylor, D. J., *On the Corinthian Spirit: The Decline of Amateur Sport* (London, Yellow Jersey Press, 2006)

Robert Bourne, MP

Burnell, R. D., *The Oxford and Cambridge Boat Race*, 1829–1953 (London, Oxford University Press, 1954)

Legg, L. G. W. 'Bourne, Robert Croft (1888–1938)', Rev. Marc Brodie, *Oxford Dictionary of National Biography* (Oxford University Press, 2004)

Ross, G., *The Boat Race: The Story of the First Hundred Races between Oxford and Cambridge* (London, Hodder & Stoughton, 1954)

'The Rowers of Vanity Fair / Bourne RC', (Available at: www.en.wikibooks.org/wiki/The_Rowers_of_Vanity_Fair/Bourne_RC, accessed 12 July 2013)

Gordon Chevallier Cobbold

Duckworth, M., 'Sunbeam's Star Turn', *The Classic Motor Cycle*, (January 2000), pp. 6–10

Mortimer, C., *Brooklands: Behind the Scenes* (Yeovil, Haynes, 1980)

Colonel John Murray 'Ivan' Cobbold

Dismore, J., *The Voice from the Garden: Pamela Hambro and the Tale of two Families Before and After the Great War* (Bristol, SilverWood, 2012)

Eastwood, J. and T. Moyse, *The Men who Made the Town: The Official History of Ipswich Town F.C. since 1878* (Sudbury, Almeida Books, 1986)

Faber, D., *Munich, 1938: Appeasement and World War II* (London, Simon & Schuster, 2008)

Country Life, No. 2017, September 1935

Military Service

Field Marshal Herbert Charles Onslow Plumer, GCB GCMG GCVO

Badsey, S., 'Plumer, Herbert Charles Onslow, first Viscount Plumer (1857–1932)', *Oxford Dictionary of National Biography* (Oxford University Press, 2004; online edn, January 2011)

Harington, C., *Plumer of Messines* (London, John Murray, 1935)

Plumer, H., *An Irregular Corps in Matabeleland* (London, Kegan Paul, Trench, Trübner & Co., 1897)

Powell, G., *Plumer: The Soldier's General* (London, Leo Cooper, 1990)

Sykes, F. W., *With Plumer in Matabeleland: an account of the Matabeleland relief force during the rebellion of 1896* (London, Constable, 1897)

Bernard Cyril (Tiny) Freyberg, VC GCMG KCB KBE DSO, 1st Baron Freyberg

Freyberg, P., *Bernard Freyberg V.C. Soldier of Two Nations* (London, Hodder and Stoughton, 1991)

Sellers, L., *The Hood battalion: Antwerp, Gallipoli, France, 1914–18* (London, Leo Cooper, 1995)

Stevens, W. G., *Freyberg V.C., the man, 1939–1945* (London, Jenkins, 1965)

Wards, I., 'Freyberg, Bernard Cyril, first Baron Freyberg (1889–1963)', *Oxford Dictionary of National Biography* (Oxford University Press, 2004; online edn, January 2011)

Peter Charles Victor Cobbold

Dickson, J., 'Peter Cobbold and the Long Nawang Massacre' (unpublished, May 2013)

Fisher, J. C. B., Consolidated report for the Information of the Sarawak Govt Agent, London, concerning 'Missing Sarawak Govt. Officers, Company Officials, their Wives and Children' (undated)

McKerracher, W., Report on proceedings before, leading up to and covering the evacuation of the Borneo Company's Staff from Sibu and the Rejang Timber Concession (2 May 1942)

Ooi Keat Gin, *The Japanese Occupation of Borneo, 1941–1945* (Abingdon, Routledge, 2011)

Brigadier Simon Fraser, DSO MTCD, 15th Lord Lovat

Fraser, S., 15th Lord Lovat, *March past: a Memoir* (London, Weidenfeld & Nicolson, 1978)

Melville, M. L., *The Story of the Lovat Scouts* 1900–1980 (Kinloss, Librario, 2003)

Messenger, C., *The Commandos, 1940–46* (London, Grafton, 1991)

Warner, P., 'Fraser, Simon Christopher Joseph, fifteenth Lord Lovat and fourth Baron Lovat (1911–1995)', *Oxford Dictionary of National Biography* (Oxford University Press, 2004; online edn, September 2013)

Obituary, *The Times*, 28 March 1994

INDEX

NB: A number in parentheses following the name of an individual is a unique search reference for that person on the Cobbold family tree at www.cobboldfht.com.

Page numbers in **bold** indicate the main biography section for that individual.

Abbey Church, Malew, Isle of Man 91
Abyssinia 109–12
Academy of Athens 173
Academy of Science, Philadelphia 157
Achi Baba 215
Achnacarry 230
Adair, Hugh 20, 21
Addenbrooke's Hospital, Cambridge 173
Adelaide 86, 89
Aden 109, 207
African Corps 119
Aigburth Cricket Ground, Liverpool 176
Air Corps 217
Airborne Division, 6th 233, 234
Airy, George Biddell 151
Albania 168, 169
Albemarle, New South Wales 94–5
Albion Hotel, Viti Levu 93
Alcock and Brown 182, 191
Alcock, Rutherford 123, 124, 126, 128
Aldeburgh Festival 83
Aldershot 131, 209
Aldershot FC 199
Aldrich (sub-commissioner, Ipswich wet dock) 16
Alexander III, Tsar 107
Alexander, Frances Gordon 52
Alexander the Great 173
Alexandra, Princess of Wales 73
Alexandria 133
Alfington, Devon 44
Alfred, Prince, Duke of Edinburgh 87
Algiers 51
Aliartus, Greece 170
All Saints, Ayr 167
All Stretton 161
Allen, Mary 42
Allied Military Mission to Greece 172
Almaty (see Verniy)
Alps, The 44
American War of Independence 119

Amhuinnsuidhe Castle 50–1
Amoy 123, 124
Amys, Anne (4148) 154
Amys, Frances Phillippa (175) 154
Amys, John (1103) 154
Anatolia 132
Anatomy Act (1832) 153
Ancre, Battle of 216
Anderson, A. W. 225, 226
Anderson Street, Melbourne 88
Andrews, John 11–2, 14
Anglesea Road, Ipswich 27
Angling 111, 112, 197
Anglo-Russian Convention 135
Anglo-Scottish Cattle Company 234
Angus Evening Telegraph, The 229
Ann Duthie (ship) 92–3
  Anna (ship) 86, 88
Antwerp 214
ANZAC 210
ANZAC Cove (*see* Ari Burnu)
Apthorp Wheelwright, Charles 147
Arbuthnot, Hester Marion (290) 181
Arbuthnot, William Reierson (1152) 181
Argentina 234
Argus, The (newspaper) 87
Ari Burnu (ANZAC Cove) 215
Arkell, William Jocelyn 161
Armstrong, Benjamin 119
Armstrong, John 103
Arran 156
Arrow (ship) 125
Ascot Racecourse 75, 76
Ashley Cooper, Patrick 140
Ashmolean Museum, Oxford 59
Aspall, parish of 10
Aspall Cyder 9, 14
Aspall Hall 1, 9, 10, 13, 131
  lunatic asylum 13
Asquith, Arthur 214, 215
Asquith, H. H. 28, 136, 214

Athens 170, 172
Athletics 177, 190
Atkin, Joseph 41, 42
Atlantic Wall, Normandy 233
Atlee, Clement 141
Auckland 44, 45
Augusta, Empress of Germany 26
Austen, Jane 65
Australia 48, 75, 84–5, 86–91, 92–3, 94–8,
    136, 172, 194, 223, 226, 234
  Army 209
  Chevallier barley and 12
  Goldrush 86–7
  sugar plantations 46
  stock rearing 89, 94–8
  transportation to 5, 35, 38
Australian Banking Crisis, 118
Authoringa, Queensland 96
Ayr 167

Bacon, Bacon, Cobbold & Co. (bank) 7
Bacon, Cobbold & Co. (bank) 23, 138
Bacon, Cobbold, Rodwell, Dunningham and
    Cobbold (bank) 7, 15
Bacon, Cobbold and Tollemache (bank) 23
Bad Kissingen 112
Baden-Powell, Robert 208–9
Badingham, Suffolk 10, 11, 146
Bahamas, The, 113
Bailey, Malcolm 176
Bailleul, Pas-de-Calais 216
Baird, George 75
Baker, Valentine 207
Balkhash, Lake 108
Ballasalla, Isle of Man 86, 91
Balliol College, Oxford (see Oxford
    University, Colleges)
Balmoral 200
Balsall Heath, Birmingham 123
Baltimore 75
Banco Italo-Britannica 139
Bancroft Theatre Company 74
Bandung, Indonesia 225
Bangalore, RMS (ship) 88
Bangkok 124
Banjarmasin, Borneo 223
Bank Islands 45
Bank of England, 54, 115, 120, 138,
    139–42, 143
Bank of Madras 181

Bank of Victoria 87
Barber, David 176
Baring, Evelyn 133
Barnby, Joseph 81
Barnes Bridge, London 185
Baron, R. N. 226
Barwell Jones Ltd. 8
Batavia 225
Bath 119, 154, 156
Bathe, Henry de 76
Bathurst, Henry 6–7
Battenberg, Louis 73
Bavaria 112
Bean, Roy 75
Beatty, Laura 73
Beaucourt, Franche-Comté 216
Beaufort Castle 228, 230, 234
Beccles 64, 99
Beethoven, Ludwig van 78
Beit, Alfred 112
Belaga, Sarawak 224
Belgian Motorcycle Grand Prix 193
Belgium 230
Bell, Gertrude 26
Bellingham, John 120
Bendigo's Creek, Victoria 86–7
Bengal 139
Bénouville, Normandy 233, 234
Bentley, Suffolk 19
Ber Street, Norwich 64
Berbera 109, 110
Bere, Thomas 59
Berlin 79
  Congress of (see Congress of Berlin)
Bernhardt, Sarah 73, 74
Best, George 177
Béthune, Pas-de-Calais 113
Birdcage Walk, London 201
Birmingham 123, 156
Birmingham Natural History and Micro-
    scopial Society 157
Birmingham University 163
Birnie, Captain 92
Black Forest 165
Black Watch 228
Blackbirding 46, 47, 48, 94
Blackburn Olympic FC 178
Blackburn Rovers FC 179
Blackwall, London 19
Blatchly, John 5

Bletchley Park 217, 229,
Blimp, Colonel (cartoon character) 206
Bloomsbury and Inns of Court Volunteers
    121
Bloxwich, Staffordshire 122
Blue Bank, Ipswich 7
Bluff Harbour, New Zealand 87
Board of Education 78
Board of Victorian Railways 89
Bobby, Rebecca 40
Boer War, Second 109, 134–5, 209, 228–9
Bognor Regis 195
Bohemia 165
Bolivar, Simon 7
Bombay 135
Bomfrey, Mrs 224
Borneo 142–3, 205, 221–7
Borneo Company Ltd. 221, 222, 224, 226
Boroondara Cemetery, Melbourne 91
Boston, Massachusetts 139, 147
Boulogne 231
Bourne, Gilbert Charles (4912) 184
Bourne, Robert Croft (1187) 174, **184–9**
Bourne, Robert M. A. (1598) 188
Bournemouth 73, 165, 182
Bow, London 77
Bowring, John 125
BP 143
Bracebridge, Ontario 100
Bradley, Percy 192
Brahms, Johannes 78
Braithwaite, John 18
Bramall Lane, Sheffield (football stadium)
    179
Bramford 78
Brandon 19
Brands Hatch 192–3
Brassey, Thomas 19
Brentwood, Essex 18
Bretton Woods 141
Bréville, Normandy 234
Brewery Tap, The, Ipswich 4
Brewster, Percy 192
Brighton 192
Brisbane 96
Brisbane Tramway Company 97
Bristol 172
Bristol University 172
Britannia Adelphi Hotel, Liverpool 230
British 3rd Infantry 233

British Academy 168, 173
British Association 164, 165
British Championship (football tournament)
    179–80
British Expeditionary Force 137, 209
British Library xi
British Medical Association, 200
British Motorcycle Racing Club (BMCRC,
    later Bemsee) 192, 195
British Museum 121, 156
British Open Golf Championship 184
British Petroleum (see BP)
British School of Athens 168–9, 173
British Somaliland 109
British South Africa Company 208
Britten, Benjamin 82–3
Brodrick, St John 109
Brompton Oratory, London 229
Brook, Norman 142
Brooke, Bertram 223
Brooke, Charles Vyner 221, 223
Brooke, James 221
Brooke, Rupert 214, 215
Brooketon Mine, Brunei 222
Brooklands 174, 190–3, 194–5
Broome Park, Kent 136
Broseley, Staffordshire 160
Broughton, Henry John Delves 229
Broughton, Rosamond Delves (2343) 229,
    230
Brown (young sailor) 92
Browne, Denis 214
Bruff, Peter 18, 19
Brunei, Sultanate of 142, 221, 222, 225
Buck, Martha 41
Buckingham Palace 112
Buffalo Stadium, Paris 194
Bulair, Turkey 215
Bulawayo 208–9
Bull, John (motorcycle accessories) 192
Buller, Redvers 209
Bulwer, James Redfoord 21
Bulwer-Lytton, Margaret Hermione Millicent
    (491) 139
Burke, Edmund 117–8
Burkhun, Russian Central Asia 108
Burma 106
Burney, Charles 62
Burnham, Frederick Russell 209
Bury St Edmunds 19, 62

Bury St Edmunds Grammar School 10, 15, 146
Bute, Earl of (Prime Minister) 10
Butler, Arthur Gray 99–100
Byron, Lord 234

Cain, Eleanor (8033) 88, 91
Cain, Horace William (229) 84–5, **86–91**, 97
Cain, Robert 86
Cain, Robert (b.1879) (1869) 88, 120
Cain, Walter (1870) 88
Cain, Willie (368) 88
Cairns, Hester (1179) 188
Cairns, Wilfred Dallas (321) 188
Cairo 51–2, 53, 134, 216
Caistor, Thomas 6
Caldwell, Diana 229
California 12
Camberley 207, 216
Camberwell Green, London 77
Cambridge 19, 131, 164, 173
Cambridge, Lord 131
Cambridge University 140, 144, 145, 146–7, 148, 174
    Athletics Club 177
    Boat Race and 184, 185–7, 188, 189
    Colleges
        Clare 167, 169, 172, 173
        Gonville and Caius 36, 144, 168
        Jesus 177
        King's 23, 25, 42, 139
        Newnham 169
        Pembroke 146
        St Catharine's 146, 147
        Trinity 196
    Football Club 177
    Lawn Tennis Club 177
Cambridgeshire Cricket Team 177, 181
Cameron, Stella Willoughby Savile (348) 138
Campbell-Bannerman, Henry 27–8, 135
Canada 84, 99–105, 113–4, 197, 198, 234
Canal de Caen 233
Candler, Ann 67
Canons, Stanmore 118
Canterbury 136
Canterbury, Viscount 87
Canton 123, 124–5, 126, 128
Cape Colony 208

Cape of Good Hope 92
Cape Helles 215
Cape Horn 92
Cape Town 208
Capie, Forrest 140, 142
Capital and Counties Bank 7
Caradoc, Caer 162
Caradoc Field Club 162
Caradoc and Severn Valley Field Club 162, 163
Cardiff 217
Carlton, Richard 62
Carnatic, The 117
Carnival Handicap (horse race) 98
Caroline of Brunswick 120
Carpentaria Downs, Queensland 95–6
Carrington, Richard 151
Cassar, George H. 137
Castle Hotel, Richmond upon Thames 193
Catchpole, Margaret 5, 38–9, 58, 66–7, 176
Catto, Lord 141
Cavendish, Blanche (449) 197, 201
Cavendish, Michael 62
Cavendish, Suffolk 62
Cavendish, Victor, 9th Duke of Devonshire (2452) 197
Cenotaph, The 204
Central Asia xii, 50, 106–9
Cesarewitch (horse race) 75
Chamberlain, Neville 200,
Chancery Lane, London 121
Chandos, Street, London 156
Charity Commission 28
Charles V, Holy Roman Emperor 61
Charlton Hill, Shropshire 165
Charterhouse School 153, 176–7
Charteris, John 211
Chatham 131
Chelmsford 82
Chelsea, London 78
Cheltenham College 176
Cherry Tree, The, Wortham 41
Chester (racehorse) 95
Chevallier family
    business interests
        Chevallier barley 1, 9, 11–3, 14
        cider making 1, 9–10, 14
        farming 10, 11
    French origins 9
    unions with Cobbold family 1, 9, 29

Chevallier, Alicia (3350) 147, 151
Chevallier, Anthony Rudolph 9, 149
Chevallier, Barrington (2027) 11, 13
Chevallier, Catherine (2120) 147, 151–2
Chevallier, Charles (2050) 10, 11
Chevallier, Charles Henry (206) 9, 11
Chevallier, Clement (2055) 10, 11
Chevallier, Clement Benjamin (1330) 9, 10
Chevallier, Frances Ann 'Fanny' (731) 11, 131
Chevallier, George (2020) 11
Chevallier, Harriet Temple (78) 9, 144
Chevallier, John (b.1774) (729), 1, **9–14**, 17, 144
Chevallier, John (b.1817) (2024) 11
Chevallier, John Barrington Trapnell (207) 9
Chevallier, Richard Edgcumbe (2122) 151
Chevallier, Temple (d.1722) 9
Chevallier, Temple (b.1731) 10
Chevallier, Temple (b.1794) (2116) 11, 143, **146–52**
Chevallier, Temple (b.1833) (2119) 147, 151
Chevallier, Temple Fiske (2054) 10, 11
Chevallier, Thomas (2115), 196
Chevalyir, Jourdam 9
Chicago 75
Child, Beatrice (225) 96–7
Chile 12
China 8, 107, 114, 122, 123–6, 128–9, 160
Chinese Turkestan 107, 109
Chiswick 187
Christ Church, South Yarra, Melbourne 91
Christchurch Park and Mansion, Ipswich 23, 25, 26, 27, 28
Christy, Millicent Adela (317) 112
Church Stretton 161, 162, 163, 165, 166
Church Stretton Illustrated 162, 163
Churchill, Winston 110, 130, 214, 217, 218, 219, 234
Chusan, China 123
Cider Act (1763) 10
Clark, Christine 12–3
Clarke, Henry Lowther 90–1
Clarke, William (2712) 66
Cliff Brewery, Ipswich 4, 5, 8, 197
Cliff House, Ipswich 4, 5, 6, 68
Clifton College 172
Coan Downs, New South Wales 89
Cobalt, Ontario 104, 113
Cobb & Co. 95–6
Cobbett, William 33

Cobbold family
  business interests
    banking 1, 2, 7, 8, 15, 17, 20, 21, 23–4, 26, 138
    brewing 1, 3–4, 5, 6, 8, 26, 196, 197
    coal 1, 5, 8
    corn trade 1, 5, 8
    farming 25, 26, 28, 95–7, 98
    football (*see* Ipswich Town FC)
    malting 3, 5, 8
    railways 2, 9, 13–4, 15, 17–20, 21
    shipping 1, 8, 19–20
    wine 8
  charity 20, 22, 26, 27, 28, 37, 64, 67, 68, 70, 98
  Members of Parliament 20, 24, 27–8, 132, 197
Cobbold & Co. (bank) 7
Cobbold & Co. Ltd. 201
Cobbold, Alfred (136) 20
Cobbold, Alfred Townshend (253) 78
Cobbold, Alice 64
Cobbold, Alistair Philip (472) 201
Cobbold, Anthony (539) xii, xiv, 236
Cobbold, Arthur Thomas (138) 88, 92, 96
Cobbold, Barbara Elizabeth 205
Cobbold, Cameron Fromanteel (490) 115, **138–43**
Cobbold, Charles Spencer Waller (293) 155
Cobbold, Clement John Fromanteel (347) 138
Cobbold, Clive (446) 181
Cobbold Commission 142–3
Cobbold, Edgar Sterling (250) 144–5, **160–6**
Cobbold, Edith Caroline (304) 154
Cobbold, Edward (108) 39
Cobbold, Edward Augustus (172) 153, 176
Cobbold, Elizabeth (née Knipe) (58) 4–5, 6, 8, 36, 37, 57, **65–70**
Cobbold, Elizabeth (née Wilkinson) (57) 4, 8, 66
Cobbold, Elizabeth Harriet, (155) 161
Cobbold, Emma 61
Cobbold, Emily Caroline (157) 4
Cobbold, Evelyn (née Murray) (308) 30, **50–6**, 106, 174, 196
Cobbold Family History Trust xii, xiii, 236
Cobbold, Felix Thornley (201) 2, 16, 21, **23–8**

Cobbold, Francis Edward (223 82, 88, 89,
    92–8
Cobbold, Frederick (99) 4
Cobbold, Fredrick Forbs (305) 158
Cobbold, George Thomas (2860) 221
Cobbold, Georgiana (291) 181
Cobbold, Gillian (1683) 195
Cobbold, Gordon Chevallier (337) 174,
    190–5
Cobbold, Henry Gallant (98) 4
Cobbold, Herbert Spencer (287) 180, 181
Cobbold, Horace John 'Jack' Templer (7593)
    222, 226
Cobbold, Isobel Amy, (208) 9, 216
Cobbold, Isobella Frances 'Fanny' (205) 9,
    131
Cobbold, Jean (573) 197
Cobbold, Joan Lindley (398) 58, **77–83**
Cobbold, John (56) 1, **3–8**, 30, 36, 38, 65,
    66, 67, 99
Cobbold, John Cavendish (575) 196, 201, 203
Cobbold, John Chevallier (114) 1–2, 7,
    13–14, **15–22**, 23, 94, 138
Cobbold, John Dupuis (307) 21, 24, 52, 53,
    106, 196, 197–8
Cobbold, John Murray (448) 52, 174,
    196–203
Cobbold, John Patteson (186) 18, 21, 23,
    24, 27, 106, 188
Cobbold, John Wilkinson (77) 4, 6, 7, 8, 9,
    13–14, 16, 17, 18, 22, 26, 92, 144
Cobbold, Katherine (125) 26
Cobbold, Lucy (182) 198
Cobbold, Mary (85) 4
Cobbold, Matthew 59, 61
Cobbold, Monty (326) 190
Cobbold, Nathanael Fromanteel (195) 24,
    138, 197, 198
Cobbold, Olive (320) 188
Cobbold, Pamela (452) 52, 54, 140
Cobbold, Pamela Maud (570) 197
Cobbold, Patrick (576) 8, 197, 201
Cobbold, Paul (260) 103, 105
Cobbold, Peter Charles Victor (7595) 205,
    221–7
Cobbold, Philip Wyndham (324) 198, 199,
    201
Cobbold, Ralph Hamilton (454) 112
Cobbold, Ralph Patteson (316) xi, 85,
    106–13, 188

Cobbold, Reginald Louis 204
Cobbold, Richard (b.1797) (106) 5, 29–30,
    36–42, 43, 57, 65, 67, 68, 153, 154,
    176
Cobbold, Richard Wilkie (170) 153
Cobbold, Robert George (7596) 22
Cobbold, Robert Henry (148) 160
Cobbold, Robert Knipe (100) 6, 99
Cobbold, Robert Nevill (470) 199, 201
Cobbold, Rowland Francis (258) 115, 206
Cobbold, Rowland Hope (407) 58, 167
Cobbold, Rowland Townshend (150) 160
Cobbold, Sarah Jane (227) 88, 93
Cobbold, Thomas (b.1680) (31) 3–4
Cobbold, Thomas (b.1708) (44) 4, 30
Cobbold, Thomas (b.1742) (51) 4, 30, 32,
    36, 37
Cobbold, Thomas Clement (191) 16, 21, 24,
    132, 197, 198
Cobbold, Thomas Spencer (174) 37, 144,
    153–9
Cobbold, William (b.1530) 57, **59–64**
Cobbold, William (b.1560) 57, **59–64**
Cobbold, William (b.1784) (88), 6
Cobbold, William Nevill (289) 174,
    176–83
Cobbold, William Rust, (71) 29, **31–5**
Cobbold, Winifred (450) 52
Cobbold's Point, Felixstowe 21, 24
Coke, Gertrude (1721) 50–1
Coke, Winifred 51
Colchester 6, 17, 18, 19, 20
Cole, Elizabeth (730) 11
Coleridge, Edward 43, 44
Coleridge, John Duke 49
Coleridge, Samuel Taylor 16, 43
Coleridge-Taylor, Samuel 78
Collier, John 27
Collingwood Battalion 216
Collins Street, Melbourne 87
Collyer, Henry 33
Cologne 212
Colonial Office 221
Comley, Staffordshire 163–4
Commandos 230–3
Compasses, The, Selborne (public house)
    32, 33
Concorde (supersonic jet) 195
Conder, Claude 131–2
Congress of Berlin 132

Conquistador (racehorse) 97, 98
Conservative Party 20, 21, 24, 188
Constable, John 66
Constantinople 135
Corbett, B. O. 178
Corinthian Football Club 178, 179, 180
Cornell, Martyn 12
Cornhill, Ipswich 7, 21
Cornwallis, Lord 118
Coronet Theatre, Notting Hill 79
Corrie, George Elwes 11, 147–8, 151,
Cotman, Thomas William 7, 21, 24
Country Life, magazine 197
Court of Exchequer 116, 117, 120
Courtauld's 141
Coward, Noël 231
Cox, Cobbold & Co. (bank) 24
Cox, G.V. 32
Craig, Edward Gordon 79, 83
Crane Hall, nr. Ipswich 17
Cranmer House, Felixstowe (*see* Lodge, The,
    Felixstowe)
Cransford, Suffolk 10, 11
CREFORCE 217
Crete 170, 213, 217, 218. 220
Cricket 43–4, 148, 177, 181, 188, 196, 198,
    207, 212
Cripps, Stafford 141
Crosse, John Green 153
Crostwight, Norfolk 61
Crown Street. Ipswich 7
Crystal Palace Speedway 193
Cumberland Goldmine, Queensland 95–6
Curzon, Lord (Viceroy of India) 107, 135
Cutlers Row, Norwich 59
Cyprus 132, 170
Czechoslovakia 230

D-Day 205, 231–4
Daily Mail 136
Dalhousie, Lord 197
Dallas, Robert 117
Damascus 53
Dandenong, SS (ship) 93
Danieli Hotel, Venice 218
Dapper, Carl von 112
Dardanelles (*see* also Gallipoli) 136, 188
Darling, River 94
Darwin, Charles 155
Davis, John Francis 123

Dawson, Harry 131
Day, Francis 158
Day, Robin 142
Dayan, Moshe 170
Dearmer, Mabel 80
Dearmer, Percy 79–80, 81
Deasy, Hugh H.P. 107
Debenham, Suffolk 9, 11
Dedham, Essex 161,
Deer Stalking 53, 197, 228
Derby, The (horse race) 184
Despard, Edward Marcus 119–20
Dickens, Charles 69
Dickson Brothers, Melbourne 93
Dickson, William Hill (228) 88, 93
Dieppe Raid 231
Dinapore 207
Diss 13, 17, 19, 62
Dodge, Johnny 214
Dolphin, The, Wortham (public house) 41
Dongola, Sudan 134
Douglas, Isle of Man 86
Downing Street, London 128
Downton, Wiltshire 120
Dove, Edward 11
Dover 176, 216,
Down, Mabel Frances (7591) 221
Drag Hunting 207
Duncan, A. Scott 199
Duncan, Isadora 79
Dunkirk 214–5
Dupuis family 29
Dupuis, Adele (187) 106
Durham 146, 150, 151
Durham Cathedral 63, 152
Durham University 144, 146, 147, 148,
    149–51, 152
Dutch Borneo 223
Dutch East Indies 221
Dykes, John Bacchus 81

Earlswood Asylum for Idiots, Redhill 154
East Anglia
    Huguenot population 9
    railways (*see* Railways, East Anglia)
    Swing Riots and 31
East India Company 10, 116, 117
East Grinstead 181
East Suffolk Council 28
Eastbourne 192

Eastbourne, New Zealand 213
Eastern Counties Railway 14, 17–20
Eastern Union Railway 19–20
Eastwood, John 199
Eaton Place, London 72
Eaton Terrace, London 138
Echuca, Victoria 89
Eckstein, Herman (6117) 112
Edict of Nantes (1685) 9
Edinburgh 50, 77, 157, 168
Edinburgh Club 157
Edinburgh Medical Journal 153
Edinburgh University 10, 153–4
Edward VI, King 60
Edward VII, King, ('Bertie', Prince of Wales)
    71, 73, 75, 76, 109, 136, 156, 186
Edward VIII (as Prince of Wales) 186
Efate 94
Egypt 51–3, 133, 136, 207, 215, 229
Eighth Army (British) 218, 220
El Alamein 139, 217, 218, 219
El Teb, Sudan 207
Elan Valley, Wales 161
ELAS 171–2
Eldon, Earl of 120
Elgin, Lord 125–6
Eliot, T.S. 82
Elizabeth I, Queen 9, 62
Elizabeth II, Queen 219
Elizabeth Street, Melbourne 88
Elliston, Sarah (139) 88
Emmanuel Church, Hampstead 78
England Football Team 176, 178–80, 188
England, Gordon 195
English Channel 121, 151, 216, 231
Enigma Machine 230
Epirus, Greece 168, 172
Epsom 6
Esh, County Durham 144, 147–8
Essendon Park, Hertfordshire 192
Este, Thomas 62
Eton College 23, 43–4, 74, 106, 116, 122,
    139, 143, 176, 184, 188, 196, 206
Exeter Cathedral 44
Exeter City FC 199
Eye, Suffolk 6, 37
Eyre, James 116

FA Cup 178, 180, 184
Faiyum Oasis, Egypt 52

Falconberg School, Beccles 99
Faraday, Michael 157
Farjeon, Eleanor 81
Faroe Islands 230
Farr, Charles Cobbold (266) 84–5, **99–105**,
    112–3
Farr Drive, Haileybury 105
Farr, Emily Ruth Kipawa (736) 102
Farr, John (158) 99
Fashoda Incident 134
F. E. Cobbold Trust 98
Felix Cobbold Trust 28
Felixstowe 2, 21, 23, 24–6
Felixstowe Cottage, Felixstowe (*see* Lodge,
    The, Felixstowe)
Feltham, Middlesex 195
Feniton Court, Devon 44
Fenne, George 61
Fettes College, Edinburgh 168
Fielding, William 119
Fifth US Army 218
Fiji 44, 46, 93
Finch (Orwell pilot) 16
First Division (English football) 203
First Home Rule Bill (*see* Government of
    Ireland Bill)
First Opium War (*see* Opium War, First)
First World War (*see* World War I)
Fishing (*see* Angling)
Fitzgibbon, Edmund 88
Fives 177
Flanders 138, 181, 212, 232
Flass Hall, County Durham 147–8
Flatman, John 42
Fleming, Philip 187
Flemington Racecourse 98
Flinders Lane, Melbourne 93
Flinders River 97
Florence 218
Folkestone 176
Fonnereau, William Neale, (2351) 26
Foot, 65th 206, 208
Foot, 84th 206
Football 174, 176–181, 182–3, 188, 190,
    196, 198–203, 236
Football Association, The 176, 178, 180,
    199, 203
Football League, The 199–200
Football Museum, Hitchin 179
Forbes, Edward 154

Fore Street, Ipswich 5, 26
Foreign Office, London 53, 108, 110, 122, 124, 128–9, 132, 234
Forest Home, Queensland 96
Fort Charog, Russian Turkestan 109
Fort George, Scotland 119
Fort Kipawa, Quebec 101–2
Fort Temiskaming, Quebec 103
Fort William 230
Foster, W. D. 158
France 119, 121, 131, 134, 139, 141, 165, 194, 230
    Revolutionary 5, 117, 119
    World War I and (*see* World War I, Western Front)
    World War II and (*see* D-Day)
Franco-Prussian War 131
Fraser, Andrew (6679) 230
Fraser, Clan 229
Fraser, Peter 217
Fraser, Simon Augustine (6675) 230, 234
Fraser, Simon Christopher Joseph, 15th Lord Lovat (2342) 204–5, **228–35**
Fraser, Simon Joseph (6659) 228, 229
French, David 136
French, John 137, 209
French Motorcycle Grand Prix 193
Freyberg, Bernard Cyril (3174) 204, **213–20**
Freyberg, Oscar 215
Freyberg, Paul (2079) 216
Fromanteel, Abraham 138
Fromanteel, Ahasuerus 138
Fromanteel, Martha (2283) 138
Fry, Charles Burgess 177, 183, 188
Fuchow 123, 124
Fuji, Mount 127
Fulford, Bessie (224) 96
Fulham 195
Fulham Avenue, South Yarra 98
Fulham Road, London 191

Gainsborough, Thomas 4
Galle, Johann 150
Gallipoli 188, 213, 215–6, 219, 229
Gardner, Daniel 3, 66
Garnham, Israel, 41
Gascoigne, Mary 62
Garrow, William 119, 120
Gebhard, Freddie 75

General Aircraft 195
Gentleman's Magazine, The 35
Geological Magazine 164
Geological Society 160, 161
Geological Survey 165
George III, King 119, 120, 121
George IV, King (*see* Prince Regent, The)
George V, King 212
George VI, King (also as Prince Albert) 186, 200,
Germany 200
Gibson, Alfred 176
Gibson, Ron 192
Gilgit 107
Gillingham, Norfolk 99
Gippeswyk Park, Ipswich 28
Gladstone, William 12–3, 24, 128
Glasgow 167
Glassbrook, Roger 148
Glemham Hall, Suffolk 197, 198
Glenapp, MV (ship) 221
Glencarron Estate, Wester Ross 53, 56
Godalming 176
Goddard, Daniel Ford 27
Gold Standard 140
Golders Green, London 113
Goldsbrough Mort and Co. 89
Goldsmith, Oliver 74
Goldsmith's Company of Norwich (*see* Norwich, Goldsmith's Company of)
Golf 181, 184
Gonville and Caius College, Cambridge (*see* Cambridge University, Colleges)
Goodenough, W. H. 208
Goodsir, John 154
Goodwood Racecourse 76
Gordon, Charles 133, 134
Gordon Creek 104
Gorée, (West African island) 119
Gorgopotamos Viaduct, Greece 170
Goss, Annie Constance (2547) 207, 208
Government of Ireland Bill (First Home Rule Bill) 24
Government of India xii, 50, 108, 109
Goward, Mary Anne 67
Gowing, Richard 38
Grace, W. G. 181
Graham, Gerald 207
Grand Junction Railway 19
Grant, James Hope 125, 126

Grant, William 121
Graves-Sawle, Rosemary (319) 113
Gravesend 44
Gray, Frank 188
Gray, W. R. 177
Great Eastern Railway 20
Great Game, The xii, 50, 106–9
Great Marsden, Lancashire 88
Great Ouseburn, North Yorkshire 116
Great White Horse Hotel, Ipswich 199
Greece 145, 168–72, 173, 213, 217
Greenwich 151
Greenwich School 4
Grenville, George (Prime Minister) 10
Greville, Sydney 107
Grierson, James 209
Griffin, A. F. R. 224, 226
Griffith, Guy 173
Guards' Chapel 197, 201, 202
Guild, Ivry (1808) 216
Guilford, 8th Earl of 197
Gulf of Carpentaria, Australia 95, 96, 97
Gulf of Pechili, China 125
Gulf of Saros, Turkey 215
Gunsborough House, Listowel 131
Gustav V (King of Sweden) 188
Gützlaff, Karl 123,
Gützlaff, Mary 123
Gwalior 207

Hadleigh, Suffolk 19, 25, 28
Haider Ali 117
Haig, Douglas 209, 210, 211
Haileybury, Ontario 99, 102, 103–5, 112–3
Haileybury School 99–100
Haileyburian and Temiscaming Mining Journal, The
       104
Hair (musical) 143
Hajj 50, 55–6, 196
Haldane, R. B. 209
Hale, Hori 33, 35
Halley's Comet 149–50
Hambro, Charles (453) 54, 140
Hammersmith Bridge, London 186
Hammond, James Vavasour, (3819) 167
Hammond, Laura Annie (551) 167
Hammond. Nicholas G. L. (3823), 145,
       167–73
Hammond Bammel, Caroline Penrose 169
Hampshire, HMS (ship) 137

Hampstead, London 77, 78–9
Hampstead Conservatoire 79
Hanbury-Tracy, Algernon 109–10
Hanbury-Williams, John 141
Happy Valley, Kenya 229
Harar 110, 111
Hardelot, Pas-de-Calais 231
Harding, Aaron 33–5
Haringey (speedway track) 193
Harington, Charles 206, 211
Harley Davidson Motorcycles 190
Harley Street, London 155
Harper Gow, Max 228, 230, 235
Harrington, John 110
Harris, Isle of 51
Harrison family, Wortham 40, 41
Harrison, John 34
Harrow School 151, 176
Harrow Weald 152
Hartismere, Suffolk 37
Hartop, Christopher 60
Harwich 3–4, 6, 19, 23
Hastings, Warren 117–8
Hatfield House, Hertfordshire 133
Haughley, Suffolk 19
Hauraki Regiment, 6th 213
Hay, Josslyn 229
Hayes Court, Kent 149
Haymarket Theatre, London 74
Hayter, Walter Louis Balzaine 181
Headley, Hampshire 35
Hejaz, The 53, 54
Hellenic Society, The 173
Helwan, Egypt 218
Henley-on-Thames 185
Henry VIII, King 59
Hepburn, Caroline (2016) 10–1
Hereford 64
Herne Bay 176
Highbury (football stadium) 198
Hill (Orwell pilot) 16
Hill-Wood, Samuel 198
Hindu Kush 107
Hintlesham, Suffolk 28
Hispano Suiza (car) 194
Hitchin 179
Hitler, Adolf 200
Hobhouse, Emily 134–5
Hodgson (ECR Director) 17
Holborn, London 191

Holdaway, Robert 33, 35
Holderness, Joan 61
Holkham Hall 50
Holmehurst Plantation, Fiji 94
Holst, Gustav 77, 78, 81
Holy Wells, Ipswich 3–4, 6–7, 21, 24, 52, 68
Hone, Ann 90
Hong Kong 122, 123, 125, 128
Hood Battalion 214, 216
Horace (Roman poet) 159
Horsa Bridge 233
Horsa Gliders 233
Horse Racing 75, 76, 95, 98, 184
House of Commons 12, 117–8, 120
House of Lords 28, 117, 125, 219, 234
Howard, Charles 62
Howard, John 233, 234
Howlett, George 40
Hudson's Bay Company 101–3, 143
Hughenden, Queensland 89, 97
Huguenots 9
Hull 156
Hulse, John 146–7
Humphrey's Depot, Ontario 101, 102
Hungary 178
Hunt, Edward 95, 96
Huron, Lake 101
Hussey, Thomas 149
Hyde Park, London 219

Iffley, Oxfordshire 184
Imperial General Staff 137
Imperial Theatre, London 76
Independent, The 228
Index Monasticus 3
India 8, 106, 107, 108, 109, 117, 118, 135, 139, 181, 197, 206–7, 217
Indian Civil Service 99, 100
Indonesia 143
Infantry Brigade, 88th 216
Inglott, Edmund 64
Inglott, William 64
International Fisheries Exhibition (1883) 158
International Monetary Fund 141
Invercargill, New Zealand 87
Inverleigh, Queensland 89, 97
Inverness 56
Inverness County Council 234

Ioannina, Greece 172, 173
Ipswich
  banking crisis (1825) 7
  Chevalliers and 13, 146
  Cobbolds and 3–4, 5, 6, 7, 8, 15, 16, 18, 19, 20, 21–2, 23, 24, 25, 26–7, 28, 29, 36, 52 66–7, 68–9, 70, 78, 92, 132, 138–9, 196, 197–201, 203
  development of 5, 15
  diamond jubilee celebrations (1897) 26–7
  football 174, 196–201, 203
  gaol 38
  garrison 5, 68
  general elections 20
  growth in population 5, 15
  hospitals 13, 27
  licensed premises 8
  Members of Parliament 20, 24, 132, 197
  public baths 25
  public parks 23, 25–6, 28
  racecourse 96
  railways 2, 13, 17, 18, 19
  society 5, 36, 68–9
  wet dock 2, 8, 16, 17
Ipswich AFC 16
Ipswich and East Suffolk Hospital 27
Ipswich Borough Asylum 13
Ipswich Borough Council 15
Ipswich Charity 20
Ipswich Conservative Association 24
Ipswich Corporation 8, 28
Ipswich Cricket, Football and Athletics Ground Co. Ltd. 198
Ipswich Dock Commission 16
Ipswich Journal, The 15, 16, 20, 21
Ipswich Lying-in Charity 67, 68
Ipswich Mechanics' Institution 20
Ipswich Savings Bank 20
Ipswich School of Art 20
Ipswich Society for Clothing for Infant Poor, 88
Ipswich Steam Navigation Company 19–20
Ipswich Theatre 67
Ipswich Town Council 26
Ipswich Town FC 174, 196, 197–201, 203, 236
Ipswich United FC 198–9
Ipswich Waterworks Company 20
Ipswich Working Men's College 20
Iraq 53

Ireland Football Team 178–9, 180
Irving, Henry 73
Isis, River 184
Isis Tavern, Iffley 184
Island Trading Company, Borneo 224
Isle of Man 86, 91, 191
Isle of Man Post Office 91
Isle of Wight 156
Italy 119, 139, 165, 201, 217, 218
ITV 142

Jacks, Philip 224, 225–6
Jackson, N. Lane 178
Jackson, Reverend 226
James, Charlotte (3348) 77
Jameson Leander Starr 208
Jameson Raid 208
J.A.P. Motorcycles 193
Japan 122, 126–8, 221
Japanese Air Force 223, 225
Japanese Imperial Army 221, 223, 225, 226–7
Jardine Matheson 128
Java 223, 225
Java, Battle of 225
Java Sea 225
Jeddah (see Jidda)
Jenkyns, Henry 147
Jermyn, Laetitia 66, 68, 69, 70
Jersey 9, 71–2, 73, 76, 167, 208
Jersey Opera House 76
Jervis-White-Jervis, Herbert (1424) 198
Jesus College, Cambridge (see Cambridge University, Colleges)
Jidda, Sa'udi Arabia 53, 54, 56
Jijiga, Ethiopia 110, 111
Jinnie M (motorboat) 104
Johannesburg 112
John Innes Centre, Norwich 14
Johnson, Samuel 3
Johnston, James 128
Jones, Arthur 73
Jupiter, Planet 150
Justerini & Brooks 112

Kaaba, The, Makkah 56
Kala-i-Wamar, Russian Turkestan 108
Kampong Kenyah, Borneo 227
Kapit, Sarawak 223, 224, 226
Kashgar, Chinese Turkestan 107–8

Kastamonu, Turkey 132
Kayan Tribe, Borneo 224
Kedington, Suffolk 11
Kendal 65–6
Kennington Oval 177, 178, 179, 180
Kensington, London 212
Kenya 56, 229
Kenyah Tribe, Borneo 224
Keswick family 128, 204
Keswick, James Johnstone (916) 128
Kevekiss, Captain 109
Khartoum 133, 134
Khedive of Egypt 207
Khotan, Chinese Turkestan 107
King Edward VI School, Birmingham 123
King's College, Cambridge (see Cambridge University, Colleges)
King's New Grammar School, Ottery St. Mary 43
King's Quay Street, Harwich 3
King's Royal Rifles 106
Kirby Hall 116
Kirbye, George 62
Kirkland Lake, Ontario 113
Kitchener, Henry Horatio (732) 131
Kitchener, Herbert Horatio (733) 11, 115, **130–7**, 209
Knebworth 139, 140, 143
Knipe, Robert (783) 65
Knight, D. F., 190
Krebs (trawler) 230
Krithia, Turkey 215
Kruger, Paul 208
Kuching, Sarawak 221, 222–3, 226, 227
Kumobun, Higasi 227
Kyoto 126, 127, 128

La Touche, James Digues 162
Labouchère, Henrietta 74
Labour Party 142, 234
Lake House, Knebworth 143
Lakeshore Goldmine, Ontario 113
Lancaster, Duchy of 117
Lancers, 16th 107
Lancet, The 155, 156, 159
Lands Department, Victoria 94
Langlo Downs, Queensland 128
Langtry, Edward 'Ned' (1248) 72–3, 75, 76
Langtry Farms 75
Langtry, Jeanne 73, 76

Langtry, Lillie (1243) 58–9, **71–6**
Langtry, Texas 75
Lansdowne, Marquess of (Foreign Secretary)
    109
Lapworth, Charles 163
Law, Edward (Lord Ellenborough) 117, 119
Lawford, Peter 234
Lawlor, Tom 103, 104
Lawlortown, Ontario 103
Lawrence, James 87
Lawrence, T. E. 53
League of Arts 81
Le Breton, Jane Penrose (1225) 58, 145, 167
Le Breton, Reggie (1238) 73
Le Breton, William Corbet (1229) 71–2, 74,
    75, 167
Le Mans 131
Leander Rowing Crew, Oxford University
    187
Leeds 77
Leibniz, Gottfried 146
Lessines, France 216
Levett-Scrivener, Egerton Bagot Byrd (3143)
    128
Levin, New Zealand 214
Levuka, Fiji 93, 94
Liberal Party 20, 24, 27–8, 188, 216
Licensing Act (1737) 143
Lilling Hall, North Yorkshire 116
Lilydale, Queensland 96
Limpopo River 209
Lincoln's Inn 23, 116, 120–1, 188
Linnean Society 69, 155
Lisle, Henry de Beauvoir de 216
Listowel 131
Listowel Downs, Queensland 97
Liverpool 17, 65, 86, 99, 176, 230
Liverpool Institute 86
Liverpool to Manchester railway line 17
Lloyd-George, David 28, 137
Lloyds Ave., Ipswich 7
Lloyds TSB 7
Loch, Henry Brougham 126
Locke, Joseph 19
Lodge, The, Felixstowe 21, 23, 24–5
Lofoten Islands 230
London 12, 25, 35, 38, 43, 53, 56, 65, 66,
    72–3, 74, 75, 77, 78, 91, 112, 113, 116,
    117, 124, 128, 133, 137, 138, 139, 143,
    154, 155, 157, 158, 159, 178, 191, 193,
        194, 197, 199, 200, 204, 207, 214,
        217, 229
    banking 7
    goldsmiths 59, 60
    railway links with East Anglia 13–4, 15,
        17, 19
    society 52, 72, 73
    theatre 67, 73, 74, 76, 143
    World War II and (*see* World War II, Blitz,
        The)
London Chartered Bank of Australia 87
London Evening Standard 206
London Gazette, The 33, 106,
London Geologists' Association 165
London Medical Society 156
London Street, Norwich 59
London Underground 211
London, University of 143
London Zoological Gardens 155
Long Eran, Borneo 225
Long Green, Wortham 37
Long Melford, Suffolk 176
Long Mynd, Shropshire 162–3
Long Nawang, Borneo 221, 224–7
Longiram, Borneo (*see* Long Eran)
Longley, Arthur 71–2
Loog Lake, Ontario 104
Louis XIV, King of France 9
Lovat Scouts 228–9, 230
Low, David 206
Lowndes Square, London 73
Loyalty Islands 45
Luard, Miss C. G. 80
Luckie, John 199
Lucknow 206
Ludgate Hill, London 35
Lytton, Alexander Edward John (2301) 139
Lytton, Edward Anthony (2300) 139
Lytton, Edward Robert, 1st Earl Lytton
    (3147) 139
Lytton, Victor Alexander George Robert, 2nd
    Earl Lytton (2298) 139

Mabbott, Maria (72) 32
Macartney, George 108
Macau 123
MacDonald, Ramsay 189
Macedonia 173, 229
MacKenzie, James 87
Macmillan, Harold 141, 142

MacPherson, Andrew 223, 224–5,
    227
MacPherson, Mrs 224, 226, 227
Mad Mullah, The (*see* Mohammed Abdullah
    Hassan)
Madinah, Sa'udi Arabia 54
Madowla Park, Victoria 89
Madras 117, 181
Mafeking 209
Magdalen College, Oxford (*see* Oxford
    University, Colleges)
Magoura, Queensland 96
Magpie Inn, The, Wortham 41
Mahakam River, Borneo 225
Mahdi, The (*see* Muhammed Ahmad)
Mahdists 134, 207
Maidstone 119
Makkah, Sa'udi Arabia 50, 53, 54–5, 56,
    196
Malaya 142
Malaysia 142–3
Maleme, Crete 217
Malew, Isle of Man 86, 91
Malew Curates' Endowment Fund 91
Malmesbury, Earl of 125
Malpas Lodge, Torquay 206
Malta 136, 212, 219
Maltby, Edward 149
Manchester 6, 17, 66, 156, 161, 178
Manchester United FC 199
Manchester University 165
Manipur, Burma 106
Manning, William 111
Manor House, St Margaret's Green, Ipswich
    4, 5, 66–7
Mansergh & Co. 161
Mansergh, James 161
Manx Society of Melbourne 91
Margaret Chessel (ship) 94
Mark Lane, London 12
Markham, Albert H 48
Marryat, Frederick 92
Marshall Aid 141
Marshbrook Gorge, Shropshire 163
Martin, Emilie (1230) 71
Mary, Princess 197
Mary, Queen 60
Masjid al-Har m, Makkah 56
Mason Science College, Birmingham 163
Matabele War, Second 208

Matabeleland 208–9
Matthews, Stanley 177
Mattocks, John 40, 41
Maunganui (ship) 214
May, Dorothy (3820) 167
May, William 16
Maxwell, John Grenfell 109
Mayfair, London 53
MCC, (Marylebone Cricket Club) 212
MCC, (Motorcycle Club) 192
McGill University, Montreal 143
Mcgregor, Gregor 7
McKerracher, W. 223, 224, 225–6
McLaren, Barbara (née Jekyll) (3175) 216
McLaren, Francis (4586) 216, 218
McQueen, Steve 214
Medina (*see* Madinah)
Meggs, Francis 32
Melanesia 16, 43, 44–9
Melanesian Mission 34–9
Melbourne 84–5, 86–91, 93, 94, 95, 96,
    161
Melbourne Cup (horse race) 98
Melbourne Exhibition 88
Melbourne Grammar School 91
Melbourne Hospital 87
Melbourne Metropolitan Board of Works 88
Melbourne Tramway Company 89
Menelik II, Emperor of Abyssinia 109, 110
Menin Gate, Ypres 211
Menin Road, Ypres 216,
Merest, James 36
Merman (racehorse) 75
Merton College, Oxford (*see* Oxford
    University, Colleges)
Messines, Belgium 211, 212
Mexican Civil War 214
Middlesex Hospital 155, 157, 158
Midland Bank 181
Midland Medical Miscellany, The 153
Milan 139
Miles (RTC employee) 224, 226
Millais, John Everett 71, 73
Millden Estate 197, 200
Millin, Bill 230, 232–3
Mills-Roberts, David 234
Milsom, John 62
Milton, John 62
Mina, Sa'udi Arabia 55, 56
Miranda Downs, Queensland 95,

Miri, Sarawak 221, 223, 225
Mitcham, Surrey 195
Mitchell, David 86, 88
Mitchell Downs, Queensland 97
Mitchell, Edward 89
Moffat, Hugh 8, 18, 19–20
Mohammed Abdullah Hassan 109
Monkira, Queensland 95
Monte Carlo 52, 76, 194
Monte Cassino, Italy 213, 218
Monte Piccolo, Italy 201
Montgomery, Bernard 220
Montreal 143
Moon, The (observations of) 150, 152
Mora Shima 226, 227
Morar, India 207
Moray Firth 119
Morley, John 135
Morley, Thomas 62
Morrison, John Robert 123
Mortlake, London 185, 187
Moscow 234
Moto (chief, Nukapu) 43
Motor Cycle, The (magazine) 193
Motorcycle Club (see MCC, Motorcycle
    Club)
Motorcycle Racing 174, 190–3, 195
Mountbatten, Louis 231
Moyse, Tony 199
Mozart, Wolfgang Amadeus 78
Mtobo Hills, Matabeleland 208–9
Muhammed Ahmad (The Mahdi) 133–4,
    207
Munich Crisis 200, 229
Munstead, Surrey 219
Murchison, Roderick Impey 156, 163
Murray, Charles Adolphus, 7th Earl of
    Dunmore (1720) 50, 51, 106–7
Muskoka, Ontario 100, 101, 103
Muskoka River 101
Muzdalifah, Sa'udi Arabia 56
Mysore 117

Nacton Heath, Ipswich 196
Nagasaki 128
Nairobi 229
Nanking 123
Nanking, Treaty of (1842) 123, 125
Napoleon Bonaparte 119, 121
Napoleonic Wars 68

Natal 208
National Archives, The xii
National Hellenic Research Foundation,
    Athens 172
National Humanities Center, North Carolina
    172
National Reform League (Australia) 89
National Trustees, Executors and Agency
    Company 89
Natural History Museum, South Kensington
    164
Neilson, Keith 137
Nelson, Horatio 120
Neptune, Planet 150
Nestorian, SS (ship) 99
Netherlands 60, 215, 230
New Armies 136
New College Boat Club 188
New Hebrides 44, 46
New Liskeard, Ontario 103, 104
New River, New Zealand 87
New South Wales 38, 89, 94, 95, 98
New Steam Navigation Company 20
New York 74, 75, 76, 195
New York (boat) 94
New York Stock Exchange 74
New Zealand 39, 44–5, 87, 136, 172, 194,
    204, 213–4, 217, 218
  Chevallier barley and 12
New Zealand Army 204, 209, 214, 218
New Zealand Church Constitution 44
New Zealand Division 218
New Zealand Expeditionary Force 217
New Zealand National Film Unit 214
Newbolt, Henry 184
Newcastle, New South Wales 89
Newgate Gaol, London 119
Newmarket 75
Newnham College, Cambridge (see Cam-
    bridge University, Colleges)
Newton, Isaac 146, 149
Ngongono, John 47
Niagara Falls 74
Nile, River 134
Ningpo, China 123, 160
Nobbs, Edwin 46
Noirmont Manor 72
Norfolk Island 45, 48–9
Norfolk and Norwich Hospital 153
Norman, Montagu 139–40, 141, 142

Normandy 9, 228, 234
Normandy Landings (*see* D-Day)
Normanton, Queensland, 96
North African Campaign (*see* World War II,
    North African Campaign)
North Hill Brewery, Colchester 6
Northern Ireland Football Team 176, 199
Northern Ontario Railway 104
Northumberland, 3rd Duke of 150
Norton Motorcycles 190–1
Norway 230
Norwich 14, 57, 59, 60, 61, 62, 64, 138,
    156, 198
  Goldsmith's Company of 59, 60
  railways 14, 18, 19
Norwich Castle 59, 61
Norwich Cathedral 59, 61–2, 63–4, 161
Norwich City FC 199
Notting Hill, London 79
Nottingham 156
Notts Forest FC 179
Nukapu, Melanesia 30, 43, 46–7, 48
Nunn, Alice Bessie (255) 78
Nunn, Richard Lindley (1146) 78
NUT Motorcycles 190

Oaks, The, Queensland 95
Oakes, Harry 113
O'Brien, Cobbold & Co. 96
O'Brien, Nick 199
O'Brien, Patrick 95, 96, 97
O'Coigley, James 119
O'Connor, Arthur 119
O'Dawg (dog) 104
Ogaden Desert 110
Okino, Lieutenant 227
Old Bailey 116
Old Carthusians 178, 180
Old Etonians 178
Old Trafford (football stadium) 199
Oldham, F. R. 226
Olympic Games (*see* Stockholm Olympics)
Oman, Charles 61
Omar Ali Saifuddin II, Sultan of Brunei 221
Omdurman, Sudan 134, 209
Ontario 84, 100–2, 104, 112–3
Operation Abercrombie 231
Operation Claymore 230
Operation Jubilee 231
Opium War, First 123

Opium War, Second 124–5
Orange Free State 209
Oriana Madrigals 62
Orion (ship) 20
Orly Airport, Paris 194
Orne, River 223
Orwell (ship) 20
Orwell, River 4, 16
Osaka 127, 128
Osman Digna 133
Ostend 215
Otley College, Suffolk 28
Ottawa River 101, 102
Ottawa Valley 103
Ottery St. Mary 43, 44
Ottoman Empire 61, 132, 207
Ouistreham, Normandy 232
Ovalau 93
Oves Poli (Marco Polo sheep) 107
Owen, Michael 176
Owens College, Manchester, 161, 165
Ox and Bucks Light Infantry, 1st 113
Oxford 116, 161, 185, 188, 189, 229
Oxford University, 145, 147, 148, 161, 174
  Boat race and 184, 185–7, 189
  Colleges
    Balliol 44
    Magdalen 32, 187–8, 229
    Merton 44, 45
    New 184, 185, 187–8
    Trinity 23
  University 116
    Football Club 177
    Lawn Tennis Club 177

Paaredeberg, South Africa 134
Pacific Islands Protection Act (1872) 48
Pacific Ocean 128
Paddington, London 154, 159
Palestine 53, 131–2, 169, 170, 212
Palestine Exploration Fund 131–2
Palgrave, Suffolk 154
Palmerston, Lord 125
Pamirs 108
Pan-Anglican Conference, London (1908)
    119
Parachute Battalion, 7th 233, 234
Paris 73, 75, 78, 112, 154, 193–4
Parker Enquiry 142
Parker, Matthew, 60

Parker, Poll 41
Parker's Piece, Cambridge 177
Parkes Collection 128
Parkes, Harry Smith (849) 114–5, **122–9**, 204
Parkes, John, 160
Parkes, Lillian Hope (259) 115, 206
Parkes, Mabel (914) 128
Parkes, Marion (912) 128
Parkin, Mary Selby (408) 58, 167
Passchendaele 211, 213
Patteson family 16, 29, 138
Patteson, Frances Duke (2464) 43
Patteson, Frances Sophia Duke (2466) 44
Patteson, Henry (1088) 16, 36
Patteson, John (1420) 43, 44
Patteson, John Coleridge (2465) 16, 30, **43–9**, 94
Patteson, Lucy (115) 16, 138
Patteson Memorial Fund 49
Payne, Ian 63
Peacock, Edward 140
Pearl (ship) 20
Pearl Harbor 221
Pearl River, China 123
Pears soap 73
Pears, Steuart (2121) 151
Peat, Jane 147
Pegasus Bridge, Normandy 233–4
Peiho, River, China 125
Pehtang, Beach, China 125
Peking 125–6, 129
Pelagus Rapids, Sarawak 224
Pembroke College (see Cambridge University, Colleges)
Pembroke, Ontario 101, 102
Peninsular War 41
Pennsylvania 75
Penrice, Porthpean 113
Pentalofos 170, 173
Pentland Firth 137
People's Budget (1909) 28
Perceval, Spencer 119, 120
Peterson, Peter 60
Petra, Jordan 53
Petrovsky, Nikolai 107, 108
Philadelphia 157
Philby, Dora 54
Philby, Harry St John 53–4, 55
Philby, Kim 53

Philip II of Macedonia 173
Philippines 143
Phipson, Richard Mackilwaine 22
Physiological Society, The 157
Piccadilly, London 39
Pickford, William 176
Pilbrow (business partner of F.E. Cobbold) 93
Pindus Mountains, Greece 168–9, 170
Pitcairn Islands 46
Pitlochry 53
Pitman, Fred 187
Pitt, Minnie Diana (318) 112
Pitt, William 117
Pitt's Farm, Ipswich 6
Pius IX, Pope 44
Plawhatch Hall East Grinstead 181
Plumer, Eleanor (2555) 263
Plumer, Fanny Hannah (Lady Parkes) (850) 114, 124, 127
Plumer, Hall (853) 128
Plumer, Herbert Charles Onslow (2546), 258–9 204, **206–12**, 216
Plumer, Julia (8620) 128
Plumer, Marjorie (2560) 208
Plumer, Sybil (2556) 207–8
Plumer, Thomas (b.1711) (2564) 116
Plumer, Thomas (b.1753) (855) 114, **116–21**, 124
Plumer, Thomas (b.1890) 208
Pocock, R. W. 165
Poland 165, 230
Polo 207
Poor Rate, The 31, 35
Porteous, Patrick 231
Porthpean, Cornwall 113
Portland, Duke of (Prime Minister) 120
Portman Road (football stadium) 176, 198, 199, 201, 203, 236
Portsdown Road, London 155
Potter, Henry 42
Potters Bank, nr. Durham 150
Pottinger, Henry 123
Powell, Geoffrey 206, 207, 209, 210
Poyais (fictitious Latin American country) 7
Pretoria 109, 209
Prince Albert (ship) 20
Prince Regent, The (later George IV) 68
Princeton University 172
Privy Council 143, 189

Probyn, Clara (261) 105
Probyn, Louise Georgina (267) 102, 103,
    105
Prussia 131
Punch 74
Purcell, Henry 79
Purcell Operatic Society 79
Putney, London 184
Pybus, Charles Small 68

Qing Dynasty 126
Quebec 99, 100, 101
Queen Red Sector, Sword Beach 232
Queen's Head, The, Wortham (public house)
    41, 42
Queen's Own Cameron Highlanders 228
Queen's Royal Rifles 113
Queensland 46, 89, 95, 96, 97
Queensland Meat Export and Agency
    Company 96
Quekett Microscopial Club 157
Quilter, Colonel 215
Quirinal Hotel, Rome 218

Rackets 112,190, 196
Radford Thomas 13
Railways
    Australia 89, 90
    Canada 104
    East Anglia 2, 9, 13–4, 15, 17–20, 21
    India 135
    Japan 127
    Liverpool to Manchester line 17
    New Zealand 87
Raleigh Motorcycles 193
Ramsey, Alf 203, 236
Randolph Avenue, London 159
Ranelagh, Lord 73
Ranjitsinhji, K. S. 181
Rannoch 197
Ranville, Normandy 233–4
Ras Makonnen 110
Reade, Peter 61
Reade Salt, The 59, 61
Reade, Thomas Mellard 165
Reading, Berkshire 119
Red Gauntlet (yacht) 72
Red House, The, Bournemouth 73, 74
Red Sea 207
Redhill, Surrey 151, 154

Reed, Joseph 87
Reef Islands 44
Reeves, John 118
Rejang River, Sarawak 223–4
Rejang Timber Concession (RTC) 224
Repington, Charles à Court 137
Reserve of Officers 109, 230
Reynolds, George 192
Reynolds, Joshua 66
Rhayader, Powys 161
Rhodes, Cecil 208
Rhodesia 208, 209
Richardson, G. S. 214
Richmond Park, London 190–1
Richmond upon Thames 193
Ridout, John 14
Rifles, 60th 108
Rijksmuseum, Amsterdam 59
River Queen (ship) 20
Riversleigh, Queensland 96
Roberts, Lord 134
Roberston, William 137
Robson, Bobby 203, 236
Rochford, A. N. 110–1
Rodwell, William 7, 15, 16
Roehampton, University of 78
Rolls House, Chancery Lane 121
Rome 44, 50, 218
Romilly, Samuel 120, 121
Rommel, Erwin 220
Rosario, HMS (ship) 48
Ross, Gordon 185
Rothermere family 61
Rotterdam 151
Rous, Stanley 199
Routley, Erik 77
Rowing 184–9
Royal Academy of Music 78
Royal Agricultural Academy, Turin 157
Royal Air Force 195, 221–2
Royal Astronomical Society 149, 152
Royal Botanic Gardens, Kew 128
Royal College of Music 78
Royal College of Physicians 154
Royal College of Surgeons 154
Royal Engineers 131
Royal Flying Corps 191, 216
Royal Geographical Society xii, 156
Royal Institution 156
Royal Marine Commando, No. 45 231–2

Royal Medical Society 157
Royal Military Academy, Woolwich 131
Royal Naval Division (RND) 214–6
Royal Naval Volunteer Reserve 214
Royal Navy 48, 73, 125, 128, 214, 226
Royal Netherlands East Indies Army (KNIL)
    226
Royal Society 121, 153, 155, 184
Royal Veterinary College 155, 157
Royden, Agnes Maude 81
Rugby School 176
Rugby Union 168, 174
RUKBA 98
Rumbold, Thomas 117
Russell, John 126
Russia ix, 106–9, 120, 123, 129, 135, 137
Russian Foreign Ministry 108
Russian Turkestan 108
Rust, Ann (52) 32
Ryan, Andrew 54

Sabah (North Borneo) 142–3
Sadleir, Nicholas 94
Sadong, Sarawak 222
St Albans 160
St Andrew's, Norwich 60, 64
St Ann's, Liverpool 66
St Barnabas', Norfolk Island 48, 49
St Catharine's College, Cambridge (see
    Cambridge University, Colleges)
St Clement's, Ipswich 70
St Helier 9, 208
St John's, nr. Auckland 45
St Laurence's, Church Stretton 166
St Martin-in-the-Fields, London 80, 81
St Mary-le-Tower, Ipswich 22, 29, 36, 70
St Mary the Virgin, Selborne 31
St Mary's Hospital, Paddington 154–5
St Mary's, Knebworth 139
St Mary's, Primrose Hill 79–80
St Mary's, St Helier 9
St Michael's, Beccles 64
St Michael's, Esh 147–8
St Paul's Cathedral, London 80
St Paul's Cathedral, Melbourne 90–1
St Petersburg 108
St Saviour's, Jersey 71, 76
St Stephen's, Norwich 62
Salisbury 217
Salisbury, Lady 133, 135

Salisbury, Lord (Prime Minister) 107, 133
Salisbury Plain 217
Samarinda, Borneo 225, 226
San Francisco 214
Sanatorium Dapper, Bavaria 112
Sandford-on-Thames, Oxfordshire 161
Sandhurst 180, 181
Sandy, Reverend and Mrs 226
Santa Cruz 45–6, 47
Santa Cruz Islands 44
Sarawak 142–3, 205, 221, 222–4
Sarawak Club, Kuching 223
Sarawak Gazette 222
Sarawia, George 45
Sarsgood, William 90
Sa'ud, Ibn 53–4, 55, 56
Sa'udi Arabia 53–6
Savanaka (racehorse) 95
Scapa Flow 137
Schotling, J. A. 224, 225, 226
Scotland Football Team 178, 179
Scots Guards 196, 200, 229
Scott, Clement 74
Scott, Robert Falcon 213
Sebright, Sir John and Lady 73
Second Boer War (see Boer War, Second)
Second Matabele War (see Matabele War,
    Second)
Second Opium War (see Opium War, Second)
Second World War (see World War II)
Sedgwick, Adam 163
Sedgwick Museum 164
Selborne, Hampshire 31–5
Selwyn, George Augustus 44–5, 46
Seraphis, HMS (ship) 207
Sergison-Brook, Bertram 200
Services Reconnaissance Department 226
Seven Years' War 10
Severn Valley Field Club 162
Seymour, Michael 125
Shanghai 123, 124, 126
Shaw, Geoffrey (3349) 80
Shaw, James (3347) 77
Shaw, John (720) 80–1
Shaw, Martin Edward Fallas (399) 58,
    77–83
Shaw, Mary Elizabeth (721) 80
Shaw, Richard (716) 81
Shaw-Stewart, Patrick 214
Shebele River, Abyssinia 110–1

Sheffield 179
Sheffield United FC 179
Sheriff Hutton, North Yorkshire 116
Shoesmith, James 35
Shooting 53, 109, 112, 175, 196, 197, 198, 200, 228
Shorting, Alice Frances (251) 161, 165
Shorting, Charles (156) 161
Siam 124
Sibu, Sarawak 221, 222, 223, 224, 226
Silk Road 107
Simonds, James Beart 155
Sinai Desert 53
Singapore 142–3, 222
Skyros, Greece 215
Sladen, Toby (1454) 56
Smith, James 69
Smith, John Owen 32
Smith, Matilda Caroline (173) 176
Smith, Rita (1682) 195
Smith, Richard 41
Smith-Dorrien, Horace 209, 210
Snodgrass, Anthony 168, 169
Society for the Propagation of the Gospel 80
Society of Antiquaries 121
Society of Arts 156
Society of United Irishmen 119
Soil Association, The 14
Solomon Islands 43, 44, 45
Somalia 109–10
Somaliland Field Force 111
Somme, Battle of the 113, 210, 213, 216
Sowerby, James 69
South Africa 76, 132, 135, 178, 234
    Boer War, Second (see Boer War, Second)
    Chevallier barley and 11
South Australia 89
South Kensington, London 164
South Pole 213
South Saxons' Tennis Club 181
South Sea Islands 93
South Yarra, Melbourne 91, 98
Southampton 72
Southern Cross (ship) 45, 46, 47
Southern League (football) 199
Southern Ocean 92
Southwold 83
Spa, Belgium 193
Spanish Flu 139
Special Operations Executive 169, 170

Special Service Brigade 231–2
Speedway 193–4
Spencer Street, Melbourne 89
Sproughton, Suffolk 25, 28
Squatting Investment Company 89
Srinagar 107
Stainer, John 81
Stalin, Joseph 234
Stamford, Lincolnshire 156
Stamford Bridge (speedway track) 193
Stanford, Charles Villiers 78
Stanmore, Middlesex 118
Stanway embankment 18
Stark, Freya 30
Statue of Liberty, New York 195
Steele, William 95, 96
Stevens, Cat 81
Stockholm Olympics 187
Stoke Newington, London 147
Stonham, Norfolk 161
Stopes, Henry 12
Stopford, Frederick 188
Stowmarket 24
Strontian, Argyllshire 189
Stuart, D. C. R. 185
Sudan 133–4, 207
Sudetenland 200
Suffield, Lord 72
Suffolk Agricultural Association 25
Suffolk Agricultural Society 20
Suffolk Alliance Company 20
Suffolk Record Office, Ipswich xiii
Suffolk Regiment 138
Sugnall Hall 118
Sunbeam Motorcycles 190–3
Supplementary Reserve of Officers 230
Suvla Bay, Turkey 188
Swan Lane, Norwich 59
Swayne, Eric J. 109–10
Swing Riots 31–5
Switzerland 126, 131
Sword Beach, Normandy 232
Sydney 92, 93, 96, 213, 214
Syer, Barrington Blomfield (2047) 11
Syer, Emily (1336) 11
Sykes-Picot Agreement (1916) 137
Syme, James 153
Syria 170

Table Top, New South Wales 98

Tahiti, RMS (ship) 214
Tai'ping Rebellion 126
Taku, China 125
Tamai, Sudan 207
Tanzania 230
Taras (racehorse) 98
Taroaniara, Stephen 47
Taula (chief, Nukapu) 43
Taveuni, Fiji 94
Taylor, D. J. 178
Taylor, Richard 3
Temiskaming, District of 103, 105
Temiskaming, Lake 101, 105
Temiskaming and Northern Ontario Railway
    104
Templer, John Charles 221
Tennis 168, 177, 181, 223
Terry, Elle 79
Tetule (or Atule, Nukapu islander) 47
Texas, 98
Thames, River 92, 184, 185–7
Theatres Act (1843) 143
Thessaloniki, Greece 170, 173
Thessaly, Greece 170
Third Division South (football) 199–200
Thomas, Rosalind 23
Thompson, Anne (2585) 116
Thompson, Henry (2587) 116
Thompson, Leonard P. 198
Thorne, R. G. 120–1
Thurso 137
Tien Shan, 141
Tientsin, 163–4
Tientsin, Treaty of, 163
Tilehurst, South Yarra, 128
Times, The 136–7, 139, 183, 185, 189
Tinne, C. E. 187
Tito, Josip 218
Todd, Richard 234
Tokugawa Shogunate 126
Tokyo 128
Tonbridge 176
Tonbridge School 161
Toronto 100
Torquay 128, 206
Tower of London 119
Townley, Margaret (3824) 169, 173
Townsville, Queensland 96
Transvaal 208, 209
Treasury, HM 10, 141, 142

Trieste 218
Trimley, Suffolk 113
Trinikat, Sudan 207
Trinity College, Cambridge (*see* Cambridge
    University, Colleges)
Trinity College, Oxford (*see* Oxford
    University, Colleges)
Tripartite Agreement (1936) 114
Tuan Muda 223
Tumble Down Dick, Wortham (public
    house) 41
Tunbridge Wells Rangers FC 199
Tungchow, China 125–6
Tunis 61
Turin 157
Turnley, Louisa (854) 206
Turton, John (2563) 118
Turton, Marianne (856) 118
Twickenham 74
Tye, Walter 10

UEFA Cup 203
Ulverstone Hall, Debenham 11
United Nations 143
United States of America 41, 73, 74–5, 128,
    136, 140–1, 163, 214
    Army 76, 200, 218, 231
    Chevallier barley and 12
Unity, HMS (destroyer) 137
University Boat Race 174, 184, 185–7, 189
University College, Oxford (*see* Oxford
    University, Colleges)
Upfield, Arthur 93, 96
Uppingham School 161
Urabi Pasha 133
US Rangers 231

Van Cutsem & Co. 112
Vancouver 222
Vanua Levu, Fiji 94
Varengeville, Normandy 231
Vatican City 44
Vaughan Williams, Ralph 77, 78, 79, 81
Venice 218
Verniy (Almaty) 108
Vickers (aircraft manufacturer) 192, 193
Victoria, Australia 84, 87, 89–90, 94, 97,
    161
Victoria & Albert Museum 128
Victoria Cross 216, 219, 231

Victoria, Mount, New Zealand 213
Victoria, Queen 26, 50, 124, 176, 196
Victory, HMS (destroyer) 137
Villa Farm, Felixstowe 25
Villa, Francisco 214
Villiers, George, 4th Earl of Clarendon 160
Villius (racehorse) 98
Viti Levu, Fiji 93
Vryburg, South Africa 209

Wade, Thomas 125, 128
Wahba, Hafiz 53
Walbank, Frank 168–9, 172, 173
Wales Football Team 180
Wall, Joseph 119
Waller family 29
Waller, Alice (784) 65
Waller, Mary Anne (107) 36, 42, 153
Walter, T. E. 225, 226
War Claims Commission 188
War Council 130
War Office, London 109, 136–7, 167, 169,
    214, 217, 228
Warner, Philip 132
Waterloo, Battle of 40–1
Waterview, Queensland 96
Watling House, All Stretton 160, 161, 165
Watling Street, London 65
Watts, William 163
Wayling, Vic 179
Wellington Barracks, London 197
Wellington College, New Zealand 213
Wellington, Duke of 68
Wellington, New Zealand 213–4, 218–9
Wells, Henry Benley 186–7
Welsh Guards 201
Weslake, Harry 191
Wesley, Samuel Sebastian 77
West Ham (speedway track) 193
West, Henry Wyndham 20
West Hoathly, Sussex 181
West Wratting Cricket Club 177
West Wratting Park, Suffolk 176, 180, 181
Wester Ross 50
Westerhuis, D. J. 226
Westhorp, Sarah Frances (151) 160
Westminster 24, 200
Westminster Abbey 212
Westminster School 176, 190
Westwood, Arthur 193–4

Wet, Christian de 209
Wetherall (business partner of F.E. Cobbold)
    93
Wex Carburettors 191
Weybridge 190
Whalley family 93
Whalley Grange, Manchester (football
    stadium) 178, 179
Wheelwright, Catherine (2117) 146, 151
Whistler, James 73
Whitchurch, Middlesex 124
White City (speedway track) 193
White Ladye (yacht) 75
White Rajas (Brooke family) 221
Whitehall, London 129, 137, 203
Whitelands College, London 78
Wilberforce, Herbert W. W. 177
Wilby, Charlotte 40
Wilby, Simon 40
Wilby, Suffolk 29
Wilbye, John 62
Wilde, Oscar 74
Wilhelm II, Kaiser of Germany 25–6
William Cain Scholarship 91
Wimbledon Tennis Championships 177, 184
Wimpole Street, London 155
Windmill Club, London 191
Windsor 44
Windsor Castle 128, 219
Withers, Thomas 164
Wolseley, Garnet 132
Wolverhampton 191
Woodbridge, Suffolk 27, 197
Woodhouse, Colonel 133
Woodcock (ship) 109
Woodward, Arthur Smith 164
Woolpit, Suffolk 29
Woorooma West, New South Wales 98
World Bank 141
World War I 53, 136–7, 181–2, 204, 205,
    206, 213, 214–6, 222, 229
  Home Front 138
  Turkish Front (*see* Gallipoli)
  Western Front 113, 196, 209–12, 214–5,
    216
    Ancre (*see* Ancre, Battle of)
    Menin Road (*see* Menin Road, Battle of)
    Messines (*see* Messines, Battle of)
    Passchendaele (*see* Passchendaele, Battle
    of)

Somme (*see* Somme, Battle of)
Ypres (*see* Ypres)
World War II 145, 195, 200–1, 202, 204–5, 230–4
  Albania and 145
  Blitz, The 201, 202, 205
  Crete, fall of 170, 217
  D-Day (*see* D-Day)
  Greece and 145, 170–2, 217
  Italian Campaign 218
  Normandy Landings (*see* D-Day)
  North African Campaign 204, 217–8
  Pacific Ocean, in the 205, 221, 223–7
    Java (*see* Java, Battle of)
    Pearl Harbor (*see* Pearl Harbor)
Wortham, Suffolk 16, 36–42
Wrekin, The 165
Wuntho, Burma 106
Wyks Bishop 3
Wynberg, South Africa 208

Xinjiang 107

Yangtze River 123, 126
Yarmouth 13–4, 17
Yarra Dredging Board 89
Yarra House, Melbourne 88
Yarram Park, Victoria 97
Ye, Governor General of Canton 125
Yokohama 128
York 209
York Herald 180
York and Lancaster Regiment 206, 210
Young, Arthur 10
Young, Fisher 46
Younger, John 88
Ypres 209–10, 211–12, 216

Zanzibar 133
Zimbabwe (*see* Rhodesia)
Zionists 170
Zola, Émile 57, 58
Zoological Society 155